# BILLION DOLLAR
# AGENT

## Lessons Learned

## Best Agent Business

**Billion Dollar Agent™ – Lessons Learned**
Website: www.billiondollaragent.com
By Best Agent Business – www.bestagentbusiness.com

Interviews by Steve Kantor, President, Best Agent Business
Copyright 2006 Lifebushido LLC – www.lifebushido.com
Published by Lifebushido

Billion Dollar Agent™ is a trademark of Best Agent Business
Client Agent™ is a trademark of Best Agent Business

Printed in the United States of America.
First Edition – December 2006
ISBN 978-0-9788854-3-4

10 9 8 7 6 5 4 3 2 1

# Lessons Learned

## Success Secrets of Top Real Estate Agents

Interviews with over 50 real estate agents
who sold over $1 billion in real estate or
will achieve $1 billion in career sales

Includes interviews with top national trainers/
coaches:
Howard Brinton, Mike Ferry, Ken Goodfellow,
Walter Sanford, Floyd Wickman

by
Best Agent Business
www.bestagentbusiness.com
sales@bestagentbusiness.com – Phone: 240-396-5282

# BILLION DOLLAR AGENT
# LESSONS LEARNED

## TABLE OF CONTENTS

# Billion Dollar Bonus

### FREE FREE FREE
### REGISTER YOUR BOOK TODAY!

## Billion Dollar Bonus

Register your book today for free bonus material and content!

As an owner of **Billion Dollar Agent – Lessons Learned** you are entitled to hundreds of dollars worth of additional content.

Billion Dollar Bonus materials includes free additional content, goal tools, sample budgets, profit models, book summaries of other business books, and samples of systems.

Our goal is to share knowledge with you to thank you for buying our book and to introduce you to **Best Agent Business** for your current or future part-time or full-time assistant needs.

We are looking for 1,000 people to grow from $100,000 in GCI to $1,000,000 over the next 1,000 days.

**Do you have what it takes?**

**Register your book today for free Billion Dollar Bonus:**

Email your contact information to:

register@billiondollaragent.com

Call us and leave voice mail at: 240-396-5282

Complete this form and fax to: 240-751-4247

Complete form and mail to:

Billion Dollar Agent

7706 Oldchester Road

Bethesda, MD 20817

Name: _____

Company: _____

Phone: _____ Email: _____

City/State: _____

# INTRODUCTION

This book is unique. All content, no fluff. This book is only for real estate agents who want to own a business.

If you are a great salesperson who is motivated to become an entrepreneur and own a profitable business that allows you to achieve your life goals and dreams – this book is for you.

Welcome to the big time. Welcome to **Billion Dollar Agent**.

This is not a motivational book. If you are not motivated already, go get a normal job and do not try to create and run a business. This book will not teach you how to be a salesperson. If you are not good at sales, get out of real estate right away. Real estate is a sales business. Every single one of the agents in this book is an excellent salesperson, as well as an entrepreneur and a businessperson.

Target market for **Billion Dollar Agent – Lessons Learned:**

- The top 20% of real estate agents who have $100,000+ gross commission income, have desire, passion, and aptitude to grow their business. These are agents who want to focus on their unique talents, get a part-time assistant, delegate, and grow their business.

- Rising rookies, who are the 10% of rookies each year who actually survive, become stable, and will hit $100,000 GCI in 1,000 days.
- Teams who are evolving from two or three people into a company of five or more people.
- Billion Dollar Agent and Future Billion Dollar Agents who are profiled in this book qualify for the next edition of this book.
- Brokers, franchise leaders, trainers, coaches, real estate schools, and real estate industry leaders, who understand that the top 1% of agents in the country are going to rapidly increase their market share by 2010.

## Goals

Goals are important. Written goals are better. Telling lots of people about your goals make them more likely to be achieved and focus your efforts. At Best Agent Business, we have the following goals for this book:

- Sell 100,000 copies of book
- Have 10,000 people actually read the book
- Find and create a group of 1,000 people with the passion, desires, goals, skills, and aptitude to grow from $100,000 net profit to $1,000,000 net profit in 1,000 days by working together and leveraging their unique talents

## Purpose for Readers

**Billion Dollar Agent - Lessons Learned** is for the 20% of real estate agents who have achieved a success of $100,000/year and have the desire and abilities to achieve $200,000 or $500,000 or more per year.

The key is to transform yourself from a salesperson to a business-person, consistently delegate to your assistants and vendors, and build systems for your business. Entrepreneurs often 'reinvent the wheel,' spending money in the wrong places. They fail to seek wisdom from other businesspeople, and are not aware of valuable products and services for their industry. Business entrepreneurs can save time and money by learning from the lessons of other entrepreneurs.

Most entrepreneurs waste time and money on learning lessons in business. It has been said that if you can make $100,000 as a real estate agent, you can make $1,000,000. It is not easy to make $100,000 in real estate, less than 20% of agents achieve that level of success. If you learn from the lessons and experiences of Billion Dollar Agent, you will consistently move up from $100,000 towards $1,000,000.

Out of over 1,000,000 Realtors in the United States, we estimate that there are less than 100 who have achieved the Billion Dollar Agent milestone, and have sold over $1,000,000,000 of real estate in their career.

Our hope is that you get the following core lessons from **Billion Dollar Agent**:

- Your past and background is not a constraint.
- You can be raised in a poor family, not have a college education, and have significant personal setbacks and still achieve this top level of success.
- Attitude is everything. If you do not have the right attitude, you should first reprogram your mind with the attitude of success.

- Persistence is key. Never give up.
- You need to enjoy many aspects of the business and focus your time on your unique talents and what you enjoy.
- Almost everyone in this book takes written goals very seriously. If you get 100 average real estate agents in a room, all of them will say that they have heard or know that written goals are important. But only one agent will actually have properly written goals with them in that room in their wallet, purse, or work folders. You want to be that 1 in 100 agents.
- Delegate as much as possible to leverage your time.

## Purpose for Billion Dollar Agent Interviewees

If you are a **Billion Dollar Agent** or a **Future Billion Dollar Agent,** who is featured in this book, congratulations on your incredible career success. We want to emphasize, again, that out of over 1,000,000 real estate agents there are less than 100 that are profiled in this book.

Here are some ideas as you read the book if you are a **Billion Dollar Agent**:

Note the similar aspects of all of you.

- Try to read at least 10 interviews of names you have never heard of in your career.
- Notice that no one in this book is 'doing it all.' Imagine the upside if you added new pillars of revenue and profit to your business model.
- Create a list of three potential ideas to study/implement.
- Contact us via your private e-mail direct to Steve Kantor and Best Agent Business with your list of top ideas to implement. We will make efforts to connect you with other people working on same topics.
- Create a BHAG – a big huge audacious goal with a time frame of perhaps three to ten years. Share your BHAG with us. As an example, we shared our BHAG in previous pages of this book.

If you have achieved $1 billion in career sales, and just became aware of this book, please go to www.billiondollaragent.com and select Interviews. Simply apply for an interview for a future edition of the book. Our desire is to track down and include everyone who is a **Billion Dollar Agent**.

## Purpose for Best Agent Business

Best Agent Business provides part-time assistants to the top 20% of real estate agents. We apply the lessons learned from the business model of **Billion Dollar Agent** to our clients who may be making $100,000+ in commissions.

# Best Agent Business

We have a unique business model which we launched in 2006. We have had hundreds of people apply for jobs. We hired less than 10% of those who applied. Our associates work from home, around the country, and act as a business team of assistants for our real estate agent clients.

Our typical client is a real estate agent who has a $100,000+ GCI or about 15-20 transactions per year. This average client uses our services for about 15-20/hours per week for about $995/month. We provide a single client contact for a weekly management call. The client manager is responsible for delegating and reviewing all work from the team of assistants.

Like the business of a **Billion Dollar Agent,** with a staff of 5-20 people, **Best Agent Business** may have a few different people doing various tasks behind the scenes using their unique talent. For example, the person who does data entry, is different than the person who does marketing graphic design, or customer service touch base calls, to your existing clients.

**Best Agent Business** helps with the following types of assistant tasks:
- Marketing coordination – database, websites, mailings, calls.
- Listing coordination – listing plans, website, feedback, calls.
- Transaction coordination – contract to closing coordination.
- Business accounting/admin/organization.

Most importantly, we only work with clients who take the basic steps of success. During the first month, we help them to work on developing the following:
- Goals
- Budget
- Business and marketing plan
- Unique talent, delegation, and leverage plan

Best Agent Business is not in the business of training or coaching. We are in the business of actually doing the work of an assistant as delegated by our client, the real estate agent. We provide best practices from the lessons learned from Billion Dollar Agent.

## History of This Book

Anything is possible. This book is an example of how a small idea can develop into something much bigger.

# Billion Dollar Agent

In January 2006, Lifebushido, founded by Steve Kantor, started a number of ventures. The primary venture, Best Agent Business, has a focus on helping the best agents, create their best possible business, using their unique talents.

In January 2006, we read about 20 of the top books in the real estate industry. We noticed that there was no single book as a compilation of interviews, from the very top agents in the country. We are not talking about the top 1%, but the 1 in 10,000 agents who have achieved or will achieve the status of **Billion Dollar Agent**.

My sister, Vicki Westapher, is a top RE/MAX agent in Colorado Springs, Colorado. After a flight, to brainstorm with her and with agents in her office in January 2006, I was on a plane trip back to Washington, DC. I had finished reading, The Millionaire Real Estate Agent (which is one of the best books in the industry). I wondered whether anyone had sold $1 billion of real estate. Since I am good with numbers, I worked out some numbers on a napkin in the airplane and came up with an estimate of a few hundred people. I then wrote a short plan to try to track some of them down, and determine if they were open for an interview for a book.

I would like to thank my sister, Vicki Westapher, a top agent with RE/MAX Properties, Inc. in Colorado Springs, for the inspiration for this book and key aspects of **Best Agent Business**.

Vicki would love to take excellent care of any of your referrals to the Pikes Peak Region and to Colorado Springs. She can be reached at vicki@makeyourbestmove.com. Tell her that her brother sent you. Thanks!

We tracked down a few hundred names from Internet research and sent out an introduction letter requesting interviews. We conducted the first five interviews, and realized that a book was doable, and would be unique in the industry. The project grew from February 2006 to September 2006. We then realized that many of these agents mentioned five national trainers/coaches. We decided to interview and include a section on trainers/coaches. In October-November 2006, when this summary of book was written before publication, we started to turn away those requesting interviews because word was spreading about the book. Also, many were interviewed. Leaders in industry conveyed to us that the book was unique and had potential of significant sales.

# Best Agent Business

I am not a real estate agent, nor do I have an interest in becoming a real estate agent. My goal is to build a very large network, **Best Agent Business**, to help thousands of top agents focus on their unique talents, delegating everything, and achieving their financial and personal goals. As you can read in my bio in the back of this book, I am a serial entrepreneur. Most recently I sold a small software company in 2004. I approach this industry as an outsider who is now entering the industry, as your typical crazy entrepreneur with lots of ideas and energy, who enjoys helping other people grow their business. Since my views are not colored by personal experience in real estate, or any specific market, franchise, or training/coaching system, they are not typical. Feel free to skip my summary and go straight to the interviews.

## Summary

Executive Summary

Imagine if you spent the time and money to track down about 50 of the top 100 real estate agents in the US, from a career field of about 1,000,000.

Imagine that they were at such a level of significance in their lives, that they freely shared their knowledge, experience, and wisdom with you, a total stranger.

Imagine that you took this person to a long lunch. Then, after an hour of small talk, you asked them questions about how they succeeded, and you just listened and took notes for another hour.

Imagine that someone transcribed their answers from lunch into written answers and you then spent a month reading over hundreds and hundreds of their ideas and answers.

Well, that is what happened to me, Steve Kantor, from February 2006 to October 2006 except that 90% of the interviews were over the phone. Here is my attempt to summarize the lessons learned from our Billion Dollar Agent interviews.

P.S. You should focus on these areas to grow from $100,000 to $1,000,000 GCI. Think of your business growing in stages from $0-$100k, $100k-$200k, $200k-$500k, and $500k-1M net profit.

P.P.S. Please note that net profit has nothing to do with gross commission income (GCI). GCI is sales or revenue of a real estate agent business. You 'make' net profit, not GCI. The only number that matters is net profit. To repeat, the only number that matters is net profit.

## Billion Dollar Agent 777

You create your own luck in life by taking ownership of your life. Through a combination of imagination, clarity, action, consistency, determination, and perseverance you can take control of your life.

You can make massive changes happen in small steps over the next 1,000 days.

Just remember the **Billion Dollar Agent 777**.

• Learn and implement the **7 Areas of a Billion Dollar Agent**

• Set goals to achieve to gain a higher level of **7 Levels of a Billion Dollar Agent**

• Focus, train, and practice the **7 Actions of a Billion Dollar Agent**

Master the **Billion Dollar Agent 777** and we hope to write about you in a few years! ☺

# 7 Areas of a Billion Dollar Agent

To become a Billion Dollar Agent, focus on these 7 areas.

## 1. Unique Talent

You must spend increasing amounts of time developing and using your unique talent. Your unique talent is the part of your job that you love. What do you, do that you love and that gives you energy, makes you happy, builds your confidence, and brings a smile to your face? What percentage of your working hours do you currently spend using your unique talents? How would it impact your profits and happiness if you increased that percentage every month?

## 2. Assistants

You must delegate everything that is not a unique talent. Every single real estate agent with $100,000+ GCI should have an assistant. Almost every Billion Dollar Agent said that it is critical to get an assistant, and they would have hired an assistant earlier in their career if they had a second chance. What are the job tasks that you dislike, those that you avoid or fail to do, that you do poorly, that give you stress, that are making you sweat just reading this sentence? Outsource and delegate those tasks to assistants and vendors. This will leave you free to focus on your unique talent.

## 3. Goals

You must have written goals for life and business for each month, the year, and long-term dreams. You must read your goals every morning.

You must invest 1% of your life, in time devoted to planning where you want to go, and what you want to achieve in your life. You only need to spend 10 minutes a day, 1 hour a week, 4 hours a month, and a 3 day retreat each year. You must have a vision, dreams, and visual reminders of your dreams. You must focus solely on positive people, news, media, self-talk, and affirmations.

You must prioritize your life by health, relationships, finances, business, and personal – in that specific order. Without your health, nothing else matters. Your relationships with your spouse, children, parents, friends, community, and spirit must come next. Your finances are more important than your income. If you make $100,000 net profit, but spend $120,000, the solution will not be to make $120,000.

Your business will thrive only if you are calm, with healthy energy, loving relationships, and managed finances. Then, you can even have time for personal hobbies and interests.

## 4. Perfect Day

You must define your 'Perfect Day'. Develop daily habits and rituals to maximize time spent on your unique talents, and eliminate time spent on anything else. To achieve greatness in your profession and business, you must do the ordinary with consistency. You must define the daily activities that generate income and move you to the next **Billion Dollar Level**. Successful people create daily habits and rituals. They schedule and time block a much greater percentage of their work week than other people. Having a detailed routine and scheduled time blocks, interestingly, allows people to be more productive and more creative; because their mind and energy has laser focus. Like Olympic athletes, they have a clear daily routine to practice and perfect their unique talents.

## 5. Focus

You must focus. You must slow down and realize that 1 hour spent planning is worth 10 hours spent doing something else. Like any sales-oriented business, the top 20% of real estate agents make way more than 80% of commissions. If you are in the top 20%, you may be an entrepreneur, as well as a salesperson. If so, you may be like many entrepreneurs and have a problem with focus. You must fight the battle of busyness, multi-tasking, fragmented thoughts, open loops, multiple to-do lists, 60 hour work weeks, poor eating habits, no exercise habits, no accounting habits, and STOP!!!. STOP RIGHT HERE AND RIGHT NOW. Stop the madness and slow down. Successful business people are filled with calm energy not tense energy. You must learn how to sit and do focused work for periods of 1-2 hours without interruptions.

## 6. Leverage

You must leverage your time so that one hour of your time can produce ten hours or 100 hours of value for your business. Imagine that your time is worth $100/hour. And, you make six touching base calls to a client for ten minutes every other month for a year and the client refers a new client which is worth a $10,000 commission. You just leveraged one hour of your time to be worth 100 hours of your time.

You must leverage prospects, clients, assistants, vendors, real estate agents, brokers, franchises, money, and knowledge. You must leverage everything, all the time, with a business plan documenting how you are going to create that leverage.

## 7. Billion Dollar Agent Level

You must honestly face the reality of your current business. You must determine which **Billion Dollar Level** you are currently at and set written goals to achieve higher levels by specific dates. There are seven levels.

# Billion Dollar Agent

The vast majority of new real estate agents do not survive this business. Many fail and go bankrupt, or shut down their business with significant losses. First, you must survive. You can then achieve stability, create a solid profit, build a successful business, and possibly achieve a level of significance like many people in this book.

# 7 Levels of a Billion Dollar Agent

What is your BDL™ ? What is your **Billion Dollar Level?** Just like you take a test to find out your cholesterol level of HDL and LDL, you can now compare notes with other agents and identify with each other by your BDL.

You must honestly face the reality of your current business. You must determine which **Billion Dollar Agent Level** you are currently at, and set written goals to achieve higher levels by specific dates. There are 7 levels. You must first survive. You can then achieve stability, create a solid profit, build a successful business, and possibly achieve a level of significance like many people in this book.

Some of the following descriptions are written, without quotes, from the perspective of a real estate agent at that specific level. You may find the next few pages stressful, gut-wrenching, insightful, inspirational, and practical -- all at the same time.

## Maybe One

Maybe I will try real estate. Maybe I will dabble in real estate. Maybe I will think about it for a few more years. Maybe I will work part-time in real estate.

Maybe I will get my license, get a job at a local franchise, and try to sell real estate. Maybe real estate is not such a good idea. Maybe real estate is not for me. Maybe the market is too soft to make sales right now. Maybe I don't like all the stuff you have to do to be a real estate agent. Maybe I did not know, that when I got a job at this firm, my pay would actually be $0. Maybe I did not know that besides getting a job that paid $0, I actually had to pay a few thousand dollars to maybe sell real estate. Maybe this isn't for me anymore.

About 30% of real estate agents are either coming or going from the industry all the time. If you are a Maybe One, decide right now whether you are still a Maybe or that you will do what it takes to get to Just Me Three.

If you are unsure, you are a Maybe and may close the book right now.

## Terrible Two

I was making about $50,000 salary in my prior job and I heard that most real estate agents make more than $100,000. It sounds like an easy job and you make a lot of money. Plus, the work time is flexible because I would be working for myself.

I didn't know that when you get a job at Coldwell Banker, or Long & Foster, or Weichert, or Century 21 that the job pays nothing. I didn't know that I would have thousands of dollars of expenses just to get started. I did not know this was such a competitive industry.

I didn't know anything about marketing and sales. I didn't know that the key to success in real estate is marketing and sales.

I didn't know that when I sold a house to someone, I actually only got 3% instead of 6% commission. I didn't know that of the 3% commission, my broker keeps about 50% of it so I really get about 1.5%. I didn't know about estimated taxes and that I was supposed to set aside a percentage of my commission check in a separate bank account and submit estimated tax payments to Uncle Sam. I didn't know I was supposed to have a budget. I didn't know that I was supposed to have a marketing plan and business plan.

I didn't know that when a friend, who is a real estate agent that I know, told me that she 'makes $100,000/year' that she was referring to her gross commission income and not the net profit of her business. I didn't know that she really makes about $60,000/year. I didn't know that my new job at the real estate company does not include health insurance and I have to pay another $5,000-$10,000/year to cover my family.

I didn't know, and that is why I failed in real estate, and I have decided to leave the job after I tried it for a few years.

About 30% of real estate agents actually try to make it for a few years, on a full-time basis. But, they never match their previous job salary equivalent, they acquire more debt, and they suffer through a terrible two years before failing and quitting.

## Just Me Three

It is just me in my real estate business; but, I am surviving. It is much harder than I had thought. More than 50% of the other agents who started with me 2-3 years ago have failed and left our company. I am happy to be surviving.

I made about $40,000 a year in my previous job and I think I am doing about the same in real estate.

I had about $60,000 GCI and I think my net profit was about $40,000. Of course I am a bit unsure about this, because I think I spend a few thousand dollars more for my car and gasoline. I don't even know if that is considered an expense. Also, I had four weeks vacation in my last job; I have not taken a one week vacation in the last three years in real estate.

But, I am pretty happy and proud to be self-employed and surviving. I guess I do not really have a business yet. But, I feel it is better than my old job, and I do have some flexibility in my hours.

If you want to survive in real estate, you must have a strong sales personality, and desire to find prospects, and close sales. One good option is to join an existing top team to learn from other agents. If you do not have sales skills and do not want to join a team, you should seriously consider exiting the real estate business and seeking a J-O-B.

About 20% of real estate agents are surviving, barely, and have created a job for themselves as a self-employed person.

## Stable Four - $100,000 GCI

I am finally at a stable point of my real estate job. It was a really hard first few years, but I can feel all the pieces coming together, and I have more confidence.

Last year, I had $100,000 GCI and I had a net profit of $65,000. I am proud that I had goals, a budget, and a business plan for last year. I think that is why my net income went up 40%.

Best of all, I finally paid off my last credit card debt and I am now saving 10% of my net profit, or about $500/month, into a retirement plan.

My current problem is that I am getting busier. This is a good and bad thing.

Now I am working about 60 hours per week and it does not seem enough. My eating habits are terrible, I have gained 20 pounds. I do not find or take the time to exercise and workout like I used to at my old job. Worst of all, my spouse has been complaining that I work all the time, and my children don't even try to ask me to do family things together on the weekend like we used to.

I feel stressed and out of balance in my life.

I read the **Billion Dollar Agent – Lessons Learned** book and I think that I only spend about 20% of my time using my unique talents. I have been thinking that I need an assistant and should hire a part-time assistant or do something.

About 10% of all real estate agents are at this level.

## Solid Five - $100,000 net profit

My business and life are solid, and getting better every year. I am very happy that I am a real estate agent, and I can see a fantastic future.

Last year, I had a net profit of over $100,000. I hired a part-time assistant which helped me leverage my time. Now I can do more of the work that I enjoy and makes me money. The assistant is getting work done that was just never getting done.

I can see the benefits of my client marketing efforts as over 50% of my business is now client repeat/referral. This has led to greater profits.

I have my goals that I read daily. I review my budget monthly. I am developing a financial plan for the future.

Best of all, I am spending about 30-40% of my time using my unique talents and loving every minute of it. I set my goal to get to the next level within 2 years.

About 10% of real estate agents are at this level.

## Success Six - $200,000 net profit

My business is very successful. I have a net profit of over $200,000 each year and save/invest 20% of my net profits. I am building my business and team by delegating to assistants and leveraging my time in all possible ways. Soon, I will be exploring getting my first buyer agent as I focus solely on listings.

My life is in excellent balance. I am accomplishing a variety of life goals. I spend over 50% of my time using my unique talents.

About 1% of real estate agents are at this level.

## Zen Seven - $1,000,000 net profit

I made it after a decade of hard work and smart work. A few years ago, my business passed $1,000,000 in revenue for the first time. And this past year, I achieved the Zen Seven level of $1,000,000 net profit.

We have consistently lived below our means and saved for retirement. Right now, my plan is that with further growth of business, I should be able to retire, if I wanted to, within another 10 years when I am 55 years old.

I spend more and more of my time using my unique talents.

I can see a future where I can reach a level of significance and contribute to other people in many ways. I have been mentoring and helping other agents for the last few years and sharing my knowledge.

My business helps to support a few different community charities. I enjoy that work, we make a difference, and it is good marketing for our business as well.

About 1 in 1,000 agents achieve this level.

## 7 Actions of a Billion Dollar Agent

### 1. Delegating and Staffing

Focus on building a business -- not a team. A business is something you own -- to achieve goals for your life. The goals are a mix of financial and personal lifestyle goals. Never forget that your goal is to create a business and achieve success in your business. If you do this, you are already mentally ahead of 99% of other real estate agents.

To be a real estate agent, you need to run a business, manage yourself, do marketing, do sales, manage the finances and accounting, organize one or more physical office spaces, use technology, and a few other things. Do you think that a **Billion Dollar Agent** does all of that by himself or herself? Nope, they delegate.

Imagine that you tried to do it all yourself and never worked more than 40 hours per week, like a normal job. Imagine that your average price of a home was $250,000, you averaged a solid 3% commission, and you had an 80/20 split with your broker. If you did 12 deals, or twice as many as the average agent, you would have $72,000 GCI and perhaps a net profit of $50,000 which is probably equivalent to a normal job of $40,000/year taking into account benefits such as vacation/holidays/health insurance.

Currently, the real estate industry focuses on 'teams'. We believe that teams will grow even faster and gain an increasing market share of all real estate transactions. Most importantly, businesses, such as those profiled in this book, will grow the fastest of all.

A team tends to imply people, who may be assistants on salary or sales agents on commission. The bigger the team is not always the better business. People cost money and if your mental focus is on building a team, then you may end up overstaffing and wasting money. Your mental focus should be achieving your goals through your business. If one of those goals is growing your business, you need to be specific about whether your goal is a net profit dollar amount or percentage, or simply a revenue figure attached to a number of transactions, or GCI, or dollar volume sold. We suggest that net profit should be the key focus, connected to personal lifestyle goals including hours worked.

You want to build a team which is a mix of vendors and part-time assistants and part-time agents to leverage your time and focus on your unique talents. Too many agents who start to get busy think that they should go hire a buyers agent. Based on the experience of a few agents in this book who had three or four full-time assistants, before ever having a buyers agent, we suggest you consider a very different staffing model than most people talk about in the industry.

## Staffing Levels

We propose levels of staffing that are typical in the progress of top agents.

| | |
|---|---|
| **Part-time agent** | You are working part-time in real estate. |
| **Full-time agent** | You are working full-time in real estate. |
| **Vendor Outsource** | You delegate and outsource to vendors as much as possible. |
| **Part-time assistant** | You have a part-time assistant for 5-15 hours per week. |
| **Full-time assistant** | You have a full-time assistant. |
| **Multiple assistants** | You have multiple part-time, or full-time assistants, so you can fully leverage your time for your unique talents. |
| **Part-time agents** | You use part-time agents for open houses and showings. |
| | You pay these people hourly, not a commission split. |

The assistants handle a mix of marketing, listing, and transaction coordination. The more specialized, the more profitable.

At this point, you may be doing 50-100 homes a year and be spending 5-10% of GCI on outside vendors and another 10-15% of GCI on assistants and part-time agents.

| | |
|---|---|
| **Showing agent** | A showing agent is paid less than a buyers agent. |
| **Buyers agent** | A full-time agent who takes a highly qualified buyer lead and works with them to buy the house until contract is signed.<br><br>Most of the rest of the work is handled by transaction coordinator. |
| **Listing agent** | Often, the agents in this book hold on to the listing side of the business for the longest. About 10-20% of agents in the book have started to delegate some or all of the listing side of the business. |
| **Management** | During the process of having multiple assistants and getting your first buyers agents, someone needs to manage different aspects of the business. Some of them may be managed by you if they fit your unique talent. Some should be managed by other people. This includes the management of marketing, sales, people, operations/systems, and accounting. You are now running a multi-million dollar business with 10-50 staff and you need 2-3 people on your management team. |
| **Leadership** | As your business grows and you have a few people on your management team, your role evolves to a leadership focus. |

## 2. Client Marketing - What is a Past Client?

A past client is the real estate industry term for a person who has had a transaction with you and that transaction closed. Thus, they are now a 'past client'. That phrase is costing you, almost all real estate agents, and even most of the people in this book a significant amount of money.

Words can kill and the word 'past client' kills your profits. Why would anyone care about a past client? Why would you even think of investing any money in a past client, or even your time and energy?

Well, past clients are the most profitable part of your business and the only asset you have if you ever wish to sell your business. The valuation of a real estate practice is closely connected to the percentage of business that is from existing clients versus new clients.

> **DELETE THE WORDS "PAST CLIENTS" FROM YOUR MIND!**

You have clients. They are your biggest asset.

This is one of the biggest lessons of this book – listen closely. The agents in this book achieve from 20% to 80% of their business from current clients. We strongly believe that the agents with the higher percentage of business from current clients are much more profitable than agents in the lower ranges.

A person becomes a client when they sign a listing agreement. If you fail to sale their house, or get fired, you just lost a client. A person becomes a client when they sign a buyer agreement and, hopefully, you have taken a buyer fee (such as $595) to be reimbursed by the seller at closing through your skillful negotiation. If you are driving around a buyer without a signed buyer agreement, you are not driving around a buyer, you are driving around a prospect.

When a client has a house listed with you or you are showing them homes to buy, they are an **active client**. So, you may have 100 clients after a few years and about 10-20 of them are active at one time. When a transaction is closed, they move from Client - Active to Client status.

A client may be at different levels:

Fired client – closed a transaction. But, you decide never to do business with them again because they are toxic. Fire toxic clients. It will make you very happy.

- Client – closed a buyer or seller transaction
- Testimonial client – provided written testimonial for marketing use
- Referral client – provided at least one referral, whether closed or not
- Lifetime client – completed two or more transactions
- Investor client – completed investment transactions
- Partner client – involved with joint venture business with you

You should operate your business to have 50% or more of your clients as testimonial clients.

On average, it seems that 10% of clients become referral clients for the agents in this book.

Imagine that you have a $200,000 GCI and are spending 20% or $40,000 on marketing. Your business is 30% existing clients/referrals. You spend close to nothing of the $40,000 on clients.

If you had average commission of $10,000 and 20 transactions, then you had 70% or 14 transactions were new clients for $140,000 and you spent $40,000 to acquire them. Thus, you actually spent close to 30% on marketing for new client acquisition.

If your average commission is $7,000 and your average client has a buying or selling transaction every 7 years, then **each client is worth $1,000 per year in GCI**. Thus, if you lose a client, you just lost $1,000 every single year for the next 10-30 years. This is big – huge – bigger than big.

## BILLION DOLLAR BONUS:

Best Agent Business developed a business model with spreadsheet and analysis to help you analyze your client base, the value of each client. We have a few different versions for different size businesses. Just send an email to bda-client@aweber.com, include your current number of clients, transactions and dollar volume closed last year, and the percentage of last year's business that was client repeat/referral.

### 3. Hunting and Farming

Are you a hunter or farmer? Do you prefer, as a salesperson, to hunt new business or to farm your existing client relationships? If you are a salesperson, your personality and unique talents are on a point along a spectrum from hunting to farming. Here are some examples:

**Hunter:**
- Calls FSBO and Expireds
- Go to FSBO home and knocks on door to meet them
- Walk around farm to knock on doors
- Calls a website lead 10 times within 48 hours to make sure that they reach them live to pursue the sale
- Loves getting the listing appointment and then closing the deal

**Farmer:**
- Stays in touch with clients and sphere of influence
- Calls people, writes hand-written notes, meets clients for lunch
- Sends consistent marketing messages to clients and sphere of influence
- Meets with sphere of influence to develop referrals
- Organizes client parties and events
- Thinks of ways to provide customer service to clients between transactions

Not surprisingly, almost every Billion Dollar Agent is a hunter – an extreme hunter. You would not go hungry on an island stranded with a Billion Dollar Agent. If there is meat running around the island, they will hunt it down, close the deal, and bring home the bacon. And they will love the hunt.

Read the book closely and notice the 10-20 people who have a strong farming personality and the special ways they leverage that unique talent.

Although the hunters in this book will hire and fire salespeople to cold call FSBOs, track down unbranded website leads, and other hunting activities, almost no one has taken the simple step of farming their client base and hiring a farmer, at $30,000-$50,000, to call, contact, and develop deeper relationships with clients.

If you were able to stop working with buyers and hire a buyer agent, then you could, if you grew big enough, stop working directly with hundreds of clients and hire a client agent. This book just invented a new role in the industry, a Client Agent™.

If you are a hunter and you are reading this, open yourself up to the possibility that your unique talent of hunting has led you to great success. But, at the same time, it may have blinded you from a huge profit opportunity of your client base. Business does not have to be either/or – you can expand your vision to be both/and and become a true Billion Dollar Agent.

## 4. Start Stop Delete More Less

The choice and consistency of your daily actions and the actions of your team will define the quality of your business.

Make a list of actions that you should start doing, stop doing, delete from your life, do more of, and do less of. Then, make another list of actions for your business for that same criteria. For example, you may stop doing something that you will delegate to someone on your team who will start to do it.


Focus.

Start doing things, which you know you should be doing, but have been putting off for a long time.

Stop doing things which are non-productive or destructive to you and your business.

Delete stuff, activity, people, vendors, piles, and old attitudes from your life and business that are holding you back. It will clear your life and provide you much more energy for positive activity. Try to delete one thing from your life every week. It sounds crazy but it is very powerful.

Do more of the activities which you believe fit your unique talent.

Do less of activities that are not your unique talent. Take a radical step and either delete from your life, stop doing it, or delegate to your team or a vendor.

## 5. Focus on Buyers and then Sellers

Most agents in this book make more profit from sellers than from buyers. They have properly put a focus on their time on getting listings and then generate leads for buyers. But because of this, many have a buyer side of their business that is weaker than the seller side.

A Billion Dollar Agent leverages the concept of focus. If they are still working directly with clients, they almost solely focus on listings. If they hire other agents, they have them focus solely on buyers. You get better at something you focus on. One of the biggest problems of an agent at $100-200k is that they are trying to do it all, especially if they do not have an assistant. They are trying to do marketing, sales, listings, buyers, transaction coordination, office management, accounting, and client relationships. It is no big surprise that they fail to do some of these at all, such as accounting and client relationships, and the more successful they get, the more frazzled and less successful they feel as they are working 60-80 hours a week.

If you are new in the business and in your first few years and not yet hitting $100,000 GCI, consider joining a top team in your city to get as much experience as quickly as possible. You are likely to make more money, get more experience, and make a better decision. Focus on buyers first. It allows you to focus and improve your sales techniques and scripts for qualifying buyer leads and all the steps of a buyer transaction. If you did 10 transactions yourself each year, it would take you 3 years to get the same experience as 1 year working for a top team and doing 30 transactions. Plus, you will make more money with the team. If, after a few years, you are ready to go out on your own, you will have savings instead of debt, a clear view of how a larger business operates, and confidence to pursue your own business.

A Billion Dollar Agent is always looking for great new salespeople. If you think you are the 1 in 100 who makes the recruiting cut for a Billion Dollar Agent team, feel free to email bda-recruit@aweber.com and describe your background, numbers, and city/state. We will provide a screening process that, if you pass, will get you an interview with a Billion Dollar Agent in your city.

If you are on your own you should leverage your time with an assistant, once you get busier, to delegate transaction coordination and marketing. If you have more buyers than you can handle at the same time, you are ready to hire a showing agent on an hourly basis. Your buyer clients, if you have a strong client marketing program, will start to generate seller leads for free and become sellers themselves in as little as 2-4 years. You can also decide on a target market or farm for listings and invest gradually in seller marketing.

## 6. Management – Financial, Systems, People

Management is not one thing. Most people think that 'management' is a single thing that businesspeople do. Management for a real estate agent involves the following:

- Personal management of your time and energy
- Financial management of your finances and business
- Systems management of the operation of your business
- People management of your team of staff and vendors

If you are not so good at managing yourself, you may not be the best at managing other people. ☺

You may be a great people manager, motivator, and team builder, but have no financial reporting or systems for your business, and no clue whether your net profit is going to be $80,000 or $110,000 this year.

You may love to create systems and operations for your business but not be a warm and fuzzy people manager.

### Financial

The weakest link for real estate agents, surprisingly, is financial. Real estate agents handle the largest financial transaction of many people, are motivated salespeople who want to make money, and have to work with numbers in their business. Yet, the vast majority of real estate agents have no, or very little, financial management of their business.

Even worse, real estate agents have a very high bankruptcy rate, often due to a lack of management of paying their taxes.

Since a real estate agent progresses from seeking survival and self-employment, to stability, to financial success, it is important to manage the finances for your overall life and your business.

Your business finances must be 100% separate from your personal finances. You need a separate legal entity, such a Schedule C business or LLC or Corporation. You need separate credit cards and separate checking accounts. Run your business like a business and you are far more likely to succeed and actually have a business in 10 years.

### BILLION DOLLAR BONUS:

As always, we are here to help. Just email bda-budget@aweber.com with your situation, basic numbers, and current budget, if any, and we will provide a budget template and also tell you how you compare with other agents at your level of GCI.

## Systems

McDonalds has a system. A Billion Dollar Agent has a system. As you read the interviews, you can probably guess which agents have more detailed systems than others. The personality of a typical real estate agent, and a hunter salesperson, is not the type that likes to sit down for hours and write documentation of systems.

You can start small. You probably have developed a checklist of steps for transaction coordination. It may be in your head or a cover sheet on your files.

Leverage includes systems. Just as one hour of planning is worth ten hours of doing, one hour of creating systems is probably worth ten hours of doing. If you create a system, you can repeat a service level consistently. You will have far fewer 'people' problems. Many people problems in a small business, as perceived by the owner, are really systems problems of lack of a system and lack of communication.

Another word for systems is operations. Operations are how things happen in your business. If the process is documented well, then you can call it a system.

## BILLION DOLLAR BONUS:

Email bda-systems@aweber.com and describe your problem/challenge related to systems and where you would like some help. Also, if you have a great system you want to share with others, email that as well.

## People

People management is one of the hardest things for a small businessperson. There are almost 1,000,000 businesses with 1-10 employees in the United States. Most real estate agents have never recruited, hired, fired, trained, and managed a staff before, especially for a business that they own.

It is not easy, and often it's not the perfect fit with the personality of a driver entrepreneur. From the very start, get help. You may also want to consider outsourcing as much as possible to vendors to delegate the recruit, hire, fire, manage, train, and document tasks to them. This allows you to focus your energy even further.

You are able to delegate tasks, without having to spend the additional emotional and management energy, to find, train, and manage those people.

## BILLION DOLLAR BONUS:

Email bda-people@aweber.com and we will point you to free resources to analyze your personality as it relates to working with employees and some resources to help interview and screen employees.

### 7. Learning

Everyone in this book is a voracious learner. Do you ever wonder why the people who are the top agents seem to spend the most money and time going to seminars and conferences and invest in training and coaching?

All top performers in any industry are constantly learning.

You need to read more, listen to more audio learning, meet more often with other top agents, go to more seminars, and invest consistently in your own education.

The more you learn, the more you will earn.

## Photos of Agents over $1 Billion

Of the agents interviewed for this book, some have achieved the level of $1 billion in career sales and the others are on track to achieve $1 billion and stated a personal goal to achieve $1 billion in the future.

To recognize the agents who have already achieved $1 billion, we are including their photos and names in a special section of this book. This was based on a review of interview notes and confirmation emails sent prior to publication.

Karen Bernardi
Tupper Briggs
Robert Browne
Mariana Cowan
Lester Cox
Jane Fairweather
Linda Feinstein
Valerie Fitzgerald
Marc Fleisher
Corey Geib
Arlene Gonnella
Noah Herrera
Pat Hiban
Ashley Leigh
Kim Lund
Jerry Mahan
Casey Margenau
Ronnie Matthews
Gregg Neuman
Stephen O'Hara
Craig Proctor
Ron Rush
Bob Shallow
Patrick Stracuzzi
Sherry Wilson

# PHOTOS OF AGENTS OVER $1 BILLION

KAREN
BERNARDI

TUPPER
BRIGGS

ROBERT
BROWNE

MARIANA
COWAN

LESTER
COX

# PHOTOS OF AGENTS OVER $1 BILLION

JANE
FAIRWEATHER

LINDA
FEINSTEIN

VALERIE
FITZGERALD

MARC
FLEISHER

COREY
GEIB

ARLENE
GONNELLA

## PHOTOS OF AGENTS OVER $1 BILLION

NOAH
HERRERA

PAT
HIBAN

ASHLEY
LEIGH

KIM
LUND

JERRY
MAHAN

# PHOTOS OF AGENTS OVER $1 BILLION

**CASEY
MARGENAU**

**RONNIE
MATTHEWS**

**GREGG
NEUMAN**

**STEPHEN
O'HARA**

**CRAIG
PROCTOR**

**RON
RUSH**

# PHOTOS OF AGENTS OVER $1 BILLION

**BOB
SHALLOW**

**PATRICK
STRACUZZI**

**SHERRY
WILSON**

## Agent Interviews

These 70+ interviews are the core content of **Billion Dollar Agent**.

Best Agent Business sent information on **Billion Dollar Agent,** and invitations for interviews for agents who qualify to a few hundred agents, coaches, franchises, and industry leaders from February 2006 to November 2006. The following are agents who qualified as either a current or future **Billion Dollar Agent**.

The interviews were based on a one hour interview with Steve Kantor of Best Agent Business. About 90% of interviews were done over the phone and about 10% in-person. Most agents were asked the same core group of questions. Steve took notes during the interview. Many interviews have a conversational style of informal answers. An assistant at Best Agent Business did a first draft edit and provided it to the agent for their revisions, corrections, and additions.

The production editor of the book then did edits for the book layout and two other assistants did final proofing of the text.

# MATT BATTIATA

## Introduction

Originally from Washington, DC, Matt is a graduate of Tulane University (BA). Before starting his real estate career, Matt was a former Tall Ship Captain (100 ton USCG license) and, more recently, the CEO and Creative Director of the Pacific Northwest advertising firm NBP Inc. A licensed real estate broker, Matt was named the #1 agent in California / #5 worldwide in 2001 (RE Int.) and has been the #1 agent in North San Diego County for 2001, 2002, 2003, 2004, 2005 & 2006. He has sold an average of 150 homes and approx $80,000,000 - $100,000,000 in gross sales per year. Matt lives in north San Diego County with his wife, and four children.

## Background

**How many years have you been in the real estate business?**

I got my real estate license at the end of 1999 and started full time in real estate in 2000.

**What is your personal background and how did you get into real estate?**

I grew up in the Washington, DC area, had always planned to become a lawyer or go into politics. And, then went to college in New Orleans. Suffice to say New Orleans changed my perspective on things and I decided I take some time off from college after my sophomore year and do some traveling. I took a trip around the world and then moved to Hawaii, where I started working on traditionally rigged schooners and tallships. I earned my captain's license at the age of 26.

I moved ashore with the intention of getting a job and making enough money to buy a boat of my own and sail around the world. I got into sales and marketing and then opened up my own advertising/sales business. Along the way I met my wife and plans to sail around the world were put on hold. In 1999 we moved to San Diego with the intention of getting into real estate. The decision to get into real estate was inspired by the example of a family friend who was a very successful agent in the Seattle area.

**What lessons did you learn from your family, friends, previous jobs, and life experiences that helped you most to succeed in your career?**

My parents are first and second generation immigrants from Italy. They had a real immigrant mentality of hard work. This was instilled in my siblings and me while growing up. My attitude towards everything in life has always been that if other people can do it, so can I. Whatever I lacked in expertise and experience could be offset by education and hard work.

**What do you enjoy most about the business?**

I enjoy the creative aspect of marketing, being my own boss and helping other people, whether they be my clients or my employees.

## Basic Numbers

**How many transactions did you close in 2005?**

I closed approx. 150 transactions in 2005 for a total of approx $95,000,000 in gross sales.

**Are you A Billion-Dollar Agent or do you believe you will hit that level during your career?**

I have averaged 120 – 150 deals per year for the last four years with an average gross sales volume of about $80,000,000. I have sold approx 700 or 800 homes in my career with a total dollar value of about $400,000,000. I would estimate that I will hit the billion dollar mark within the next 3-5 years.

**What is your current staffing including: yourself, listing agents, buyer agents, managers, and assistants?**

I have a different model than most real estate teams, in that I do not have lots of agents working for me. My staff is as follows: an office manager, a transaction coordinator, 2 listing coordinators (one of whom also works as a graphic designer for me and the other as an Interior Design Stager), an appointment setter, a courier and a receptionist/customer care manager. I have two full-time listing agents and I use my staff as showing agents for our buyers. I bonus my staff for any buyer deals that they put together.

## Marketing

**New Customer Marketing – Lead Generation – Prospecting**

**What are your top five methods for new client lead generation and about what percent of new customers are generated from that approach?**

We spend 25% of our gross revenue on marketing. I only do 2 types of advertising – TV and direct mail.

Television: 70% of our advertising budget is television advertising for buyers and sellers. Traditionally I have focused on listings and have just recently shifted our attention to the buyer side of the business as well due to the shift in our area to more of a buyer's market.

Direct mail: We have a database of 35,000 homes and we hit them consistently every two weeks with high end, professionally designed color postcards.

## Client Marketing – Repeats/Referrals

### What percentage of your business is referral?

We think that the amount of business we receive from client repeats/ referrals is relatively low, maybe 15%. We sell a lot of homes to people who leave the area. When the market was appreciating we did a lot of transactions with investors.

# KAREN BERNARDI

THE BERNARDI GROUP
COLDWELL BANKER RESIDENTIAL BROKERAGE
BOULDER, CO

### From Hippie Waitress to Multi, Multi-Millionaire

Twenty-three years ago, Karen Bernardi, a self-described 'footloose hippie,' drifted to Boulder, Colorado from her home in Plainfield, Indiana. Without a college degree, she had trouble finding work besides bar tending and waitressing. She was in debt.

Today, Bernardi is among the nation's top-producing residential salespeople. Her outgoing personality helped, but Bernardi believes it was determination and willingness to work hard and do things differently regardless of the opinions of others.

She was so pressed for money in the beginning. Back then, she asked the owner of her company if she could live and work in one of his properties until she could make it on her own. Within five years of starting in real estate, her commission income jumped to $300,000 annually.

In 1989, she met real estate trainer Mike Ferry, who taught her to organize herself better and to focus on listing and prospecting – while leaving administrative and service work to trained, licensed assistants. Her sales volume shot through the ceiling. For the last sixteen years, her gross commission income has exceeded $1 million annually and for the last ten has been over $2 million!

## Background

**For how many years have you been in the real estate business?**

I have been in real estate about 21 years.

**What is your personal background and how did you get into real estate?**

I was broke. It is something you can do without a college education. Someone suggested I try it. I was a waitress.

**What lessons did you learn from your family, friends, previous jobs, and life experiences that helped you most to succeed in your career?**

It was my father and mother talking one night over dinner. Mom asked whether he had sent back the overpayment on an insurance check. Honesty was just what they did. Later in life, I learned people are not that honest. The best thing I learned is basic honesty.

**What do you enjoy most about the business?**

I was not enjoying it as much recently and now I am enjoying it more. I still like being good at something. I like being like an expert.

## Basic Numbers

**How many transactions did you close in 2005?**

I closed 146 transactions and my sales volume was $58,075,921.00. It took me five months. My numbers are lower because I fought breast cancer. In previous years, I did 90 million and 197 million.

**Based on that, what is average price of a sale?**

The average house price was above $400,000.

**Are you a Billion Dollar Agent or do you believe you will hit that level during your career?**

Yes, I have reached the Billion Dollar level.

**What is your current staffing, including yourself: listing agents, buyer agents, managers, and assistants?**

I have three buyers' agents and one other listing agent as well as a contracts manager, an office manager and a listing manager. I have a driver. This helps so I can work and make phone calls while in the car.

## Goals

**Do you believe goals are important to your success? If yes, describe your approach to goal setting for your business and life?**

In my opinion, the best way to do it is to set the goals and have a concrete plan. I have a full written plan. I went to some seminars to help me get started. I have written goals for everything.

It keeps me in motion and keeps me happy. I am not happy unless I am achieving. I am someone who wants to have a goal. I need to be in motion.

## Marketing

**What are your top five methods for new client lead generation and about what percentage of new customers are generated from that approach?**

We have one of the Arch Powerline numbers. I have been using it for 1-2 years and it is a good thing to do. It saves about 7% of our brochures.

I have a good reputation. People have heard of me through the years. I take it very seriously if there is a customer complaint – and I fix it!

We send out a packet the moment a listing has expired and I have a telemarketer that calls them. I would guess that 15% were from expireds. I just won a $5 million listing off an expired call.

I get about 10% from "For Sale By Owners" houses. I believe it is a supply and demand issue.

You will not know the true price of a house until it gets all the marketing.

I do a presentation based on Mike Ferry seminars, which is a factual approach. I like that it is factual and not emotional.

**What marketing advice would you give to someone at $100,000 who wants to get to $200,000 and more?**

They need a real schedule, so that real estate does not become your life. I travel a lot and take a lot of vacations. They should call people and ask them for business even if they do not like calling expireds.

I spend one hour on lead follow-up and an hour of new calls. New calls include expireds. I have a headset and a handset. I make two calls at once.

I spend about 5% on marketing. I suggest 5-10% is a good amount.

Make sure you decide what works to sell a home - not the client. Tell the client what works. You have to take control of the situation and act like the expert.

## Client Marketing – Repeats/Referrals

**About how many past clients have you worked with?**

I have probably worked with over 3,000 clients. I currently have about 4,000 in my database.

**What percentage of your business is referral?**

50-60% of my business is referral and reputation based.

Boulder is not a high-priced market. I have to have a larger number of transactions to get to that.

**What client marketing activities do you do with past clients?**

I mail to them once a month. I get a rainmaker list of people who give referrals on a regular basis. I mail a full-page ad from the newspaper and mail once a month. Now I am working on rebuilding my website.

**How do you encourage referrals?**

I do not need to do anything really, except ask!

## Listings

**What percentage of your transactions are listings? What would be ideal and why?**

Listings are 62%. I would always love to have more listings.

**Specialized Markets and Approach**
**Are you involved with any special niche markets that are more than 10% of your business and part of your success?**

No. I'm fairly broad-based.

## Growth of Business

**What single quality has made you more successful than others?**

I have a good system of how to do what I do. I take customer service seriously.

**What does the average real estate agent fail to do which are among the reasons why they are average?**

They do not look at it like a job; they are lazy. They look at it as social and that someone should list with them because their sons play soccer together. It is important to maintain a high level of integrity.

**As you grew your business, what were your biggest challenges and what were the solutions that worked the best?**

It was important to keep my emotions in control. I always try to keep my customers' interests ahead of my own.

**Did you make any big mistakes that you want to warn others about?**

Always sign your own checks. You always catch something when you do that. Why are we spending this for that purpose? Keep track of your own money and what it's doing.

**What would you have done differently if you could begin your career again to speed the process of getting to your current level of business?**

I did not realize, until later in my career, how important it is to have multiple accounts. I did not know to have builder accounts and relocation accounts and big networking clients.

I would pay my staff well but not too well.

## Building a Team

**How did you first start to delegate and outsource and build a team?**

I was in business about 3-4 years before I got an assistant. I could not type, so I had to get someone. And, I paid her a percentage of income.

I used to pay my agents a base salary and a percentage of the whole group. I never put them on a salary. The structure is 39% of what they sell. They pay their own gas and insurance. They do not take listings. The listing agent does homes in the lower end. I have people who have been with me for 15 years.

## Learning

**What books have you read or classes have you taken that have helped you to succeed?**

I have taken some management classes, and read many sports books written by coaches. These books have helped me learn to manage employees.

## Delegation and Leverage - Assistants

**We see a challenge of agents right at the point of needing to delegate, outsource and hire their first part-time assistant to leverage their time. Why do they fail to take the next step? What would be the benefit for them to take that step?**

You have to look at it like a business. It takes courage. They need a little courage and they need to put a little money into their business instead of spending all their money. They will have expenses and they cannot keep all the money. When an agent sells 15-20 transactions annually, it is time to delegate to increase their sales.

# PAUL BICIOCCHI

FORUM PROPERTIES, INC

POTOMAC, MD

## Background

**For how many years have you been in the real estate business?**

I have been in business for 30 years.

**What is your personal background and how did you get into real estate?**

I was a marketing major at University of Maryland. As seniors, there was a group of us (4-5 people) debating what to do with our futures. I had a friend, Joe Robert, whose father had just started a real estate company. So we all decided to go into real estate.

**What lessons did you learn from your family, friends, previous jobs, and life experiences that helped you most to succeed in your career?**

The old phrase, plan your work and work your plan. It is important to have a strategy of where to go and how to get there.

**What do you enjoy most about the business?**

I enjoy the aspect of helping people make decisions that affect their family and their future. It is not just a sales transaction. This is their home. It is a very personal type of enjoyment that I get. Not only did I make a good commission, but also the people made a good investment. That is important to their family life.

## Basic Numbers

**How many transactions did you close in 2005?**

We closed about 78 transactions for about $62 million. In my career, I have done about $600 million so far.

**What is your current staffing, including yourself, of listing agents, buyer agents, managers, and assistants?**

I have one full-time assistant.

## Goals

**Do you believe goals are important to your success?**

I think goals are important. But they are not my strong suit.

## Marketing

### New Customer Marketing – Lead Generation – Prospecting

**What are your top five methods for new client lead generation and about what percentage of new customers are generated from that approach?**

I pick up new customers because of listings and getting a buyer.

**What is the one most effective form of marketing that you have consistently done?**

If properly executed, an open house is an excellent way to pick up new buyers and sellers. Here is why. You get a great quantity of people, perhaps 40 people. When I meet and greet someone, I ask whether they came from my sign or the ad in the paper. If they read the ad in the newspaper, it tells me that they took the time to sit down and circle what homes they wanted to see. This is the person I want to stick with. Someone down the street who saw the sign is less interesting as a potential buyer. If I have 8 people in the house at the same time, the best prospect is a couple circling ads to see. About 20 people come to a successful open house; half are neighbors.

## Client Marketing – Repeats/Referrals

**About how many past clients have you worked with?**

I'm not sure. My only wish is that I had kept track of my past clients in a database back in 70s, 80s, and 90s. Then, I would be retired right now. We only started to keep track of past clients about 14-15 years ago.

**Of those, about how many do you have in current database?**

I have about 1,200 names in my database overall. I am not sure how many are past clients; maybe 500 past clients.

Out of those 500 past clients, about 10% of that group have sent me personal referrals. Everybody has 5-6 clients that send them lots and lots of business and not because you send them a gift or a referral fee. Very good salespeople are very good lead producers for referrals.

**What percentage of your business is referral?**

About 80-85% of my business is referral.

**What client marketing activities do you do with past clients?**

I send desk calendars out annually. I do a quarterly newsletter to my client base and I hope to send out a better e-mail database process. Everyone wants to know what is being sold in the neighborhood.

# Listings

**What percentage of your transactions are listings? What would be ideal and why?**

About 20% of my transactions are listings. This is because I am David not Goliath; I end up being more of a buyer agent.

# Growth of Business

**What single quality has made you more successful than others?**

Honesty and service are important qualities.

**What does the average real estate agent fail to do which are among the reasons why they are average?**

They truly do not know how to sell and close a deal. People think selling is talking and pushing people. I think to be a good salesperson you should listen twice as much as they talk.

**If you could go back and do things differently, what would you have done at $100,000 that would have sped the growth of your business?**

I would incorporate all the possible technology into my marketing and my base; I was very lucky. You must understand how to sell and how to close. Closing is basically solving objections.

# GLADYS BLUM

GLADYS BLUM GROUP REAL ESTATE SERVICES

SALEM, OR

## Introduction

Gladys has been working in real estate since 1977 and in Salem real estate since 1979. She has been Salem's #1 Realtor since 1985 and has been nationally recognized throughout her career.her success doesn't come by luck or accident. She earned it one person at a time. Gladys' passion to help people is a trademark known and respectedthroughout the Salem community. Her team of outstanding professionals has also been recognized for their commitment to service and excellence. The Gladys Blum Group is truly the most trusted name in Salem Real Estate and is ready to serve you with the latest in technology & service.

Gladys is a family person. She is married with three sons and eight grandchildren that keep her active and happy on the home front. She is also a giving person. She is involved in her local church and directs a puppet ministry for children using teenagers as her puppeteers. She has a compassion for the needy in the Salem area and is extensively involved in charitable and business organizations that strive to meet that need and make the community a better place to live. She presently serves on the following local boards: Salem Leadership Foundation, Family Building Blocks, Salem Bible College, and United Way. She serves on the commission for Marion County Children and Families. She also serves on the Leadership Youth Committee and is active with the Salem Chamber of Commerce. This year (2006) she was awarded the honor of Salem's First Citizen.

## Background

**What is your background and how did you get into real estate?**

I worked for 9 years in banking and 6 years in accounting. I took a job doing books for a broker. At the time, the office had only 4 agents. Since they were making more money in less time than I was, I decided I wanted to become a Realtor.

**For how many years in business?**

I have been in the business for 30 years.

**What about your background, lessons from your family, friends, and previous jobs helped you succeed in your career?**

Working in the banking and lending fields helped me understand the financial part of the business and how to qualify people.

The accounting background gave me an understanding of what it takes to run a business such as budgeting, etc.

**What do you enjoy most about the business?**

Helping thousands with "The American Dream" of owning a home. I love to solve problems and see the end result: happy clients! Accomplishing what seemed impossible to many clients is a great feeling.

## Basic Numbers

**How many transactions did you have in 2005?**

I had 250 transactions in 2005.

**What was the dollar volume for 2005?**

The dollar volume for 2005 was $43 million.

**Currently, what is average home price?**

The average home sells for $180,000.

**Are you over a billion for career sales, what do you estimate?**

I would say, probably not yet. I am closer to $600-700 million.

**Who is on your current staff including: assistants, buyer agents, listing agents, other?**

I have eight people total, in the following capacities: one listing agent (myself), two buyer agents, one person in Marketing and prospecting for new business, one in escrow, one manager, one direct assistant and one receptionist.

## Goals

**Do you set written goals for your business and life?**

Yes, goals are important and they must be written. When I was with Mike Ferry we worked hard on goals, a business plan, and daily schedules. I had been in the business about 4 or 5 years before I started following written goals. I believe it is a critical part of the business, although only a small percentage of Realtors actually set goals.

**How do you work with goal setting?**

I break down the number of contacts and listing appointments necessary to meet my goals. Because of my longevity in the business, a large amount of my business just falls into my lap. A daily schedule is set to match my goals.

# Marketing

### New Customer Marketing – Lead Generation – Prospecting

**What are the top 3-5 methods you use for new client lead generation?**

1. The Internet: We presently have three websites that we maintain. A seller can sign up for a free evaluation online. Along with their market evalution, which is immediately sent to them, they are put on a campaign follow-up list to get a weekly email. Buyers have the same option. Depending on the buyers' interests, they are assigned to a buyers' agent. We gather criteria. My buyer agents have between 800 and 1,000 people in their follow-up campaign at any given time. Approximately 80% of our buyers come from our Internet marketing. The most important thing is to get in touch immediately – quick response is critical. They may be out there requesting information from several websites. The first one who responds to them wins so you need to be very quick to respond.

2. Expireds: There are very few expireds in our present market. If you have an expired, call them and try to make an appointment to meet them. If we cannot get an appointment, we deliver a package to them with our marketing plan. We also work old expireds. Every expired will continue to hear from us until they list with someone else or list with us. We compiled all expireds and put them into a mailing system. We touch base about every quarter.

3. FSBO: We created a website that they could advertise on. It was called sellingbyowner. We meet with them, take pictures and put it on the site. They are also placed on an email follow-up campaign.

**What do you do which is the most effective of your marketing efforts? What do you do, if anything, that you feel is fairly unique?**

We've really tried it all...homebuyers seminars, selling by owner seminars, door knocking, telemarketing. At this point of my career, the business comes to me due to doing the best job with every client. They don't forget and they keep coming back and sending their friends and family members. I also believe that my involvement in the community has been a huge payback.

**To give advice to someone at $100,000 and wants to get to $200,000 and more, what do you think they should do more of and do less of for marketing?**

Advice: Be on the phone. Talk to as many people as you can. A top producer never spends time running around with buyers. They should be on the phone with people including expireds. Spend 2-3 hours per day on the phone.

I would spend the morning hours on the phone (9am-Noon). Morning is best because otherwise, you will put it off.

Work your past clients and friends who know and love you. Don't get too hung up with personal marketing. It's costly and not very effective.

## Client Marketing – Repeats/Referrals

### About how many past clients do you have in your database?

I have about 3,000 past clients in my database. I moved to Oregon in 1978. We have a custom database called Market Master that has retained all of our client information.

### What do you do for client marketing to past clients?

We do a client contact "keep in touch" greeting card quarterly. It is a very classy card, with a handwritten note done by someone else. We make sure that it is hand addressed and hand stamped. At Thanksgiving, we give out a Pocket Pal, purse sized calendar. At Christmas, we send out a calendar that is a wall-sized format. Sometimes we will call them. At a minimum, we call on an annual basis. We have them broken into As, Bs, Cs. There are approximately 300 that I call "A's. They keep sending us business and we take good care of them. Our "B" group may not give us referrals but still consider us as their Realtor when they are ready to buy or sell.

### About what percent of your business is repeat?

I would say about 75-80% is repeat and referral. Many will refer their kids or siblings.

### What were your most effective ways of generating consistent referrals from your existing clients and past clients?

The most important thing is to stay in touch and do a good job during the transaction. When we come to the closing, we ask for referrals. That's the time clients are most thankful and appreciative of your services. We provide a gift at closing. We send out a "How Did We Do?" report card after closing and again ask for referrals. Then we will call twice after closing to make sure everything is okay; once at a week after and again at a month after closing. We remind them to send us their friends and family members who need real estate service.

## Sales

### What is your closing ratio of qualified leads for listing proposals?

It is about 80%.

### What are the top lessons learned in sales situations?

I have learned to be honest with pricing and not do anything to buy the listing. It is also important to be upfront with everything.

We have a marketing plan and a service plan. It is something that both parties sign so there are no surprises. We have learned to under-promise and over deliver.

## Listings

**What is your ratio of listings versus buyers and how has that changed over the years?**

Before 2005, it was always 2/3 listings and 1/3 buyers. In 2005, the market totally flipped and became a sellers' market. This changed our ratios to 50/50.

**Do you have any comment on a suggested balance for someone at $100k or $200k?**

My goal has always been 200 listings and 100 buyers.

## Specialized Markets and Approach

**Beyond the basics, are you involved with any specialized niche markets that are part of your success or more than 10% of your business?**

Our market area includes around 250,000 population so it doesn't really give us the opportunity for niche marketing. We actually deal with everything from manufactured homes to farms and ranches. We try to position ourselves as a household name for all real estate needs.

## Growth of Business

**What single quality has made you more successful than others?**

Telling the truth...no matter what! I am a great listener. I treat every client equally. I believe that being low-key instead of high pressure has worked well for me. I strive on learning new ideas and methods. I want to always be on the cutting edge.

**What one thing would you tell a beginning agent to pursue to achieve success?**

They always have to keep the pipeline full of leads; you cannot stop even if you have 10 deals in escrow. You need to make those contacts all the time. If the pipeline is empty you are in deep trouble.

**What were the biggest mistakes that you made that you would warn others about?**

I think the biggest problem has been staffing. Your office is as good as the weakest person…the person who takes that initial call, the person who makes your weekly client calls, the person who handles the transactions in escrow. I had a tough time letting someone go who really wasn't doing the best job.

**What would you have done differently if you could begin your career again? If you could go back and do things differently,what would you have done at $100,000 that would have sped the growth of your business?**

I really have no regrets. I had a fabulous broker who believed in me and pushed me to do the things I did best…working with sellers. I hired my first assistant my second year in the business at a time when it was unheard of in our industry. I was not satisfied when I reached $100,000 because I learned to think big through Mike Ferry's teaching. I learned goal setting and each year I set my goals higher, because I knew I could do it. Mike taught me to treat real estate as a business and do a business plan. I learned early on that it is crucial to rub shoulders with people who produce at your level or higher. I was in a Mastermind group from all over the US and we met quarterly. We were accountable to each other and shared problems and solutions. That same group is meeting today.

## Building a Team

**How did you first start to delegate and outsource and build a team?**

I have never had a problem with delegating. Some top producers do not like to delegate. It is important to give it up and let your assistant do the job. In my position, I do not do anything but list. I list the property and I am done. I cannot worry what everyone else is doing. I need to trust them with their job and that it is in good hands. I was probably the first person in the state of Oregon to have an assistant. It was easy passing on all the paperwork to her. The next person I hired was a buyer's agent; then a second one. I also hired a full time staff member to handle transactions in escrow. Next I hired a marketing expert. Then I needed someone to manage my staff so I hired a manager. Now I do what I do best. Work with sellers.

**In what order did you add your first part-time and full-time staff?**

1. Office Assistant (part time and then, full time)

2. Buyer's Agent

3. Transaction Assistant

4. Prospecting and marketing

5. 2nd Buyers Agent

6. Manager

## Learning

**What are the best books you have read in the past 10 years that helped you with your business and life?**

Richest Man in Babylon

Wealthy Barber

The Purpose Driven Life

Jesus Christ CEO

# MARTIN BOUMA

THE BOUMA GROUP - KELLER WILLIAMS REALTY

ANN ARBOR, MI

## Introduction

Martin has been a resident of Ann Arbor since 1977 when he moved to Ann Arbor to attend the University of Michigan. Graduating with a degree in Biochemistry he worked for a while at St. Joseph's Hospital as a Respiratory Therapist. Little did he know that a successful career in real estate was awaiting him in Ann Arbor.

To best serve his clients, Martin and his <u>enthusiastic team</u> input each of his listings into a marketing machine that sells more homes than any other Realtor in the area. His team also provides service that is second to none and, most important of all; he manages expectations by telling the truth and backing that up with facts. Thorough market knowledge, exceptional follow-through, and good old common sense are the hallmarks of Martin's continued success

Martin Bouma has been the #1 Realtor in Ann Arbor and Washtenaw County for several years. However, he also understands that while he might be proud of that fact, all it really means to you is that he has some real experience in this business.

But what does all that experience really mean to you? He always has the latest data about the market at his finger tips, so that when a house doesn't sell, he knows exactly why. With Martin you can be confident that you have gotten top dollar for your home. But it isn't just negotiating prowess that has gotten Martin to the top of his industry. Martin's competence, integrity and top-shelf skills combined with his warmhearted and down-to-earth personality have made him the most sought after agent in the area.

## Background

**How many years have you been in the real estate business?**

I have been in the business for 21 years.

**What is your personal background and how did you get into real estate?**

I obtained a biochemistry degree from the University of Michigan and wanted to attend medical school. I didn't get into medical school and started to work as a respiratory therapist at a hospital. My father owned real estate and I wanted to learn more about it, so I got my real estate license. The broker that sponsored me in the business encouraged me to try selling, and the rest is history.

I started with 40%, 8 years ago. I do not have high turnover and I hire very carefully. If they do not reach quota, I put them on probation. I've learned that you cannot motivate someone; either they have the drive and passion or they do not.

I believe that I have higher numbers because my buyers agents have been with me for many years. They start to get repeat business. Sometimes they do 5-6 deals per month. Once you get to 4-5 buyers per month you become limited by time restraints. You can't properly service your buyer clients if you're closing more than 4-5 buyers a month. Rapport and trust are very important.

## Goals

**Do you believe goals are important to your success? If yes, describe your approach to goal setting for your business and life?**

Completely. I follow the Keller Williams model. I know what I want to make and I work backwards and I know my conversion ratios. You start with what you want to make and I am driven by that. Every week we review our goals.

I know that if I do a certain number of things everyday, I will get there. I have a goal of 28 listing appointments per month. If I go on 28 appointments per month, everything else will fall in place. The hard part in this market is getting the number of listings when many sellers are unrealistic on price. I want saleable listings, not overpriced listings.

## Marketing

## New Customer Marketing – Lead Generation – Prospecting

**What are your top 5 methods for new client lead generation and about what percent of new customers are generated from that approach?**

For buyers we use the Internet. About 76% of our leads come from the Internet, 2% come from print, 10% from signs and the balance is from open houses and miscellaneous. We are totally systematized, and track every lead into the office. We go three deep in our questioning to determine exactly how they contacted us.

We have multiple websites. We use Number1Expert for lead generation and drip e-mail campaigns. I have my own personal site, bouma.com. I have an IDX site which is homesofannarbor.com. We have two informational sites, the condohotline.com and subdivision.com. These two sites have in depth information, on most subdivision and condominium complexes, in Ann Arbor. It shares active and sold information, floor plans, by-laws, etc. Consumers love the sites. They can get some information for free and for in-depth information we ask for their e-mail.. We capture all the e-mails and put into drip e-mail campaigns. We use Top Producer as our database manager.

We do not force people to give them our name and number. We would rather get one quality lead, then 100 bad quality leads. A brand new agent can get an IDX site and do Google PPC and anyone can be on my level right away. When a lead comes in we give it to the buyer's agent. They will attempt to contact the person via e-mail or phone. If it is a bad e-mail or phone, they will toss it. If it is a legitimate e-mail/phone, they will keep it for a week and hand it off to marketing for drip e-mail. For example, in October we had 68 leads that replied to an e-mail or we reached live. Overall it seems as if about 1 in 8.5 of those leads convert to a transaction.

Some agents have the ability to connect with people and some do not. Much of it boils down to the ability to build trust and rapport. The better you are at that — the higher your conversation rate!

## Client Marketing – Repeats/Referrals

**About how many prior clients have you worked with?**

Our prior client mailing list is about 1,500.

**What percentage of your business is referral?**

Our listing side is 65% and buyers it is 25%. Overall it is 40-50% of our business. I track every dollar and from where my business comes. When I look at how much money I get from prior clients, I feel I can increase it to 60%.

Some people are heavily prospecting-based, and they have a massive mailing campaign that is passive marketing. Who cares if you spend $500,000 on marketing if you get $1,000,000 back? You just really have to watch your Return on Investment.

Many agents are afraid of their prior clients. Even for me it is harder for me to call a prior client, then it is for me to call a FSBO or Expired. My fear is rejection. If a prior client rejects me on the phone, it is very personal because they are rejecting my company and me. But, when I do call prior clients, they are all happy to hear from me.

I call all of my current sellers once a week. I can contact about 15 sellers per hour, with many of them being voice mail.

We spend about $12,000/month or a little less than 10% of revenue on marketing. We are spending about $150,000/year on marketing. About one-third goes to print advertising. I spend, maybe $25,000, on prior clients. This is going to up significantly next year.

**What client marketing activities do you do with prior clients?**

We deliver a bouquet of flowers at their job on the 1st anniversary of their home purchase and a handwritten note every year thereafter. On their birthdays, our clients get a card with a coupon for a free ice cream for 4 people. At Christmas our prior clients receive a Christmas music CD. We also mail a yearly magnet calendar. We also mail our clients on a monthly basis.

## Growth of Business

**What single quality has made you more successful than others?**

This last year we hired a systems coach who spent 2 hours a week with my staff. He analyzed the workflow of the office and helped us systematize the whole office. Every staff person has a task matrix. We have a primary and secondary backup person. We have work procedures for each task. It has massively decreased my management time. This has totally streamlined the workflow and allowed me to stop micro managing.

We started six months ago and we thought it was a quick job. The most fascinating thing is that Becky worked with me for 12 years and we had different views of what people were doing. Now what happens is that if one of my staff is gone, someone can step-in and handle their job. Everyone who is primary backup knows they have to step-in. The whole documentation system is a few hundred pages. There are very few agents that are as systematized as my office.

**Did you make any big mistakes that you want to warn others about?**

The biggest mistake we make is hiring the wrong people. Making the transition from salespeople to business people is very hard.

Someone with three great employees will far exceed someone with three good employees. Too often we hire the wrong people, and take too long to fire them. They do not learn how to manage people.

The other big mistake we make is that we don't track where our business comes from.

## Building a Team

**In what order did you add your first part-time and full-time staff?**

Assistants – Marketing, Listing Management, Transaction Closing Coordination
Buyer agent
Listing agent

**If you had to do it again, today, from a starting point of making $100,000 per year, what would you suggest for delegating, outsourcing and staffing?**

Start with a business plan or model, and develop systems to implement your plan. Then hire the right people to implement your systems. This will result in the fulfillment of your business plan. Tweak as necessary.

# TUPPER BRIGGS

TUPPER'S TEAM
RE/MAX ALLIANCE EVERGREEN
EVERGREEN, CO

## Introduction

Born in Denver, Tupper Briggs earned his degree in accounting and then served in Vietnam before returning to Colorado as a CPA. The job lacked the people contact he desired, so he made his transition into real estate. He made a pact with himself that he would provide the finest level of service to every client he was fortunate enough to serve. Over the years, he has constantly asked himself what clients really want and has diligently directed his business accordingly. He is pleased with the resulting growth his business has experienced due to this philosophy. He is forever searching for new technology; better ways to stay in touch and improved marketing tools to serve clients beyond their wildest dreams. He delights in having clients say "WOW".

## Background

**For how many years have you been in the real estate business?**

I have been selling real estate for 34 years.

**What is your personal background and how did you get into real estate?**

I went to college, earned a degree in accounting and became a CPA. I was pulled into Vietnam and served as a finance officer. When I returned to Denver, I examined my experience with the CPA firm and the army. I realized that I was an entrepreneur at heart. I had heard about real estate and got into it. I did not realize that the personality of a CPA probably is not best suited for sales. Still, I was bound and determined to be successful. I took a Dale Carnegie course and every other course in selling skills I could. I discovered that there are many heavy-handed sales tactics. But, I also learned that sales is essentially putting yourself in your client's shoes and then, giving them what they want.

Fats Waller wrote a song in the 1920's with the lyrics, "Find out what they want and how they want it and give it to them just that way." Our entire office lives by that.

**What lessons did you learn from your family, friends, previous jobs, and life experiences that helped you most to succeed in your career?**

I grew up with three sisters; so I learned that negotiation was part of survival. I learned I didn't care for structured organizations. I learned that 99% of people are nice and mean well, and only 1% is not. So it pays to give the world the benefit of the doubt and keep your mind open to the wonderful possibilities that meeting each new person offers.

**What do you enjoy most about the business?**

At this point, I know so much about real estate that it is truly fun to come across inevitable new situations that require the skills and knowledge I've acquired to creatively solve problems.

Every single day something new is happening. Just today, we found out a title company paid off the wrong loan for a home, so we'll need to help them sort that out.

## Basic Numbers

**How many transactions did you close in 2005?**

We closed 187 transactions that totaled $65 million. The average transaction volume was about $365,000.

**Are you a Billion Dollar Agent?**

I estimate I attained this level about three to five years ago.

**What is your current staffing including: yourself, listing agents, buyer agents, managers, and assistants?**

I have five partners besides myself. I call them partners because they both list and sell. We have six agents and five staff people who support us.

## Goals

**Do you believe goals are important to your success? If yes, describe your approach to goal setting for your business and life?**

Absolutely! I can remember taking a goal-setting class in my salad days. I set a goal and then made it. I set another higher goal and made it again. I thought all I had to do is set the goal and I would achieve it. As I've made bigger goals, I have now realized that there is more to achieving goals than that. I can only set goals for things I have control over. If I know our numbers and we meet our goals for lead-generation, we will meet our overall production goals.

## Marketing

**New Customer Marketing – Lead Generation – Prospecting**

**What are your top five methods for new client lead generation and about what percent of new customers are generated from that approach?**

The web is by far our best source of buyers. We do pay-per-click on Google and Yahoo and we use search engine optimization. We have a number of websites to attract visitors from different directions. We have software to search the entire MLS using IDX. It allows people to enroll in our automated Buying Buddy system. Then they are e-mailed if a new property comes on the market. We understand the importance of immediate contact, so we have auto-responders and check our e-mail frequently during the day. We also understand that people browsing the Internet want to keep us at arm's length, until they've chosen a more active engagement with us.

Every morning I wake up to ten to twenty inquiries that need responses. Of those, about twenty percent turn into viable clients. Of those, maybe another twenty percent end up being transactions. We spend $1,500 to $2,500 per month on pay-per-click. Some of the leads eventually turn out to be viable, but not immediately. We stay in touch with them through our website. This way, they'll remember us when they become real buyers down the road. We currently have over 650 people at different stages of investigating our market in Buying Buddy. Once clients engage us, we follow up religiously.

Listings are about 75% of our business, and about 25% are buyers. 85% of our buyer business originates from the web.

We publish a four-color, sixteen-page newspaper that goes out once a quarter to every post office box and home in our entire marketing area of 26,000 households. We feature articles that are genuinely newsworthy. There is very little "We are great! List with us!" The cost of the newspaper is zero-based because our favorite businesses advertise in the newspaper. The cost to mail it is about $3,500 and we bear that expense ourselves.

As for print media, we always do full-color, full-page ads and we always feature the address and price of our listings in our ads. We also do just listed and just sold cards, but since our area consists of rural routes, our neighborhood mailings go out to a few hundred homes at a time.

## Client Marketing – Repeats/Referrals

**About how many past clients have you worked with?**

We have 3,000 past clients and vendors in our database. We do not keep individuals who have moved out of state in the system.

**What percentage of your business is referral?**

25-30% of our business comes from repeat and referral business.

**What client marketing activities do you do with past clients?**

Every time we sell a home we call the buyer to make sure everything is okay and make sure any problem is taken care of. Sending a plumber or handyman to the new buyer's house can be the best $50 ever spent, because they'll remember us when they eventually sell.

A week after closing we send out a survey questionnaire. We get about 75% back and 99% of them are glowing. We are quite proud of that.

We send a letter thirty days later to make sure the buyers are settling in okay and we send a copy of the warranty deed after it is recorded.

After six months, we send a coffee table book to celebrate their six-month anniversary in the home along with a note expressing our hope that they are enjoying their new home.

We send a copy of the settlement sheet the following January to assist them with their income tax preparation and send an anniversary card every year thereafter. We also send out monthly postcards featuring heartwarming Chicken-Soup-For-The-Soul kinds of stories. There is a picture of us on the front and the story about us on the back. We get lots of positive comments on them.

## Growth of Business

**What single quality has made you more successful than others?**

We care, we have fun, but we are very competent and we wear that on our sleeves. None of our promotion is heavy self-promotion. All of our marketing is done with the purpose of connecting with the public. We do very little 'sell, sell, sell'. When we ask people why they choose us, they generally say they saw our signs and ads everywhere. We try to be different than our competitors' self-promotional approach.

**What does the average real estate agent fail to do which are among the reasons why they are average?**

Realtors tend to be reactive. In reacting to one situation, they may not be ready or focused to react to another situation. We create systems and checklists to insure we stay on track and provide uniformly superior service despite the interruptions. We make it appear that we work 24/7 and we have organized workflow so we can cover everything.

# ROBERT BROWNE

## Introduction

Widely recognized as one of New York's most successful real estate experts, Senior Vice President, Robert M. Browne, cuts a distinctive figure in the Manhattan broker community. Whether tending his rooftop garden over Central Park, commuting to showings on his bicycle, or closing the largest residential real estate deal in New York City history, Robby approaches work and life with his own unique combination of intelligence, passion, and humor.

Equal parts seasoned professional, experienced negotiator, and charming raconteur, Robby has sold major properties in all parts of Manhattan, and is renowned for his ability to usher clients successfully through the selection process of the city's most discriminating co-op boards. Recognized by New York Magazine as one of New York's 21 most powerful and successful brokers (August 18, 2003), Robby works closely with partners, Maria Pashby, Chris Kann and Greg Sullivan, and is a member of Corcoran's elite $100 Million Circle.

## Background

**For how many years have you been in the real estate business?**

I have been in the business since 1986.

**What is your personal background and how did you get into real estate?**

My mother started working as a residential real estate broker, while my father was in a lengthy job transition. That was in Louisville, KY where I grew up. I was 10 years old and my three older brothers were in college. My mom became a top salesperson in Louisville within a few years. I remember giving her referrals from the kids I knew at school; and, I remember when she sold her first $100,000 house. I enjoyed doing Sunday open houses with her, but also saw how hard she worked.

I graduated from Phillips Academy in Andover, MA, Princeton University, and then, after some work experience, Harvard Business School. I worked part-time in the admissions office at Harvard University. From 1971-1988 I co-owned a travel company that took high school kids all over Europe. I was a teaching fellow at Phillips Academy, worked for Senator Mathias from Maryland. I worked for a year and a half for the 1984 Los Angeles Olympic Organizing Committee. I went to medical school for a year, then moved to New York to produce a Broadway Musical.

All of this experience was relevant to beginning my career in real estate, in 1986 in New York City. I can remember the floor plans and prices of almost everything I've sold in the City over the years. There are so many different ways of living in Manhattan and I find it fascinating. Usually, I can nail the price of any apartment that anybody asks me. However, I have no ability to remember movies, songs, or history. Selective memory, I guess.

Everyone said I should go into real estate because I was always telling people what properties to buy without having a license. At that time, I kept walking by a real estate office on Columbus Avenue. I needed a job, but I had seen my mother work so hard, and I initially rejected residential real estate sales as a career. I wanted a "real" career, like a doctor, or publisher of a magazine, and I wanted a guaranteed paycheck. Ultimately, I walked in to the realtor and was hired (my desk was in the basement). That was about the time the listing system was switching from index cards to computers. I may have been lucky with that, because I loved computer searches. If someone told me they wanted a one bedroom apartment in a certain location, I would push a button on the computer, and find everything available in seconds. My attitude has been, that the customer is "always right", and I provide the additional information, and tenacity to make it happen. I worked 24/7 for about 10 years, and I really enjoyed the process and results.

**What lessons did you learn from your family, friends, previous jobs, and life experiences that helped you most to succeed in your career?**

I think all of the experiences I have had, mostly following my heart, have contributed to making real estate so rewarding for me. It is surely not as easy as some may believe. I would think it is next to impossible to do part time.

**What do you enjoy most about the business?**

My former bosses have said to me, "You have both the contacts and ability to close; other agents have contacts but not the ability to close; still others can close but do not have the contacts." I like the puzzles and the steps in the real estate process in Manhattan; I enjoy making people happy with both purchases and sales. I am able to let go if a deal does not work. That is difficult to do, but important if you want to continue moving forward.

## Basic Numbers

**How many transactions did you close in 2005?**

There are 4 of us on our team. We had about 75 transactions.

**What was your total dollar volume in 2005?**

Our total dollar volume was over $250 million. Last year we (Chris Kann and Greg Sullivan and I) had a fourth partner, Maria Pashby, and we were the top producers and had the biggest dollar volume in New York.

**Based on that, about what is average price of a sale?**

Our average is about $2.5 million.

**Are you A Billion-Dollar Agent or do you believe you will hit that level during your career? Are you over a billion for career sales or what do you estimate?**

Yes, I am over $1 billion.

**What is your current staffing, including yourself, of listing agents, buyer agents, managers, and assistants?**

I have two listing/buyer agents and one assistant. We do not write offers, everything is verbal and goes to attorneys. We do cooperatives apartment sales which make up about half of our business. Every cooperative sale requires a board package which is an enormous amount of paperwork..

## Goals

**Do you believe goals are important to your success? If yes, describe your approach to goal setting for your business and life?**

I have not really set goals.

## New Customer Marketing – Lead Generation – Prospecting

**What are your top 5 methods for new client lead generation and about what percentage of new customers are generated from that approach?**

I do not have any conscious methods for attracting new clients. I do make sure that any presentation of a property I have listed, is presented clearly, and accurately on the web.

## Client Marketing – Repeats/Referrals

**What percentage of your business is referral?**

About 80% is client repeat/referral.

**What client marketing activities do you do with past clients?**

We do not do client marketing. I try to get together with friends (and clients) whenever possible. I enjoy entertaining and helping other people in any way I can.

## Growth of Business

**What single quality has made you more successful than others?**

I think always telling the truth has been one of the greatest keys to success.

# JIM BYRNES

ALAIN PINEL REALTORS
MENLO PARK, CA

## Background

**For how many years in the real estate business?**

I have been in the real estate business for 9 years. It is my 2nd career.

**What is your personal background and how did you get into real estate?**

Wow! It was a long, circuitous, sometimes arduous, sometimes effortless, journey to my real estate career. After almost flunking out of high school, I then worked as a draftsman for $350 per month. Going into and out of the Army, I decided that I could "do" more, I could "have" more, and most importantly I could "be" more! Fear is a great motivator!

I first elevated my educational goals and went from almost a high school drop out to a college graduate with honors and a degree in psychology and an M.B.A. It was then that I learned that your thoughts create your reality and success. I told myself that I was going to be a college graduate with honors before I even took the first class.I didn't know how to, but the mechanisms just showed up when they need to be there.

With confidence, I then landed a sales job in the Commercial Building Products Business and for the next 20 years had a "successful," somewhat predictable, linear career. I went from sales, to sales manager, to operations manager, to general manager and part owner.I built the business to a $200 million dollar a year sales volume with 178 employees to a profit point that was double industry standards. I thought that life couldn't get any better. Then, it even got better.We sold the company to an English conglomerate and I became "Group President."The inherent mistake I made is that I thought that I had created this success.Ifailed to realize that many people, events and forces contributed to this successful outcome. External forces then took over my life in challenging and redefining ways. First, the English conglomerate sold the company to another English conglomerate who had a very different vision and business plan.

Within six months, I was fired for not following all of the new company's directives.Within the next 12 months the company was gone.A viable 30 plus year leader in the industry destroyed by a conglomerate that knew nothing about the local and regional business and cultural dynamics.

At the same time as my firing, we had just completed the "Dream House from Hell."It took twice as long and cost twice as much.

# Billion Dollar Agent

A Realtor friend advised me not to tear down a perfectly good home for a great home, but I didn't listen. In retrospect, that would be the beginning of my calling, my purpose, my passion...."to help people make theirbest real estate decisions - to help people create their lifestyle within a realistic affordability model."

We reluctantly sold the home, I was then diagnosed with cancer, had no job and then we got divorced. I went from a 4000 sq. ft. home to a 12 x 14 foot room with books in one corner and a saxophone in another.I share this with you so this does not happen to you.Pay attention to what you are doing, and how you are doing it. Don't just be a participant in life, be an observer of your life and others.You must create a bird's eye perspective of your life and others and learn from other people's experiences.

It was again time to reinvent myself.It was now "Half Time".I had played the first half of my life. I was now in the locker room before the second half was going to begin. Would I do the same and what would I change?

I made a commitment that the second half of my life has to be lived with magical people, places and things. I did not want a job that was OK or good.I wanted a profession that I could be passionate about and would align with my core values and beliefs. I went to NYC for a year as a consultant. It was successful but I am a California boy and California Real Estate has always interested me.

So as a result of some positive experiences, some negative experiences, some defining moments and a lot of everyday experiences that I should have paid more attention to, I began my real estate career with passion, purpose but not much of a plan.

What lessons did you learn from your family, friends, previous jobs, and life experiences that helped you most to succeed in your career?

Define who you are and who you want to be and how do you want to be remembered. Then select your everyday activities and behavior with this end in mind. Be passionate and proud of who you are, what you do and most importantly how you do it. In other words, love what you do and do what you love.

Life is not a linear journey up or down.Life is full of cycles and wondrous opportunities if we just take the time and perspective to recognize them....take action....and share these opportunities and successes with others.

I'm not perfect, but I'm better than I used to be.

**What do you enjoy most about the business?**

I enjoy helping people make their best real estate decisions and helping them create and enhance their lifestyle within affordability boundaries.

**Are you a Billion Dollar Agent or do you believe you will hit that level during your career? Are you over a billion for career sales or what do you estimate?**

I have sold almost $400 million in my 9 years in the real estate business. I will reach the Billion Dollar mark within the next 9 years, due to not only my focus and attention on professional and personal goals, but also from the nurturing and support of Real Estate/Life coaches like Floyd Wickman and Patti Kouri, Mentor Groups with Ted Jacobsen and Laura Stuckey and with the help and guidance of the higher source.

**What is your current staffing including: yourself, listing agents, buyer agents, managers, and assistants?**

I have one assistant. My goal is to keep it simple and direct. I want to personally touch my clients' lives toward their greater success and enjoyment.

## Goals

**Do you believe goals are important to your success? If yes, describe your approach to goal setting for your business and life?**

Goals are your dreams combined with your passion, purpose, a defined plan, some playfulness, and a timeline. Goals are a progressive journey of constant and never ending improvement and abundance.

Goals are an extension of your core values and beliefs. Your professional and personal goals are most successful and significant to yourself and others when they are in alignment with your higher self and when they benefit others.

Your thoughts create your goals and reality. I think high not low. I think positive not negative. I think abundance, not scarcity, I think great not just good.

Consequently, my approach to goal setting, in business and life, is to set goals that will greatly enhance my life and the life of those around me.

Your professional goals are the "legs" of your business. These legs create and support your production and operational success of your business. Each goal must begin with a positive statement. For example, "I have (or it's on it's way), a world class referral network that drives my business and creates 75% of my business." Then, the goal needs an strategic element of — what will it take and am I willing to do it. Then the goal needs specific action steps, to achieve it within a specific time frame.

Your personal goals are not the legs of personal success. Your personal goals are the legs of your significance, your legacy. Like professional goals, our personal goals involve passion, purpose, a plan, playfulness and have short, medium, and long range timelines.

However, the significant difference between professional and personal goals is that your personal goals are much more important and significant than your business goals. Your business goals are only a partial blueprint to achieve you personal purpose, goals, desires, wants and needs.

The beauty of Real Estate is that you can combine or integrate both business and personal goals, every day and every way with proper thought and actions.

## Marketing

### New Customer Marketing-Lead Generation-Prospecting

**What are your top 5 methods for new client lead generation and about what percent of new customers are generated from that approach?**

Historically, Open Houses have been my best method for new client lead generation.It still represents 50% of my business development. My open houses are a blend of entertainment and education.My mind set is that I am hosting a party for the neighbors, potential buyers, and sellers.To make the "open house party" successful and enjoyable, I do the following action items:

- Send open house card invitations to the neighborhood with a start time of 1/2 hour before the public open house. When the general public arrives the house is full of people interacting, talking, laughing.
- I bake cookies and use them as an icebreaker.
- I provide a real estate sales activity analysis of the neighborhood. It includes the last 6 months of sales activity and is helpful for buyers and neighbors.

The report contains summary pages, statistical analysis, a one page color photo and summary of each house, and a map locating all homes 4 sale, sale pending, and sold in the area. It creates great take-home value for all open house visitors regardless of their immediate intent.

My second (and growing) best source of lead generation are referrals. Referrals currently represent 30% of my business. Referrals include my Power Partners, Prior Clients, and people within my Sphere of Influence.

Website hits and follow up account for 10% of new business. Many are buyers that have to sell their existing home.

Just Listed/Just Sold and local newspaper advertising of homes for sale account for 7% of my new client business. However, this is very expensive and should decline as my referrals and Internet business contacts grow.

Sign calls are still alive but with a weak pulse at 3% of new business leads.

## Client Marketing

**What percentage of your business is referral?**

About 30% of my business is referral with the intent to double this percentage in 2007.

**What client marketing activities do you do with prior clients?**

I have a Customer Appreciation Program for my past clients. It includes a 1 year home warranty for buyers and a gift for sellers at the close of escrow. I ask each client for a letter of recommendation based upon my value added services.Also, I ask them if they know anyone who might be thinking about buying or selling their home. I send quarterly newsletters with current neighborhood home sale market activity, real estate and mortgage trends, and maintenance and repair tips for their home. I also send a contractor resource booklet for their review and use.It includes many trades and services they will need to help maintain or repair their interior or exterior of their home. I have a client appreciation party for all my past clients once a year. I have a special event for my Power Partners that bring multiple clients to me once a year. Magical Power Partners, Prior Clients and Sphere of Influencers are also invited to dinner and other events on an individual basis.

## Growth of Business

**What single quality has made you more successful than others?**

I make my clients #1 goal, my #1 goal.

**What does the average real estate agent fail to do which are among the reasons why they are average?**

They fail to think, believe and affirm that they can be a world class Realtor.

They have no goals, or have low achievement goals.

They put their own needs in front of the needs of their clients.

They do not approach real estate like a business.

They have no plan or timelines.

They do not have a list of daily proactive real estate activities that help create and grow their business. They confuse "hygienic" activities (i.e., going on tour or floor time), with "intention" activities (i.e., prospecting your sphere of influence, or holding an open house, sending out a mailer or newsletter) with home benefits for the reader.

They pretend to be in real estate and they pretend to get paid. They do not have a real estate/life coach. A coach will help them define and align their business and personal goals. A coach helps to create a strategy to implement the daily, monthly, and yearly action items that are necessary for greater success and enjoyment. Get a coach! I did and it more than quadrupled my business in the next 12 months and doubled my business in each of the next 2 consecutive years!!!

# BILL CAIN

RE/MAX UNIVERSAL REALTY INC.
PLYMOUTH, WI

## Background

**How many years have you been in the real estate business?**

I have been in the business for 26 years.

**What is your personal background and how did you get into real estate?**

I grew up in a small town -- Plymouth, Wisconsin. I got interested in construction and doing housing projects. I worked in steel construction and different things. We built one house in the winter, when it was slow, and we sold it in the spring. Then, we got paid in the spring when it sold. I worked in the trades. I wrote a business plan in my sophomore year of high school for a real estate company. It was a dream. I guess it was about 9 years later and I got into real estate. I saw that everyone in construction did not make it past age 40. I started an auction business out of high school. I went to auction school and was a good ring man and did the cattle and all sorts of auctions. People asked us if we could sell their farms. Auctions worked well to list the houses also.

**What lessons did you learn from your family, friends, previous jobs, and life experiences that helped you most to succeed in your career?**

I learned about hard work and honesty. I learned to do it right the first time. I grew up as the oldest of a family of seven. I learned to work, it was just the way it was. I learned about working on farms. I always had a job doing something since 7th grade; I worked in a cheese plant. Almost everyone during college or high school days worked in a brat factory or a cheese factory. I learned the things I did not want to do in a variety of different avenues. I tended bars and I did lots of door to door sales.

**What do you enjoy most about the business?**

I like the variety, the different people, how I can help people. I like to help them accomplish their goals and life changes.

## Basic Numbers

**How many transactions did you close in 2005? What was your total dollar volume in 2005? Based on that, about what is average price of a sale?**

We closed 366 transactions for about $62 million. Our average is about $180,000.

**Are you a Billion Dollar Agent or do you believe you will hit that level during your career? Are you over a billion for career sales or what do you estimate?**

I have been with RE/MAX for about 15 years. My estimate is that 5 years ago maybe $40 million. I guess that I am over $500 million.

**What is your current staffing, including yourself, of listing agents, buyer agents, managers, and assistants?**

We have 5 buyer's agents. We have a front desk person. We own the franchise for RE/MAX. We have a closing assistant, a technology person, and a marketing person. I am doing a lot of real estate auctions. We are selling most houses the same day. I am also a certified personal property appraiser. I get in more doors when a business is splitting up. I get to meet more people and develop more relationships. I get in the door, a lot, between auctions and appraising. I hired an office manager, a month ago, so he can work on managing the agents as a sales manager.

## Goals

**Do you believe goals are important to your success? If yes, describe your approach to goal setting for your business and life?**

Coach Ken Goodfellow worked with me for many years. He has a printout of 20-30 sheets to analyze where each closing comes from and doing budgeting. It is very important. Every seminar I went to - Howard Brinton, Mike Ferry, I was a tape-aholic; I bought every set. I self-taught with the tapes and listened to them between appointments. I built a library. Tapes have been wonderful for me. I have done that for 20 years. Positive attitude is important, and also never stop learning. Attitude is 100% of the game. With a good attitude you can groom a good salesperson and a good smile and a good handshake. I think some of it is an instinctive competition in the belly.

You get in the zone like a professional athlete and you know they train and train and train. You need to invest. In this business you have to work at it and build one relationship at a time. Honesty and a fair reputation are important. Don't be afraid to try different things.

## New Customer Marketing – Lead Generation – Prospecting

**What are your top five methods for new client lead generation and about what percentage of new customers are generated from that approach?**

When we get a new listing, Just Listed and Just Sold are great. The Just

Listed card does better than newspaper. We may mail 50 postcards or we may mail 500 postcards - usually we mail 50 to 200.

The Internet is incredible in all aspects. We do internet emails for our auction business. We have a good sphere of people. We do a lot by email and are repetitious by being in front of them. We do a lot of benefits. We do 40-50 benefit auctions per year for different groups and we donate our time and get in front of hundreds of people. That makes us different. I sometimes get in front of 800 people. We raise hundreds of thousands of dollars doing benefit auctions.

We have done billboards in the past. I ask them why they called us and they say, "I see your signs everywhere". By just being out there and around we carry anywhere from 200-400 listings at times. We do some subdivisions and we are at about 125-150 houses on the market. Signs are a big item. Listings are about 'circulate to percolate'. Start working more on FSBO and Expireds. We have never done a lot of it. Do referrals. The newspapers are having less and less impact.

We spend about 15% on marketing. We are trying to get it back to 10%. I am at 18-20% this year.

## Client Marketing – Repeats/Referrals

**Of those, about how many do you have in current database?**

We have about 5,000.

**What percent of your business is referral?**

Last year it was about 80%. Using Coach Ken we really analyzed the transactions.

**What client marketing activities do you do with past clients?**

I do an annual Christmas party. We have a new facility. We will get about 200-250 people. We will invite all the builders as well. We will invite 1,000 people.

I will take some clients out to dinner or go out fishing. You've got to be working a client once a week. I help their church with auctions. I donate my services and help them raise money. I have a pottery collection. I have about 50 different pieces and I know some people that enjoy pottery. I give unique gifts. A couple of times a year we will give out 1,000 flags for parades.

## Growth of Business

**What single quality has made you more successful than others?**

I guess hard work. It is not we can't do, it is how we can get it done. Positive attitude is the one thing.

**Did you make any big mistakes that you want to warn others about?**

I guess other people saying 'you can't do it.' For some people, a lot of it is jealousy. You work your tail off and find out who your true friends are. Adding staff one-by-one and taking risks to grow out of your comfort zone and learn how to do it.

Shoot the gun instead of aim, aim, aim. You have to dream. Try some things within reason.

# RON CAMPBELL

THE CAMPBELL TEAM

CAMPBELL AND CAMPBELL REAL ESTATE SERVICES

ALBUQUERQUE, NM

## Introduction

Ron Campbell has an extensive background in sales and marketing that spans over 30 years and includes management, ownership, franchising, and mortgage banking. He is a national speaker and a member of several elite groups of real estate brokers/owners who are ranked nationally as the best in the business. He has set real estate records locally, statewide, and nationally that still stand after almost a decade. He is a licensed real estate broker in New Mexico and the only one to rank in REALTOR® Magazine's Top 100 for three consecutive years - 2001, 2002 & 2003! The Campbell Team has closed over 2700 transactions worth in excess of $360 million of residential real estate since 1990.

## Background

I am a Howard Brinton star, A Bill Barrett Top 50 member and a coach for Coach Ken out of Canada. I have a life, work four and a half days a week, manage a large team, coach 27 clients and sell forty to sixty homes a month on the average.

Mike Ferry was my personal coach for two years in along with Coach Ken (the New York Times recognized sales manager for Mike Ferry). I have also been associated with Howard Brinton and the excellent Tom Ferry.

**For how many years have you been in the real estate business?**

I have been in real estate since 1991.

**What is your personal background and how did you get into real estate?**

At one-time, I was one of the largest mobile home dealers. When the interest rates rose to eighteen percent and the oil field markets shut down, dealers were on recourse financing. Homes were being repossessed. In ninety days I had a $2.3 million loss. I went bankrupt in 1986 and lost everything. I started over at the age of 40. I had a wife and three kids. I was sick of the mobile home business. I sold cars for a few years to figure out what I wanted to do. The books I read said people made money on real estate so I went into real estate in May of 1990.

The first three companies I went to work for shut their doors. The third company was an ERA franchise. He shut his door sixty days later. I was an entrepreneur and picked up the franchise for $2,500. I joined with a partner who was another top agent in the city fed up with current circumstances. We opened our own company and an ERA franchise. I put my destiny back into my hands not someone else's. In 1991 I was named international rookie of the year. I sold 176 houses by adopted principles out of my background. I was the first to advertise a house with a down payment and a monthly payment. I did not go after listings, I found someone who wanted to buy a house.

I took out ads for entry-level houses; $50,000 houses with a down payment and a monthly payment. I had so many phone calls that, the third month, I hired two Buyers' Agents and a Personal Assistant. I was the first Realtor in the city with a Buyers' Agent. My background in finance gave me the information to learn how to qualify people. I had a credit bureau terminal in my office, set everyone up for an appointment on Saturday and had them lined up to see me. I knew that monthly payments and down payments are the key.

An attorney in town had billboards about "I sue drunk drivers." His name was Ron Bell; my name is Ron Campbell. His number was 828-BELL so I choose 821-RONN and put up a huge billboard. Then I bought a $35,000 electronic message center that was 35 feet long that I could control it with a modem from my office.

When I was growing up I always looked over at McDonalds to see if they had sold a million hamburgers yet. I am going to have a electronic signboard showing the number of houses I have sold. Every time I sell a house, I will change the numbers from my office. Human nature looks for change.

Joe Stumpf used a picture of my billboard for many years as innovative advertising.

**What lessons did you learn from your family, friends, previous jobs, and life experiences that helped you most to succeed in your career?**

After I filed bankruptcy, I was down mentally. I had always had perfect credit. I read one book called Why Smart People Fail. I decided that I was a victim of the time and circumstances and it had nothing to do with me. When you lose everything you find out who your true friends are. We had a non-dischargeable debt of over $175,000. I was motivated to make money to pay off the debt. I have always been one to plow ahead, take risk, and damn the torpedoes. I have a high confidence level.

## Basic Numbers

**How many transactions did you close in 2005?**

In 2005 I reached $448,363,301 in sales with 2005 being a little over 80 million. That represented 3035 homes sold overall.

I have now surpassed 500 million in my career. In 2005, we had about 480 transactions with average price of about $200,000.

**What is your current staffing including: yourself, listing agents, buyer agents, managers, and assistants?**

I have twelve buyer agents, of which six are required to man a shopping mall location for eighty hours a week. I have no listing assistants other than my son. Out of the 480 deals and 240 listings, I win about 80% of the listing appointments. It is about 40 deals per buyer agent.

I expect two sales a month from the buyer agents. I think a typical deal is eight to twelve hours. Someone else does transaction coordination. I take pride in the fact that my team is different from most teams. I have found that it is very common for buyer agents to wait for the rainmaker to give them leads. In my case, every Tuesday night we have Team Tuesday. My buyer agents show up at 5:00 and from 5:30 to 7:30pm we knock on doors, or we will telemarket around the houses we have sold or we work Internet leads.

Every time we sell a house we put 200 door hangers around the house. We go to whitepages.com and produce a telemarketing list and scrub against do not call list and then we telemarket every Tuesday night with a "Would You Take" system which is a script we have developed. We recently just sold a house down the road and we possibly have another buyer.

I have a Monday morning sales meeting each week and I am always talking about what it means to be successful. I own my company and I am independent so I train to retain. I train people to be good agents and then independent agents. I put them on a 80% split until company has received $12,000 then they go to 90% until $18,000 and finally 100% split until anniversary date.

## Goals

**Do you believe goals are important to your success? If yes, describe your approach to goal setting for your business and life?**

I set my goals in October of every year for the next year. I am looking at my sales board; I track everything by month. Our goal is $125 million in sales. Last year goal was $100 million and we did $80 million.

## Marketing

### New Customer Marketing – Lead Generation – Prospecting

**What are your top five methods for new client lead generation and about what percentage of new customers are generated from that approach?**

One-third of all our sales originate from the Internet. I have 15 to 25 leads per day. I use a service called Number 1 Expert. We have multiple Internet sites. I have full-time person working Internet leads. This is an inside sales person. I have had an inside sales person since October. If a buyer agent leaves you, there is no clue of what he is taking with him. Tracking sources of leads is critical. I wanted to be able to track the leads and know the source of the leads. The only job of the person was to work the lead. We went with a software program called LeadTrax which is an online system. This lead automatically enters into our lead tracking system; we don't need to re-enter it. Any buyer agent can go into the fishing pond for the leads sitting there and they can assign themselves any number of leads. They are given thirty days to generate some sort of response or else they go back to the fishing pond for a later date. Most of the agents go to the fishing pond and drop personal notes while they are waiting. We have seen a huge difference. We have a drip system like everyone else and they can tell it is a canned response. We have a personal letter that goes out from us, over and above from Number 1 Expert. It tells a full page about us.

This is a pearl. On our Internet sites, you have to login to send an e-mail. I am not interested in hits. I am interested in inquiries and leads! About 40 percent of leads that came in have names and phone numbers and 60 percent have e-mails only. This was really frustrating. We immediately, if we have e-mail only, send out a survey broken out in four phases. The first phase is really generic, the second gets more personal and by the fourth phase we ask what type of Realtor they want to work with. When we send the survey out we asked for a phone number to contact them and we get back 40 percent from the 60 percent that only provided an e-mail address.

Two percent of Internet leads convert to a closed transaction.

One-third of all sign calls, proactive efforts and marketing material responses convert.

## Client Marketing – Repeats/Referrals

### About how many past clients have you worked with?

I have worked with over 3,000 clients. We have 2,200 in our database. Our metro market consists of 750,000 people. There are about 1,000 homes sold monthly or 12,000 per year. I average about forty to fifty sales per month. Our market share is about four to five percent.

125 past clients did a deal with us in 2005.

### What percentage of your business is referral?

25% of my business is by referral.

### What client marketing activities do you do with past clients?

I am not a superstar with past clients.
We write handwritten personal cards on their birthday.

We do anniversary cards for the home sale.
We sometimes drop them something in the mail about the market.
We send holiday cards.
We also try to make two calls a year to these people.
My wife makes the calls; she sits out at the kitchen table and handwrites the card.

We know our past client. We know every client. We go to every closing.

## Growth of Business

### What single quality has made you more successful than others?

Consistency. I know how to do the same thing. Every morning I do the same thing, day after day; I tried to find an excuse not to do it. I have no choice. I know that I have to be consistent at what I do and do it every day. I prospect two hours every day. If I do not prospect my business will go down. I have a dedication to do the same thing day in and day out.

# DeLena Ciamacco

## Introduction

DeLena Ciamacco was born and raised in Columbus, Ohio. DeLena attended Columbus Public Schools and then the Ohio State University for 6 years with studies in International Business, International Marketing, and Criminology/Sociology. In 1989 she decided to take a temporary detour from her original path (of attending Law School at Capital University) to pursue a career in Real Estate.

DeLena began to sell Real Estate with a local conventional real estate brokerage. Quickly, she realized to grow, she would need to affiliate herself with a much larger, International Company. She chose RE/MAX and that is when her career as a Realtor began to soar. In 1993, just after her second year with RE/MAX, DeLena ranked #5 among RE/MAX Realtors in all of Ohio. In 1994 she became one of the Top 100 Re/Max Realtors in the World (and has been ranked in "The Top 100" ever since). In 1998 she took over the number #1 Re/Max Realtor position in Ohio.

## Background

**For how many years have you been in the real estate business?**

I have been in business as a Realtor for 17 years (since 1989).

**What is your personal background and how did you get into real estate?**

Personally, I always thought I would be a Lawyer, or possibly join the C.I.A. I attended the Ohio State University (Go Bucks!) for 6 years with studies in International Business, International Marketing, and Sociology/Criminology. I took a little detour from my intended path because one of my girlfriends said: "let's get our real estate license". It was a three week course. I had nothing to lose, but a few weeks, so I agreed. The first few months were challenging, but I LOVE a good challenge. My friend dropped out of Real Estate after just a few months, but I have been selling ever since! I would not trade this profession and everything I have learned for anything.

**What lessons did you learn from your family, friends, previous jobs, and life experiences that helped you most to succeed in your career?**

My family has had a big influence on me. My parents are both Italian immigrants. They came here with nothing.

# Billion Dollar Agent

My father built a large commercial construction company and my mother stayed at home. My entire family has always been committed to working long, hard hours at anything we do, because that is how we were raised and what we saw our father do. I become bored quickly if I am not always moving at 150 miles an hour! My brother and sister are the same way. While in college, I managed a clothing boutique and a tanning salon. The clothing store owner taught me how to "soft sell", how to politely not take "no" for an answer, and how to try harder and learn from my mistakes when rejected.

## What do you enjoy most about the business?

I go nonstop all day from the minute I get in here until the time I leave. I had an assistant cover my work to do this interview. I work 12-14 hours a day, 7 days a week and love every minute of it. It does not feel like a job to me. I have always told myself, "If I stop liking what I do, I will get out of it!" I love that you can make as much money (or as little, for that matter) as you want and get rewarded for your actions in this business. I have also witnessed many clients, family members and friends, have no control over their job loss, down sizing, or transferring, etc. I know as long as I am willing to work hard, remain honest & ethical and always do what I tell my clients I will do, I will never be "fired" from my job! What more could I ask for?

## Basic Numbers

### How many transactions did you close in 2005?

My numbers average about $60-100 million a year. 2005 was a little slower, maybe $80 million and just over 200 transactions.

### Are you a Billion Dollar Agent or do you believe you will hit that level during your career? Are you over a billion for career sales or what do you estimate?

For the last 10 years, I have sold over 300 homes (except for 2005) per year. I would estimate my sales volume to date is over $500 million and I most definitely plan to hit the Billion dollar mark soon!

### What is your current staffing including: yourself, listing agents, buyer agents, managers, and assistants?

I have a team of 16 people. There are 6 licensed agents and 10 unlicensed people. 5 agents work with buyers and sellers and 1 works with buyers only. I personally do both, but mainly sellers (listings). Of the total annual transaction we close as a team I, personally, am responsible for approximately 70% of them. My personal buyer assistant handles my personal clients. My "personal clients" can best be described as family members, friends, my sellers who have homes to sell & buy, personal referrals (if my time does not permit) and prior clients. My buyer assistant handles all the showings for my buyers.

I prefer to negotiate the contracts and to attend the closings.

All "cold calls" and some listings I just do not have time to work go directly to my other 5 licensed assistants.

I am a "hands-on" person. I communicate with my clients directly and get extremely involved in the day to day activities of my business. The responsibilities of my unlicensed assistants include: production, printing, and mailing of my marketing pieces; calling for feedback on showings and reporting to my Seller clients; entering Buyer clients into our automatic update data base; answering calls, maintaining files, supplies, submitting my ads to the various publications; and providing copies of those ads to my clients, and, of course, keeping me informed always! Our goal is to always maintain over 100 listings. I spend over $500,000 a year in advertising. As busy as I am, I write every ad for each of my listings. An assistant, who has never viewed that listing and probably lacks a marketing background, cannot accurately depict the important features of that home. I create systems and manuals for everything we do. Consistency in everything we do is critical to me.

## Goals

**Do you believe goals are important to your success? If yes, describe your approach to goal setting for your business and life?**

Absolutely! I set goals every year. At the start of the year I write down what I want to accomplish for the upcoming year and attach it above my computer so that I see it every day.

As a former Re/Max office owner, I did goal setting with the agents every year. I encourage everyone to set their goals slightly higher than what they feel they can achieve because it has been my experience that most people tend to underestimatethemselves & their ability.

For me, setting goals high is motivating! My Goal categories are broken down to two groups: Business and Personal goals. Unfortunately, very seldom do I meet my personal goals because I love the feeling of working extra hard to achieve my business goals. I know I will always have those "golden" years to enjoy my personal goals.

I think I learned about goal setting during my school years, or perhaps by accident. Either way, it works for me and always has. Although it may be against the "norm", I have only been to 1 or 2 seminars. I really like to create and discover things that work for me and it keeps my systems unique to the masses.

## Marketing

**New Customer Marketing – Lead Generation – Prospecting**

**What are your top five methods for new client lead generation and about what percentage of new customers are generated from that approach?**

My most successful marketing campaign has to be my Just Listed and Just Sold cards. I direct mail 5,000 to 10,000 pieces each month. When we ask clients how they heard about me, they often mention my postcards. Consistency is the key to marketing and probably life in general. I have been consistently marketing for 17 years. I always try to stay in front of people. In this business, there are so many Realtors, the public will forget about you quickly if they are not constantly reminded of who you are and what you do.

We direct mail anywhere from 1,000 postcards up to 10,000 for each listing. We decide how many to send by price range, market location and/ or my desire to gain market share in a particular area. The average number of cards sent is 2,000. I will send them to the immediate neighbors, move-up neighborhoods, executive rentals, and in some cases, entire zip codes! We do everything in house. We have our graphic design programs, mail machines, color printers, commercial cutters, etc. When sending as many direct mail pieces as I do, it definitely pays to be able to not only cut production time by 75% but also to produce a card at 25% of what it would cost you to outsource it.

Besides mass mailings, I try to submit numerous full-page ads to the majority of the local print publications. I also buy about ½ hour two times daily on the local cable channels highlighting my listings.

I do very little personal promotion. I would estimate less than 1% of my total marketing budget is spent on promoting just myself. I think word of mouth and personal referrals is the promotion anyone could hope for … and it's free!

## Client Marketing – Repeats/Referrals

**About how many prior clients have you worked with?**

We have about 4,000 prior clients, friends, family members, etc. in our database.

**What percentage of your business is referral?**

I would estimate that our client repeat/referral number is 60%.

**What client marketing activities do you do with prior clients?**

We send a "Home Journal" to my entire database monthly. The Home Journal publication is outsourced, but we prepare, label it and mail it in house. It contains tips about the market as well as home selling tips and recipes.

I send out annual Holiday cards to the same database.

We send out "Thank you for referring…" cards to anyone who refers a client to me. Many years ago, a client referred someone to me. I called her and thanked her but failed to send her a note.
She then told a mutual friend that I did not even send her a note.
That was the last time it ever happened. I immediately designed a "Thank you for referring a Buyer/Seller" card and we immediately mail one to anyone who refers a person to me! I learn quickly from my mistakes and never repeat the same mistake twice. I truly believe that is a large key to success in any business!

## Growth of Business

### What single quality has made you more successful than others?

I think my drive, self-motivation, and positive attitude towards everything, has made me successful. I have found most people prefer to be around a positive, uplifting personality. I also prefer to use my own creative, innovative ideas instead of those designed by others. I enjoy creating systems that are unique to the way I do business, my personality and standout compared to the competition.

### Did you make any big mistakes that you want to warn others about?

Employees/competent staff are the biggest challenge. Locating people, with a strong work ethic, is so difficult to find in today's world. Your staff is an extension of yourself. Everything trickles down from the top. If you are a hard working, honest, fair and diligent boss your staff will mirror that. If not, cut them lose …and fast! When hiring, go with your "gut instinct". If your "gut" does not feel good about a potential employee right upfront there is usually a reason. I have made many major business decisions right from my "gut"!

## Building a Team

### How did you first start to delegate and outsource and build a team?

Delegating is extremely hard for most people. We always think we can do it better or faster than anyone else. You must remember, however, there is only one of you and your time is not best spent doing tasks an hourly employee can do for you. I hired my first assistant when assistants were not even being used in our local industry. I hired my first assistant back in 1991. I was only in the business for 2 years when the RE/MAX office receptionist wanted to work for me as a personal assistant. I did not see the value then and I certainly was not making enough money (at least that is what I thought) to have an assistant. She was extremely persistent, so I agreed to hire her on a part-time. I quickly realized I needed her full-time.

She freed up my time by handling all the day to day activity so I could get out there to do what I knew I did best, SELL!

For each assistant I hired after her, my business grew and grew and grew.

To this day I still have a tough time delegating to assistants because I am such a "hands on" person but I have become much better at it.

If an agent wants to get to $100,000 level or beyond, they MUST hire an assistant. They must free up their time to sell. Every assistant helped me get to the next level. I would suggest you train your new assistant from the ground up. Create manuals and systems as you go and do not be afraid to just "turn them lose". They will be much more effective if you loosen the reins, so to speak. Remember, they are your direct connection to all prospective clients calling into the office for you.

# KRISTAN COLE

THE KRISTAN COLE TEAM
RE/MAX OF WASILLA
WASILLA, AK

## Introduction

Kristen is originally from Nebraska. She moved to Alaska in 1969 when her dad went to work for the Alaska Railroad. After graduating high school, she went to college in Arizona, but returned to Alaska to begin her career in real estate. Whether she's devoting time to her career or her hobbies, Kristen always holds herself to the highest standards. Determined, dedicated, and focused, she always strives to be her best in every situation. That's why, as a real estate professional, she's committed to providing the best service for her clients and for her team. Besides closing 365 sides in 2005 with the help of her team of 14, she's a pilot; an avid outdoors person; a former Miss and Mrs. Alaska; and she and her husband, Brad, are raising five children.

## Background

**How many years have you been in the real estate business?**

This is my 23rd year in the business.

**What is your personal background and how did you get into real estate?**

My mother was a real estate agent. My parents pushed me to get my business degree in college, but initially I rebelled and studied engineering until I was totally miserable. I then switch majors and double majored in real estate and finance at the University of Arizona. I now have my MBA as well. I started in real estate right after college. I went to work for RE/MAX where my mother was a RE/MAX broker owner. Two years later I I got my broker license and decided to buy the company. I bought my Mom out and owned the company for three years, then sold the company and just became an agent. I am a type D personality. At that time in my career, I struggled with baby-sitting agents who just wanted to complain rather than going out and getting something done. I knew I could grow my business further if I could just focus on selling real estate.

**What lessons did you learn from your family, friends, previous jobs, and life experiences that helped you most to succeed in your career?**

My previous job, while I was still in high school, was a gas station attendant. At 16, that was a lot of hard work. There was only full service then so, we filled the gas tanks, checked the oil, etc. The most important thing I learned from family growing up was from my dad. My Dad taught us to work hard, and to have a good work ethic. That helped a lot early on in real estate. I was willing to put in as many hours as needed. I worked for a long time as a single agent. Then I discovered a better way and in 1998, I starting working on systems. I went to work at 4 or 5 in the morning. I would sometimes work until 9-10 at night and I worked 7 days a week. I knew that if I was willing to put in the work in the front end, there would be a huge pay off in the long end. Once the systems were in place (it took about a year), and the team was hired, my life changed dramatically. I no longer worked in the business ... I worked on the business.

**What do you enjoy most about the business?**

After 23 years in the business, I can say I enjoy seeing the growth in my team and I enjoy the long-term relationships I have developed. It's no longer about the next transaction as it was early on. For a long time now it has been about developing relationships. That change in my thinking from being inward focused to outward focused really changed my business from transaction based to relationship based. It's those relationships today that bring the most joy.

## Basic Numbers

**How many transactions did you close in 2005? What was your total dollar volume in 2005? Based on that, about what is average price of a sale?**

We closed 365 transactions for about $56 million. Besides residential real estate, we also sell raw land and commercial property. Our average sales price for a home is $249,000. There are 500 agents in our local board and my team alone represents about 19% of the total volume.

About 5 years ago I took a hard look at how I could increase our volume and GCI without necessarily increasing our numbers. Increasing our numbers is fine, but I wanted to increase our GCI and our net income. We began charging a higher commission for residential sales.

We also started marketing to the commercial property and land owners. I am a CCIM so it was a natural. Also the average sales price on commercial buildings and properties is much higher than residential sales and the commissions are higher too. We charge 10% for commercial and land sales. So by increasing our land and commercial sales, we were able to increase our GCI and our net. Our gross GCI in 2005 on $56,000,000 was just over $2,200,000. So, by adding commercial and land sales into the mix 5 years ago, it netted us an extra 1% of our gross sales. That means our average commission is 4% on each transaction instead of 3%.

**Are you a Billion Dollar Agent or do you believe you will hit that level during your career? Are you over a billion for career sales or what do you estimate?**

I estimate we have closed over $375 million so far, and I plan to reach one billion before I retire.

**What is your current staffing, including yourself, of listing agents, buyer agents, managers, and assistants?**

I have two listing partners, five buyer agents, two listing coordinators, one marketing coordinator, one creative ad coordinator, two closing coordinators (one of them is a virtual closing coordinator who lives 120 miles away), and an executive assistant who focuses on the financials. I no longer go on listing appointments. I started training a listing partner in late 2004 and completely handed off listings about 15 months ago. The average buyer agent pends 3-4 sales per month. This year we added staff to prepare our foundation to be able to successfully close a $100 million a year in sales. I believe you need to put the foundation in first anytime you intentionally go into huge growth mode. There is no sense in attracting more business unless you have the infrastructure to take care of it. Otherwise you will have frustrated clients who do not feel like they got the attention they deserved and you will have frustrated team members who feel like they are working at 120% all the time. Anyone can work at that level for short periods of time, but it can't be sustained at that level. So we added a creative director, an additional listing partner, an additional listing coordinator and two more buyer specialists in the last 12 months.

All the buyer specialists are on the same graduated contract. I pay all of their costs except cell phone and their vehicle. They start at 30%/70% split. They then move up in increments of 5% as they close more sales. The best buyer agent in 2005 reached the 65%/35% level by end of the year.

At the end of the year, they all go back 2 levels, then they can work there way back up throughout the year again. I feel this is the fairest way to adequately compensate them and at the same time have a safe guard in place so that if the market shifts and slows down, I am not left paying huge splits and still be left paying all of the costs. The listing partners earn 25% of each listing closed. The listing partners were both buyer specialists before becoming listing partners.

## Goals

**Do you believe goals are important to your success? If yes, describe your approach to goal setting for your business and life?**

I think goals are incredibly important. Goals are written dreams with a deadline. My husband and I go to Maui in October every year for 10 days. There we strategically think. We look at the big picture — big rocks, for our business and for our personal lives. 20% of what I do creates 80% of our business. My genius is lead generation and leadership. I have a knack or intuitive spirit for seeing what's coming before anyone else. So I am able to change course in advance of everyone else knowing what's happening and what's coming. If I know what's coming in six months, then I know where we need to be and I know what activities to put in place to make sure we get there first. You have to begin with the end in mind. You need to know where you are going before you set the course. I recognize that clarity of vision is more important than certainty of outcome. Clarity creates its own influence and its own momentum. I also help each one of my team members set goals. They post them at their desk as a colorful picture collage of their top 5 goals they want to reach. I have found that by visually putting them at their desk besides writing them down, the higher the outcome that they will achieve them. My husband and I have wheels of life where we note our goals and then add the top three things that can help us achieve each of those goals. We have a master wheel of life, a leadership wheel of life, a market place ministry wheel of life and a family wheel of life. Those wheels represent our master plan, our work plan within the team, our plan at home and our plan within our community.

## New Customer Marketing – Lead Generation – Prospecting

**What are your top five methods for new client lead generation and about what percent of new customers are generated from that approach?**

I publish a monthly 8 page full color newspaper that is inserted into our local paper. I write something about real estate, a lot about premier community citizenship and I share all of our giving back program. One of our team members always writes an article about current events. Our vendors are featured and, of course, all of our homes are also. The circulation is 8,600 people and it costs me $735 per month. I used to have the paper published out of state; but, I found I could get more vendors to advertise in my paper, as a preferred provider, if I had the local newspaper publish it and insert it into their paper. Our paper is now completely underwritten by our vendors. We can track 25-30 new clients who either list or buy property from us, as a direct result of this paper.

I have a new website being designed that will be live by January 1, 2007. It will be a great community asset and something different from any other sties. Visitors will be able to communicate with us through blogging and podcasting, and they will be able to search all properties in the MLS with many advanced search tools. It will also contain a lot of local useful information on the communities in our area, and allow visitors to sign up to use our moving truck, apply for our scholarships, or just ask me a question. This web site will not be stagnant, but instead very fresh and up to date which will keep buyers and sellers returning to the web site. Currently 19% of our new business comes from the Internet. We believe this new flagship web site will increase our new business even more.

I also send direct mail. I use expresscopy.com to mail out full color laminated cards. We not only send Just Listed and Just Sold cards, but we also send cards that constantly place us as the experts in the mind of the consumer. Examples: "Top 10 Reasons To List Your Home With Kristen Cole", "Experience is not Expensive, it is Priceless", "We Wish We Would Have Called Kristen First". Direct mail is a great way to increase listing business. As we all know, if we have the listings, we will get more of the buyers. Our Internet web presence is very important to us and that is why we are having our website redesigned.

We spend about 8-10% or our gross GCI on marketing.

## Client Marketing – Repeats/Referrals

**Of those, about how many do you have in current database?**

We have over 30,000 records in our data base and 2,500-3,000 of those are clients we have done business with before. We actively stay in contact with those clients.

**What percentage of your business is referral?**

I have tracked this for the last 8 years and in any given year it is 68-73%.

**What client marketing activities do you do with past clients?**

We send a postcard every 6 weeks to our client base. The post card says, "Thank you. Thank you. Thank you. at the top and then says thank you for referring clients, or purchasing a home or property from me either in the past, present or future. As a very special thanks I am offering only to my clients, the chance to win _____. " This year we have given away a ski trip for two, a King Salmon fishing trip for two, an Ipod, a portable DVD player, a digital camera, and six $50 gift cards to American Eagle and Old Navy. We allow them to enter our drawing by e-mailing me.

When they e-mail me, it gives me a chance to e-mail them back and reconnect with them. Of course I will let them know, I will get them entered to win.

Moreover, I look up each person who e-mails me, in our data base, to pair them up with a buyer specialist. The buyer specialist then contacts them at the end of each drawing to let them know who won, what the next contest is and to be looking for the post card in the mail. Then they will ask "By the way, who do you know who may need to buy or sell next?". We remind them about the free moving truck, our scholarships for seniors, and our giving back program. If the client does not know of anyone at that time, the buyer specialist gets permission to call them back by asking, "Would it be okay with you if I called you in 5-7 weeks to see if you know of anyone at that time?" It is the law of reciprocity. If you are always giving to your clients, they naturally will want to give you something back. Our data base is set up so that the call automatically comes up on the right buyer specialist's schedule, reminding them to call the client again. Also, we record all the communications in our data base. At anytime that the client calls, anyone on our team knows the communication we have had with them. I am sending this postcard out to about 1500 clients who are local. The cost of the card is about $600 with postage, and the cost of giveaways is $300. I am spending $900 every 6 weeks, or about $8,000 per year. What I love about this program is my communication with them is always warm, because they are responding and they e-mail me. It's also a warm call for our buyer specialists to make, because these are people who have already done business with us before and/or have referred clients to us.

It's a really great way to stay in touch, give our clients gifts, and ask for more business.

We found a retired lady who makes specialty cakes. She has two kitchens in her home. When our clients have birthdays, she makes them a cake and delivers it to their place of work. She charges me $15 to make the cake and deliver it. That has been a HUGE wow for our clients. It is so personal and all their co-workers want to know who just sent them a cake. Our clients tell them, "my Realtor Kristen Cole did". The delivery to their workplace is key.

We have a client party once a year. We give away a trip for two to Mexico, including airline tickets, and one weeks hotel accommodations at a 5 star hotel. We also have other drawings and almost always combine our client party with a coat, blanket, toy, or food drive so that clients can bring something to the party that can help our community.

These three ideas are the reason why we have 68-73% repeat and referral business. Oftentimes, as Realtors, we spend so much money on new business, when it's much cheaper to keep the clients we already have!

## Growth of Business

**What single quality has made you more successful than others?**

Hard work and leadership. No one wants to pay the price, but everyone still wants the goal. Get up early, work as if it depends on you. Pray as if it depends on God, be outward focused not inward focused. Make sure that others get what they want first and you will get what you want. Be a great leader. Leadership is the difference between success and failure. Everyone, whether it's your clients, your team members, your spouse or your children want to know the answer to three questions: Can I trust you? Are you committed to excellence? Do you care about me? Everyone wants to feel special. These simple truths, executed consistently with positive intention, will attract abundance. Success is something you attract by the person you become.

**As you grew your business, what were your biggest challenges and what were the solutions that worked the best?**

- I self discovered that if I wanted the business to grow, the single most important thing I could do was work on myself. I had to stop managing things and start leading people. All of us can be great because we can all serve. I discovered that as our business grew and I no longer listed and sold property, my clients changed. Today my clients are my team members. How I lead them means everything. Leadership has everything to do with character. Character counts, character is the game. Character makes you successful, not competence. You can lead without character, but character is what makes you a leader worth following.

- My gifts and determination may dictate my potential, but it is my character that will determine my legacy. Andy Stanley said this, "you can create an enviable lifestyle by leveraging your leadership skills alone. But, you cannot create an enviable life without giving serious attention to who you are on the inside." Arthur Ash said, "true heroism is not the urge to surpass all others at all costs but, to serve all others at all costs". You can pay people to perform, but you can't pay them to excel. The more I learned to serve and lead with character, the more successful my team members became. On September 12, 2005 when our son was in a near fatal car accident, I saw my team *walk out* their commitment to me. I didn't go back to work for six months after the accident and even when I did go back, I was still gone a lot taking care of my son. We had the best year ever during that time as my team and my husband stepped up and served me. I am eternally grateful to them.

# JENNIE COOK

C21 LEADING EDGE
MARKHAM, ON, CANADA

## Background

**For how many years have you been in the real estate business?**

I have been in the business for 25 years.

**What is your personal background and how did you get into real estate?**

I was a real estate receptionist in the evening. I did that for seven years because I had small children at home. I received my license in 1981 and fell in love with the business and never looked back.

**What lessons did you learn from your family, friends, previous jobs, and life experiences that helped you most to succeed in your career?**

One of the main things was caring. I have a very caring philosophy and have a theme 'work with someone who cares.' I always put myself in the position of the client. Building trust is important. I surround myself with successful people. I learned very quickly that having a mentor was very important. Floyd Wickman was my mentor.

**What do you enjoy most about the business?**

People. I love building relationships with people. I like helping first time home buyers. I love the interaction with people; it is so rewarding to see them so happy. I always put my clients first, and foremost.

## Basic Numbers

**How many transactions did you close in 2005?**

I reorganized my business so I could have more personal time. In 2005 I closed 100 transactions. Our average price is $380,000.

**Are you a Billion Dollar Agent or do you believe you will hit that level during your career? Are you over a billion for career sales or what do you estimate?**

I estimate $600 million and I am making the lifestyle choice to phase down my personal involvement in the business but retain an income flow.

**What is your current staffing including: yourself, listing agents, buyer agents, managers, and assistants?**

Myself and two partners, one support person. That has been since 2003.

# Goals

**Do you believe goals are important to your success? If yes, describe your approach to goal setting for your business and life?**

Absolutely. I believe you need to set short-term and long-term goals. They must be in writing. You must review them. I pay particular attention to monthly and yearly goals.

I always believed in goals; but, it hit home at a conference given by Century 21. At the conference Floyd Wickman was introducing the Sweat Hog program, which I signed up for. I remember during that time, learning how important written goals are.

# Marketing

## New Customer Marketing – Lead Generation – Prospecting

**What are your top five methods for new client lead generation and about what percentage of new customers are generated from that approach?**

1. Print Media, 2. Just Listed / Just Sold cards, 3. Web Site, 4. Subscription to Real Estate TV, 5. Target Marketing (350 Homes). I did a special promotion, where I hired a student to take pictures of each home in summertime, and at Christmas I sent a personalized Christmas card to that area with a picture of their home.

They would phone me and say, "this is amazing, and we love it." Sometimes they brought out a few years of pictures. It was probably the best thing I did. I got 12-15 transactions a year from that area.

My family and I also delivered a monthly-personalized newsletter. It was a great start having the family involved and their support.

## Client Marketing – Repeats/Referrals

**About how many past clients have you worked with?**

We have about 2,000 past clients.

**What percentage of your business is referral?**

Our referral percentage is about 75%. This made business more valuable as I phased out of my role and phased in two partners.

**What client marketing activities do you do with past clients?**

When a transaction closes we give a gift and spend a few hundred dollars on a print. At the end of a transaction we had a professional photographer do inside and outside photos and do a personalized album with all the photographs that were taken as well as a virtual tour of their home as a memories album.

That memories album has been very amazing. We do birthday cards and get the birthdays of everyone in the family. In the birthday card we put a few coupons for Tim Horton coffee. We do anniversary cards and Christmas gifts. We try to do something, which has some real use or value. It is something that people carry with them all the time. I think the biggest thing and least expensive has been the album. They move on to their new home.

On moving day we have something delivered like a tray of sandwiches and pizzas to get through the move easier. Calendars and gifts every Christmas.

## Growth of Business

**What single quality has made you more successful than others?**

I am a people person. I am a good listener. I ask my clients to talk to me about their needs and wants. This process narrows down the number of properties they need to view.

**What does the average real estate agent fail to do which are among the reasons why they are average?**

**They fail to treat their business like a business**

They fail to stay in touch.
They fail to listen.
They fail to communicate.
They fail to care.

They fail to build trust.

**Did you make any big mistakes that you want to warn others about?**

Getting involved with negative people is a big mistake. We always had mentor groups and that was a positive thing.

# MIKE COSTIGAN

THE MIKE COSTIGAN GROUP
RE/MAX COMMUNITIES
MARIETTA, GA

## Introduction

At the age of 22, Mike Costigan was attending college and working part-time selling newspapers door-to-door. Without any certainty in his future career path Mike's mother one day "challenged" him to get his real estate license, hoping that he could make something of himself. A few years later Mike's career as an agent took off. Currently, at the age of 37, he is the #1 agent at the one of the world's largest RE/MAX offices-RE/MAX Communities in Marietta, GA. He is ranked #2 in the state of Georgia and amongst the top 20 RE/MAX agents in North America. Mike has been awarded the RE/MAX Hall of Fame Award.

## Background

**For how many years have you been in the real estate business?**

I have been in the business for 14 years.

**What is your personal background and how did you get into real estate?**

My background is in sales. My father has also been in sales all his life; I have sales in my blood. I've done plenty of nose-to-nose, toes-to-toes selling very hardcore stuff and I've always been the top guy-it was always in me. I worked in telemarketing while I was in high school. I sold newspapers door-to-door in some rough neighborhoods while I was in college. That was when my mother veritably "challenged" me to get my real estate license. I get my competitiveness from her.

There was no way I would not prove to her that I could do it. I worked my tail off for about six years. I sold tons of homes but I was killing myself. I took about a year off to regroup during which time I sold cars. Man, was THAT great training. I don't care what anyone says about car salesman; it's by far the best training there is. Car guys are far ahead of most industries when it comes to making sales. I was the top guy my 1st month and had a great time while I was there but I knew I wanted to get back into making real money. I was an even better salesman after the cars, but I needed to figure out how to create some leverage. I learned a lot from Craig Proctor about building a business and stayed with his program for about nine years.

**What lessons did you learn from your family, friends, previous jobs, and life experiences that helped you most to succeed in your career?**

I have developed copywriting as a skill, which has become a hobby of mine. All great businesses start with one thing — marketing. If you can't market you'll fail — period. I have really developed a skill for this, and I know it allows me to have an unlimited potential. In fact, I routinely generate too many leads for the stage I'm at in my business. But it's good to know that I can always create an overabundance when I need to. I have learned a lot from my father about work ethic. You do not need to be a brain surgeon. But you do need to work very hard at what you're doing and be in front of people everyday. I learned that you can't be everything to everybody. You also need to create leverage by surrounding yourself with people who are better than you are at their respective jobs. I also learned that you need to have both honesty and integrity. B.S. only gets you so far.

**What do you enjoy most about the business?**

I enjoy the marketing, writing the ad copy, and doing the TV and radio spots. I still do a small percentage of the listings. I haven't been in the car with a buyer for years and I can't say that I miss it. I think you go through different stages of what you like in your business. Right now for me it's the marketing which I think is by far the most important.

## Basic Numbers

**How many transactions did you close in 2005? What was your total dollar volume in 2005?**

I closed 287 transactions and did about $61 million in total dollar volume. I am on track for 325 transactions this year for a volume of over $70 million.

**Are you a Billion Dollar Agent or do you believe you will hit that level during your career?**

**Are you over a billion for career sales or what do you estimate?**

I am 37 years old, so I have another 10-15 years. I have sold about $300 million, or so. I will easily hit a billion by the end of my career.

**What is your current staffing, including yourself, of listing agents, buyer agents, managers, and assistants?**

Right now I have eight agents on my team, including myself. I have a lead listing agent and three secondary listing agents. I have three buyer agents and someone who does both. I carry a tremendous amount of listings, so I have three people to specifically take care of them all.

I have one person who is my listing coordinator, in charge of communicating with contract people and getting them set up. I also have two client care managers who stay in contact with listings. I have someone who markets to expired listings every day.

I also have a brother in the business who acts as an inside sales person and general office assistant. Apart from the business contractors, I have a closing coordinator and a photography team. I run about 75% listings and I run only about 25% buyers. So, most of my business is focused on generating and taking care of sellers.

The client care people really are key in my business. They serve as liaisons between the listing agents and the clients. We have over 300 listings right now and each client care manager has a 10-day call with every client. They track every showing. and they create a report every week for me on every listing, that I review with each agent in a group meeting. It is our job to make sure our pricing is appropriate. We monitor traffic and lack of traffic very closely and work on adjustments every day. It is a vital means of getting homes sold. We stay on top of each one so we know we are serving them properly by giving them sound advice constantly. We are very direct and it pays off for everyone.

I have discovered a lot of this mentality through the help of Russell Shaw. He's really helped me to reel in a business that was growing out of control. With his help I realized the necessity for being selective in choosing clients. In other words, don't waste your time on antisocial people or listings that don't have a high probability of selling. It clogs up your business and you end up not serving your "good" clients well. We have tons of potential clients to choose from-it is crucial that we choose wisely. Russell is a very giving guy. I couldn't thank him enough.

## Goals

**Do you believe goals are important to your success? If yes, describe your approach to goal setting for your business and life?**

That has changed quite a bit in my business lately. I've always been very "seat of my pants" so to speak. I think this is probably a very common thing among people who are truly salespeople at heart. But as my business has grown, I have learned that it is critically important to have goals. I write out my goals every year. I am in the midst of planning now for 2007. I set goals that are fairly high that I have a good chance of hitting. In my business life, I think I am very good at training myself to be successful. I once read something Donald Trump said: "Dress for the job you want not for the job you have." I take that to heart every day. I see today as a very small stepping stone in what I will accomplish. When you ask about a billion I automatically think two billion.

With my team, we have taken goal setting, and more importantly, constant goal measuring, very seriously this year. We are going to have three levels of agents and start everyone over at level one. We did income and productivity goals and looked at some personal goals for everyone individually. We will be monitoring whether their goals and progress lead us to a mutually acceptable end result.

At level one, we will meet twice a month for 30 minutes. As they progress through levels, I will be more hands off.

## New Customer Marketing – Lead Generation – Prospecting

**What are your top five methods for new client lead generation and about what percent of new customers are generated from that approach?**

By far, radio is my strongest lead generator. I use conservative talk radio stations. I am very recognized in Atlanta for this. Second, would be expired listings and network television runs very close behind.

I was shocked the other day when I saw how well expireds matched up with my other marketing. It's something I kind of forget about because of the insignificant cost compared to radio and TV. I simply send out a 6-piece direct mail sequence ala Dan Kennedy to about 35 new expireds every day. It starts out with an introduction letter then ends with an "are you crazy" letter if they haven't called by day 6. Expireds accounted for about 8% of my business last year with very little cost. It goes to show that you don't always need to spend big money to get great results. You just need a good message delivered in good copy.

We spend about 25% on marketing.

## Client Marketing – Repeats/Referrals

**What percentage of your business is referral?**

I will admit that our prior client repeat/referral business is terrible. It is the weakest part of the business. We are going to be working on it. I am weak in this area, probably due to laziness.

As I said, I found a way to generate so many "now" leads that I did not pay attention to prior clients. There is a mentality that they will not buy for 6-7 years so I just forget them. Well, this is changing dramatically as we speak. I am very interested in prior client marketing. I know very surely that I can generate tons of business in a very inexpensive manner by re-selling people we have already taken very good care of.

## Growth of Business

**What single quality has made you more successful than others?**

Confidence and obsessiveness have made me more successful. This is my business 24 hours a day. I wake up routinely at two am and shake my wife to tell her I have a great idea. She moans and goes back to sleep while I lay awake all night writing the ad in my head.

I also have perseverance. I view failures and challenges as opportunities and learning experiences. To quote Jim Carey, "The times when you are the most terrified, those are the mastery times." Anyone without guts in real estate or any business for that matter is in big trouble. You cannot make decisions out of fear. Push forward and keep your momentum going at all costs.

I've got to mention a second big reason for my success... being surrounded by great people. I belong to a mastermind group of unbelievable guys and gals across North America. Some of them have become very close friends and it's such a healthy thing for my business and personal life to be able to connect the dots with other successful people. The power of the mastermind is unlimited. I cannot overemphasize the growth opportunities that come out of it.

I am also very happily married and the love for my wife and my 20-month-old son give me even more drive. I couldn't do it without support and tolerance from her and seeing my son smile makes me want to work hard so he can have whatever he wants out of life.

**What does the average real estate agent fail to do which are among the reasons why they are average?**

I have been through at least ten buyer agents. Here are the reasons I think they are average: They are lazy, they fail to return phone calls, they fail to listen to clients, they fail to develop consistency in their responses, they fail to see beyond their own needs, they fail to stretch their thinking in terms of what they can accomplish, they fail to innovate, they fail to think out of the box, they fail to take it seriously - they take it as a casual business, they fail to market, they fail to do good lead generation, they fail miserably at effective marketing, they fail to gain practical knowledge, they fail to look at themselves in the mirror and realize where their business is, they fail to be honest with themselves, they fail to watch profitability, and they follow a lot of people over the cliff.

Among the agents I have gotten rid of, 100% are people who failed to learn canned responses, and they also failed to make phone calls. They say different things to different people. They fail to listen to the clients in the end and they fail to listen to me.

# Mariana Cowan

The Mariana Cowan Homeselling Team
Coldwell Banker Supercity Realty
Halifax, Nova Scotia, Canada

## Introduction

Born in Vancouver, B.C., Mariana moved to Halifax, Nova Scotia in 1985. There she started her real estate career in the fall of 1986. Mariana has been described as one of the most recognizable faces in the real estate industry. She has devoted herself to being one of the top Realtors. Mariana built her reputation on continuing education, along with introducing ground-breaking methods for marketing, and selling properties using her Homeselling Team Concept.

## Background

**For how many years have you been in the real estate business?**

I have been in real estate for 20 years.

**What is your personal background and how did you get into real estate?**

While in University, I majored in psychology and business. At age 23, I was looking toward a career that would include helping people, plus provide my family with a high-quality standard of living. After selling my own home privately, I realized that real estate was my niche.

**What lessons did you learn from your family, friends, previous jobs, and life experiences that helped you most to succeed in your career?**

The greatest lesson was the gift of learning, from my grandfather who is a wise man. At a very young age, my grandfather who, at that time was the Dean of Graduates of UBC and later Chancellor of the University of Victoria, taught me appreciation and values. He also taught me about the love people possess, and how to learn from them, which is still with me today.

When I first started the in Real Estate Business, I read every book on business including the #1 influential book Napoleon Hill's Think & Grow Rich. This book shows how to sow the seed and reap the benefits. Being a successful real estate agent means more than just selling homes; it means taking the time and effort to invest in your business and the people around you.

**What do you enjoy most about the business?**

The biggest satisfaction for me, in this business, is helping clients build their dreams into reality, whether it is to maximize their investment, or put them into a new home.

My goal is to make my clients happy while providing them with the best in customer service.

# Basic Numbers

**How many transactions did you close in 2005?**

In 2005, we closed about 272 units for GCI of $1,400,000.

**What was your total dollar volume in 2005?**

Total sales volume is about $60-70 million.

**Based on that, about what is average price of a sale?**

Our average price was about $250,000.

**Are you a Billion Dollar Agent or do you believe you will hit that level during your career? Are you over a billion for career sales or what do you estimate?**

Over the past 20 years I have been very fortunate to sell, on average, 250-300 homes per year. My office has sold over a billion dollars in gross sales.

My goal when I leave the real estate industry is to consult. We invest in commercial real estate ventures such as shopping plazas, raw land, and subdivisions.

**What is your current staffing, including yourself, of listing agents, buyer agents, managers, and assistants?**

We currently have four buyer agents and seven administrative staff. My staff includes:
Receptionist who takes care of the daily running of the office, answering incoming calls, mail, greeting clients, filing, typing, etc.
Listing Coordinator who deals with customer care, inputting listings, keeping track of listings, contacting clients each week individually, etc.
Closing Coordinator who assists in presenting and closing deals made within/outside our office.
The inside sales person who manages and tracks all of the buyer client leads, Bookkeeper who keeps track of all office details concerning finances, payroll, vacations, etc.
PR who takes care of the marketing, advertising and communications.
Photographer/Webmaster who assists in taking photos, creating web designs, looking after office technology, etc.
Previously I had been acquiring all of the listings myself. I now have 2 people working with me on obtaining listings. For the buying side of my office, we do approximately 25 deals per buyer agent.
My biggest challenge is proper documentation of leads and what progress is being done with these leads.

## Goals

**Do you believe goals are important to your success? If yes, describe your approach to goal setting for your business and life?**

Yes, goals are very important to my success. I set realistic goals annually, as well as make five and ten year plans. I review both personal and business goals on a quarterly basis. I have learned from working with Craig Proctor, that holding myself accountable and being focused helps me to obtain these goals.

## Marketing

### New Customer Marketing – Lead Generation – Prospecting

**What are your top five methods for new client lead generation and about what percent of new customers are generated from that approach?**

Advertising/Marketing myself, and my Business
Using the 120 Day Guarantee in our advertising/marketing
Past clients
My website
Word of mouth

### Client Marketing – Repeats/Referrals

**About how many past clients have you worked with?**

We have about 1,500 past clients in our database.

**What percent of your business is referral?**

I estimate it is about 33%.

**What client marketing activities do you do with past clients?**

Dawn Coolen is our Listing Coordinator who keeps our clients updated on all feedback, issues, etc. During their listing transaction. She also provides them with assistance on information, feature packages for their home, etc.

## Growth of Business

**What single quality has made you more successful than others?**

I think that being able to delegate, and leverage myself with people, has made me more successful.

**What does the average real estate agent fail to do which are among the reasons why they are average?**

They fail to follow-up.

They fail to listen to what customer wants.

They fail to invest in marketing.

**As you grew your business, what were your biggest challenges and what were the solutions that worked the best?**

The biggest challenge for me has been finding the appropriate people to fill each position within my team. For a team system to work you need people who believe in the part of the team instead of the "team"

# LESTER COX

## Introduction

Lester Cox has been the #1 producing Realty Executives Agent in Arizona for the last two years; he is currently ranked #7 worldwide and is the recipient of the R. Dale Rector Award, given to just one agent and the highest award given by Realty Executives in Arizona.

## Background

**Fow many years have you been in the real estate business?**

I have been in the business for about 35 years; I started in 1971.

**What is your personal background and how did you get into real estate?**

I was in the Air Force from 1966 to 1970. I really did not have much choice. As I was getting out of Air Force, I was in upstate Michigan and it was very cold. They had a program where you could reintroduce yourself into civilian life. One of the jobs was spending half of your day working at some other career. I knew I liked the real estate business so I worked in a real estate office with Kowalski Real Estate. It was a laid back office. I learned about land contracts and abstracts.

I didn't really have any money. I tried to get a job in the mortgage title business and work my way into real estate. The best job was working in a paint store for $1.25/hour sweeping floors. I went on interview and I wondered why I went to real estate school!

**What lessons did you learn from your family, friends, previous jobs, and life experiences that helped you most to succeed in your career?**

My family was involved in home improvement sales and I did door-to-door sales starting at age 16. I learned to have confidence; just knock on doors and meet people. I knew nobody in Phoenix. I had no mentors. I picked out a neighborhood and did only thing I knew how to do; I became that neighborhood expert.

**What do you enjoy most about the business?**

I learned a long time ago not to sell or do real estate for the money; you do it to help people achieve their dreams and money is a byproduct. I still have a passion for this business. I enjoy helping people achieve their goals in real estate. I have clients with whom I have done 15-20 transactions.

## Basic Numbers

**How many transactions did you close in 2005?**

In 2005, my team worked together to close 479 transactions with over $88 million in gross sales.

**Have you sold a billion dollars yet and if not, do you think you will during your career?**

I have never calculated totals, but having been in the real estate business for over 35 years. With the various home builders that I have represented as sales manager and other executive positions, I'm sure it must be over a billion dollars by this point. If not, a billion yet, I must be darn close and barring some fatality, I surely will surpass this mark.

**What is your current staffing, including: yourself, listing agents, buyer agents, managers, and assistants?**

My agents are dual; they do both listing and buyers. Right now I have two offices, one in Tempe in Realty Executives and another in Arizona City, which is another broker under Pacific Arizona realty. I have 17 licensed people including 6 administrative staff and myself. My wife works with me too. When we did 479 transactions, we had about 12 agents. My current role is managing and I did about 30 transactions. I am turning over more personal referrals to my staff.

## Goals

**Do you believe goals are important to your success? If yes, describe your approach to goal setting for your business and life?**

Goals are important and they must be written. I do a goal setting session at the end of every year. I have a dream book where I have my goals for the next year, five years, and 10 years from now. I work with my team and make them write their goals and do a dream session with them. If you eliminate money as a factor what do you want in your life?

I read my goals about every month or two months. I was fortunate enough that, in 1974, Tom Hopkins was teaching at real estate school where I got my license. Tom Hopkins was the first one who told me about written goals. About 4-5 years ago I really got into it. When I started to build my team, I went to Craig Proctor coaches. I had been to all the different gurus and I am not sure why I grasped the Proctor system so much but it was because he was doing it himself. That affected me enough to open the book and really get into it. I joined a graduate level and Brian Moses got passionate about it.

# Marketing

## New Customer Marketing – Lead Generation – Prospecting

**What are your top five methods for new client lead generation and about what percentage of new customers are generated from that approach?**

Internet is number one. I have a huge Internet presence. I have four different websites, over 400 different URLs for tracking. I track from where our business comes; if the phone rings, I know why it rings. We probably generate 100-125 new leads per week from various Internet sites. About 2-3% end up as deals, maybe 4%. I do know that they expressed an interest. Internet leads are probably about $5-6 per lead.

I have a cafeteria; if you do not like turkey I have ham. I have four different sites. If one approach is not working, I have another approach. The sites offer various reports and school information and some are unbranded. We did not do PPC; we use classified ads to drive websites. My websites average over 500,000 hits per month. My average time on the website is 5-7 minutes. Our overall marketing cost was about 8%.

**What do you do, if anything, that you feel is fairly unique and successful?**

I return phone calls.

**What marketing advice would you give to someone at $100,000 who wants to get to $200,000 and more?**

If the guy is at $100,000, he probably has a net of 60-70k. He has probably not done a marketing plan or a marketing budget. I would guess he is not spending enough in marketing; this is typical. He cannot visualize the return on investment in good marketing. He also may not know where their business is coming from.
He needs to analyze where customers are coming from.

## Client Marketing – Repeats/Referrals

**About how many past clients have you worked with?**

I would guess as many as 10,000 past clients.

**Of those, about how many do you have in current database?**

We have about 1,500 past clients in the last four years.

**What percentage of your business is referral?**

Our referral business is about 35%. We have identified this as a challenge. We receive about one in ten deals from clients.

**What client marketing activities do you do with past clients?**

In prior years we did a bi-monthly newsletter and mailed it to our past clients. We just lost track of what we should be doing.

We are trying to fix that by staying in touch now through a new newsletter with 16 pages and interesting stories and good advertising. That is like a newspaper.

We are enrolling clients in a free magazine with the Cox Team label. We are starting with a 4-6 times a year. We also have an electronic newsletter once a month. In addition, we have a client follow-up service with Sharper Agent twice a month. We get those fairly quickly. We also send out things that give people value like a discount.

## Listings
**What percentage of your transactions are listings?**

I think it is a 40/60 split - 40% listings and 60% buyers.

## Growth of Business
**What single quality has made you more successful than others?**

I hate to lose and I am extremely competitive. My Dad told me when I was 10 or 11 years old, if are going to do it, do it right. It takes the same amount of time. If I am going to be in real estate, why not do it with all my energy? I am passionate about what I do.

**As you grew your business, what were your biggest challenges and what were the solutions that worked the best?**

I may be paying too high of a split. Listing agents I pay about 45% which may be too much. I like getting up and feeling good about myself and know that my team members are like family.

**If you could go back and do things differently, what would you have done at $100,000 that would have sped the growth of your business?**

I would have gotten a coach, that is probably the biggest mistake in my career. I just did not grasp the idea of holding someone accountable.

The first impact is that a coach is bringing a compilation of experiences from hundreds of different coaching clients. It sets you on a fast track of learning.

It keeps you on track and setting goals and avoids mistakes that others have made.

## Learning
**What are best books you have read in past 10 years that helped with your business and life?**

I probably read Think and Grow Rich six times. I read Power of Positive Thinking when I was in my first slow period.

# SANDE ELLIS

THE ELLIS TEAM
RE/MAX REALTY GROUP
FT. MYERS, FL

## Introduction

Sande Ellis credits her success in real estate to hard work and good advice. She was impressed with a speaker who once said, "People don't care how much you know until they know how much you care." Her strong interpersonal skills and diligent efforts made her the top residential sales agent in the Fort Myers/Lee County area. Sande says, "You might say real estate is our passion, it's what get us up and going every day. Our team truly cares about people, their needs and wants." Among Sande's many achievements and awards are being named one of the top 100 agents in the world by the National Association of Realtors, Top 100 Agents by RE/MAX International, Top 10 Agents RE/MAX of Florida, the RE/MAX Lifetime Achievement Award and the RE/MAX Hall of Fame Award. She has held many offices in the local Realtor Associations. Sande says that while it is an honor to step on stage and accept an award for your team; it feels better to stand on stage and impart something that will change the life or the business of another.

## Background

**For how many years have you been in the real estate business?**

21 years.

**What is your personal background and how did you get into real estate?**

I had taught school and had worked as a field coordinator for the Arthritis Foundation. Then Mike, my husband, was transferred to Florida. I had always wanted to go into the real estate business. I did not know anybody or anything about Fort Myers, FL. The fact that I knew what I didn't know turned out to be a tremendous advantage. I did not expect anyone to list or sell their home with me because they knew me. Everyday was an adventure.

Remember these were the days before GPS. I got excited when I got lost. Either I had found a new way from here to there, or it was something I never wanted to repeat. As a child I had enjoyed doing puzzles. And now, I was doing people puzzles. I was taking the information that I was given and putting it together in such a way that a buyer or seller might transform their lives. Sometimes I had to seek more information to make the pieces fit. I learned to "always be asking."

**What lessons did you learn from your family, friends, previous jobs, and life experiences that helped you most to succeed in your career?**

I always knew that I could do anything that I wanted. I was involved in sports. Someone said to me, "It is not that you are so good; it is that you work so hard." I believed that. I was simply more disciplined. I enjoyed the feeling of the second wind after a really tough workout. And when I became a Realtor, I knew I was bringing everything that I had into the business with me. I would work harder than the rest and learn from the best. I attended seminars. I learned something from each that I attended. Fortunately, I happened upon Howard Brinton at a CRS meeting. I left the meeting with sides splitting and a new appreciation for a particular trained pig. If you have not heard the story, there is still time. Today we are Stars in the Star Power network (www.gostarpower.com). It is truly an honor to share what we have learned and tweaked. We also recognized the need for a business and life coach. We have learned much about ourselves that has helped us to be better for our customers through Dr. Fred Grosse. We have traveled half way around the world to meet others interested in taking their lives and their business to a whole new level. Sometimes you might need a nudge or someone that suggests you need to get out of your own way. These are the Dr. Fred groups. You could belong to one or all as all of the participants are the seeking the same quality of life. RE/MAX has been a keeper of the flame. Dave and Gail Liniger, Margaret Kelly, Vinnie Tracey, and others recognize and promote the entrepreneurial spirit. These are people who can move you off your seat and challenge you to do the same for others.

**What do you enjoy most about the business?**

I don't need drugs to feel high … high on the business and high on people. I enjoy the diversity. I may be working on a lot, a $2 million waterfront property, a commercial building and several CMAs all in the same day. I love the negotiating aspects of the business. I enjoy the people, the challenges. I enjoy growing and learning. I learn something new every day … usually several "somethings." It is amazing to me; it intrigues me. I can work 16 hours a day and still come home and read a book on real estate or leadership or growth.

## Basic Numbers

**How many transactions did you close in 2005?**

We closed about 400 units. This year we are mirroring last year, which is great in this market in Florida.

**What was your total dollar volume in 2005?**

Our total dollar volume in 2005 was $125 million.

**Are you a Billion Dollar Agent or do you believe you will hit that level during your career? Are you over a billion for career sales or what do you estimate?**

If you had not asked I would not have known. We will be a billion dollar agents in 2007.

**What is your current staffing, including yourself, of listing agents, buyer agents, managers, and assistants?**

We have 14 people on the team. We have a listing manager, closing manager, and marketing manager. My son, Brett Ellis and Shaun Henderson and myself do listings and negotiate the contracts. I work with the team. Brett does the media presentations for us with TV stations. Brett hosts the weekly radio show; he is a phenomenal speaker and trainer. My husband, Mike, runs our Pine Island office and handles the Ellis Team financials. We have seven buyer agents including son, Kevin Ellis, and one courier.

We recognized early on that, "none of us is as smart as all of us," and that we had fun working together. We knew we had to leave our egos at the door. A sense of humor is a common thread … a must for any Realtor or organization. It is evident that a family that truly cares about each other, their team, and their clients, will nearly effortlessly achieve their goals. One of the finest things that Mike and I were able to do was to recognize the incredible talents in the family we had raised. If you know Brett and Kevin you know what I am saying. Without their great talents, and their sharing of the same, we might not be Billion Dollar agents. Our youngest son, Sean, is a real estate attorney. Imagine that. It is here that the plot thickens. Sean is married to Anna. Anna is the featured speaker on our team video. Anna's sister Gina is our closing manager. Shaun Henderson is her husband. You will see why Firestone thought we wreaked of family. Cindy Diaz is our Listing manager. She is bilingual. Dale Peck is marketing manager. Both Cindy and Dale can boast that they have no genealogical link to the Ellis family. We ask our buyer agents and team members a lot of questions to take them out of their comfort zones so we can get to the heart level with them. When you have the right people on the bus you have flexibility, and people can cover for others for illness, vacation, or whatever. Nicole Dalton has had many positions on the Ellis Team. Because of her versatility she now is Office Manager for the Pine Island office. We hire only about 5% of people we interview and most of them stay with us.

## Goals

**Do you believe goals are important to your success? If yes, describe your approach to goal setting for your business and life?**

I love Brian Tracy and The Psychology of Achievement. I believe in setting goals. However, you must give the goal life. Let's say that your goal is 400 transactions per year. Perhaps you did 200 transactions last year. Your mind does not know that what you tell it is not true. When you set a number, like 400 transactions a year, I think that somehow, in the night, something makes that happen; opportunities just land in your lap. The affirmation must be in the present tense. "I close 400 transactions each year." You have to say it, write it down, and do it. When I do a coaching call, I ask people to tell me what their number is and put it out in front of them. Similar to taking a picture of the car you want, laminating it, and putting it in the wallet. Whatever it is, put that visual out there for you!

When you help others set goals it is important that the goal set come from the agent. You can coach and encourage if you think the goal is too low. Again always be asking ... seeking to understand. For example: we have an excellent buyer agent, Fran Jurek, who had family members this year with distressing health situations. And, Fran would be handling their issues. Nobody could or would do that better. Fran has done a phenomenal job for us when available. Might Fran decide to do her business in another way someday? She might. We all have to recognize that team members and buyer specialists have a "use by date."

We feel that it is important that the goals not be limiting to the person's abilities. We had a new buyer agent, new to the business, earn $250,000 for himself. Think if I had given him a $200,000 goal. It would have sounded good. He would have made it. We would have applauded and we would not have known what it might have been.

The diversity among our buyer agents is incredible. I mentioned that our son Kevin is a buyer agent. His passion is art. His integrity and caring for people stand out. Mark Hilderbrand was a day trader and financial planner. Mike Kornell owned his own printing business in Wisconsin. His son, Tim, was a lender. Dave Kellogg was a radio and tv personality. He worked for Voice of America. Brian Hall owned a Florida business. Fran previously owned a real estate company. Her family are mostly contractors.

## Marketing

### New Customer Marketing – Lead Generation – Prospecting
**What are your top five methods for new client lead generation and about what percentage of new customers are generated from that approach?**
A few years ago the radio station asked us to do a real estate show every week on Saturdays. We said "sure". But, inside we questioned that anyone would want to listen to us. What happened? Realtors, buyers and sellers listened. We decided, that if Realtors would put us on their busy schedule, we would do our best to keep them updated as to changes in the market, laws, controversial items, etc.

We took the first segment on the radio show to talk about properties. Now, it is a one-hour show and we talk about properties in the first and second half of the show. When the market was hot, we only had 4 properties for sale. The radio show has been phenomenal. About 20% of our new customers come from that. We have sponsors for the show and they pay the station for the advertising. We pay for the engineering, and now we tape the show in the office to save us the travel time to the station, etc.

We also do television commercials. After 9/11 we hired Firestone Advertising to do a tv commercial. They came up with a jingle that was folksy. It would remind you of the Andy of Mayberry and Aunt Bea. Firestone said you wreak of family. Use it. We have done several commercials. We attempt to make the commercials timely. At one point last year anybody could put a sign out and sell their property. We actually did a commercial showing a disgruntled homeowner who had used a discount broker and someone who was a happy client because they had used the Ellis Team. And, of course we concluded with the now well known jingle "Always call the Ellis Team. It's a family affair. Always call the Ellis Team. We'll handle you with care." The jingle is played between segments of the radio show as well.

We also use the newspaper. It used to be very effective and we continue to do one-page ads every week. At least once a month we run double truck ads. Today we are only getting 10% of our business from the newspaper, though. Fewer and fewer people read the newspaper. Newspapers have also been relying on the Internet for increased exposure.

Our Internet site is second to none, even though Brett is Internet savvy, we hire an Internet guru.

**What marketing advice would you give to someone at $100,000 who wants to get to $200,000 and more?**

Get the name and the face out there. Figure out something unique about your marketplace or yourself. Why would someone call you?

If you cannot find any reason other than how or why. how would a buyer or seller find one? Invest in the Star Power scrapbook (www.gostarpower.com). Agents have come up with humorous reasons to be memorable. There is no need to reinvent the wheel. Seek and tweak. We send out advertising calendars (Bruce Shay or Mulch). I recommend sending out 100 magnetic calendars (I prefer the 10x13 size) - people love them.

The name "Ellis Team" is in front of them all year long. People call us every year looking for their new calendar or insert. We now send out about 6500 per year.

## Client Marketing – Repeats/Referrals

**What percentage of your business is referral?**

I truly hesitate to give out these percentages. It is not that we don't ask the question and want the answer. Here is how it goes: How did you happen to call the Ellis Team? Well I heard a TV commercial. I loved that ad. When I looked you up in the yellow pages, you had the biggest ad. But, my brother-in-law told me to call you. You sold two properties for them; and they were really pleased. You sold my neighbor's house also. And when we moved here our agent referred us to you ... said not to use anyone else. And, like everybody, else I listen to the radio show every week. I really got tickled when you and Bert had different thoughts on insurance or something. I do appreciate the calendar that you send out every year.

Believe me, this is typical.

**What client marketing activities do you do with past clients?**

We send out calendars and notepads. We send out things that service the client. We have done client parties in the past. Parties are enjoyed but, I feel there is more bang for the buck by spending those dollars for more contact or mail outs. We send out a newsletter that goes to approximately 40,000 people and we make sure our past clients receive that as well. Occasionally a past client will see all of the things that we do and somehow decide that we are too busy for them. Nothing could be further from the truth.

## Growth of Business

**What single quality has made you more successful than others?**

If I had to give a single quality, I would say it is integrity. Without integrity you have nothing. I do not mean that others do not have it; we probably take it to a new level. If we say we are going to do something ... we are going to do it.

**What does the average real estate agent fail to do which are among the reasons why they are average?**

The average agent fails to see rejection and problems as opportunity. They fail to get back to their clients promptly. Some let their egos get in the way and fail to realize that the issue has nothing to do with them. They fail to ask the proper questions in a non threatening manner.

They don't spend enough money to get their name out there, and won't spend money in a down market. They fail to get the education that they need. Finally, they fail to hire staff to assist them so that they can grow.

**Did you make any big mistakes that you want to warn others about?**

One time we paid for a marketing piece that did not arrive for 18 months. It was outdated and with so many errors, that we could not use it.

Mistakes are opportunities also. Always be asking , "what did we learn from this? Would we do it again? Same or different conditions?" For the most part our funds were limited. I thought about a marketing piece. I made a decision to do it. I did it. It worked. Sometimes I think that the fact that I believed in it so much was the reason that it worked every time. Not working was simply not an option.

## Delegation and Leverage - Assistants

**We see a challenge of agents — right at point of needing to delegate, outsource and/or hire their first part-time assistant to leverage their time. What percentage of agents do you think are in that zone and why do they fail to take the next step? What would be benefit for them to take that step?**

If an agent does not have an assistant, they are one. What else could they do with that quality time? Some people hide behind busy work instead of doing sales work. Just do it! They may be afraid of rejection, but rejection is opportunity.

Assess yourself! Hire to your weakness. Ask questions that take people out of their comfort zones. Most interviewees are programmed to tell you what you want to hear. You must ask questions that will take them to the heart level for their responses. Those who operate at the heart level, are "real" to their customers. Allowing one to be real saves valuable time and effects communication.

# FRED EVANS

RE/MAX GOLD COAST REALTORS
VENTURA, CA

## Introduction

Fred believes that everyone in America has the chance to grow and get ahead on the strength of their own efforts. After earning a marketing degree from Cal State in 1969, Fred spent 16 years in retail management with Sears and Roebuck. He declined a promotion to company headquarters and joined a national real estate firm. His star rose quickly, due to his people skills, energy, desire and persistence. At the height of his career, he left that firm to pursue growth opportunities with RE/MAX. In the past 20 years, Fred and his team have assisted over 2,200 families achieve the American dream of home ownership! Today, Fred lives with his wife in the beautiful seaside city of San Buenaventura.

## Background

**For how many years have you been in the real estate business?**

I started in 1985 so about 21 years.

**What is your personal background and how did you get into real estate?**

I was in retail management in Sears for 16 years. They wanted to promote me and I decided I did not want to move to Chicago. I changed careers to stay here in Ventura County, CA. I went with Coldwell Banker, which was a Sears company at the time. I always had a knack for fixing things up and making money. I decided to just go for it at the same time. In 1989 I had a chance to buy a RE/MAX franchise with a partner.

Making the switch to RE/MAX from Coldwell Banker was not easy. I was the top agent in Ventura County and I was making good money in 1989. It was a good part of the cycle. I just caught on very fast and I used many marketing skills I learned from retail. I advertised a lot and sold many of my own listings.

My wife did not think I should leave Coldwell Banker. But, I really did not know my potential until I was out on our own. I hated floor time. I thought it was a poor use of my time. Some of the agents would sit on the floor and not even know the properties people were calling on. That is what is unbelievable about real estate; many Realtors can't promote what they are selling.

**What lessons did you learn from your family, friends, previous jobs, and life experiences that helped you most to succeed in your career?**

My mother came from the Philippines. She was a war bride and grateful to be in America. She taught us to work and do our best.

When I was a kid, I raked leaves for a quarter. My mother would tell me to just do a good job and see what they would pay. I learned about service and under promising and over delivering. Do more than they expect and it leads to good things. With Sears, we did not argue with the customer, we gave them what they wanted. People wore holes in the jeans and then asked for another pair. At Sears, if you break a Craftsman Tool, you get a new replacement free. That is the type of stuff, basic customer service, and good will.

My mom had a positive attitude. We are so lucky to be free and to have the opportunity to do anything we want with our unlimited potential.

**What do you enjoy most about the business?**

I love the marketing aspect of unique properties, especially when other agents have failed. Many people are afraid to invest money to sell a house. I think it is persistence concerning following a marketing plan. I love the satisfaction of helping the younger couple, first-time buyer, and the feeling of just getting started. I remember our first Realtor and how she helped us to get started.

## Basic Numbers

**How many transactions did you close in 2005?**

Last year we had over $100 million and 153 transactions, which generated about $2 million in gross commissions. The average transaction was about $653,000.

**Are you a Billion Dollar Agent or do you believe you will hit that level during your career?**

In the last 20 years I did over $1 billion.

**What is your current staffing including: yourself, listing agents, buyer agents, managers, and assistants?**

I do all the listings. I have ten buyer agents and one of them is a husband/wife team. I have my office manager, a transaction coordinator, and a receptionist. My oldest son changed careers. From working at the post office, to doing all of my marketing and stocking the buyer boxes and handling the bulk mailing. A few of my buyer agents are new.

For a buyer agent, we do a 60/40 split with 60% going to agent. It is helping me get more free time. I am still making plenty of money and I have been able to take more vacation time.

## Goals

**Do you believe goals are important to your success? If yes, describe your approach to goal setting for your business and life?**

I used to do some "believe and desire and visualize" techniques when I got into real estate. I wanted to get a Lexus, so I focused on earning enough to get a Lexus.

I set goals at Coldwell Banker to get a free ad in the paper that stated I was the top agent. We have a monthly chart and their goal is to sell one house per month. We have a contest for a cruise and if they sell four houses in four months they get a cruise to Mexico. I set some personal goals for myself. I look at numbers and the dollars just come. Right now we are not meeting our goals. In the RE/MAX system, I am still in the top 100 in the whole country. We were number 84 out of 115,000 agents. I am down 35% from last year.

We have to stay focused and break it down to a daily routine. I always try to see five properties and call five people about buying or selling.

## Marketing

### New Customer Marketing – Lead Generation – Prospecting

**What are your top 5 methods for new client lead generation and about what percentages of new customers are generated from that approach?**

I realize that the Internet is probably the most cost effective method to generate new leads. I am using the Realtor.com banners. They see my banner on the top and on the side every few minutes. They can click right to my website. It is very expensive but I think it is worth it. We committed to that for this year.

I am still doing my normal Just Sold and Just Listed but I do it in large quantities. I usually do 3,000 to 4,000 pieces a month of Just Listed and Just Sold. It always pays off; I get two or three listings from that each month.

It is hard to measure and keep track from where the business came. That is the biggest thing I need to do better is figure out what is working and cut some out to have a better bottom-line.

I spend 20% on marketing.

I hired a financial coach to help me stay more organized.

## Client Marketing – Repeats/Referrals

**How many do you have in current database?**

We send out about 1,500 Christmas cards every year.

**What percentage of your business is referral?**

I would say that at least one-third is repeat/referral. That is something that I need to do a better job in analyzing. When I send out my batch of holiday cards, we usually send gifts as well.

That really pays off. We get lots of cards and e-mails back and future business comes in for the New Year.

**What client marketing activities do you do with prior clients?**

Every three or four months, I send out a newsletter.

# Listings

**What percentage of your transactions are listings?**

Last year it was 30% buyers and 70% listings.

Specialized Markets and Approach

**Are you involved with any special niche markets that is more than 10% of your business and part of your success?**

I specialize in ocean view properties. In Ventura there are many nice homes overlooking the bay and coastline. I do some of the more unique higher-end properties. I have been able to spend the money to get something sold.

I had a $2 million house listing that I spent $25,000.

# Growth of Business

**What single quality has made you more successful than others?**

Mass exposure of my name. I really push the client properties and my own name. Whenever I advertise in booklets for fundraisers I always put in houses at the same time. I put properties there. The football or symphony programs, I always put properties along with myself.

**As you grew your business, what were your biggest challenges and what were the solutions that worked the best?**

My biggest challenge was delegating. I quit Sears because I was not very good at delegating. I was not able to delegate well or fire people when I needed to fire them. It was great building a business myself and now I am back in a management league even though I don't want to be in that role so much. How high do I want to go with this thing? I know I could do more if I kept getting more organized. When is enough, enough?

I want them all to make a good living so they will stick with me. The challenge is delegating and giving quality service through other people. You don't know what the other agents are saying. It is important to have really good buyer agents that will not compromise their standards.

**What are questions you would like to ask of other billion dollar agents?**

What technical systems do you have in place to generate the volume you are doing?

What automatic systems are you using to speed up time and avoid communicating by phone?

## Delegation and Leverage - Assistants

**We see a challenge among agents: that are right at point of needing to delegate and outsource and hire their first part-time assistant to leverage their time.**

**What percentage of agents do you think are in that zone and why do they fail to take the next step? What would be the benefit for them to take that step?**

I was the same way until my partner encouraged me to add a few buyer agents. I was wasting all the leads and throwing in the trash all the future deals. They have to realize that if they cannot handle it all themselves they have to decide whether to grow or not. If you need to borrow the money to grow the business, then do it.

Many people will not delegate because they do not think others will do it as well as they can do it. They have the ability themselves but they cannot pass it through other people. A big part of it is personalities. It has taken me a long time to slowly delegate.

# JANE FAIRWEATHER

THE FAIRWEATHER COLLECTION
COLDWELL BANKER
BETHESDA, MD

## Introduction

Jane's remarkable experience allows for more product knowledge, more accurate pricing, proven marketing strategies, greater name recognition and stronger negotiating power. Jane also employs a team of expert assistants, who specialize in research, marketing, administration, finance and sales, allowing Jane to devote most of her time to negotiating on behalf of her sellers. Jane also has an unparalleled referral rate through which a considerable percentage of her 2,000 plus satisfied customers provide her with instant, credible access to new buyers and sellers.

A 22-year veteran of the business, Jane Fairweather is a staple in the Maryland Real Estate business. Together with her team of highly specialized assistants and buyer agents, Jane sells an average of 160-190 homes per year. She has been named the # 1 Coldwell Banker agent in the Washington Metropolitan Area for the last six years.

## Background

**For how many years have you been in the real estate business?**

I have been in the business for 22 years.

**What is your personal background and how did you get into real estate?**

I was a business major and had a management-consulting firm for 12 years doing various government and state contracting jobs. I had kids and stopped traveling and took up real estate. I considered catering and a few other things.

**What lessons did you learn from your family, friends, previous jobs, and life experiences that helped you most to succeed in your career?**

I learned how to run a business by being self-employed. I knew this was a sales business and that it was just about the numbers. I also knew that marketing was the key. Instinctively, if they don't know who you are why would they call you? When you start in real estate you have no listings. Listings are what put your name out in the marketplace. You have to spend money on marketing to get listings. You have no money but a lot of time.

So, I did direct mail and handwrote and stamped the cards myself. I learned how to bag by bulk mail rules and lugged them to post office myself. As the kids got older they helped me with them.

**What do you enjoy most about the business?**

I enjoy the excitement that comes with every day. Every day is different. I enjoy the variety of people and my team. I love my team. I love every single smart, professional and enthusiastic member of my team. Each person makes a huge contribution to the success of the whole team. I am blessed to work with such superior people.

## Basic Numbers

**How many transactions did you close in 2005?**

We did $128 million and 168 transactions. For Coldwell Banker, I was in the top 20 nationwide.

**Are you a Billion Dollar Agent or do you believe you will hit that level during your career?**

I would estimate I am probably $1 billion plus.

**What is your current staff including: yourself, listing agents, buyer agents, managers, and assistants.**

I have an administrative assistant who is receptionist/front desk expediter and sales person. I have two listing coordinators, one is licensed and the other is not. I have a full-time marketing director who runs all Jane Fairweather marketing, special events, and community service projects (not listing marketing). I have a full-time closing coordinator. I have an executive assistant who shadows me and assists with listings and sellers. My listing assistant is in training as my backup listing person. My goal is to have him cover for me so I can take more time off for fun and vacation. I have a very senior buyer agent who is my partner; she is the lead on buyer sales. She also covers for me. I have another buyers agent who does open houses and floor time. I have a financial / administrative manager — my husband David. He deals with payroll, retirement plans, health plans, legal. My daughter runs the property management division and property development division. She is also a buyers agent. All but one of my staff are licensed including my runner/courier who is also a junior buyer agent. He covers entry level buyers and renters.

## Goals

**Do you believe goals are important to your success? If yes, describe your approach to goal setting for your business and life?**

I write a huge business plan every year. It's probably six chapters and 90 pages. A lot of people set goals on production. I believe we also need to set goals on customer service, community outreach and community service, public relations, marketing, future business development, wealth development, and planning for retirement, etc.

We set goals for all areas in my business. If you do your homework in all the other categories, you will reach your production goal. It is a three-month process and my entire team works on the business plan. When it is complete everyone has bought into it.

## Marketing

### New Customer Marketing – Lead Generation – Prospecting

**What are your top five methods for new client lead generation and about what percentage of new customers are generated from that approach?**

I have two telemarketing companies that do cold calls for me and give me warm leads. I then prospect those leads. This is 11% of my business. They are calling five zip codes in the Bethesda, MD area. The leads are long-term. I work them over a number of years. I create relationships with these people over time, I may not sell their house for five years, but they may refer other people to me. Selling is a relationship building process. I spend about $1,500/month or $20,000/year on telemarketing.

I do direct mail. We do something every month. We send some combination of just sold and just listed cards, restaurant cards, high school scholarship announcement cards, redskin cards, etc.

We do a year-end sales report that people save.

**What is the one most effective form of marketing that you have constantly done?**

My sign is singularly the least expensive, the most distinctive, in the marketplace. The best thing I have done is to create a distinctive and memorable sign. No one thinks out of the box in real estate.

About the third year I was in real estate I came up with "The Fairweather Collection" as my brand name. I remember I went to list a woman's home and she was extremely creative. She said to me, "you need a brand". I will come up with something for you. She did; she came up with The Fairweather Collection and the weather vane and arch. I put the arch on top of my sign and then created a 2.5 times larger nametag rider than the standard tag at that time.

My sign is recognizable from a mile away. It's easy to remember and gives my brand a powerful advantage in the market place.

**What do you do, if anything, that you feel is fairly unique and successful?**

We do an annual report that is a detailed market analysis of all the sales of the previous 12 months. This report goes to every neighborhood in our zip codes.

We also send out quarterly updates by email. It is a newsletter with useful information that I hope they will keep. I want my image to be that I am knowledgeable and that I am the go-to person for good information. I also do a great deal of public speaking on the real estate market and loads of press interviews. I am regularly quoted in the Washington Post and I often do interviews on CNBC and Fox News.

**What marketing advice would you give to someone at $100,000 who wants to get to $200,000 and more?**

You are not being paid to be an administrator. Offload all administrative non-client tasks to someone else. If you are not listing or selling, you are not doing your job. Your time should be spent being face-to-face with buyers and sellers. After you reach 30-50 sales you need to offload the buyer part of your client interaction to a buyer agent. You should then concentrate on listings.

I hired my first assistant when I was doing 35-40 transactions. She was fantastic. About two years later she decided to take a job closer to her home. I asked her to write down everything she did, a task list for every job. All of our systems are documented in a procedures manual. I learned early on that I needed to institutionalize and systemize every job.

## Client Marketing – Repeats/Referrals

**About how many past clients have you worked with?**

We have worked with thousands and thousands.

**Of those, about how many do you have in current database?**

In the current database we have about 10,000 clients.

**What percentage of your business is referral?**

About 60% of my business is repeat and referral. About 31% is name recognition, 28% were past customers. A few were relocation.

**What client marketing activities do you do with past clients?**

We do direct mail; we send them reports. We also send them calendars. I do not do client parties. I do referral gifts to them when they send me business. We call them.

**How do you encourage referrals?**

We just keep doing a great job for their friends and family and we stay visible in the community by doing good works for charity.

## Sales

**Do you track all incoming leads for buyers and sellers and about what percentage turn into a closed sale?**

My buyer agents close around 60% of buyer leads.

I probably close about 70% of listing leads.

## Listings

**What percentage of your transactions are listings? What would be ideal and why?**

We are usually 60% to 70% listings. Many of my sellers move away.

## Specialized Markets and Approach

**Are you involved with any special niche market that is more than 10% of your business and part of your success?**

No, we cut across the board. We are all things to all people. I do not want to be riding just the high-end wave. I have tried to spread out the business so I still have a business if one segment goes down.

## Growth of Business

**What single quality has made you more successful than others?**

I am a big thinker.

**What does the average real estate agent fail to do which are among the reasons why they are average?**

They are small thinkers. They think this transaction, this direct mail card, this moment. They do not plan. They do not have a long-term vision. Thus, they do not execute a long-term vision. Most agents spend their lives working on their deal, which is singular. They never look up and see where they are going.

Agents who are making 100K usually have several issues. They cannot delegate or they will not delegate. They are afraid to let their deal go. They think no one else can do it as well as they can. They can never multiply the value of their hours if they don't learn to delegate and lead.

**Did you make any big mistakes that you want to warn others about?**

My first big mistake was not having systemized the job of my first assistant. When she decided to leave, I had to scramble around to find out what she did so I could rehire and not have lag time. Every job should be documented and institutionalized.

**If you could go back and do things differently,what would you have done at $100,000 that would have sped the growth of your business?**

I would not have done anything differently. It takes years of creating one relationship after another. It takes 7-15 touches for someone to get a piece of your brain and imprint your brand on them. You cannot go from 50 to 200 transactions over night.

Strong, stable businesses grow incrementally, having strong foundations on each level before they move to the one above. Business maturity is like aging; it cannot move quicker than the natural order of things. You need to crawl before you walk and walk before you run. So it is with growing your business.

## Learning

**What are best books you have read in past 10 years that helped with your business and life?**

I read at least 10 books every summer. I read books about selling, managing, customer service, and leadership. I started pretty early on with a coach. I was open to criticism. I was a sponge for information. I thought the best books for teaching about business, sales, and customer services, were:

The e-Myth by Michael E. Gerber, Raving Fans by Ken Blanchard, Selling the Invisible by Harry Beckwith, Visionary Business by Marc Allen, Man's Search for Meaning by Viktor E. Frankl, Customers For Life by Carl Sewell, Bringing Out the Best in Others by Thomas K. Connellan, The Guerrilla Marketing Handbook by Jay Levinson & Seth Godin, The 22 Immaculate Laws of Branding by Al Reis & Laura Ries, Don't Fire Them, Fire Them Up by Frank Pacetta

Most importantly I surrounded myself with smart people doing more or better business than me. I needed to reach up and grab the next step of the ladder – many smart agents helped lift me up to their level. I am grateful to them all. I try to do the same for other agents striving to learn and grow.

# LINDA FEINSTEIN

ERA JENSEN & FEINSTEIN REALTORS, LLC

HINSDALE, IL

## Background

**For how many years have you been in the real estate business?**

I have been in the business since 1987.

**What is your personal background and how did you get into real estate?**

I was a nurse and I liked working in a chaotic ICU and in the emergency room. I married a physician and we had 6 children in 9 years. A seventh child came later. When I was the PTO President, I thought a lot about real estate. I did 3 or 4 deals, unlicensed for friends, in 1986 and one of them was a $1.2 million transaction. My husband said, "if you were licensed, you would make X dollars."

When my 6th child started pre-school, I told my husband I was going to get my license and was just going to dabble in the business. I was just like a racehorse set off at the Preakness. My goal in finding an office was that it had to be an office that required no training, and I could just start working. I did not want to sit in class, after obtaining my license.

In terms of the market, even though I was an agent for only a few days, I knew what to do and could do it. My 10th day in the office the person answering the phone went home sick. A couple from Colorado were walk-ins and I sold them a house. They were working with another agent and the agent dropped them off for lunch - the office was next to the restaurant. They said their agent was not listening to them. This business is more than listening, it is taking in the big picture. Understanding what makes people happy. It is really important to be a good listener. A lot of times people say one thing, but that is not what they mean.

I really have a problem with agents who are condescending because they are at a certain status in their life. We are in a service industry. A few weeks ago, I was showing clients 40 rentals because I am a full service Realtor.

**What lessons did you learn from your family, friends, previous jobs, and life experiences that helped you most to succeed in your career?**

I think that throughout my whole life I have been very determined not to give up. In that sense, that is what has made me successful. I like when a client calls me in for a market analysis of his home, and he calls in three agents. I like that I need to excel and there is competition. I grew up living in a two-flat apartment above my grandmother. I knew you could study hard and get ahead; studying and focusing and never giving up.

My 3rd child has a handicap and we always focus on what she can do, not what she cannot do. She is 27 and works in a daycare center with children.

My father was a real 'people person' and he was a very positive person with a positive personality. I inherited that from him.

**What do you enjoy most about the business?**

I enjoy the deal. Not just the monetary portion, but getting the deal together. I am not going to sit back and celebrate that deal if there is another one to obtain. It is not so much the size of the deal, just the meeting of the minds.

## Basic Numbers

**How many transactions did you close in 2005? What was your total dollar volume in 2005?**

I closed 132 transactions for $127 million for average price over $900,000. That was about $1.7 million GCI. I am netting about 60% net profit.

**Are you a Billion Dollar Agent or do you believe you will hit that level during your career? Are you over a billion for career sales or what do you estimate?**

Yes, I have sold over $1 billion.

**What is your current staffing, including yourself, of listing agents, buyer agents, managers, and assistants?**

I have one full-time secretary. I have one agent who helps with open houses and works 25 – 30 hours per week. I have another part-time agent who helps with open houses, and brochures. I do most of my showings myself. My two part-time agents are doing about one full-time equivalent. I pay them hourly. Also, I pay agents to do open houses for me.

I am at about 65% listings and 35% buyers. I try to do the showings.

## Goals

**Do you believe goals are important to your success? if yes, describe your approach to goal setting for your business and life?**

I went to a Mike Ferry seminar when he was speaking in Chicago in 1989 or 1990. I went to this seminar and heard him saying that floor-time was a waste of time. I was in an upper-end office, and floor-time was quite good. I did quite well. I listened to him, though, and gave up floor time, and it forced me to get the business elsewhere. I was not going to sit at the desk for three hours and wait for phone to ring. Mike Ferry was instrumental in changing my life and helping me go after expireds.

# Marketing

## New Customer Marketing – Lead Generation – Prospecting

**What are your top five methods for new client lead generation and about what percentage of new customers are generated from that approach?**

Direct mailing. Agents have to understand that direct mailing is not something that gives results overnight. All it can do is get you in the door. It is up to you once you are in the door.

Internet and newspaper advertising. We do more and more with the Internet. Today I gave an emotional talk about going after expireds. In my most focused period I would stay up until 12:01am and I would have the letter written. I would deliver the letters in the morning after working out. I was doing at least 16-17 expireds per day. I hand-delivered the letters. I had read an article from the Chicago Tribune that said that it costs no more to use an excellent agent than a mediocre one. Many times people are depressed when their home expires. I would call them a day or two later. At first, for every 17, I would get maybe 1-2 listing appointments. As my inventory built up, so did the callbacks. The business goes to the people that have the most.

## Client Marketing – Repeats/Referrals

**Of those, about how many do you have in current database?**

We have about 3,000 past clients.

**What percentage of your business is referral?**

About 80% of my business is referral.

**What client marketing activities do you do with past clients?**

I try to send a holiday present to people who sent a referral. I always send a thank you note and fruit basket or something. I have a card mailing system where my past clients get 3-4 cards per year and they are handwritten. I hire a company to do the card mailing system. It is a nice fuzzy approach. It is not stamped ERA. It is a soft sell. I don't like doing silly things like pumpkins at Halloween. I think that dilutes the industry. I do not do organizational parties. I like taking a client out to dinner after closing a transaction.

## Growth of Business

**What single quality has made you more successful than others?**

I would say, probably putting the client's needs before my own. No matter how tired you are at the end of the day, if you promised something to someone you need to do it. If you have four more phone calls to make, you had better make them.

**What does the average real estate agent fail to do which are among the reasons why they are average?**

They fail to do client follow-up.
They fail to keep in touch with warm fuzzies.
They fail to understand what it is the client is looking for.
They fail to be flexible enough to get the deal done.

# VALERIE FITZGERALD

## Introduction

For Valerie Fitzgerald, who branded herself with the memorable "Want Your Home Sold? Got Valerie?" slogan, there is a human side to real estate. She manages to make it home for dinner almost every night to be with her 17-year-old daughter. Over the last fifteen years, Fitzgerald has single-handedly managed to build a multi-million dollar real estate business. She has also found the time to establish her own charity foundation, speak around the country at numerous business conventions, and appear on television shows like "Entertainment Tonight" and MTV's "Cribs." Valerie also ranks among Coldwell Banker's Top 10 agents nationwide, and earned the attention of the Los Angeles Business Journal for the highest sales volume for residential real estate in L.A. County for 2000. She was also recently nominated for the publication's 13th annual "Women Making a Difference".

Valerie says: "You need to have the dream of how you want your life to be, and then you need the heart to go and get it. Don't ever give up - if you shoot for the moon and miss, you are still amongst the stars."

## Background

**For how many years have you been in the real estate business?**

I have been in the business for 18 years.

**What is your personal background and how did you get into real estate?**

Previously, I was a model with the Ford Agency in New York for 10 years. As I transitioned out of modeling, I moved from New York to Los Angeles with my three-month-old baby to run a division of a cosmetics firm. The company went private and I lost the job, which was frightening. I didn't know what to do next to support my daughter and myself. A friend who lived in Florida came to visit me and suggested I try Real Estate.

I did not have friends in Los Angeles or a business degree. I had not finished college and I knew nothing about real estate. My challenge was figuring out a way to get my real estate license and take care of my baby daughter. I took her everywhere with me, to school and later to open houses. She came to all my appointments, even to the office where I started out. To this day, on showings, agents ask me how my daughter is. So many of them remember those days.

**What lessons did you learn from your family, friends, previous jobs, and life experiences that helped you most to succeed in your career?**

I think one of the biggest things I learned from being a model was how to deal with rejection. Modeling is full of rejection. In real estate you have to learn to handle rejection, as well as manage people and their emotional and financial issues. When you are a new agent trying to find your own way in the world, it is hard to manage other people's issues at the same time. It took me time to understand the emotional and financial patterns that exist in many transactions. I learned not to take things personally. I also learned about blind faith.

**What do you enjoy most about the business?**

I enjoy the diversity. Every day is different, the people, locations and the properties. I am also very entertained. It is a very entertaining business with all the various needs, wants, and desires of people on a daily basis. Real estate can be similar to being in a movie every day.

## Basic Numbers

**How many transactions did you close in 2005?**

We closed about 63 transactions in 2005.

**What was your total dollar volume in 2005?**

We sold a total of $160 million in 2005.

**Based on that, about what is average price of a sale?**

The average price of a sale in 2005 was about $2,500,000.

**Are you a Billion Dollar Agent or do you believe you will hit that level during your career? Are you over a billion for career sales or what do you estimate?**

My career sales are over $1 billion.

**What is your current staffing including: yourself, listing agents, buyer agents, managers, and assistants?**

In addition to myself, I have six administrative assistants, and seven buyer agents. I have an escrow coordinator, an office manager, a marketing assistant, an office administrator, a weekend assistant, and a personal assistant who is the call and showing coordinator. I also have a Director of Sales. My team, in total, is 14 people. My personal split of time working in my business is 75% listings and 25% buyers.

When you show a buyer or list a home for sale in our area, called the Westside (Southern California), you have to physically be there for every appointment. Most markets across the US have lockboxes or the sellers show them. This means I personally drive 4-5 hours a day.

## Goals

**Do you believe goals are important to your success? If yes, describe your approach to goal setting for your business and life?**

I think goal setting is vital. I have each buyer agent set a goal number and add 20-25% to their number as a goal for the next year. I have been setting goals for 10-12 years.

When you first start out in real estate, very few agents grasp the "independent contractor" theory to put money away to pay their taxes. My original goal setting began by mistake. At first, after making some money, I realized I had forgotten "Uncle Sam". At the time I had made about $200,000, but owed $100,000 for taxes. So quickly I had to learn how to live and work and pay this off. It took me two years. Many times in business, you find out what you don't know by making mistakes.

Several years ago I started looking at our market which is comprised mostly of houses. I felt the market strongly lacked what other major US cities have, luxury high rise living. There existed very little to offer to people who traveled, or were young and didn't want the responsibility of owning a home yet, and a place for people who owned large homes and didn't want to buy another house while moving.

I spent a 1 ½ years learning this market and speaking to developers. I am very happy to say that a major New York developer had the same viewpoint. He is building an incredible, luxury high-rise "estate living" building, for which I am the sales and marketing consultant.

This is a dream come true for our community. There will be a major lifestyle shift here where it is desperately needed. Finally, we will have estate living without having to have the responsibilities of maintaining a house.

## Marketing

**What are your top five methods for new client lead generation and about what percentage of new customers are generated from that approach?**

As a result of our exceptional customer service, we frequently get referrals from our past and present clients.

I do two full pages in the LA Times every week on Fridays and Saturdays. It gives me a solid, consistent presence and a memorable brand image.

We do about 55,000 mailers a month, that can be a newsletter, a Just Listed or Just Sold card, a brochure, or other promotional material.

My strong online presence, through my own extensive website, www.valeriefitzgerald.com, generates a number of very strong leads from all over the world. It gets about 15,000 hits a month.

I have a talent staff of associate agents who I assign to sit at our properties that are open on Sundays. It's a great way for them to bring new business into the office.

**What do you do, if anything, that you feel is fairly unique and successful?**

One thing I have done for many years is a tag line, "Want your home sold? Got Valerie?" This along with my name has been the foundation of our marketing and branding strategy. We believe in keeping things simple and memorable.

## Client Marketing – Repeats/Referrals

### What percentage of your business is referral?

Past clients are probably 25% of our business. Referrals are 33% of our business, and new business is 33%.

### What client marketing activities do you do with past clients?

Each month, past and present clients receive our newsletter, as well as our monthly promotional mailers. They often highlight our #1 ranking for Coldwell Banker Beverly Hills.

I will call 20-30 of my past clients. That has always been a priority with us, as has coaching. I have asked myself, "Do you call through all 1,500 people as a client base?" On yearly basis, I may actually speak to only maybe 100. We also send clients holiday gifts and cards.

## Growth of Business

### What single quality has made you more successful than others?

I think we are extremely organized. That is a word that stands out for me. We have our job descriptions; we have tremendous harmony in our group. We have been together a long time and we have a lot of fun. There are no egos involved, we pull together and we can do each other's job.

What does the average real estate agent fail to do which are among the reasons why they are average?

The average real estate agent fails to qualify their client.

They fail to qualify the motivation of the seller and buyer.

They also fail to set goals.

### Did you make any big mistakes that you want to warn others about?

I wasted time working with people who were not qualified. I said yes to everything, I spent too much money, and I didn't have good time management. It is important to be organized and in control of your schedule.

## Building a Team

### In what order did you add your first part-time and full-time staff?

At first, in the beginning of my career, instead of paying my taxes, I hired a full-time assistant.

Soon thereafter, I hired a second full-time assistant, when most successful agents had only one. Next, I tried to bring in associate agents, but we weren't prepared to manage them. Then, I hired a transaction coordinator because of the tremendous amount of paperwork. Then we hired our own full-time marketing coordinator. Since this time in the last 7 years or so, we have built a little company that has an office administrator, two other assistants, a sales director, and a great talented team of buyer's agents. We also use four virtual assistants when outsourcing projects.

## Delegation and Leverage - Assistants

**We see a challenge of people right at point of needing to delegate and outsource and hire their first part-time assistant to leverage their time. What percentage of agents do you think are in that zone and why do they fail to take the next step? What would be benefit for them to take that step?**

I think that they feel that they cannot afford an assistant, and they are unsure what to tell the assistant to do. I had made three sales and decided I needed an assistant, when no one had an assistant at that time. I made a list of everything I liked doing and of things I did not like doing. When I first earned $65,000, I took half the money and hired an assistant instead of paying my taxes. Had I thought it through at the time, however, I'm not sure I would have leveraged myself and my business that way.

## Connections and Referrals

**Are you part of any mastermind coaching groups?**

I have been with Ken Goodfellow for eight years – www.kengoodfellow.com. He has helped me grow my business beyond my wildest imagination.

# Marc Fleisher

## Introduction

Marc sold a record-breaking $150 to $277 MILLION in residential real estate in Washington DC and Montgomery County each year from 1999 through 2005. That's over $1 BILLION in seven years! His sales volume in 2000-2004 earned him the title of Top Producer in the Nation (upper-end homes) from REAL Trends, Inc. and Realtor Magazine.

For the past six years, Marc has been recognized as the #1 Long & Foster overall Top Producer in both residential resale's and new home sales, and the #1 agent in the metropolitan DC area (Montgomery County and Washington, DC) among all companies (for sales and number of transactions). With 25 years of experience, Marc is very highly regarded by both his peers and clients for his integrity, knowledge and enthusiasm. Marc employs seven extremely competent assistants to ensure that each seller and/or buyer has complete attention and thorough service. His team helps Marc maintain the highly detailed effort from start to finish that he is known for. Personally, Marc has boundless energy and a hard work ethic that he applies toward every real estate transaction.

Whether as a buyer-broker or as a seller's listing agent, Marc has consistently maintained a twrack record of success for the clients he represents.

## Background

**How many years have you been in the real estate business?**

I have been in the business for 30 years and I have been full-time for 27 years.

**What is your personal background and how did you get into real estate?**

I have always been entrepreneurial and involved in sales. I got my license in 1976 when I was selling Indian Art and Western Artifacts. I began a business in 1979 that involved the rental and sale of roller blades. I met my wife-to-be and she suggested that if I was going to sell anything, I should spend my time selling *expensive* things. I was very competitive, always selling. I have never worked for anybody.

I first got my license when one of my business associates, who was a commercial real estate broker, encouraged me to pursue my license.

**What lessons did you learn from your family, friends, previous jobs,**

and life experiences that helped you most to succeed in your career?

Many friends owned their own business. I have an affinity for type A people. I enjoy meeting people and interacting with them. I always was excited about completing a transaction on any level.

**What do you enjoy most about the business?**

I enjoy the flexibility to enjoy my life, take off and still be successful. Rather than 80-90 hour workweeks that I used to face, I currently work about 35-45 hours per week. I am taking off at least 10 days a month for travel and myself. I find that I can still conduct business with my Blackberry while traveling.

## Basic Numbers

**How many transactions did you close in 2005?**

I sold $277 million based on 157 transactions. Of those, approximately 115 were listings and on 30% of those listings, we were the only agent involved in the sale.

**Are you a Billion Dollar Agent or do you believe you will hit that level during your career?**

Yes, I am a Billion Dollar Agent. In fact, in the last 5 years I sold over $1 billion. I estimate my career total to be approximately $2.3 billion.

**What is your current staffing including: yourself, listing agents, buyer agents, managers, and assistants?**

We have 7 people on my team. I have 2 buyers agents and myself. Up until 1995 it was myself and one other person. We promoted one of my assistants to full-time buyer agent this year. Our percentage of clients was 72% sellers and 28% buyers. I believe that 2/3s listings are more profitable than 50/50. The number of listings you can focus on will speak volumes to your business. It is easier to manage 50 listings at a time than service 50 buyers. I would never be where I am without my team - they are the best in the United States in my mind. I have a listing coordinator, contract coordinator, marketing administrative person. I also have an assistant to the contract coordinator who deals primarily with inspections and property condition items for both homes about to go on the market as well as the results of home inspections for properties under contract. I negotiate approximately 8,000 repair items/issues annually due to the home inspection. All members of my team must be licensed.

## Goals

**Do you believe goals are important to your success? If yes, describe your approach to goal setting for your business and life?**

No. I am often asked to do seminars and I hear from other agents that their managers always try to get them to establish goals. I find setting goals can be self-limiting. Why set yourself up to be satisfied with a certain level of production when you should be able to exceed it?

Ten years ago I was driven to be the number 1 agent in my market in terms of sales volume. Now I am driven more by the bottom-line. I am much more interested in the net profit. Mostly I am driven by the fact that I enjoy what I do.

## Marketing

### New Customer Marketing – Lead Generation – Prospecting

**What are your top 5 methods for new client lead generation and about what percent of new customers are generated from that approach?**

Of the $4.8 million GCI earned last year, I spent about 10% on marketing. I don't specifically have a marketing plan to generate new leads versus networking my past clients. My marketing is always about the property at hand.

It is always about continued exposure in the marketplace using the right vehicles. I can justify spending dollars on marketing since the public associates my marketing efforts with my overall success.

## Client Marketing – Repeats/Referrals

**About how many past clients have you worked with? Of those, about how many do you have in current database?**

I have been very fortunate to maintain a relationship with many of my past clients, but having said that, I have no doubt that I have not been aggressive in nurturing that aspect of my business. Therefore, I would not be surprised if I have fallen out of touch with at least 50% of my past clients. Currently we have about 1000 previous clients in our Top Producer database.

**What percentage of your business is referral?**

I would guess 35-40% with the remaining clients coming to me as a result of their awareness and familiarity with my marketing efforts and reputation.

**What client marketing activities do you do with past clients?**

We stay in touch with them once a year with a market update and at tax time we send the previous year's clients a copy of their settlement sheet for tax purposes.

## Growth of Business

**What <u>single</u> quality has made you more successful than others?**

No one single quality stands out, but I would say honesty, patience, persistence, and salesmanship have gotten me to where I am today.

**What does the average real estate agent fail to do which are among the reasons why they are average?**

They are self-serving and do not put their clients' interests first.

They fail to follow-up.

They fail to negotiate well.

They are insecure.

They are surprisingly not well-versed in either current legislation or market conditions.

They lack mathematical skills.

They are not familiar with tax implications.

They set themselves up for disappointment and do not know how to recover.

They fail to be honest.

They are not committed to a full time career as an agent.

You cannot get from one level to the next if you focus on the minutia rather than establishing a team of assistants and delegating tasks to others as capable if not more capable than yourself.

My unique talent is working with buyers and sellers and negotiating contracts. I solve problems. I expect my assistants to be able to independently solve problems arising from their own responsibilities.

# MARY ANNE FUSCO

PRUDENTIAL DOUGLAS ELLIMAN
WESTSIDE OFFICE BROADWAY
NEW YORK, NY

## Introduction

In just eight years, Mary Anne Fusco rose from a position of real estate novice to deserved fame as one of New York City's most recognized, honored and talented agents. A top producer who leads a team of six skilled professionals, this market-savvy Prudential Douglas Elliman Executive Vice President also boasts a superior reputation among the most successful and innovative marketers of multi-million dollar properties. Mary Anne enjoys and excels at the challenge of matching buyers up to their perfect home. She is known for her uniquely effective marketing prowess and negotiating strength that attain the best price for her clients. This extremely loyal, sincere and dedicated residential specialist is committed to the unique goals of each buyer and seller she represents, plus employs honest, direct, straightforward guidance that inspires confident decisions and assures optimal results. Mary Anne has been honored and praised for her mentoring work to others throughout the country.

She is an active member in a number of professional organizations and charities, including Real Estate Board of New York, Association of Real Estate Women, National Organization for Italian-American Women and Habitat for Humanity. Mary Anne has additionally been a member of the Women's Commerce Club since 1985, and served on its board for two years before leaving Atlanta for New York City in 1995.

## Background

**For how many years have you been in the real estate business?**

I have been in real estate for eight years.

**What is your personal background and how did you get into real estate?**

By profession, I am an English teacher of high school and college. I am an entrepreneur and had a number of businesses in areas such as wholesale garments as well as a construction company in Atlanta, GA. I moved to New York and worked in sales for a corporate entity. I left when I could not buy part of the corporation, and I decided to investigate real estate since the industry had always flirted with me in Atlanta.

**What lessons did you learn from your family, friends, previous jobs, and life experiences that helped you most to succeed in your career?**

139

What I began to realize early in real estate is that almost everything I have ever done was basically sales. If I were not selling a verb, a noun, or life lessons while teaching, I was selling a construction company, or reassurance and self-dignity in the weight-loss business. People would come in with tears and go out with hope. The bottom line was sales. Whether I like it or not, this is what I do best. You really have to love and believe in what you do. I knew the bottom line was mentoring and caring more about the other person than what I thought about myself.

**What do you enjoy most about the business?**

I enjoy the action. I enjoy the quickness of the business. The business perpetuates; you need to be on your feet. It is not a job for sitting at the back of your chair. I have been accused of sitting at the first third of a chair! It is a very spontaneous and reactive business. I view it similar to a tennis player with a tennis racket in his hand. As a real estate agent you need to have tunnel vision and focus and respond to the needs of others as they appear. The quickness of the business is a real rush for me.

It is a very satisfying business because you get to feel that people are entrusting you with the biggest asset they have. When you can turn around and make them smile, there is enormous satisfaction.

## Basic Numbers

**How many transactions did you close in 2005?**

Last year I closed more then 40 transactions.

**What was your total dollar volume in 2005?**

In 2005, I sold about $28 million. This year I should end up with $40 million or more.

**Are you a Billion Dollar Agent or do you believe you will hit that level during your career? Are you over a billion for career sales or what do you estimate?**

I surely believe that I will be a billion dollar agent. With my new affiliation with the number one company in New York City and Long Island, Prudential Douglas Elliman, my goal will be realized. I have sold about $180 million to date.

**What is your current staffing, including yourself, of listing agents, buyer agents, managers, and assistants?**

I have three assistants, an executive assistant who handles the business and paperwork, I have a marketing assistant, and another person who shows the properties and looks after my finances.

I have an associate who is my right hand and a buyer specialist.

## Goals

**Do you believe goals are important to your success? If yes, describe your approach to goal setting for your business and life?**

Goals are imperative. I am a teacher. I am a marathoner as well. Goal setting is paramount to everyone's success. If you do not know where you are heading, you are lost. You must know where you are and then plan where you want to go. Day to day, month to month, one year and five year plans are what I work to design. I am goal setting and running a business at the same time.

Ultimately, my five-year plan is a focus. My goal is to get to $150 million sold per year.

## New Customer Marketing – Lead Generation – Prospecting

**What are your top 5 methods for new client lead generation and about what percentage of new customers are generated from that approach?**

New York City real estate is a completely different creature. It is better to choose a narrow market, at first. Dig trenches narrow and deep. I choose an area to target. Once I have chosen the target buildings, the goal is to get 15% market share or better from a building.

Lateral farming is a necessity. For example, we do Just Listed and Just Sold cards in related areas. All of a sudden there is awareness of our team and that we are active. We have done that on the East Side and West Side of Manhattan. I have also created a newsletter that is a very soft sell which gives information, every two months or so, of events in the area.

We go into all our new buildings and search for specific units, thereby generating sellers for our new buyers. This has been an enormously successful tool. We will say, "we are searching for a 2 bedroom and 2 bath in your building". It has given us new listings and helped our buyers.

We also give seminars of topical interest, like "Merlot and You". We invite speakers to buildings and pick a venue in the city. All this drives people to us in a non-threatening way.

## Client Marketing – Repeats/Referrals

**What percentage of your business is referral?**

About 35-40% of business is client repeat/referral business. I have worked very hard to develop my referral business through our elite and master sales conferences.

I am pleased that so many people remember me. I contact them at least six times per year.

**What client marketing activities do you do with prior clients?**

My marketing plan divides my market into groups: Platinum, Gold, and Silver. My sphere of influence and prior clients are platinum and the other groups are categorized by the activity of a farm area. A group may hear from us two or three times a month. Formally, they will be contacted once a month with various postcards and schedules. I have a different type of newsletter called Jubilee News, which is a warm newsletter. The newsletter goes out quarterly. It is a very intimate type of newsletter. I give an annual party to clients to say 'thank you' to my clients and customers. In addition, I run a coat drive for the homeless across the city. We collected 200 coats last year. Our goal for this year is 300 coats. We also give people a gift for donating to the charity we support.

## Growth of Business

**What single quality has made you more successful than others?**

A moral ethic and an enormous care factor, linked with being knowledgeable of my market, has made me more successful. I think that people are impressed with an honest attitude, a no-nonsense approach, and the enormous caring that I give. One must know the market intelligibly, then do the job better then one ever could dream.

**What does the average real estate agent fail to do which are among the reasons why they are average?**

Average agents fail to prepare themselves to be knowledgeable in their market. They fail to seek the answers and have an awareness of their own market. They fail to seek out and surround themselves with tools necessary to be knowledgeable. They fail to invest in their business. They fail to realize they have to share of themselves with other people to get others to come to them. They fail to create venues open for people to get to know them. Finally, they fail to pick up the phone and make the call.

**Did you make any big mistakes that you want to warn others about?**

The greatest challenge is also the greatest gift. I am talking about the success that I had from making $20,000 in the first year, and then $86,000 in the second year. In the third year, I met Floyd Wickman and he helped me increase my business by 240%. Once your business gets very big, it is necessary to seek proper coaching and assistance. The challenge then is how to handle that growth.

The key items were:

1. To be knowledgeable and make sure you know your business.

2. To market and stay in front of your people is paramount.

3. To keep in contact with your people often.

## Delegation and Leverage - Assistants

**We see a challenge of people, right at point of needing to delegate and outsource and hire their first part-time assistant, to leverage their time. What percentage of agents do you think are in that *zone* and why do they fail to take the next step? What would the benefit be for them to take that step?**

I think that by the time you are closing about $15 million in sales you need help. What prevents people from getting help is the fear of people duplicating themselves; or, they do not know how to train an assistant. People in real estate do not like to spend money. In business, you have to spend money to make money.

# COREY GEIB

THE COREY GEIB TEAM
RE/MAX HOME STORE
LAS VEGAS, NV

## Introduction

I currently am, and have been for five years in a row since 2001, the number one team leader worldwide in commissions paid, for RE/MAX. I am a single father of three boys. Roby 19, Mitchel 13, and Jacob 8. We all love football and golf.

## Background

**For how many years have you been in the real estate business?**

I have been in business for 17 years.

**What is your personal background and how did you get into real estate?**

I began in real estate at a young age; I was about 20. I lived in a small town at the time. My sister had a license but did not work in the business for long. I liked the concept. I was in Santa Clarita, California and got my California license in 1989. I moved to Las Vegas in 1994. I got my Nevada license in 1997.

**What lessons did you learn from your family, friends, previous jobs, and life experiences that helped you most to succeed in your career?**

I treat every day the same; whether it is a 9-5 paid job or a commission paid job. If you treat sales like a real job you will succeed.

There is a problem with the freedom associated with sales that can get you into trouble; you need to treat sales like a real job. I think that structure is very important.

**What do you enjoy most about the business?**

In general, I just like working. I love the business. We used to work with many first time buyers. Now it is mostly repeat and referrals. I liked helping first-time buyers. I love homes themselves; the character, style and architecture.

## Basic Numbers

**How many transactions did you close in 2005?**

My team volume was $201 million with 688 units sold and $6,259,467.80 in commissions. Personally, I did about 74 transactions.

**Based on that, about what is average price of a sale?**

The average price of a home was about $320,000.

**Are you a Billion Dollar Agent or do you believe you will hit that level during your career? Are you over a billion for career sales or what do you estimate?**

I estimate my career team number is maybe 1.3 or 1.4 billion dollars.

**What is your current staff? Include: yourself, listing agents, buyer agents, managers, and assistants.**

My team is about 12 people who are all agents. We let them do everything and they are able to do it all. They list and sell. We generate the leads. We have about four assistants. Some of the team members have part-time assistants. We have generated and built this team out of mostly buyer leads. For the past five years it was 90% buyer transactions. Now with repeat clients, we are starting to do many listings. Ninety percent of my personal business is listings.

In 2005, we had about 40% listings.

For myself, I help the other agents with their daily struggles and then I handle the referral business that I get. I try to take as many referrals as possible. We produce our own magazines and I design those as well as coordinate printing and distribution.

## Goals

**Do you believe goals are important to your success? If yes, describe your approach to goal setting for your business and life?**

We do goals at the beginning of the year. We do personal and team goals. We go over those at the start of the year and look again at the end of the year. I think it is extremely important for goals to be written down and visualized. I am a strong believer in almost daily review of goals. We set monthly goals for the team. We break it down to financial, family, vacations, etc. The first five years I was fairly lost trying to make a sale. It was not until 1997 or 1998 that we really got going. I sold 80 homes and then 105 homes and generally average approximately 80 units a year personally.

## Marketing

### New Customer Marketing – Lead Generation – Prospecting

**What are your top five methods for new client lead generation and about what percentage of new customers are generated from that approach?**

We use the magazines for first-time buyer lead generation. We do have an Internet presence that is growing and becoming a larger part of our business. We advertise in newspapers to generate buyer leads. We do just listed and just sold postcards on each transaction.

Depending on the neighborhood, I try to keep it at 200-250 residences. We use a company that narrows farming to specific demographics. We use INFO-USA. People get the 3-5 year itch so we target that group. We may have an investment opportunity, so we contact people with multiple investments. We may go after doctors and lawyers living in town.

**What do you do, if anything, that you feel is fairly unique and successful?**

The market helped us a lot; our average price was $122,000 way back then. We were anywhere and everywhere. We were generating close to 1,000 leads per month. We converted one out of five turned into sales.

We have fantastic phone training. Before the agents can speak to anyone, they need to learn every property that is in the magazine. They need to know the inventory before they can be in front of clients. You have to know what you are selling; and I test them. If the clients are here in Las Vegas and willing to make that phone call, we need to know how to handle it.

Almost all magazines put a picture and price. We sell according to a monthly payment. If we told you something was $50/month, or $10,000 total, you would be more interested in the $50.00 per month since it doesn't seem so expensive. Then we have APR disclosures as well that disclose what programs we are using to get the low payments.

**What marketing advice would you give to someone at $100,000 who wants to get to $200,000 and more?**

They have to stay focused. You can take that $100,000 and turn that into $200,000. You have to pickup the phone and call past clients. If you have made $100,000, then you have enough past clients. They will get you introductions if you just ask.

I set up the expectation during the escrow process; I tell them I will be calling them. I try to call everybody at least once in a 90-day period. It is like putting $5 or $10 bucks in your gas tank. Always be putting a few calls into your prospecting tank. I used to hate to be 'stuck in traffic'. Now I love it because I can make my calls.

I usually do it between 9-10am. I get about 50% voice mail. It seems funny because once I am on a regular rotation, they are offended if I do not call.

If I get voice mail, I will not call them back I will just leave a message letting them know I was thinking of them. Out of 386 past clients, I had 70 deals. That is one in five, or one in six. Maybe 50 of 396 have referred a deal to me. I always try to increase that number.

I have made a lot of people a lot of money. I have a personal coach who I work with. His name is Tim and he drives home that I am in complete control of my business. I had not picked up an ad call in over two years. There were people I was afraid to call because it had been so long. I called to apologize for not calling them and now I just pop them into the rotation.

## Client Marketing – Repeats/Referrals

### What client marketing activities do you do with past clients?

We are a huge proponent of picking up the phone and calling your past clients. I send postcards and letters to past clients. One thing I must get better at is having my team members contact their past clients more often or set up a system to reach all clients of the team. We are working on it.

## Growth of Business

### What single quality has made you more successful than others?

Hard work and focus. I lost many top producing agents who were affected by the amount of money they were making. They decided to not work as hard. I have not let commissions affect my drive. I still enjoy coming to work. It drives my girlfriend nuts. If you treat it like a job, you will see the results. I am also brutally honest with people, I will not tell them what they want to hear, I will tell them what they need to hear; good or bad, but the truth.

### What does the average real estate agent fail to do which are among the reasons why they are average?

They do not talk to enough people and tell them what they do. They wait for business to come to them. The more people you talk to, the more people will want to use you. I think many Realtors don't talk to people because they don't have enough product knowledge to feel confident in what they are talking about.

### Did you make any big mistakes that you want to warn others about?

Getting lazy. It all comes down to hard work. There are guys who outwork me for sure, but by now I try to work smarter not harder just based on my time availability.

### If you could go back and do things differently,what would you have done at $100,000 that would have sped the growth of your business?

I would have started calling past clients a lot sooner. I did not call past clients back then. It probably cost me hundreds of past clients. When I saw a past client and found out I lost a sale because they lost my contact info, I would go crazy. There is no excuse for your clients to be unable to get a hold of you.

## Building a Team

**How did you first start to delegate and outsource and build a team?**

The owner and previous team leader Michael Vestuto started our team. Because of numerous magazine leads, it grew out of necessity.

He gave leads to other agents at a split. We brought more agents, then more and more. We were selling 1,300 homes a year with eight guys. Because our team was growing, we needed structure. Everyone is on the floor everyday. I have a calendar with days off. I only let four agents off per day. If they all took the same day off we wouldn't have phone coverage. We have lots of incoming phone calls. The assistants are administrative. They set up listings, virtual tours, paperwork with title, etc.

**What are the best seminars/conferences that you attend?**

I go to Tom Hopkins every year without fail.

# CHAD GOLDWASSER

THE GOLDWASSER TEAM
KELLER WILLIAMS REALTY
AUSTIN, TX

## Background

**For how many years have you been in the real estate business?**

I have been in business for eight years.

**What is your personal background and how did you get into real estate?**

I was in the service industry and knew I was going to be successful at something. I started to manage a restaurant and decided I did not want to do that. I started to invest in real estate and earned my license. I felt I could do well in business.

**What lessons did you learn from your family, friends, previous jobs, and life experiences that helped you most to succeed in your career?**

I learned a lot about business from my Dad who owned an aluminum company in the Midwest. Unfortunately, at a certain point, he lost the company and passed away when I was just 14. I learned a lot about being smart and about what you are doing. I learned a lot about not letting money and success go to your head. I also learned a lot from my Mom who reared four boys while working full-time.

**What do you enjoy most about the business?**

I enjoy sitting down with people and helping them get homes sold. I enjoy leading my team and figuring out how to grow the business. I love goal setting and motivating the team.

## Basic Numbers

**How many transactions did you close in 2005?**

Last year was $42 million from 210 transactions. When I started out, I started as a buyers agent from another agency and the first year I closed 66 deals and went on my own. Then I went from $5 million to $9 million and onto $12 million. That is when I started building my team and things really took off. We went from $12 million to $22 million to $36 million. My wife is my business partner and we continued to grow during a transition year.

This year our goal is $80-100 million with 400 transactions.

**What is average price of a sale?**

The average price of a house sale is $225,000.

**Are you a Billion Dollar Agent or do you believe you will hit that level during your career?**

I am 33 years old and I expect to hit a billion dollars in my career.

**What is your current staffing including: yourself, of listing agents, buyer agents, managers, and assistants?**

I have myself and one other agent doing all of the listings and I have 12 buyer specialists. I have a listing manager, closing manager, courier, bookkeeper, marketing manager (my wife), and a director of operations who handles staff administration. I also have a production manager who does all flyers and gets properties listed on to the Internet.

## Goals

**Do you believe goals are important to your success? If yes, describe your approach to goal setting for your business and life?**

About five years, I thought I was doing really well. After all, I was only 28 years old, had a very successful business and many opportunities. I attended a breakfast meeting at RE/MAX where Rick DeLuca was speaking. He asked us, who had a business plan. Only one person responded, yes. He basically said, 'have you written it down because that is the first step?' I bought everything he had, took an afternoon and sat at my house and followed his instructions. I broke down my numbers and the activities I would do to hit those numbers. I was super excited because it was my first business plan. The next day my wife typed it up for me and laminated it. One I put above my visor and the other above my office desk.

Now it is about setting goals for the team and teaching them to write their own business plans. I love helping other people. I like giving them opportunities.

## Marketing

### New Customer Marketing – Lead Generation – Prospecting

**What are your top five methods for new client lead generation and about what percent of new customers are generated from that approach?**

I have a huge base of builders. I started going to "move-up sales" for a builder in Austin. After I was doing sales for him for a few months, I asked to attend their meeting. I brought donuts and introduced myself to the sales team. I have been going to that meeting for the past three years. This morning I got in front of 60 builder reps and brought breakfast tacos and met the sales people. My best listing lead venue is builders.

We started doing some radio advertising with Matt Wagner. We do a popular Austin real estate update for one minute and that has started to produce.

Our web presence is huge. Our website generates probably 3,000 buyer leads per month. Maybe 10% of them are good. Even with 12 buyer agents they cannot keep up with web leads. We only have one website. It is ranked highly. We signed a deal with a company named Home Gain five years ago and it has continued to grow. This part of their company is more pay-per-click. I would guess 10% give us a good phone number and good e-mail address. We enter their information into an e-mail drip system.

We do a lot of farming particularly in one specific neighborhood. We market to about 4000 homes in that area. We started with 300 and have built up our database. We take the entire team and literally knock on doors. We knock on Tuesdays from 6-8 PM or Sat from 9-11 is. When all 14 of us are working together we are able to talk to 700 homeowners in just a few hours.

**What marketing advice would you give to someone at $100,000 who wants to get to $200,000 and more?**

They should consider building a good relationship with a builder rep where they can work with move up buyers.

## Client Marketing – Repeats/Referrals

**About how many past clients have you worked with? Of those, about how many do you have in current database?**

We have about 2,000 past clients. In Top Producer, we have scheduled calls every few months or so. I am making a lot of calls and lots of personal notes. My goal is 12 per day. I learned that early on.

**What percentage of your business is referral?**

Probably about 25% of the business is referral; less than I wish.

**What client marketing activities do you do with past clients?**

We do client parties. We need to do something for kids and something for adults. I like live music; so we decided to do a benefit concert. It was called Rock and Restock. It started out as a benefit for the capital area food bank. We did it right after Christmas. The first year there were 170 people present — two live bands. It was awesome. We hosted 200 people at the last one. And we raised $5,000.

## Listings

**What percentage of your transactions are listings? What would be ideal and why?**

I would guess that buyers were probably 60% and sellers probably 40%. At the end of last year and the beginning of 2006, there were six buyer specialists and then we hired three more and trained them.

## Growth of Business

**What single quality has made you more successful than others?**

My ability to change who I am as a leader and as a person to attract other leaders and people and my ability to see the future and make it happen. Leadership.

**Did you make any big mistakes that you want to warn others about?**

Do not grow too fast. We have grown and had to come back down and did that a few times. We keep reaching and moving forward. On occasion, we move too quickly and we hire too quickly. We are trying to slow that process down. Like Jim Collins says, "get the good people on the bus". Be careful about how you grow.

## Building a Team

**How did you first start to delegate and outsource and build a team?**

For agents, my first approach was a friend who had been in sales and seemed like a decent person. He came to me and saw my success and he had no real estate experience. I hired him and an assistant at the same time. The assistant became a buyer's agent in six months. The second year we did a lot more interviewing and my lead guy is a past client of mine and has no previous real estate experience. I think you need a great heart and patience to serve people.

**If you had to do it again, today, from a starting point of making $100,000 per year, what would you suggest for delegating, outsourcing and staffing?**

You need to understand you will go through ups and downs. For me, it's when people leave. Last year, my two administrative people came into my office and both sat down, like in high school. Then, they resigned with a two-week notice. What I have found, anytime there is adversity and challenges, this is an opportunity to grow and get stronger. The business will continue to flourish if you can do that. No matter how great the company is, it is still going to happen.

# ARLENE GONNELLA

WEICHERT REALTORS - SHORT HILLS

SHORT HILLS, NJ

## Background

**How many years have you been in the real estate business?**

I have been in the business for 23 years.

**What is your personal background and how did you get into real estate?**

I was a college graduate and I was working for a bank. My husband was working for an investment bank. He had better hours and made more money, and I was traveling a lot. When I had children, I got my real estate license. I have 5 children.

I hit the ground running. I have been doing it for 23 years. I thought it would be interesting, and I had bought about 5 houses that we lived in and sold. I thought I had some experience in that.

**What lessons did you learn from your family, friends, previous jobs, and life experiences that helped you most to succeed in your career?**

I think having empathy for other people has helped me succeed. This is not about selling a house. It is about understanding what a family's needs are and helping them get what they want. It is a people business more than a house business.

**What do you enjoy most about the business?**

I enjoy working with different people and getting to know other people. I like the unpredictability; I am unsure who I will meet in a day. I like to multi-task. Everyone has a different personality. I like to do many different aspects of things. I do not delegate, for the most part. I have a tech wiz and I am very hands-on.

## Basic Numbers

**How many transactions did you close in 2005? What was your total dollar volume in 2005?**

Last year was 53 transactions and volume was $89 million. I am #1 in the country for Weichert

**Based on that, about what is average price of a sale?**

Average price is about $1,600,000.

**Are you a Billion Dollar Agent or do you believe you will hit that level during your career? Are you over a billion for career sales or what do you estimate?**

I am probably right at $1 billion. The last decade I have done about $60-90 million and prior decade almost always above $30 million.

**What is your current staffing, including yourself, of listing agents, buyer agents, managers, and assistants?**

I have a full-time assistant to drop-off things and she does not handle the people. I have a full-time tech person that does all my brochures and mailings and that stuff, she does both computers and marketing.

I work 7 days a week. I work about 80 hours per week. I need to do that to service my client base. I eat sleep and breathe it. It is a ritual. I enjoy the people that I work with. I think people want me and I do not like to delegate for that reason.

## Goals

**Do you believe goals are important to your success? If yes, describe your approach to goal setting for your business and life?**

Yes, but in many ways I cannot anticipate what I am going to do. It is not something that is predictable. An estimation would be very imprecise. How can I anticipate that someone is going to get divorced?

### New Customer Marketing – Lead Generation – Prospecting

**What are your top 5 methods for new client lead generation and about what percent of new customers are generated from that approach?**

I don't really advertise myself with the homes I presently represent. I bought the inside cover of our magazine in town which comes out 7 times per year. In that it has advertisements for those homes. At the bottom there is a very small picture of my face which is a 10th of the size of the house picture.

I may have 4 pictures at a time, or 1 house for super duper listings.

It is a constant thing. We have a town newspaper. I take out a half-page color ad in 40 out of 50 weeks. The emphasis is not on me, it is on the house and on the bottom my picture is very small. It says #1 in town and #1 in Weichert company.

## Client Marketing – Repeats/Referrals

**Of those, about how many do you have in current database?**

We have hundreds of past clients.

**What percent of your business is referral?**

About 30% are client repeat/referral. This is not an investment community.

**What client marketing activities do you do with past clients?**

It is just the advertising I have in the newspaper. It is all very personal. When I get to know someone, I get to know them as a person. I keep up with their family.

As I think of them, I give them a call. I may call about 1/3 of past clients to touch base.

## Listings

**What percent of your transactions are listings? What would be ideal and why?**

It is pretty much 50/50 for sellers and buyers.

## Growth of Business

**What <u>single</u> quality has made you more successful than others?**

Maybe it is that I truly enjoy working with people. Sometimes I find it appalling the way other agents will describe their relationship with their clients. If I did not enjoy working with someone I would not do it. I have a lot of empathy and I am persistent.

**What does the average real estate agent fail to do which are among the reasons why they are average?**

I think they give up, and maybe they do not love what they are doing - if you really do not care, it shows. There are endless amounts of phone calls and tracking you need to do, and it is important to follow up. If you really do not enjoy it, it will show.

# PHYLLIS HARB

DICKSON PODLEY REALTORS

LA CANADA, CA

## Introduction

Phyllis has achieved *Platinum* Designation, the highest ranking RE/MAX offers its agents and reserves for a select group based on their closed sales.She is a Department of Real Estate Course Instructor. This means Phyllis is certified to teach mandatory continuing education courses to Real Estate professionals.

## Background

**For how many years have you been in the real estate business?**

I have been in the business since 1989; before that, I was in the mortgage-banking field.

**What is your personal background and how did you get into real estate?**

I was in mortgage banking for 10-15 years; and honestly, I just fell into that because I did not have good typing skills. I had the opportunity to assist the loan processor. In the late 1980's, the banks were being merged out of existence and jobs were disappearing. My mom was a Realtor and introduced me to the business. It seemed like a good fit and a way to use the skills I had learned while in mortgage banking.

**What lessons did you learn from your family, friends, previous jobs, and life experiences that helped you most to succeed in your career?**

The Golden Rule is very important in real estate... to both clients and other agents.

**What do you enjoy most about the business?**

I enjoy problem solving. You have a sense of accomplishment to solve a problem. It is great to see the look on a buyer's face when they find the perfect home and even better to be invited to their home year after year.

## Basic Numbers

**How many transactions did you close in 2005?**

I closed about 24 transactions in 2005.

**What was your total dollar volume in 2005?**

My total dollar volume was $18 million. Back in 1992-1998, I sold many foreclosures. I sold about 200 transactions per year with the average sales price of Freddie MAC loan limits being around $225k. We made about $40 million a year then.

**What is your current staffing, including yourself: listing agents, buyer agents, managers, and assistants?**

My assistant just got her real estate license. She will now be my Buyers' Agent and part-time assistant. If we need, we will get someone else full-time in the office.

## Goals

**Do you believe goals are important to your success?**

I do not set goals. I want to be successful, make enough money, enjoy my life, and career.

## Marketing

**What are your top five methods for new client lead generation and about what percentage of new customers are generated from that approach?**

I mail to my farm, advertise in Homes & Land, and in local papers. I also get business from the Internet. I pay someone to optimize our site for Internet search engines — so I rank high. Of the five listings I have right now, three are referrals, and two are past clients.

I have a farm that is my sphere of influence: past clients, and vintage/old homes. I prefer to sell older character homes. I scan properties for ones that were built before 1940 and are at least 2,000+ square feet. They need to be in neighboring communities where I like to do business and where I have a presence. There are 600 homes that fit that criteria. I prefer listings to buyers. My mailing effort is every 3-4 weeks. I have a year of mailings ready to go, so I am not worried about what to mail next. We try to make them up a year in advance. Turnover rate for owners is every 7-10 years. I started trying to list these 600 houses ten years ago and I got 1-2 listings a year. Having those 1-2 listings also exposed me to other sellers. I try to keep my mailing list to 1,000. When I have a new listing, I mail to everyone on that block. This strategy has been successful in the long-term.

**What marketing advice would you give to someone at $100,000 who wants to get to $200,000 and more?**

You need to spend money to make money. You need to have a presence.

It is probably a good idea to take a client out every two weeks for breakfast, lunch, or a happy hour to keep a personal relationship. Remind them at end of meeting that you love referrals.

I spend $3000-4000 on Internet marketing and $5000 on mailings. My print advertising is $8000 per year and is least effective.

## Client Marketing – Repeats/Referrals

### About how many past clients have you worked with?

Other than the foreclosures I have had about 300 past clients. One client has 17 condominiums and I sold five of them.

### What percentage of your business is referral?

I would have to say well over 50% - 80-85% is referral. However, it is constantly changing. Every now and then, I get an influx of sellers from my web site.

### What client marketing activities do you do with past clients?

I just started to take clients out for lunch or dinner. There is a cluster of clients that make up about 40% of my referral business. When someone sends us a referral, I send a thank you with a gift certificate (movies/Sees Candy) and thank you note. After closing, I follow up with a bottle of Dom Perignon.

### What advice do you have for new agents regarding their repeat or referral business?

When agents first start in the business, they do not think they have enough past clients to get repeats or referrals. So, they do not focus on them; this is a mistake. You need to focus on your past clients, no matter how few there are.

## Listings

### What percentage of your transactions are listings? What would be ideal and why?

About 90% of my transactions are listings. I only work with buyers who are referred to me. I have usually always done it that way.

### When your team makes a listing presentation to a prospective seller, about what percent of appointments convert to a closed listing?

I win about 75% of the deals.

## Growth of Business

### What single quality has made you more successful than others?

Hard work.

**What does the average real estate agent fail to do which are among the reasons why they are average?**

They fail to be there. If someone emails you, respond quickly. If someone asks a question and you do not know the answer, find the answer. It is important to wake up in the morning and go to work. Do not start your day at 10am or 11am. The most successful get to work early and start either planning or returning calls.

**What did you do correctly to begin your career and to speed the process of getting to your current level of business?**

I am glad that I owned my email address and it was not tied to a broker. I am glad I owned my own phonenumber. If I switch brokers, only my address changes. Clients call the same phone numbers, email to the same address.

## Building a Team

**How did you first start to delegate and outsource and build a team?**

When I first started marketing foreclosures, I hired another agent to assist with the marketing.When the foreclosures started coming in, I hired one assistant for accounting, another for BPOs and inspections, and another for escrow follow-up. Then I had five people working for me.When the REO business changed, I had two assistants left over that I kept.

## Learning

**What are best books you have read in the past 10 years that helped with your business and life?**

I like Mike Ferry's book. I was a part of some coaching program about four years ago.

**We find many Agents, who are right at the point of needing to delegate, outsource and hire their first part-time assistant but hesitant to do so.**

**How important, would you say it is to take this next step in order for them to take their business to the next level. How would they benefit?**

When you get an assistant it allows you to have a life and it allows you to be more productive with your time. There are a lot of tasks that are not so useful. Having someone to help you like an executive administrator is very useful.

# Phil Herman

## Introduction

A lifelong resident of the Miami Valley, Phil wouldn't dream of raising his family anywhere else. He believes there's a quality of life here that begins with the ideals of its great people. "Our values, dreams and aspirations just seem to be the same wholesome, true and solid goals that our parents and grandparents strived for," Phil explains.

For Miami Valley residents, one of the top goals seems to be the American Dream of home ownership. And that's an area where Phil has become quite an authority — his other passion is his career as a real estate professional. In fact, this very passion has driven him to the top of his field. His nationally renowned performance is the direct result of his extensive knowledge and expertise backed by an unwavering commitment to go the distance for each client.

The road to becoming Dayton's top home seller was not an easy one for Phil, either. From day one, Phil immersed himself, with his typical zeal, taking every real estate class he could find. He read every real estate book he could get his hands on, and spent hours studying with some of the top agents in the country. But true to form, Phil's hard work eventually paid off. He started doing innovative personal marketing and set up systems to ensure outstanding service. Soon Phil was breaking records with his phenomenal performance. Phil is flattered by the requests he receives from companies and agents to share some of the secrets to his success.

## Background

**For how many years have you been in the real estate business?**

I was licensed in 1977 and celebrating 30 years in business in 2007. After 30 years and nearly 6,000 transactions, I think I can really get good at this!

**What is your personal background and how did you get into real estate?**

At age 25, I was renting a house from a well-known builder and developer named Pat McAllister, who was a jack-of-all-trades in the real estate business. I looked up to him and saw him as being successful. Pat said he thought I'd be great at selling real estate. He suggested I give it a try. I valued his opinion and followed his advice.

**What lessons did you learn from your family, friends, previous jobs, and life experiences that helped you most to succeed in your career?**

I am from a family of six children. My father was a letter carrier, and it was challenging to raise a family on his salary. I learned a work ethic early on. Life experiences have taught me much about perseverance, always being a student of the game, being humble and always being open to change and improvement.

**What do you enjoy most about the business?**

The business is about making money and having fun! One without the other does not work. I notice when people are making money they have smiles on their faces! Any successful business is about balancing work and fun to create profit. In real estate, helping people achieve their American Dream of home ownership is still fun for me!

## Basic Numbers

**How many transactions did you close in 2005?**

We sold several hundred homes last year with the total dollar volume around $40-50 million. Our average sale price was about $170,000.

**Are you a Billion Dollar Agent or do you believe you will hit that level during your career?**

To the best of my knowledge, I am in the $500-700 million range.

**What is your current staffing including: yourself, listing agents, buyer agents, managers, and assistants?**

We have about ten of us on our team. We currently have about four buyer agents, a listing assistant, plus three other people who can list on the staff. We have a full-time telemarketer, courier, listing manager, contract manager, bookkeeper, general manager, and personal assistant. On the team, I see my role as the leader, visionary, and the "rainmaker". I spend about 25-50% of my time on listing work and the rest on management and leadership.

I have three coaches who coach me on a regular basis. One is a Ph.D./MBA psychologist; another is a Ph.D./MBA "business" coach. The first is more for my psychological health and well-being. His primary function is to help me grow as a human being and keep me in check. It is important to keep priorities straight. The second, my business coach, probably makes $15 million a year; he has been in multiple businesses and retired multiple times. He is the business genius. He coaches about 40 top coaches. The third person that coaches me is Coach Ken, who lives in Canada and has a coaching firm. With him I talk a lot about the nitty-gritty, day-to-day business issues.

## Goals

**Do you believe goals are important to your success? If yes, describe your approach to goal setting for your business and life?**

For me, it is as simple as this: you cannot hit a bulls-eye if you do not have a target to shoot at. It gives you a sense of purpose and focus. It ignites the passion and drive from within; it's the juice. I think top-level achievers are more goal-oriented. You figure out what you want and then put a plan to reach it so you have a sense of direction. When you have enough "whys" you figure out how. The more "whys" you have, the more motivated you are to find the "how to".

I grew up across the street from a park. In my day, there were hundreds of kids in the park. No, matter what season, the two best players among 50 kids would play pickup games and they would alternate picking players for their teams. You did not want to be number 50! I would always surround myself with people who were bigger, faster, and smarter than I. I wanted to meet with them and find out how they were "baking that cake". I remember meeting a guy named Darrell who hit the ball better than anyone, and I asked him to improve my hitting. This 18-year-old worked with me as a 13-year-old and told me, "Try to read what is on the ball as it is coming at you." That experience taught me to find the best of the best. I remember going to a 1988 Tony Robbins Seminar called "Date with Destiny" at his house. That seminar appealed to me and ignited and added fuel to the fire for me. Since then I have continued to seek out people at the top of their game so I could learn and be the best possible student, then put into action what I learn. The key to personal power is action!

## Marketing

### New Customer Marketing – Lead Generation – Prospecting

**What are your top five methods for new client lead generation and about what percentage of new customers are generated from that approach?**

The best marketing is to take a listing, price it right, sell it, and earn another listing because of the first.

I have branded my name. I had a long-term approach to my business. I reinvested all my business profits back into the business. It was branding me – Phil Herman – that has helped generate business.

I have done TV, direct mail, billboard, and newspaper advertising. I have about 140 listings in my current inventory. I spend 10-20% of my time on marketing. I really see myself as being in the marketing business and I happen to work in real estate.

**What do you do, if anything, that you feel is fairly unique and successful?**

I try to establish a position in the consumer's mind that I am the leader. No one else can post "Dayton's Top Real Estate Professional 22 Years Straight."

**What marketing advice would you give to someone at $100,000 who wants to get to $200,000 and more?**

They need to spend more of their money on marketing and they need to spend more time on prospecting. I personally call expired listings every day. I call buyers. I do personal prospecting which makes it powerful. One without the other is not powerful. You need to market and you also personally prospect. We have a telemarketer who makes 300 dials out of our office every day, calling new and old expired listings and FSBO's.

## Client Marketing – Repeats/Referrals

**About how many past clients have you worked with? Of those, about how many do you have in current database?**

There are a few thousand in our local database. We mail to them monthly and we call them periodically. We call them once a year. It would be better to call them even more often. We try to pick the top 100 of the past clients who refer us often, and really stroke them. If each one of those 100 clients referred us to one new client, we would have 100 deals. I just picked a number 100 to pursue. The top 100, our passionate group, we call and mail them more often and find value-added things for them. They help our business grow just by being our "fans". I have a jeweler who has referred a lot of business to me but has never done a transaction directly with us.

**What percentage of your business is referral?**

I would estimate about 20% of our business is repeat/referral.

## Listings

**What percentage of your transactions are listings? What would be ideal and why?**

I would estimate about 2/3 are list side and 1/3 are buyer side sales, typically.

## Growth of Business

**What single quality has made you more successful than others?**

A competitive spirit.

We have sent emails on a regular basis through our website; they go out

# Noah Herrera

Noah Herrera Team
RE/MAX Central
Las Vegas, NV

## Background

**For how many years have you been in the real estate business?**

I have been in the business about 19 years.

**What is your personal background and how did you get into real estate?**

I have been in real estate since I got out of high school when I was 18 years old. I always had a passion for real estate. I took courses when I was 13 and 14 years old. My parents owned a lot of property. They came here as immigrant workers and retired in the late '30s due to real estate.

**What lessons did you learn from your family, friends, previous jobs, and life experiences that helped you most to succeed in your career?**

I learned to work hard and put in a full days work. Be passionate about what you do, take pride in what you do. Be the best in what you do or don't do it.

**What do you enjoy most about the business?**

I enjoy being able to change someone's life. I enjoy the satisfaction in making a difference with one person. When I was a few years in the business, I wanted to build a team and a bedrock of the business. I enjoyed putting systems in place, hiring, having key people, all the aspects of a business. Now I have a business that pretty much runs itself.

## Basic Numbers

**What was your total dollar volume in 2005?**

I personally closed about $105 million based on 524 transactions. I have two people on my direct company who work with me. We have offices in four states, with agents and with sales teams. That happened about four years ago.

The market was starting to pickup across the country and I saw a need for more clients to purchase and invest in different states. So we went to the hottest real estate area and set up groups. The problem with referrals is they are a personal reflection of me. If the client is not taken care of that is an issue.

The total production of the three of us was $150 million in Las Vegas. Over the four states, it is probably over $200 million.

**Are you a Billion Dollar Agent or do you believe you will hit that level during your career? Are you over a billion for career sales or what do you estimate?**

Yes, we have sold more than $1 billion. I would estimate around 1.5 billion.

**What is your current staffing including: yourself, listing agents, buyer agents, managers, and assistants?**

We have myself, a partner, another agent and we have two assistants. It is good structure due to trust, focus, and training. Everyone who works for me is part of my unit. We work well as a team. We have one vision and one goal. Everyone is empowered. I ask people to — fail forward fast. People get caught up in mistakes and get worried. All my people are empowered to make decisions.

## Goals

**Do you believe goals are important to your success? If yes, describe your approach to goal setting for your business and life?**

We have weekly, monthly, quarterly and annual goals. The reason they are important is we have to quantify on a weekly basis. In this business, you either move forward or you move backwards. For us, there is no moving backwards. Many people do a little of this, and a little of that, and only track at end of year. They only analyze at the end of the year.

When I was 17, I read Think and Grow Rich, by Napoleon Hill. It says you are in charge of your own destiny. That was influential. Real estate is what I do to provide for my family. It also gives me a life so I can spend time with my family. I constantly read. I am a seminar junkie. I went to Stephen Covey classes. I am always trying to improve myself.

I think only 1% of agents are running a business. We have systems in place to get stuff done.

## Marketing

### New Customer Marketing – Lead Generation – Prospecting

**What are your top 5 methods for new client lead generation and about what percentage of new customers are generated from that approach?**

We run large ads in the paper. It is more effective to do seminars in front of 50 people, such as how to buy a home for first-time people. We do something with a housing authority.

People try to market one-on-one. If you associate with an organization or a charity, you can do a presentation for 50 people for the same effort as for two people.

We have our own magazine that we print and publish of 16 pages and that goes to 320 locations. They are in various supermarkets and other distribution sites. We contract with them to distribute our magazine. With Homes and Land, we lose control of placing and real numbers. They say they are printing 40,000 but how do we know that. We do about 50,000 quarterly. We do not own the magazine. It is with an office and we control about 15% of it. Marketing costs are 14.3%; that's just new leads, not client marketing.

**What marketing advice would you give to someone at $100,000 who wants to get to $200,000 and more?**

You have to determine if real estate, and sales, is what you want to be doing. By doing a few simple ads in magazines and direct mailings will take the business up 25%.

## Client Marketing – Repeats/Referrals

**About how many prior clients have you worked with?**

We have probably had 5,000 clients over the years.

**Of those, about how many do you have in current database?**

We have about 5,000 clients in our database. Most of our clients we have are ongoing clients.

**What percentage of your business is referral?**

About 70-80% was repeat/referral. About 350-400 deals per year, which is about 1 in 15 from our client database.

**What client marketing activities do you do with prior clients?**

We have several events that we do such as client appreciation days, parties and fundraisers for various charities. I sit on three different boards for nonprofit organizations. All my clients know that they can call me and I will pickup the phone.

We do mailers that we mail out, gifts at closings. We send clients a nice gift.

**How do you encourage referrals?**

When someone sends a referral, we send the person a thank you card.

**Do you have other significant referral sources other than prior clients?**

We work with many doctors and lawyers.

# Sales

**Do you track all incoming leads for buyers and sellers and about what percentage turn into a closed sale?**

Every call that comes in we probably have an ad on it. Every call that comes in I hear exactly what is said. I hear what the agent is saying. Out of the calls we get, the capture rate is 40%, the conversion rate is 65-70%. Capture rate is when I have them on the phone and I have them come in. Conversion is qualifying and getting a client.

We have very little or no Internet leads. We do not focus on that because so many agents are doing Internet for Las Vegas. I look at everything by how much it will make me per hour or minute.

# Listings

**What percentage of your transactions are listings? What would be ideal and why?**

Listings are only 10%. We use many Internet-based tools. The client says what they are looking for. We will take out 20 buyers at a time, in a bus. We have pre-negotiated deals with builders. New homes are about 40% of our business. The record is about 30 deals coming from one bus tour. I think we are successful because we give our clients something of value; everyone wants to feel special. Everyone wants to work with someone who can do something that no one else can do. Our bus tours are usually first-time buyers. They account for 37% of our business.

# Growth of Business

**What single quality has made you more successful than others?**

Being brutally honest.

**What does the average real estate agent fail to do which are among the reasons why they are average?**

They fail by not communicating with their clients and not being 100% truthful. The majority of the agents look at things with their eyes instead of how the client sees things. Most agents do not want to work.

**As you grew your business, what were your biggest challenges and what were the solutions that worked the best?**

I was not organized and I did not have systems in place. It is important to track transactions and keep clients informed.

There was a point where I had 250-300 calls per day and I started blundering and falling on my feet.

**If you could go back and do things differently,what would you have done at $100,000 that would have sped the growth of your business?**

I would have taken more calculated risks in advertising. I would have started to do more charitable events and sponsorship. I would have handed out more business cards (I made over $100,000 by passing out business cards over the years).

## Learning

**What are the best books you have read in past 10 years that helped with your business and life?**

I am a voracious reader. I read 5-6 books a month. Most agents think they know everything. They refuse to continue learning.

# PAT HIBAN

KELLER WILLIAMS REALTY
PAT HIBAN REAL ESTATE GROUP
ELLICOTT CITY, MD

## Introduction

Pat has been married for 14 years, has 2 children and a black Lab. In his spare time, he enjoys running, biking, weight lifting, Tae Kwon Do, and journaling.

## Background

**For how many years have you been in the real estate business?**

I have been in business for 19 years.

**What is your personal background and how did you get into real estate?**

I was in college and went straight to real estate. It was not a methodical decision. I got a degree in Sociology and my goal was to be a probation officer, but there was a year waiting list. I went to some sales interviews because I was hungry for money and nobody hired me. I heard you could sell new homes. Nobody hired me. I got a real estate license, and was a substitute teacher during the whole time. I sold real estate part-time and made $13,800 in first year. I think that crime intrigued me and helping people also intrigued me.

I went from Long & Foster to RE/MAX and then started my own firm and then became the regional director for Keller Williams. I am in charge of 17 offices and will open 38 more offices.

**What lessons did you learn from your family, friends, previous jobs, and life experiences that helped you most to succeed in your career?**

Most of what I have learned is self-taught. I read books. I am a Nightingale-Conant freak. I have a thirst for learning. Much of what I know and learn is from other people. These people were not mentors but authors, such as Tony Robbins.

My favorite book was As A Man Thinketh, by James Allen. I gave it out last month to a group of people at a leadership meeting. The other book I like is the 80/20 Principle.

My real estate mentor is Howard Brinton and my life mentor is Dr. Fred Grosse.

**What do you enjoy most about the business?**

My favorite part of the business is that everyday is a different day; and I am not doing the same things repeatedly.

## Basic Numbers

**How many transactions did you close in 2005?**

We closed $208 million and about 496 units; about 60% listings and 40% buyers. The average sale is about $400,000.

**Are you a Billion Dollar Agent? Are you over a billion for career sales?**

Yes, we are over $1 billion in career sales, probably about $1.2 billion.

**What is your current staffing including: yourself, listing agents, buyer agents, managers, and assistants?**

We have 52 people overall. I have four listing agents. Each of those listing agents have two client-care coordinators and one courier. That equals about 14 people for listings. We have ten Buyer' Agents and one client-care coordinator. We have two IT guys and four marketing people. The marketing people are split into groups by postcards, brochures, advertising, and department manager. I have eight part-time agents who are open house agents. They make $100 per open house from 1-3. The office gets the buyer leads. We have someone else setup and take down. I have a mortgage company with two people processors, and one mortgage officer, and a Title Company with two people. I have a full-time accountant and full-time office manager. I stopped going on listing appointments about four years ago. It was very hard to get to that point.

I am setup more like a GEICO insurance company. They took out the insurance agent, paid $10/hour for call center operation, took all the savings, and poured it all back into marketing.

Now, we have listing agents who are paid 12.5% of total commission. Our average listing agent did 100 houses each. Last year we had three agents doing 300 houses. Listing agents, made between 140-250k. I asked for advice from Rachel DeHanas and found out she was giving 25% to listing agents; it was too much.

For the buyer agents, they get 37.5% if we give them the lead and 50% if they have the lead.

## Goals

**Do you believe goals are important to your success? If yes, describe your approach to goal setting for your business and life?**

I have always had goals. I have set them since day one. I am an affirmation guy. I put on an affirmation CD and listen while going to work and going home. It is about five minutes long. I am all about goals. I have about 30-40 goals. I read the goals into a microphone; and burn them on a CD.

Think and Grow Rich influenced me for goals. When I first got into business I took Floyd Wickman's Sweathogs. He was very into goal-setting.

# Marketing

## New Customer Marketing – Lead Generation – Prospecting

**What are your top 5 methods for new client lead generation and about what percentage of new customers are generated from that approach?**

We spend about 20% on marketing.

We do a lot of television. We probably do 20 listings appointments per month from television. TV is about 20%. We have done TV for 5 years. We do some print ads. We send postcards.

Signs are about 21%. We get a lot of name recognition from signs.

Repeat and referral business is 43%.

**What marketing advice would you give to someone at $100,000 who wants to get to $200,000 and more?**

They are going to have to grow through others. They need to hire a team and focus on dollar productive activities.

## Client Marketing – Repeats/Referrals

**What client marketing activities do you do with past clients?**

We have a customer appreciation party. We have a big party for them with games for the kids and stuff. We send them cookies on their anniversary. We have a deal with a cookie company that makes a 17-inch cookie on the anniversary of the house purchase. We send past clients a calendar at end of the year.

## Growth of Business

**What single quality has made you more successful than others?**

I think a belief system that it will work. I think many people see things that other people do and for whatever reason thinks that it won't work for me. For me, I see things other people do and think it will be better for me. You do not need to be creative ... just do what other people are doing. Some of it is naiveté, I think. Because other people do not do what is so simple.

**What does the average real estate agent fail to do which are among the reasons why they are average?**

They fail to be dollar productive.

They fail to know what makes money.

They fail to get in their 20% of time to make 80% of their income.

They fail to focus on the 20% of their time. That should be prospecting, meeting with buyers and sellers, negotiating. It would not be driving documents and being a courier.

They work 12 hours a day and they did not do anything dollar productive.

They don't practice rapport-building skills. The bottom line is that people have to like you. If they do not like you, you are not going to get anywhere.

**Did you make any big mistakes that you want to warn others about?**

A big mistake people make is they hire people that they like. They hire people that are like them. We tend to like people who are similar to us. Just because you like someone does not mean they are good at a job. You should probably surround yourself with people who compensate for your weaknesses.

You need to interview yourself first and find out where you have weaknesses. Then hire someone who is strong to counter your weakness. Agents are social beings and they love to meet people. Every interview is a sales pitch. The agent likes the interviewee. They really need to hire people that they may not like. However, they make that mistake and then they have six of the same person.

**If you could go back and do things differently, what would you have done at $100,000 that would have sped the growth of your business?**

Start building your team now. You can't get anywhere by yourself. You are only going to reach some level by yourself — then you need to hire someone.

They should first hire a full-time staff person and then hire a courier to do outside the office stuff and then hire a buyer agent.

They should hand-off all non-dollar productive tasks to the assistant.

# MELISA AND DOUG JAMES

RE/MAX INFINITY
THE WISE LISTING TEAM
CENTENNIAL, CO

## Introduction

Now in their 28th year in real estate, together Melisa and Doug James have taken The Wise Listing Team to the top of Realtors nationwide. Today, their team helps Doug outsell the average agent in Colorado by more than 30 to 1. At the same time they are selling these homes for more than 2.4% MORE MONEY than "average" Realtors. And, 98.4% of their clients say they would enthusiastically do business with him again.

The James' attribute their winning success to Doug's father's legacy to Doug of a 'stick-to-it-tiveness' and 'get it done' attitude. The James' have a sincere desire to help their clients achieve their goals.

Doug is with RE/MAX Infinity in Centennial, Colorado and together with Melisa formed The Wise Listing Team. Doug also works directly with high-level real estate mastermind meetings, that he coaches and participates in, with some of the best Realtors across North America. By defying all normal, common, and ordinary practices, The Wise Listing Team started the highly successful 'Guaranteed Home Sale' revolution.

Doug's career took a turn in the right direction when he read about a successful real estate agent from Canada named Craig Proctor. Doug picked up the phone and called Craig. Today Doug says, "The rest is history."

## Background

**How many years have you been in the real estate business?**

We started our 28th year recently.

**What is your personal background and how did you get into real estate?**

Doug – After college I moved out to Colorado and I was searching for a lifelong profession. I was looking to get into insurance with Northwestern Mutual Life and maintained a strong interest in real estate. At the last minute I decided to sell something that was tangible; so I chose real estate.

Melisa – I have been in the business for ten years. Actually, I came from an administrative assistant type position background and ended up in real estate.

Because I was let go while we were on our honeymoon, I decided to help Doug. At that point he had a part-time person only. I did everything except cold call and sell.

**What lessons did you learn from your family, friends, previous jobs, and life experiences that helped you most to succeed in your career?**

Melisa – For me it was to be tenacious about what it is that you want to accomplish. Never let the word NO set you back; do it right the first time. The only person I could truly count on was myself.

Doug – The legacy my father left me were the words 'stick-to-it-tiveness.' My background was "get it done and get it done now; do not procrastinate". People are more apt to respond favorably and positively to you, as you show willingness to help make something happen rather than procrastinate. They'll see you are just like everyone else. Their biggest downfall is, that they do not do what they say they are going to do. Thus, they are branded by consumers as not delivering.

**What do you enjoy most about the business?**

Doug – I enjoy the challenge of helping someone accomplish their real estate goal they could not accomplish without my expertise and experience. Right now, on 40% of our business, we are the second or third agent to work with these people.

Melisa – What is most rewarding for me is to empower others to help them grow and achieve their goals. Then they realize they had it within them.

## Basic Numbers

### How many transactions did you close in 2005?

We closed about 100 transactions and about $29 million. The average is about $300,000.

### Are you a Billion Dollar Agent or do you believe you will hit that level during your career? Are you over a billion for career sales or what do you estimate?

In the last five years we have done $121 million and previous about $220 million, so about $350 million plus. My goal is to work 8-10 more years.

### What is your current staffing, including yourself, of listing agents, buyer agents, managers, and assistants?

Our staffing is two listing agents, Doug and another agent. That agent also works with buyers. We have another part-time buyer agent who is mainly inside sales position.

Doug only works with referrals if they are buying 600k and up or a direct referral. Because our market is in such bad shape, we slimmed down.

## Goals

**Do you believe goals are important to your success? If yes, describe your approach to goal setting for your business and life?**

Absolutely, we try to sit down once a year and write down things most important to us financially and personally and set numbers accordingly. We need to work on having a better focus.

Melisa uses goals every month to move the team forward. I set goals for various types of projects.

We went through Tony Robbins conferences and events and learned that goal-setting is personally very important. We did that two years ago and set some very large goals for ourselves.

We guess that only about 10% of Realtors have written goals.

## New Customer Marketing – Lead Generation – Prospecting

**What are your top five methods for new client lead generation and about what percentage of new customers are generated from that approach?**

Internet direct responses marketing – branded and unbranded. We use Google and Overture. We do both search optimization and pay-per-click. I do not work on that, I hire people who know what they are doing. We get about 300 per month. If I am looking at it from the unbranded site that brings in the majority of the leads, less than 10% are qualified leads ready to do something from now and next six months. Of those 10%, less than 4% of the 10% will do a transaction. We've have been told there have been different companies analyzing the entire market over the last two years. When they bring data in through unbranded only about 5% can afford to do something and they spoke to 17 agents. If 100 people call us, only 50% will do something in 12-14 month period. If we can get half of 5% and convert them — that is a lot of people. At least half to two-thirds of people have a credit issue. The branded leads are much more qualified. They do not have to be sold so much.

Direct mail – We send out about 1,300 over the net postcards per week, and over the net home evaluations, that drive traffic to website. That is to a different group each week, the fourth or fifth week of the month they would get the message again. We hit them once a month. Our target is about 5,000-6,000 homes.

That campaign only pulls about ½ percent. It is unbranded.

Television – It is since January of this year. One trainer had taught us that an unbranded lead was very powerful because we got so many. But we found that they were very hard to convert, having no idea who they reached, and they did not value us as professionals. With TV, it branded us and set us apart as more professional.

We were so tired of the convincing. We have not made our millions from it. But, it has increased our business. By May 1st I have listed more houses as a result of TV than all of last year. We already had 45 listings taken. It is hard to track cost per lead via television.

**What is the one most effective form of marketing that you have constantly done?**

The Internet has been the most effective form of marketing for us.

**What marketing advice would you give to someone at $100,000 who wants to get to $200,000 and more?**

I would tell them two things. Make sure you have a very strong Internet presence. Be sure that you absolutely have that name advertised on everything that goes out. It is not enough to have a website. It must be user-friendly, and marketed. Spend your money on branded marketing; pick great USPs, *Unique Selling Points*, to set you apart.

The direct response post card campaigns, if done to right neighborhood and branded, is good. Moving up the market income-wise is possible to do classified advertisements. Ads for hot new horse property use a sort of generic description. An ad to get more buyers of a certain type, use classified ads not on your own properties.

For farm sales, it needed to be a two-person household, both employed. They needed to have 75k combined income, and be at least 35 years old, and no older than 65. One more criteria is, they had to live in that house for three years. This was a move-up market. This is more fine-tuned farming. Another criteria we used was, to take first group of people and then ask the vendor, Melissa Data, to find out which real estate agents are doing what business in those streets. Did someone already own the brand on that street? Then, we took the map and drew in magic marker who owns a block. In my mind, if an agent had fewer than 50% we could still market to them. In Colorado, farm owners move every fourth year or so.

## Client Marketing – Repeats/Referrals

**How many clients do you have in current database?**

In our database, we have about 4,500 active people. These are not all previous clients.

**What percentage of your business is referral?**

About 40% is repeat or referral. It used to be higher than that; but, we are growing the new business.

**What client marketing activities do you do with past clients?**

Each quarter we send them a gift, a guilt gift. We send a small gift with a letter about being a loyal client and referring our name.

We have sent emails on a regular basis through our website; they go out once a month filled with helpful tips. We have done that for three quarters.

We sent out 1,300 to past clients and others in Colorado.

Twice a quarter we send a helpful letter about something they may find of interest.

We believe we are average. Jay Abraham has some great things that we can say to the client when they are in high states of emotion that help brand us and get us the confirmation that we did a fabulous job for them. For example, at closing we can present them with a request for referrals. We reinforce asking for referrals.

In the past we have done calling to touch base. But, this year the number of appointment calls has gone up so dramatically — that our inside sales person has been the primary person making calls. My calls are to follow-up on closings. We try to touch base with past clients twice a year with phone calls.

We hope satisfaction level is above 90%.

I want to do a better job having a conversation when the client is at a high-level state.

## Listings

**What percentage of your transactions are listings? What would be ideal and why?**

Our business was about 60% listings and 40% buyers.

## Growth of Business

**What single quality has made you more successful than others?**

Doug – to never give up and stick to it. I bought my first real estate car, a Cadillac Seville in 1979. I bought it from another broker who was in business 30 years. He said you are going to want to quit many times and you need to stick to it.

Melisa – I think what sets us apart is our desire to help the client achieve the goal. We will do anything to help them sell their house or buy a great house.

**As you grew your business, what were your biggest challenges and what were the solutions that worked the best?**

I think we realized we should have hired an assistant sooner than later. That was probably the biggest mistake. The other mistake was spending money before we had it in the bank. It took time to get things implemented and working and getting the money back in.

Picking team members that were the wrong person to put on the bus and wrong seat on the bus.

One of the most critical things is having a good business model and a budget that people can look at.

That plus associating with great Realtors. The best model is <u>Millionaire Real Estate</u>. They need to be pushing towards keeping 40% of what they make. In reality, with 100% company you are wearing more hats and if you do not know how to do them, you are drowning quicker.

There are only a few who are concerned about net profit. It is so easy when you have little direction and no coaching to overspend on things like lead generation.

**What would you have done differently if you could begin your career again to speed the process of getting to your current level of business?**

I would recommend to get connected to a great real estate coach. The biggest thing it did was allow us to rub shoulders and associate with the best of the best. That sort of interaction is essential. You can always get better if you associate with someone doing way more than you are. If not, you associate with mediocrity within your office and you stay there.

The mastermind groups around the cocktail tables at conventions were great. We always sought out the top agents. I had that desire from day one but we had people around us at 30-40 sales a year.

# JAY KINDER

COLDWELL BANKER CROSSROADS
LAWTON, OK

## Introduction

I was literally born into real estate. My father, John Kinder, started getting into real estate in 1977, the same year I was born. I have been surrounded by it and loving it every second since. I grew up in Lawton and quickly became passionate about helping the community develop and grow.

Real estate is what I do. I am hooked on constantly gaining more knowledge about the industry so that I can best help my clients. When I'm not coming up with new innovative ways to market our resources or training members of the Jay Kinder Home Selling Team, I am out and about across the country attending conferences and events to gain more information and contribute ideas on the business systems for real estate teams.

As for hobbies, I enjoy Harleys, football, fast boats and ATV's... when I have the time. I do devote every weekend available to my two great kids and family.

I love working with the Jay Kinder Home Selling Team because it is a great group of people. They are not afraid to think outside the box while still maintaining the enthusiasm and perseverance that is necessary in the real estate business.

## Background

**For how many years have you been in the real estate business?**

This is my ninth year.

**What is your personal background and how did you get into real estate?**

My Dad was in the business and I was mowing yards. Rather than my going to college, he sent me to places to go to learn real estate. My Dad supported me and threw me a few bones for business to keep me alive. After about two years in the business, I was on my own.

**What lessons did you learn from your family, friends, previous jobs, and life experiences that helped you most to succeed in your career?**

I had one job; I mowed lawns for four years. Early on, the harder you work the more money you make. My Dad was always working; he made it to baseball games but he was working.

**What do you enjoy most about the business?**

People. I love people. I love the people who work with me and people we help.

It is awesome to be around an energetic passionate group of people every day. It makes you look forward to coming to work.

## Basic Numbers

### How many transactions did you close in 2005?

Last year, we closed 431 transactions totalling about $42 million. So, it averaged out to be about $100,000 per house. My area consists of 100,000 people and about 266 agents; we have 15% market share. There were about 3,900 deals last year. Our business in 2006 is up 49%, whereas other offices are down 8%.

### Are you a Billion Dollar Agent or do you believe you will hit that level during your career?

My career total is about $200 million and I am 28 years old.

### What is your current staffing including: yourself, of listing agents, buyer agents, managers, and assistants?

We have ten administrative staff members. I have one marketing director, two closing coordinators, one office manager, one business manager, one inside sales for lead coordination, a courier, listing coordinator, receptionist, and a foreclosure specialist.

We have 12 agents, two do listings with me, and ten are buyer agents.

We are currently at about 20% profitability. My top three business goals are:

1. Creating additional revenue generators
2. Completing the systems by writing them down and making it replicable
3. Improving profit margin

Every person has something they are in charge of that brings in income to the company. Each team member is an investment. I expect a return on each investment, so I created a revenue stream that each person is to control.

## Goals

### Do you believe goals are important to your success? If yes, describe your approach to goal setting for your business and life?

Absolutely, every year I write down and plan my goals. My business was soft the one year I did not do it.

You should review goals at least monthly. We track our numbers at every meeting we have with the business manager and accountant.

Coldwell Banker had a goal planning worksheet. Every year, my Dad passed it out to us and it asked many thought-provoking questions like: where did my last ten deals come from? As I started to look at where my business was coming from, it showed a pattern.

## Marketing

### New Customer Marketing – Lead Generation – Prospecting

**What are your top five methods for new client lead generation and about what percentage of new customers are generated from that approach?**

TV, Radio, Print. We also have a good Internet marketing campaign and we spend $1,000 per month. We spend about 15% on marketing. We have lots of leads; but we need to improve our conversion rate. I want better quality leads. TV has given us the 'come list me' business that we were used to. They call and say please come list my home. It is hard in this business to find out where leads come from. We ask them what was the last thing they saw that led them to call us. We go "two deep" with questions, to find out from where the lead originated.

**What do you do, if anything, that you feel is fairly unique and successful?**

We wrapped a Hummer in advertising for our office. Radio advertising has helped me get from 100 to 300 transactions (where we negotiated a first rotation). With the morning show, we have a conversation interview every morning. That audience learned that I was part of the show: Time for the real estate update with Jay Kinder. We pre-recorded 10 or 15 shows at a time for the first rotation.

**What marketing advice would you give to someone at $100,000 who wants to get to $200,000 and more?**

Their focus needs to be on getting listings. Your time is best spent with sellers who want to sell. If they are turning a good profit they should go to relationship style radio because it is not that expensive.

## Client Marketing – Repeats/Referrals

**About how many past clients have you worked with?**

We have worked with about 1,500 clients.

**Of those, about how many do you have in current database?**

I would estimate we have about 700 in the database. I dropped the ball on past clients.

I think it is 25% for repeat/referral. Out of 400 deals, about 100 were repeat/referral, which is about one in seven of my client database.

**What client marketing activities do you do with past clients?**

We do nothing with past clients. We do not mail or call; I was embarrassed to say that until now. We are making a change. We are adding a full-blown system for generating referrals from our past clients. This is long overdue.

## Sales

**What are your top tips for turning qualified leads into closed sales? What do you do better than the average real estate agent?**

Lead conversion of Internet leads has a lot of potential. We are getting about 400-500 phone leads and 400 Internet leads. We have started to use a lead coordinator to handle incoming leads. We convert almost all seller leads from phone calls. I would estimate 70% of sellers convert to listings from listing presentation. Of the Internet leads, about 70% are buyer and 30% seller leads. We are converting about 10% of Internet leads. I am probably paying about $12 per lead.

# Wade Klick

RE/MAX Results
Plymouth, MN

## Background

### What is your background and how did you get into real estate?

My father was a carpenter and I grew up assisting him in building homes and remodeling. After college, I worked selling health club memberships. Then, I joined my Dad, built a few houses, and managed rental and foreclosure properties. Then I started to sell the foreclosure houses and represent new home builders. Now I am doing building and real estate.

### For how many years have you been in the business?

I have been in the business about 14 years.

### What about your background, lessons from your family, friends, and previous jobs helped you succeed in your career?

When I was in health club sales for Bally, I learned about prospecting. I used to put out boxes to sign up for a two-week free membership and convert them to a membership. Selling real estate is similar, how many people you get in contact with and what your conversion ratio is. That's what sales is all about. How many people are you in contact with? How many can you convert into an appointment? And, how many can you convert into a sale? Each one is a different skill set.

A new agent works about 60 hours a week and they need to make 100 contacts a day. Of the 100 dials, they need to get 50 contacts and turn one in 20 into an appointment. So, there are 2.5 people out of 50 coming in the door as an appointment. If one of the 2.5 show up, they will most likely convert 25% of appointments into a sale. Thus, four days equals one sale.

Another key is having good scripts so you know exactly if they are ready to buy a house. Ask key questions when speaking to a buyer. Do you currently rent or own the property you are living in? If renting, what is your lease situation (month to month or not)? Are you working with any other agent or have you signed an agreement?

I would spend about four hours per day on the phone making sales calls. When I was in growth spurts, I did Mon-Thu from 4pm-9pm and Friday 3-6pm, Saturday from 10am-1pm and Sunday from 4-9pm.

So you need to get people to call you. When I started, I was one of the first people to use the 1-800 system. It was very effective 10-12 years ago. I would receive 1,000 calls a month; now, maybe I only receive 20 calls through the system. I used to pursue the HUD market; now, I am working new construction.

**What do you enjoy most about the business?**

The most passionate thing that I have is projects. I am not emotional about it. I like finding market niches and creating systems to exploit them. I would find farms and sell it to a developer with a clause to give me the right to sell the lots to builders I represent, and receive a fee. I would then sell the builders' new home and lot to a consumer, again for a fee. The consumer would usually have a back up home that I would list. I try to make each transaction four or five deep.

## Basic Numbers

**How many transactions did you have in 2005?**

I had between 200 and 225 homes.

**What was your dollar volume for 2005?**

I would estimate it to be around $60-80 million.

**What is your net income?**

I would estimate it is around $2-3 million GCI. I went to a seminar in Vegas at RE/MAX and someone stood up whose real business is a coaching program. The biggest business is selling coaching for agents. Now I no longer show my gross as commission income; I developed a profit-sharing plan and trust. I was able to do transactions without taking the income. I bought and sold the land in a profit-sharing plan, tax deferred. Agents can choose to show a huge gross commission or do things differently. If I completely took all of my income from all entities, it may be $3.1 million and I netted perhaps $2 million. My expenses are only 1/3 of my gross.

**Currently, what is average house price?**

The average price is $275,000-$300,000.

**Are you over a billion for career sales, what do you estimate?**

The highest year was $85 million from 1999-2005 for a total of around $500 million. Now I am building a shopping mall worth $5 million.

**What is your current staffing: assistants, buyer agents, listing agents, other?**

I have two full-time agents who work with me. I have people who do open houses. I have two assistants who do administrative work. I am trying a virtual assistant.

## Goals

**Do you set written goals for your business and life?**

Yes, I have had written goals before I started in real estate.

I started in 1987 with my first plan. I read a book called, More Wealth Without Risk by Charles Given. Then I went into the goal setting and brainstorming section. I asked myself the question "If you could have anything, what would it be?"

I grew up in an environment that was dysfunctional. There were many arguments about money and I knew that was not going to be an issue with me. Now, money is important but it is not what drives me.

## Marketing

### New Customer Marketing – Lead Generation – Prospecting

**What are the top three to five methods you use for new client lead generation?**

My top method is creating a supply and demand chart for areas I want to target for listings. I go into MLS and look at a given area. My first column is the price ranges of the area, the second column is how many homes have sold in last 12 months. I will divide that by 12 and get average by month. I will look at how many houses were sold last month and how many are in the current, market inventory. I will divide and compute how many months worth of supply is there. Then, I will look for areas with three months or less of supply. If I find that, I will look at areas, to find the land, and find builders.

With existing home market, where homes are going to sell the quickest is where supply is the shortest. The people who go broke are the high-end agents in real estate market, when interest rates go up, they have more trouble.

To give advice to someone at $100,000 and wants to get to $200,000 and more, what do you think they should do more of and do less of for marketing?

Sit down and view a day from your business. Take every transaction and find out from where each originated. Did it come from past clients, expired listings, FSBO, new construction, etc? Figure out what percentage of income came from that particular group and look at it from a time aspect. How much of my time was spent on creating that income. Just focus on a few profitable areas. Focus on *one* thing only, *two* at most. What if 'they' were doing just expireds? But instead, they were doing eight things. Focusing and spending 100% of their time on expired listings until they do not have any anymore expireds. Then, what was second top generated activity?

If they run out of leads, go to 3rd and 4th. Another approach is to move outwards with one focus geographically.

## Client Marketing – Repeats/Referrals

**What do you do for client marketing to past clients?**

We send out a monthly letter. I used the Brian Buffini system for the past year. His stuff was more professionally packaged but I did not find an increase. Now I am going to try an e-mail drip marketing campaign using a virtual assistant. I am going to hire someone to do drip marketing and e-mail campaigns and analyze it to see if I have an increase or decrease. We do CMAs twice a year. For the best clients, I will go meet them and play golf and hang out together.

Of the people in the database, there are a maximum of 100 people who get the monthly mailing and some people who get quarterly mailing. Some people also get a phone call. Of the 1,000 people, I will call about 50-75 people.

Prior to six years ago, we were in a big buyers' market just like we are switching to now. I used to get many referrals. When I went into new construction, I was able to make big jumps in income. The referral or repeat business from new construction people dropped considerably. The builders and buyers were sort of opposing parties.

**About how many past clients do you have in your database?**

The highest year was 400 and now we are at 200-300. On average, over the last ten years, we have had between 200 and 2,000 total. I clean house quite often. The ones I do not remember anymore are removed. I may have 1,000 people now.

**What percentage of your business is referral?**

About 80% is referral because we deal with the same sellers, builders, and home investors. I generate the business that I create.

## Listings

**What is your ratio of listings versus buyers and how has that changed over the years?**

Ratio is about 75% listings.

## Growth of Business

**What single quality has made you more successful than others?**

I always did things differently than the majority of agents.

In my marketplace, the things I have done are good for 1-2 years and then someone copies the approach. The business is going to the Internet. If you control land, you are the King.

Having the listings is more valuable. I need to increase my Internet business. I have 50-100 listing inventory and many lots and land listings. How can I get that consumer before they get to another agent? What incentives can I put in place?

**As you grew your business, what were your biggest challenges and what were the solutions that worked the best?**

Adapting to market changes; I adapt to take advantage of changes.

# Brad Korb

## Introduction

Meet Brad Korb, an individual who knows the importance of maintaining *focus*. He believes that true success comes from making goals for what matters most in life. Whether he's with his family, interacting with his community or helping his real estate clients, Brad enjoys successful results because of his unique ability to visualize a goal and make a plan to accomplish it. This determined approach is what continues to take Brad's career as a real estate professional to new levels of success. For more than two decades, he's focused his attention on helping families reach their goals of buying or selling.

## Background

**For how many years have you been in the real estate business?**

I have been in the business for about 27 years since 1979.

**What is your personal background and how did you get into real estate?**

I was working in fast food and was going to open my own sandwich shop and I decided that was not what I wanted to do. My parent's friends suggested I go into real estate. I could be my own boss and work with the clientele I wanted.

**What lessons did you learn from your family, friends, previous jobs, and life experiences that helped you most to succeed in your career?**

I learned about hard work and perseverance. If there is a will there is a way. Back in the early 1990s, I felt like I was the undertaker. That was when the market was in the downturn. People had been saving all their lives for a down payment and they no longer could afford to keep their house going. I had to tell them that all their equity was lost or they had to bring money to the table. It was really hard to look people in the face and explain the reality of what the current situation was.

**What do you enjoy most about the business?**

It is really nice when people call and say thank you. "Thank you for the job you did, I feel that you and your team had compassion". They asked to talk to me at first and then would talk to my team.

## Basic Numbers

**How many transactions did you close in 2005?**

I closed 100 transactions for about $56 million.

**Are you a Billion Dollar Agent or do you believe you will hit that level during your career?**

I have been doing this for 27 years; I have closed approximately 700 million already.

**What is your current staffing including: yourself, listing agents, buyer agents, managers, and assistants?**

Right now it is myself and I have three active buyer partners. I will probably hire two or three more. I have challenges with people who like to work hard. I have one assistant and I have a runner/courier. I have my own escrow company. I am a satellite RE/MAX office that is just my team. The more I do not control, the more things can become messed up. The more I can control it, the more deals I close. I have a listing/marketing coordinator, sales manager and receptionist as well.

I have 36 buyers and about 64 listings. The commission split with buyer partners starts at 40% and if they sell my listings it would be 45% and then it goes up. We take 6% off the top for marketing. I am now going to a 50/50 split and 6% for marketing and a $595 for E/O and transaction fee. They ramp up, then kick back, and coast. Our average commission is about 2.75% which is about $7,000 a deal X 18 = $135,000.

## Goals

**Do you believe goals are important to your success? If yes, describe your approach to goal setting for your business and life?**

Goal setting is critical. I just got back from a four-day Focal Point with Brian Tracy. What they say is 97% of people with written goals achieve them. Only 3% of people without written goals achieve their goals. Write your major definite purpose in life every day and write 10 ways to get to it. I write my 10 goals on the treadmill. The Focal Point is a quarterly class in San Diego.

If you write it down and look at it daily it has an impact. You should have all kinds of goals. I have business goals, workout goals, spiritual time goals, family time goals, and financial goals. It is a pie; it is not all business. What are your goals with your wife? What are your goals with your business? I work on balance. In fact, Friday is a date night for my wife and I!

I wasn't happy with what I was doing and got into Brian Tracy about thirteen years ago. In addition to Brian, I also rely on my business coach Bob Corcoran of Corcoran Consulting & Coaching. He is there to hold me accountable to my goals, both business wise and in my personal life. Also, I read many positive motivational books and authors who have accomplished great things.

## Marketing

### New Customer Marketing – Lead Generation – Prospecting

**What are your top 5 methods for new client lead generation and about what percentage of new customers are generated from that approach?**

My newspaper, the Burbank Bulletin, is a great way to generate leads. I have been running it for 3.5 years. It has about a 30,000 person circulation and it is a community newspaper. If you own a piece of real estate in Burbank, or are a prior client, or member of Chamber of Commerce it will have a benefit to you. I use Custom House publishing. The cost is about $12,000-$15,000 for the year. I started to offer advertising to various vendors as well. I cover a little of the cost of the paper by allowing a lender, title, home protection and termite companies to advertise in it. Before this, I was doing a postcard to the town giving away pumpkins.

I use an IVR system heavily. First, I recommend a Flyer front and back: I made a colored flyer with my listing on the front and the rest of my listings on the back. We use the Xerox Tektronix with wax paper. I then use my 800 number through Proquest Technologies to track the calls. I also do a full-page ad in Homes and Land and a few other places. The highest calls are from flyer fronts and backs though.

We spend about $4,000 a month on print advertising. It is the worst for generating leads but it looks pretty in my listing package and helps to build my brand.

**What marketing advice would you give to someone at $100,000 who wants to get to $200,000 and more?**

First, they need to create a schedule that they follow weekly and that they have posted at their desk. For example, I get up and workout, I do my affirmations, then I go to the office and start prospecting. I do not even look at my e-mails anymore. I have someone pull them. They need to go to an office and prospect. Expireds are great. They already signed a contract and paid a commission. I start with Expireds and then do lead follow-up. What I have found talking to agents in other offices is that most people get up and they do not have a routine or schedule. Second, they should have a database, such as Agent Office or Top Producer and be using action plans for each listing and pending sales that they have.

I arrive at 9:30am and say hi to everyone. I come in and shut my door and prospect until 11am. I then go out and meet with my assistant. They pull my voice mails for me. I give out messages and review the pile of e-mails that they have pulled. I give out the work that others can do for me and figure out which callbacks needed. After lunch I am off to prospecting again until 3:45pm. Then I will review messages again.

I start with Expireds and then whatever is in my Agent 2000 tagged for that day. There are 13,000 other agents working on the expireds and you need to hit them first. Last year, out of 60 listings, I had perhaps 7-8 from calling Expireds. If I talk with them I then hand carry a package to them.

## Client Marketing – Repeats/Referrals

**About how many prior clients have you worked with?**

We have close to 3,000 prior clients.

**Of those, about how many do you have in your current database?**

All 3000 of course!

**What percentage of your business is referral?**

Year to date my referral business is about 47%.

**What client marketing activities do you do with prior clients?**

I send them my monthly newspaper. We do client parties and sometimes a movie. In addition, I call them about once a year.

## Growth of Business

**What single quality has made you more successful than others?**

Paying the price. What price are you going to pay to get the business? You need to stay and pay the price and do the business. You need a pure work ethic and a determination to succeed.

**Did you make any big mistakes that you want to warn others about?**

Bringing in an assistant sooner so you are not doing it all. Get that stuff off your plate and spend your time on high dollar productive activities. Going to someone to be a marketing makeover to appear as a brand is phenomenal. Branding yourself is important.

# Ashley Leigh

Ashley Leigh Team
Linton Hall, Realtors
Gainesville, VA

## Background

**Scope of Business:** The company provides residential real estate sales assistance to the general public. In addition, the company provides settlement services to its clients through its partnership with "Metropolitan L, Title & Escrow." Furthermore, the company assists its buyer clients with mortgage services through its "in-house" lending affiliate, GMAC Mortgage Company.

**History:** Linton Hall Realtors was founded by Ashley Leigh in August of 2003. Prior to starting his own brokerage firm, Ashley Leigh was the number two producing residential real estate agent in the state of Virginia within the Long and Foster, Realtors. Ashley was an independent licensed salesperson with Long and Foster for eight years.

**Office Locations:** Immediately after creating an independent company, Ashley opened an office located in the Braemar Shopping Center, Bristow, VA. This space is 2,000 square feet and is presently the smaller of the two office branches operated by the company.

Linton Hall Realtors' largest of their two offices is located in Gainesville, VA. This office is situated near the corner of John Marshall Highway and Lee Highway. This office is nearly 5,000 square feet. A small portion of this office is sub-leased to the company's "in-house" mortgage affiliate, GMAC Mortgage Company.

**For how many years have you been in the real estate business?**

I have been in business for ten years.

**What is your personal background and how did you get into real estate?**

I took a vocational course in real estate in high school in Fairfax County. It prepared me for the licensing exam. My mother was a Realtor and my father was a real estate attorney. I went to James Madison University and earned a degree in finance with a concentration in real estate finance. I went into the restaurant business with McDonalds and dreamed of owning a franchise. McDonalds deferred me and I abandoned my dream of owning my own McDonalds. While with McDonalds, I learned about systems, checklists, and training.

I came back home from Louisiana and decided to update my license and start in the business. I joined Long & Foster because the managing broker of the office lived across the street from me.

The first year I was connected with a team that produced $5 million. I signed a one-year contract and left the day after it expired. An agent who was doing $10 million picked me up. I stayed with him for five years. I learned salesmanship. Plus, I also learned what needed to be done to take a $10 million business to the next level. This included creating better systems and delegating through talented team players, coupled with the assistance of technology.

I was with Long & Foster for six years and left because of restrictions on my growth potential. I wanted to come to this area and open up a sales team office with Long & Foster but they declined.

So I decided to start my own brokerage and my firm is independent. The pluses and minuses are that I get to make all the decisions. You learn to juggle and balance. You have to be committed and willing to sacrifice personal time in order to make transitions and not to lose sight of your sales. There are no restrictions by being independent.

I would recommend any new agent to join a team.

**What lessons did you learn from your family, friends, previous jobs, and life experiences that helped you most to succeed in your career?**

I learned a good work ethic from my parents – work hard and good things will happen. From college and McDonalds I learned 'work smart.' Work hard does not yield maximum potential. I work about 30 hours per week. I peaked at 55 hours per week with no vacation and working while sick; I worked seven days a week. I cut my hours when I realized I could leverage my time through others.

**What do you enjoy most about the business?**

I like the payoff and freedom of where I am now. I like the tangible lifestyle that I have created. I like to follow a vision and see it come to life.

## Basic Numbers

### How many transactions did you close in 2005?

In 2005 it was 388 for $183 million and the year before was 401 for $167 million. The average price was about $475,000.

### What is your current staffing including: yourself, listing agents, buyer agents, managers, and assistants?

We have a case processor, a full-time point of sales/marketing coordinator (listing assistant), a marketing assistant who is also a part-time listing assistant, an accounting person, an accounting assistant part-time, a courier, and a receptionist. It is a total of 5-6 administrative staff. We have four listing specialists and five Buyers' Agents.

We have a total of ten licensed agents for an average of 40 transactions per agent.

One part of our model is getting new people trained so they get very productive. We increase their compensation to retain them. It works well for both parties.

## Goals

### Do you believe goals are important to your success?

I think vision is more important than goals. I have never been goal-oriented. The first vision was to be successful and net $1 million. The second vision was to create a lifestyle for myself. The third vision is to maximize what I have created and focus on where to take it from here. I need to figure out what that means. Does that include opening more offices or a brand new business venture?

## Marketing

### New Customer Marketing – Lead Generation – Prospecting

**What are your top five methods for new client lead generation and about what percent of new customers are generated from that approach?**

Our target market is about 35,000. That is the geographic farm around my office.

We advertise in local newspapers and we publish a customhouse newspaper. The custom newspaper costs $11,000 per month to 35,000 potential customers. The other local newspaper is $9,000 per month.

We also do mailings. In 2005, we mailed out 500,000 postcards. We are mailing a monthly postcard to all 35,000 in our farm. We touch our market three times a month – once with a postcard and once with a customhouse newspaper. We spend about $200,000 on postcards. We are sending success, just listed, just sold, and services. We mail 'neighborhood specific' in about 15 different postcards.

We have over 100 active listings and listings under contract. We have a toll-free hotline, 24 hour-recorded message, and virtual tour. We use AMS.

We are spending very little on Internet advertising.

We get about 350 leads per month. About one in ten turn into business.

**What marketing advice would you give to someone at $100,000 who wants to get to $200,000 and more?**

At some point you need to carefully hold your marketing accountable and continue to test and look at the returns. When something is working, it does not mean it is the best dollar spent.

There may be a better option for the dollar. It could be that there is a cheaper way to produce the same dollar of revenue. Or, perhaps you'd be better off not spending that dollar at all, and stick it into your personal account so that you have saved something over time.

## Client Marketing – Repeats/Referrals

**About how many past clients have you worked with?**

We have worked with several thousand.

**Of those, about how many do you have in current database?**

We have several thousand.

**What percentage of your business is referral?**

I would estimate about 20% to 25% of the business is past client referral. We do not track it currently.

**What client marketing activities do you do with past clients?**

If they stay within our marketing area, we do not really do anything. We used to have client parties but it got to be expensive and too big. It is probably more of a hassle than an expense. It was one more thing I did not like to do.

## Listingfs

**What percentage of your transactions are listings?**

In our business, about 60% are listings and 40% are buyers. Buyers are more profitable. The only way to get buyers is to have listings. The best marketing dollar spent is to create a listing to get a buyer. The new listing may create a new buyer and new seller.

## Growth of Business

**What single quality has made you more successful than others?**

Perseverance. It is a *no fail* mentality; work until you make it happen. You can't just take a breath when you are building it, you have to continue to go full-tilt until you realize your vision. Live and pursue your vision with constant and never ending passion.

**Did you make any big mistakes that you want to warn others about?**

Do not worry about what others are saying. The biggest mistake is that you cannot start leveraging yourself too soon. I was probably a year or two behind myself in bringing people aboard and giving up sales to work on more systems. Had I started the team concept earlier, I would have prevented myself from reaching near 'burn-out'.

**What would you have done differently if you could begin your career again to speed the process of getting to your current level of business?**

I would have started growing the team sooner and quicker both on the administrative side and on the agent side.

# Sɪᴅ Lᴇᴢᴀᴍɪᴢ

Lᴇᴢᴀᴍɪᴢ Rᴇᴀʟ Eꜱᴛᴀᴛᴇ Co.

Twɪɴ Fᴀʟʟꜱ, Iᴅ

## Introduction

Born and raised in the Magic Valley, Sid has invaluable knowledge of the local community. He has about 20% market share. Real estate tips – a wonderful checklist can be found on their extensive website.

## Background

**What is your background and how did you get into real estate?**

I was raised in a family of six children on a dairy farm ranch and always had an interest in investing in real estate. I took some night classes that had 30-40 of us in the class. I took a class for investing advice. People told me, 'you should do this, it is right up your alley'. I was involved in a family partnership and had an opportunity to leave the ranch. I moved to Twin Falls and started in real estate.

**For how many years have you been in business?**

I started in 1991 so I have been in real estate about 15 years.

**What about your background, lessons from your family, friends, and previous jobs helped you succeed in your career?**

My biggest mistake is that I did not start earlier. I was 30 years old when I started. I was working on a farm and worked seven days a week from 7am-10pm. When I got into real estate, it was tough because our market was slow. I call it 'going to the well.' No matter how bad it got, I had an inner strength that I could make it. I used to work about 85 hours a week. I left the ranch with no money. I had strong family values of working hard. There is always more than one solution to a problem. Problems came up; we had more payments than income. People say, 'gosh those are completely different life styles.' Real estate is really a business not just sales. Besides selling houses, we have 50 investment properties. The rental division is my retirement plan.

**What do you enjoy most about the business?**

I have three people in our office that I am mentoring and I take much pride in that. One person in operations became an agent. I had said, "you give me three years in escrow and I will get you into sales." I take a lot of pride in the rental department too. I have a husband and wife team that run that for maintenance.

I like to find out what their real goals are, such as financial independence. Our goal is to help them get financial independence.

I see Realtors in their 60s and 70s and they have no retirement program, etc.

## Basic Numbers

**How many transactions did you have in 2005?**
We had 300+ transactions. It was close to 50-50 buyers versus sellers (45% being listings and 55% buyers). I am happy with that split. I carried about 100-130 listings for myself. Now it is more in the 90s.

**What was your dollar volume for 2005?**
The total was between $33-35 million.

**What is average home price currently?**
The average is $110,000. This year our goal is over $40 million.

**Are you over a billion for career sales, what do you estimate?**
Our total transactions are around 2000. I have done 300 over the last 3-4 years.

**What does your current staff consist of including: yourself, assistants, buyer agents, listing agents, other?**
We have three buyer agents and two people listing. We have an escrow and client care person. We have a receptionist and do some mailings. We are also an independent company, a trust, and a bookkeeping firm.

## Goals

**Do you set written goals for your business and life?**
I have personal goals that I set for myself. The first of January I set them. At the office, we close down the office on December 30th and we plan everything for the coming year including the number of listings, sales, etc. We also look at how much money we spend on TV, radio, etc. We talk about what programs we going to put into place. I ask people about personal and professional goals, etc. Then we look at how our goals relate to the office numbers. I used to take it a step further and have a two-hour lunch brainstorming. It is amazing when you write down your goals and are conscious of them. The likelihood of you're being successful is so much higher. I guess under 3% of people write out goals. When working at the ranch, I always had goals in my mind. All year long I was thinking. When I started in real estate, I told my broker that I thought I would like to be a million dollar agent. I had to sell 25 properties between then and the end of year. I read once that it is worth taking 20 minutes a day and visualizing your goals and what you are trying to accomplish. What is the most productive thing I could do? We get all caught up in busyness. You should have things you want to accomplish each day.

I had written real estate goals. It has had a huge impact on my business.

## Growth of Business

**What would you have done differently if you could begin your career again? If you could go back and do things differently,what would you have done at $100,000 that would have sped the growth of your business?**

My biggest mistake - I wish I had an assistant the day I started. I was scared to death I would not be able to pay my rent or my staff. It took me 5-6 years before I finally said I think I can afford to pay someone but I was scared to death. When I hired my first assistant, it had been six years. Six months later, I added a second one. The secret to making money is LEVERAGE. That is the key. When I am investing, if I can buy two properties with 50k, it is better than one property. If I can get myself in front of ten people versus five people a day with appointments, I am going to make more money. I only have so many hours to work. Working smarter brings more success.

**In what order did you add your first part-time and full-time staff?**

1. Assistants – Marketing, Listing Management, Transaction Closing Coordination
2. Buyer Agent and then Listing Agent

## Management and Systems

**How do you organize and run your business? What do you use for client database?**

We use Agent 2000, which is an Online Agent. We have been using it for eight years. It is a good program but the training portion of it is weak. We are going to do some training systems. Most people do not know all the benefits of the program. We also use it for rentals.

**What are the top vendors you use for other items (marketing mailings, postcards, coaching, seminars, other)?**

We use Howard Brinton for Starpower. One of my biggest achievements was being selected for this training. Once you are selected, you get to train other people at conferences. By training others, I become a better mentor.

**What is the best new tool, idea or vendor you have used in past few years? How do you typically hear of new products and services?**

I found several companies through e-mail leads. We get hits on our website but tracking them is difficult.

We get about 50 leads a day. We need to manage the leads and funnel them into accounts.

## Accounting

**What accounting system do you use?**

We use Peachtree. We use it for rentals as well.

**Do you target an overall cost structure and profit margin?**

Once a month, I sit down with an accountant and have a spreadsheet of dollars that came in and dollars that went out.

## Numbers

**If you spend a dollar what do you get as a return? What percentage are you spending on marketing?**

Every ad we run is well targeted for the seller. If we find the seller who picks on image and buyer picks based on inventory then I find the inventory and win the buyer.

## Learning

**What are the best books you have read in the past ten years that helped you with your business and life?**

One book that has helped me a lot is Body for Life. Real Estate agents are thought of as not exercising enough, eating fast food too much and maintaining a stressful life. It makes you think about what you are doing. I workout every morning. I am not a health nut but I am aware of what I eat. I try not to eat after 6pm.

I also read many personal improvement books and listen to books on CD.

**What are the top three recommendations you would make for a skilled agent who has been in the business 3-5 years and is making $100,000 and wants to double to $200,000?**

Personal promotion. You have to work smarter, more efficiently and have systems for everything you do. Building a business is like building a house. You spend all this time getting all this business in and when it comes, you are unable to handle it.

You need to provide excellent customer service to generate great referral business.

Branding is very important. You need to have consistency in market advertising and branding and a slogan and jingle. You need to have continuity.

## Delegation and Leverage - Assistants

**We see a challenge of people right at the point of needing to delegate and outsource some work. Hiring their first part-time assistant would help leverage their time. What percent of agents do you think are in that zone and why do they fail to take the next step?**

I think fear as well as cost holds them back.

## Questions for other agents

**What questions would like to ask other billion dollar agents?**

How much are they saving? Where is their retirement? Do they have a plan for retirement and investing? If the real estate market stopped tomorrow, what is their plan? How are their investments allocated? Is there a goal they are pursuing? Are they diversified into multiple businesses?

# Patrick Lilly

Coldwell Banker Hunt Kennedy
New York, NY

## Introduction

Growing up in a small Maryland town, Patrick loved scouting out new homes with his father. He collected floor plans in three-ring binders for his imaginary real estate company "The Chesapeake & Patrick." Little did he know that a successful career in real estate was awaiting him in New York.

The owner of his own boutique agency in the Flatiron District of Manhattan for a decade, Patrick joined forces with Coldwell Banker Hunt Kennedy in 1996. One of Manhattan's top brokers with 22 years of experience, Patrick specializes in luxury apartments, lofts and townhouses. Patrick is a frequent speaker at real estate conferences and seminars, and he is both a business and life coach.

Providing superior service has always been Patrick's primary objective in his real estate career. To best serve his clients, The Patrick Lilly Group created a customized marketing plan for each seller and buyer they represent. Market knowledge, exceptional follow-through, and good old common sense, are the hallmarks of Patrick's continued success.

## Background

**For how many years have you been in the real estate business?**

I have been in real estate for 22 years.

**What is your personal background and how did you get into real estate?**

I was getting my MBA at NYU and did my internship in advertising. I had no idea how little advertising paid. Upon graduation in 1984, the highest job offer I received was $23,000. At the time, I was bartending making $75,000 cash. There was no way I was going to take that job. A few months later I had lunch with my friend Steve Straub who managed a real estate office in the city. He offered me a job, at which time I turned up my nose thinking, "I have an MBA, I am not going to sell apartments!" Steve then informed me he made $60,000 his first year in the business. My nose went back into place and I started working with Steve three days later.

**What lessons did you learn from your family, friends, previous jobs, and life experiences that helped you most to succeed in your career?**

Our family had a wide range of difficult people; complex individuals who also had some interesting challenges in their lives.

Learning to communicate with them and motivate them at a very early age helped me. One niche that I do well with is crazy women, who no one else can handle.

**What do you enjoy most about the business?**

I enjoy the money. It gives me the lifestyle that I want. I enjoy the freedom of not being 9am-5pm. I enjoy learning something new around every corner. There is nothing routine about this job. I can set my heights as high as I want. I can make my life what I want it to be.

## Basic Numbers

**How many transactions did you close in 2005?**

I completed about 35-40 transactions.

**What was your total dollar volume in 2005?**

Last year my total dollar volume was $30 million, which was not a great year. So far, 2006 is already on track to double 2005's output.

**Are you a Billion Dollar Agent or do you believe you will hit that level during your career?**

I am over $750 million so far.

**What is your current staffing including: yourself, listing agents, buyer agents, managers, and assistants?**

My staffing consists of two team members right now. One person does most of the showings and administrative work. Another person is primarily a Buyers' Agent who assists my listing agent when he is overworked.
I used to have a larger team. Managing a large team took my time away from what I do best. I am more productive with a smaller team referring out excess buyer leads.

## Goals

**Do you believe goals are important to your success? If yes, describe your approach to goal setting for your business and life?**

I believe goals are key to your success. I believe strongly that people who have a random pattern of business achieve random results. I was first exposed to goal setting about six years ago when I started studying with Dr. Fred Grosse, a life coach. He is based in Arizona and New Zealand. He opened my eyes for the need to set goals. It amazes me I did not think that way before meeting Fred.

I coach here in New York and I am teaching all of my clients about life and business goals.

I create written life and business goals each year. Business goals support my life goals.

# Marketing

## New Customer Marketing – Lead Generation – Prospecting

**What are your top five methods for new client lead generation and about what percentage of new customers are generated from that approach?**

Years ago, I used to spend a lot more money on marketing and advertising. The last five years I have been tracking results. I have now changed how I market.

My circle of influence is the best. I will do four touches a year with them, usually one by phone and three by mail. These leads cost the least.

Furthermore, a huge chunk of my leads are broker-to-broker referrals. Between 35-40% of my business is incoming broker referrals; possibly the highest rate in the country. I work this segment by going to every real estate convention that invites me, throwing parties, going to dinners; you know, schmoozing. If someone needs a New York connection I want them to think Patrick Lilly. I have thousands of brokers in my database. I do not consistently farm the same group. I do a mailing to one group and then another. I get about 30-50 leads per year incoming.

My largest farm is Manhattan Townhouses. Properties range from $2,000,000 to well, …very high. I own TheTownhouseSpecialist.com that I feed through monthly mailings to my database of 3,350 townhouse owners. I pay per click on Google and Yahoo. I spend about $500/month.

I have recently pursued relocation accounts, landing Macy's.

**What marketing advice would you give to someone at $100,000 who wants to get to $200,000 and more?**

It is important to understand what successful real estate brokers do and then mimic it in your own market to be successful. The way you get there is education/coaching.

Another secret is some sort of specialization, to be the expert, whether it is a farm or a specialty. Once you have a niche and are considered an expert in your field, then business will start coming to you.

## Client Marketing – Repeats/Referrals

**About how many past clients have you worked with?**

I am not sure.

**Of those, about how many do you have in current database?**

I have about 500 past clients. The first ten years I did not even know to put them in a database, it never occurred to me.

**What percentage of your business is referral?**

About 35% is broker to broker, 35% is repeat/referral clients and about 30% is new clients.

**What client marketing activities do you do with past clients?**

I do four touches per year. One is a phone call and three mailings. I hope the mailings have real value to them. One of the mailings is a state of market.

## Sales

**Do you track all incoming leads for buyers and sellers and about what percentage turn into a closed sale?**

About one out of five incoming leads will turn into a transaction. I am happy with that. From the Internet, I get about one townhouse lead a week for clients in the $3-5 million range. In all, we are averaging between ten and 15 leads each month.

## Listings

**What percentage of your transactions are listings? What would be ideal and why?**

I would estimate that 55% of my transactions are listings. I feel that listings are king and they bring you buyers.

**When your team makes a listing presentation to a prospective seller, about what percentage of appointments convert to a closed listing?**

We have an 85-90% success rate on listing presentations.

## Growth of Business

**What single quality has made you more successful than others?**

Coaching has been helpful.

**What does the average real estate agent fail to do which are among the reasons why they are average?**

They are not looking at what makes a successful broker. They are not comparing themselves to others and learning. They just go ahead and do what they know. They won't spend the money to learn. Successful teams, systems, and efficiency can be easily learned.

**What would you have done differently if you could begin your career again to speed the process of getting to your current level of business?**

Do not get down on yourself when you make a mistake, just tell yourself you will not make that mistake again.

For the first ten years of my career, I did not take my job seriously. I thought real estate was beneath me. When I realized it was my career, it sped up dramatically. I wish I were smarter in the early years. I wish I had a coach at the start.

## Building a Team

### How did you first start to delegate and outsource and build a team?

First, I mistakenly thought that if I let the universe know that I needed an assistant, the right person would come to me. Then, I would meet several individuals, hiring those that I personally liked. I ended up with very nice and fun assistants who were good to average, but never great. Now I have a good team, because I changed my ways. Now I call references. I give them the DISC profile test. I also let the rest of the team interview them. I trust their perceptions better than my own when it comes to hiring.

## Learning

### What are the best books you have read in past ten years that helped with your business and life?

I read voraciously and there is a shortage of real estate books. Gary Keller's Millionaire Real Estate Agent is very good.

## Questions

### What are questions you would like to ask of other billion dollar agents?

How happy are you? I think a lot of successful real estate agents are not happy because they do not have balance in their lives.

# KIM LUND

## Introduction

**Kim Lund** is the founding owner and Broker, of RE/MAX Cayman Islands.

During the last 20 years in Grand Cayman, he has specialized solely in property management and real estate sales. Due to his passion for real estate and investment, Kim's knowledge of the Cayman Islands real estate market and opportunities is unparalleled.

In more recent years, Kim has again taken the initiative by forming "The Lund Team" within RE/MAX Cayman Islands. This unique concept utilizes the experience of four dedicated and results-oriented RE/MAX team members, who combine their vast Cayman real estate knowledge and skill to ensure that clients get the very best results - whether buying or selling.

The Lund team affords a competitive edge that only a team of top producers can provide.

## Background

**For how many years have you been in the real estate business?**

I was in property management first from 1983 until 1990 and full time real estate brokerage up to now.

**What is your personal background and how did you get into real estate?**

I evolved into real estate in 1990. I graduated in Ontario, Canada and took a year off and traveled after high school. I went to college and graduated in 1980 with a degree in business. I worked in Florida for about two years and met my wife, whose father was from the Cayman Islands. We decided to move to Grand Cayman or Florida. I was in management consulting and investments previously. Being Canadian, I did not have to pay any taxes when living in the Cayman Islands. I got involved in property management right after we moved to Grand Cayman.

**What lessons did you learn from your family, friends, previous jobs, and life experiences that helped you most to succeed in your career?**

If you are going to do something, do it the best you possibly can and with the highest quality.

I had a brother who was three years older than me. I was always competing with him. We were extremely competitive. I had to work twice as hard to keep up with him and it motivated me to try my best at whatever I did.

That went a long ways toward being ambitious and competitive.

**What do you enjoy most about the business?**

I enjoy the diversity. You meet some phenomenally successful people and you can learn from their achievements. Every transaction is a different challenge. You have a chance to evolve, from what may be mundane boring properties, to something a lot more interesting - which are larger multi-million dollar deals with a lot more complexity.

## Basic Numbers

**How many transactions did you close in 2005?**

We were hit by a hurricane in September 2004, which wiped us out for 6 months. In 2006 I will have about 80 transactions for about $115-120 million. The average is about $1,500,000.

**Are you a Billion Dollar Agent or do you believe you will hit that level during your career? Are you over a billion for career sales or what do you estimate?**

I started in real estate in 1990. I have averaged over $100 million a year. Sometimes it was $200 million. I should be around $2 billion.

**What is your current staffing including: yourself, listing agents, buyer agents, managers, and assistants?**

Right now I have one assistant and three other agents that list and sell with me. Having said that, up until this year, it was myself, an assistant, and one other agent.

## Goals

**Do you believe goals are important to your success? If yes, describe your approach to goal setting for your business and life?**

I am probably one of the odd balls. For me personally goals are not important. I find myself driven anyway. I want to do as much as I can possibly do. I tried setting goals for a little while, but found I am driven to do better and more than the last success anyway.

## Marketing

### New Customer Marketing – Lead Generation – Prospecting

**What are your top five methods for new client lead generation and about what percent of new customers are generated from that approach?**

I saturate the market in Cayman with everything from flyers, to newspaper ads, to magazine ads, to TV commercials, to editorials, to property signs, etc. From the time someone gets on a flight to come to Cayman up until the time they leave, they see my marketing everywhere. I deal almost specifically with the overseas visitor and investment market and not the local resident market.

For new clients I need to be out there in every possible area where they will see me, from my referral network for condos, to advertising in every magazine and publication.

## Client Marketing – Repeats/Referrals

### What percent of your business is referral?

About 90% is repeat/referral. The only new business is from new developments that I am marketing.

### What client marketing activities do you do with past clients?

I have a newsletter that I have produced for about 15 years. That has been my most successful tool by far. It is a market overview that I send via e-mail and mail about 3 times a year. I get tremendous response. A lot of people are passionate about Cayman; but they are away from Cayman a lot of the time. By sending this newsletter, with all the information about the market, I get tremendous response to that.

## Growth of Business

### What single quality has made you more successful than others?

Drive, without question. Drive. There are two types of people in the world, ones with drive and ones without drive. If you have it, you won't give up. Persistence, if nothing else, will help you find a way to make something work. As long as you have strong drive, no one can stop you.

# RICHARD MACHADO

FIDELIS, THE BUYER'S AGENT
THE SMART HOME BUYING TEAM
NEW BEDFORD, MA

## Background

**For how many years have you been in the real estate business?**

I have been in the real estate business for nineteen years. I originally had started out as a commercial/ investment REALTOR® specialist. I started my career specializing in 1031 tax-free exchanges and large commercial/ investment properties. These properties were low volume and very high profit/commission sales, so it was more of a boutique style business. In 1999-2000, I bought a residential franchise called Fidelis and we became primarily a high volume residential business that focused on building systems. It was Fidelis that introduced me to Michael Gerber's book "The E-Myth" and the idea of building a business, and not owning a job. These systems did not solve the main problem with buyer agencies, indeed with traditional agencies as well, and that is marketing, lead generation, and conversion. For that solution, we owe a significant amount of credit to Craig Proctor and his direct response marketing systems. That has been one of the main keys to our success.

**What is your personal background and how did you get into real estate?**

My significant other back in 1985 was watching an advertisement for the Tommy Vu foreclosure program. I attended one of the seminars and became involved in the investment end of the business to start. Did a few foreclosure purchases, a couple of subdivision developments, and I acquired my real estate license as a result of this involvement. I was also a partner in a number of small business ventures. We had an accounting firm and a restaurant/night club, an import/export business, to name a few. I found that real estate had a lot in common with the day-to-day functions of owning a more traditional business. And it was especially similar to dealing with the hiring and firing of employees along with the importance of delivering a superior customer service experience.

**What lessons did you learn from your family, friends, previous jobs, and life experiences that helped you most to succeed in your career?**

My educational background focused on accounting and finance. My goal was always to own a business and this background helped me to be grounded in real estate, and to look at it quite differently than other REALTORS®.

I immediately approached the business as a business, and looked to delegate what I could, and hire the right people.

I also learned a lot about setting and achieving BHAG goals, as well as extreme dedication and persistence from my experience in competing as an elite Triathlete. I helped to put together a local team to race in triathlons every week during racing season, and usually did between 25-30 triathlons per year, mostly Olympic distance and longer, including 13 Ironmans.

This taught me the value of intense mental preparation, the importance of training, and incredible persistence, and working hard to obtain a goal. I averaged four hours of training per day, and raced at an elite level, becoming one of the top Triathletes in New England.

I developed an intense mental toughness and positive "can do" attitude that has allowed me to surmount most any challenge. The Ironman is a true BHAG, so it prepared me for just about anything.

I am a high "I" and a high "D" in the DISC test, fitting the "entrepreneur" profile precisely. I seem to be most comfortable on the creative and vision side of things, and tend to avoid the detail work.

**What do you enjoy most about the business?**

I like the idea of building a business using systems that run themselves, and I enjoy my leadership role in leading a team. Although I think we still are a long way from building a complete and effective business system, I'd like to be able to eventually hire people to replace me. I'd have those people and systems run the business without me being actively involved. This is my exit strategy for my business, rather than selling it.

I also really like helping people to reach their goals. Also, I'd like to focus on training my agents to succeed.

Having very little "S" or "C" means I tend to avoid much of the detail work, preferring to delegate that to others. I am more of a big picture kind of guy. I like setting challenging goals and motivating my team to achieve them.

## Basic Numbers

### How many transactions did you close in 2005?

Last year was one of transition, and we had some challenges and lost a couple of good agents, as I stepped out of the business and worked more on the business. We only closed 78 transactions totaling $22 million in 2005, down over 40% from the previous year. This year our target goal is 150 transactions, almost double the volume. Since we've been there before, I think that's easily achievable.

**Are you a Billion Dollar Agent or do you believe you will hit that level during your career? Are you over a billion for career sales or what do you estimate?**

In commercial real estate, I averaged between $15 to $27 million a year in sales. During my career, I have amassed $150 million in commercial and $70 million in residential sales.

This amounts to a career total of $220 million. My annual goal is an average 50% per year increase in volume and business over five years, no matter what the market condition. We are only just beginning to achieve our "quantum leap" in residential sales, so the upside is pretty audacious.

**What is your current staffing, including yourself, of listing agents, buyer agents, managers, and assistants?**

We have two assistants, three inside sales agents, and seven outside agents, including myself. We also have a credit repair specialist.

Our office policy is that we don't ever work with a buyer who has not signed an agreement and paid the retainer. We have three inside sales agents who we pay $100 per set appointment. We also collect a $595 up front retainer fee on every transaction.

We are also very good at converting the appointments to contracts, as our offer is very compelling. If we have a qualified appointment – that is someone who is ready, willing, and able to buy within the next 3-6 months, we'll convert every one to a client.

We have two numbers by which we scale the performance of our agents. There is a minimum number of 24 transactions per year for Buyer Agents. The optimum level is sixty per year, which is where we'd like to see everyone at. We encourage the use of assistants once they get to the 2-3 deal per month level, and that really spikes their performance. If Buyers' Agents perform five transactions in a month for three months, they receive a free laptop computer. My estimated personal volume for the year is 25 transactions, but I am scaling that down as I hire and train more buyer agents.

## Goals

**Do you believe goals are important to your success? If yes, describe your approach to goal setting for your business and life?**

Goals are extremely important. We go over and help our agents set their goals. We like to explain to them that there is a point at which they should plan to hire an assistant. We use an acronym called DIPA (direct-income-producing-activities).

That focuses agents on the important activities that will earn them the most return on time invested. Helping them to leverage themselves with people (assistants) and technology can really increase their profit potential.

We do an exercise with them called "the time of your life" that we were taught by Craig Proctor. In it, we strap a watch timer on their wrists that goes off every 15 minutes. They wear it for three days, and will write down on a provided sheet EXACTLY what they are doing at each 15 minute interval. When they are done, we attach a dollar value to each activity, and create job descriptions for an admin position for them. This is very effective in demonstrating to them that most of the work they do can be delegated to a $10/hour assistant.

We have set goals for income that we would like to make and what we'd like to accomplish. I put together the list with my wife Kimberlee and we have many goals. She is much better at getting them into writing and keeping us on track than I am. This is probably one of my weak points – and the devil really is in the details. I acknowledge the importance of setting and achieving goals, but she is much better at keeping us on track.

I usually get off track by doing, doing, doing it. I'd like to implement a lot more planning and systemizing for my business, and that's part of our ongoing process.

## Marketing

### New Customer Marketing – Lead Generation – Prospecting

**What are your top five methods for new client lead generation and about what percentage of new customers are generated from that approach?**

The Internet has made a huge difference in our business. I am what you'd call an early adaptor, or a geek, so I'm good with and understand technology. We are using this important resource to do many innovative things to attract business. We have live video and audio on the net. We include a lot of client testimonials. We learned much from Craig and Dan Kennedy – we are members of his Gold plus inner circle - in terms of the things we should be doing and the associated benefits. We list an amazing number of benefits that other agents in our area can't possibly compete with. We have 85 to 95 URLs/domains and each one showcases fairly similar offers for buyers. A majority of the landing pages are similar, as we make the same offer in slightly different ways to buyers. We have different domains for tracking different campaigns. We have nine different visual domains. We are constantly testing different looks and offers. We generate anywhere from 250 to 600 leads per month.

Our inside sales agent is required to get to a new lead, whether Internet or otherwise, within fifteen minutes of their leaving their contact information. We have technology that immediately notifies an agent via computer screen when a lead comes in.

We've found that if someone is on a website and they do not find what they need, they will go to another website within that 15 minutes. They just continue surfing until they find what they want. You need toinitiate contact within that fifteen minute period. When we respond via e-mail or phone, within that time period, they are AMAZED at the response. Most of our competition takes a week to respond to Internet leads or email. When potential clients get a phone call right away, they are quite impressed.

The ISA's number one goal is to get a buyer listing appointment or consultation scheduled. They also need to make sure these prospects are well qualified.

Qualifying questions include:

• Are you looking to buy in the next 3-6 months?

• Do you have a written pre-approval (not pre-qualification)?

• Do you have an agent to help you with that move when the time comes?

• Are all decision makers going to be present at our meeting?

We require that they be pre-approved from one of our lenders. If not pre-approved, we give them incentive to talk to our lender in return for $5,000 cash back at closing. If they are serious about buying, then they usually respond to one of these offers. It only takes ten to fifteen minutes on the phone to pull their credit and obtain the pre-approval.

The pre-approval is faxed to our office, not to the buyer. This way they must come to our office to get their pre-approval. Otherwise, once pre-approved, you'll find that many go out and buy a home before they get into the office, so you want to make sure you get in front of them first.

One of the important things in obtaining good quality leads is giving them a reason to leave their correct contact info. On the landing page, we give them many reasons to do so.

One of the most important things we learned in our coaching with Craig Proctor, and our Grad coach, Brian Moses, is that without value, price is always an issue. In this case the "price" is valid contact info, so we need to establish a high threshold of value for them to pay that price.

It usually takes more than one call to gain a lead. Thirty to forty percent will book appointments on the first call and the remainder will usually schedule after e-mail and direct mail.

Only one-third of all prospects are qualified to buy, due to our sorting and sifting out many "zero down" and "distress sale" prospects. The Internet leads tend to be a lot more qualified. The 800 leads are usually less qualified, and only one or two out of ten may be qualified to get a mortgage.

We have a credit repair specialist on the team to assist in these situations, and offer a free credit repair program.

Out of 100 leads, we'll eventually convert about 20% when we do finally reach them. Unfortunately, we only reach about 10% of these prospects, and need to continually market to them in order to get them into the office. The biggest problem is reaching the prospects, so it can take quite some time to do that. Our branded Internet landing pages have a three to four percent conversion rate. With a qualified appointment, we'll close nineteen out of twenty set appointments. That is an exceptional closure rate! A "qualified" appointment is one where the buyer is ready, willing, and able to buy within the next 3-6 months, has been pre-approved by one of our lenders, and arrives with all decision makers present (i.e. no "one-leggers").

With an experienced agent, about 85-90% of these buyers will eventually complete a transaction. The newer agents have a lower closure rate until they get up to speed on their skill sets.

We also hold home buyer seminars that typically attract anywhere from 25 to 80 people. We've built quite an effective marketing system to draw this kind of attendance. The seminars are about two hours long and we teach them how to avoid the most costly mistakes, and give them an excellent overview of the entire home buying process.

We also do 800 number classified ads for distressed sales and classifieds that are driven to our unbranded websites and unbranded 800 lines. These unbranded classified ads seem to be very effective at generatingleads.

We also have an open house program. The average Open House draws very few people. But, ours generate anywhere between ten and 50 buyers, which can provide a lot of buyer leads. We picked up this program from Brent Gove and post a lot of signs for each event. We typically use eighteen to twenty five signs per open house. Since we don't take listings, we do these open houses for other listing agents and for sale by owner properties. Our focus is on buyers, so these opportunities are fantastic for us. We pinpoint good high-traffic locations and make sure signage is in these high traffic locales. The key to the program is blatantly obvious signage, with reminders a quarter mile before each intersection. Usually when people put up signs, by the time you see the sign, you have driven past it. You need to over-sign in order to make it really obvious and draw prospects to an open house. All of these open houses are usually vacant, which makes it easy to control security.

We focus on looking for motivated sellers. Vacant properties owners are usually quite motivated, and we can help move the property for them. We are also helping the buyers to locate motivated sellers who are doing price-reductions. The open houses can usually convert to a few buyer consult appointments almost immediately.

We just started this effort. We are learning the program and got 41 people at our first open house, and five consult appointments. We have buyer agents, a mortgage person and an inside sales person in attendance.

The bank sponsors these events.

The "For Sale by Owner" (FSBO) program generates three income streams. One is the free referral program to get the top agent in the area. The number one mistake that sellers make is picking the wrong agent by using a friend, relative or someone they know. We help them to avoid that mistake, by referring the best agent in their market.

We explain that they should choose an agent based on objective performance criteria, as that's the best way to get a top agent.

We offer to do the research and refer an agent based on these criteria, and research the local agents performance criteria for them, including number of days on market, average list price to sales price ratio, and total number of transactions. In this way, we have the ability to find the top performers in their market by researching the MLS.

We usually get a 25% to 35% referral fee from the listing agent. We explain to the seller how it would be best to get a top professional's pricing for their home, and explain that in return all that agent will want is a shot at their business when they do decide to list their home. They get a free CMA/estimate and usually list with that agent when the time comes, because it usually is one of the top agents in their area. We call it our free "Smart Home Seller" referral system, and it's a real benefit for the sellers, as they end up with the best possible agent, picked by an expert who knows agents. This helps them avoid the usual pitfalls of choosing a friend or relative, or some other part time agent who is going to use them to practice on.

Our second income stream in this lead generation model is property previews by our buyer agents that can turn into a full commission if we have a buyer that fits that property. We help our buyers buy a lot of FSBO properties.

We've found in our experience that most FSBOs are overpriced, and we'll usually discover this during the preview. We tell the seller that the house is significantly overpriced, but if and when they do decide to sell at market, we have 137 buyers under contract that we'd love to show their home to. Unfortunately, as we do represent the buyers' best interest, we can't recommend an overpriced home for their consideration.

The third income stream from FSBOs is "yard signs" and the resulting buyer leads on the sign calls. FSBO signs usually outperform regular listing agents' for sale signs by a margin of three to one for generating buyer lead calls. This is because buyers perceive FSBOs as a bargain.

We use our 800 number property tree and sell that as a benefit to the sellers. Well have a complete and detailed description of their property, helping to rule out buyers who are not qualified.

We have it professionally recorded and also eliminate all those pesky

REALTOR® calls from other Realtors who are pestering them in order to get the listing.

Since our goal is to talk to the buyers, we end up with all the buyers who aren't interested in that particular property. Since most buyers end up ruling out the home they call on, this works great for us and for the buyers. The sign is a generic FSBO sign with an 800 number and extension. There is no email address. We use AMS for the 800 service. The buyers can also punch one and talk to the seller directly. Either we can show the property or they can show it themselves. A lot of sellers opt not to talk to the buyers. I'm in the process of hiring someone to run the FSBO program. If I could get someone good to run the FSBO program, it would be a significant profit center for us.

I think that the magic formula for us was marrying an exclusive buyer agency business model to Craig Proctor's direct response marketing program. If you can solve marketing problems and generate tons of leads, it becomes so much easier. Since Proctor's program is designed primarily for traditional agents, we've had to reverse engineer the systems to fit our EBA business model. But the changes have been dramatic to our bottom line.

We are sending out seven to ten outgoing referrals per month on average. We collect a 25% to 35% referral fee from the listing brokerage. On a typical referral in our market, we average about $2,000 per referral. We can get anywhere from $1,000-$4,500 per referral, based on the list price. Our company net profit margin is between 30 and 37%. About five to seven percent of net profit is listing referrals.

Lastly is our back end sponsor program. Since we are so good at marketing and lead generation, we can provide a significant benefit to vendors who are trying to reach homebuyers. I think this area has huge growth potential. We offer four different sponsor levels. Basic, Silver, Gold, and Platinum, modeled after Dan Kennedy's programs. Different levels offer different packages of benefits, including the ability to market to our buyer prospect/past client database.

These levels currently are $250/$500/$1,000/$2,000, and offer different benefit packages to appeal to different types of businesses.

We are reaching on average from between 250 to 600 buyers per month. The sponsors can access these buyers who have already raised their hands and said they want to buy a home. This is of tremendous value to sponsors, as they can now market to a super qualified target audience.

We approach these businesses who are trying to reach new home owners. Some examples include large appliance sellers, antiques dealers, landscapers, home inspectors, handy men, contractors, banks/mortgage companies, attorneys, basement waterproofing, furniture dealers, etc.

The list is almost limitless.

Since we control the buyer side, we can control the money. If we recommend a sponsor, they are likely to use that sponsor, so there are significant benefits to our sponsor partners.

The sponsor level would be appropriate for the business potential, each of these sponsors sees, in being able to market to our prospects. So mortgage companies, who make anywhere from 50 to 100 basis points per transaction ($1,500 - $3,000), are likely to be Platinum Sponsors. While home inspectors, with lower margins, are more likely to fit into the basic category. We are currently generating $9,000 monthly with our Sponsor program. I think if I can hire the right person to manage this program, we could easily be doing well over $30,000 monthly just on our back end sponsors.

# JERRY MAHAN

JOHN L. SCOTT REAL ESTATE
THE JERRY MAHAN COMMUNITIES
PUYALLUP, WA

## Introduction

Jerry Mahan has been in the real estate business for over 28 years. For the past fourteen years he has been affiliated with the John L. Scott office in Puyallup, Washington. In 2003, Mahan closed over 500 transactions with over $200 million in sales. He was deemed the 12th most successful real estate salesperson by REALTOR magazine.

Mahan specializes in new construction, land and residential real estate, and credits much of his success to his team. "I believe, after 25 years, that I am more of a coach of agents. I've assembled a team that tries to create the Nordstrom effect of performance, by offering outstanding service to our clients while saving them money."

## Background:

**For how many years have you been in the real estate business?**

I have been in the business since 1978, for 28 years.

**What is your personal background and how did you first get into real estate?**

I attended Central Washington University and graduated in 1977 with a degree in business administration. After graduation, I taught tennis and ran several tennis tournaments in the south Seattle area. I had always been interested in real estate and decided to give it a try. At that time, there weren't a high percentage of young adults involved in real estate. I was only 24 at the time I started.

**What lessons did you learn from your family, friends, previous jobs, and life experiences that helped you most to succeed in your career?**

My successful work ethic stems from my mother and my past jobs. I worked long hours, sometimes 16-17 hours a day, 7 days a week. Fax machines weren't handy so all offers were presented in person, taking more time, effort and motivation. As the years went on, I set more and more goals.

**What do you enjoy most about the business?**

The thing I enjoy most, about this business, is there are no limits to what you can do. Early on in my career, I helped people find homes and enjoyed being a part of their lives and helping them accomplish their goals. Today,

I build houses and develop property.

I still enjoy helping and connecting with people; and, I pass my excitement onto my sales staff.

## Basic Numbers

**How many transactions did you close in 2005? What was your total dollar volume in 2005? Based on that, about what is the average price of a sale?**

In 2005, we closed 550-600 homes for approximately $200 million. We average about $400,000 per transaction.

**Are you a Billion Dollar Agent or do you believe you will hit that level during your career? Are you over a billion for career sales or what do you estimate?**

About 8 years ago, I advertised over $1 billion in sales. We had many years over $100 million. I have been the number one agent for John L. Scott for 12-15 years.

**What is your current staffing, including yourself, of listing agents, buyer's agents, managers and assistants?**

My staff consists of 4 assistants and a sales manager; we also have many outside vendors that create different services for our company website and other things. I have an office manager who coordinates and directs my sales and operations within the company, two transaction coordinators and a graphic designer. I also have a team of 20 agents who sit at my new construction communities.

We typically carry 15-25 communities at any given time.

## Goals

**Do you believe goals are important to your success? If yes, describe your approach to goal setting for your business and life?**

Definitely. No question about it. Every year we sit down and set goals for the company and try to structure what we plan to sell each year and the number of homes we have. I'm involved in 3,000 properties currently. For builders to be successful they have to have the raw materials, which is land and ultimately lots.

One of the biggest things for me was to learn how to delegate. Let people take the load off your shoulders. Oftentimes, they get better at it than you are. I take 2-3 months off a year because I have confidence and feel my employees are well trained.

## New Customer Marketing-Lead Generation-Prospecting

**What are your top five methods for new client lead generation and about what percentage of new customers are generated from that approach?**

We are looking at starting up and opening a resale division to appeal to the general public. We feel the agent of the future will offer even more services than today's agent. To be at the forefront of the competition, you have to think ahead to the future.

We promote our company and services on billboards, off-site signage, and ads in real estate magazines. However, we are looking at using the Internet more and more in the future. We have found that over 65% of today's home buyers are turning to the Internet to search for homes.

**What do you do, if anything, that you feel is fairly unique and successful?**

We were the first to use billboards, hold broker open lunches and offer a buyer bonus. Soon after, we found that the buyer bonuses helped builders sell homes. People needed money to buy houses, even in the higher price ranges.

We were also one of the first companies to promote on the Internet. A typical agent puts up one sign in a community, but we offer people more signage to gain more buyers to that house. We also use some of the new construction techniques for resale signage. We have found that prospective buyers look in a 5-10 mile radius, thus signage is very important.

## Client Marketing-Repeat/Referrals

**What percentage of your business is referral?**

Referrals are not a large part of our business, but always welcome. Our clients are our builder's and through them we receive our repeat buyers and agents.

## Growth of Business

**What single quality has made you more successful than others?**

I believe we're more successful than others because we're persistent and always on the edge of change. We try to be ahead of the industry and always pay attention to our competitors.

We focus on relationships and provide a range of services for each community and client. For example, we would provide a concierge group of services to care for the client, such as electricians, plumbers, restaurants, etc. We create a website for each community as well.

The agent of the future should manage communities with all of that information and become the only person someone needs to call for anything.

There is normally a 10% turnover per year in houses. If you go to 500 homes, that is 50 deals per year in that neighborhood. I was getting 80-90% of market share in my community. As much as you can, try to control that market. You should at least hit 50%. Most agents work for a while and then switch; the longer you stay in a community, the more business you should get.

**What does the average real estate agent fail to do which are among the reasons why they are average?**

They fail to come up with a plan and stick to it.

They fail to come up with new ideas.

They fail to implement new ideas.

They get stagnant.

They don't run it like a business.

They fail to devote the necessary time to a new business. Nearly 80% of all new businesses fail and the same goes for new agents.

On the flip side, the best agents have the following traits:

1. Honesty.
2. Integrity.
3. Puts client interests before their own.
4. Persistence.
5. Going the extra mile and going beyond what's expected.

**Did you make any big mistakes that you want to warn others about?**

The biggest challenge was credibility when I was young. When I first started, they would not hire me because I was too young. The job paid zero; but I had trouble getting hired. At that time, real estate was not a reasonable profession. Another error I made starting out was not following up as much with clients once their transaction was closed.

Growing the business was hard. I did all the FSBO's and cold calling. I built my business through referrals, which soon led to builder business. I probably sold 50-60 homes myself and listed homes.

**What would you have done differently if you could begin your career again to speed the process of getting to your current level of business?**

I would pinpoint markets that I wanted to go after. I would also want to take ownership of those market shares. In the beginning, it was like throwing darts all over the board. I would start with areas or communities that I would want to dominate. In our company in 1980, I was the first one to hire an assistant.

I would use those assistants to get my name out and offer better service to those communities. The only way to be superior is to offer more professional services. You should be able to take over certain market areas.

## Delegation and Leverage-Assistants

**We see a challenge of people right at the point of needing to delegate and out source and hire their first part-time assistant to leverage their time. What percentage of agents do you think are in that zone and why do they fail to take the next step? What would be beneficial for them to take that step?**

I think someone should get an assistant at about 25 homes. At this point, they're so busy doing their job that they do not have time to market themselves. We get so caught up in new customers that we forget to service people who bought homes from us. Look at the dollars you are bringing in for 25 homes. This could be $150,000 a year. Take $25,000 of that and invest in an assistant that can do all your paperwork and marketing. Your time is worth $XX per hour. If you had someone else doing those appointments for you, what is it worth to you? I was paid when I went out and took people in cars or had listing appointments. I did not get paid sending information to people. My job was to help them locate a home or sell a home.

# CASEY MARGENAU

CASEY MARGENAU & ASSOCIATES
RE/MAX DISTINCTIVE REAL ESTATE, INC.
MCLEAN, VA

## Introduction

With more than 25 years in sales, over a decade as a Top Producer in Northern Virginia, and RE/MAX's #1 Agent Worldwide, Casey Margenau uses his wealth of experience to ensure the financial success of his clients. Casey's in-depth market knowledge allows him to custom tailor a marketing strategy for each property that provides the greatest exposure to achieve the goal of higher offers in the shortest time frame. Many area builders rely on his expertise when making development plans to optimize resources. As a Certified Relocation Specialist, Casey is able to access the corporate relocation purchaser and a vast, worldwide referral network. His professionalism and attention to detail have led him to the very top of his field.

## Background

**For how many years have you been in the real estate business?**

I have been in business for 17 years.

**What is your personal background and how did you get into real estate?**

I was in sales. I had a marketing degree and started off selling door-to-door. I really started off selling bicycle parts to bike shops. Then one of the bicycle manufacturers hired me. Then I sold automobiles. I managed and trained salespeople in the auto industry and managed an automobile dealership.

**What lessons did you learn from your family, friends, previous jobs, and life experiences that helped you most to succeed in your career?**

A strong work ethic comes from family. My family is made up of many successful business people who work hard.

**What do you enjoy most about the business?**

This is a multifaceted business that allows you to wear many different hats. It is a true profession; and many people who enter the business do not realize it is hard work. As a professional sales person, I have noticed that sales is a business that lazy people gravitate to.

I had money set aside for law school but I did not want to go through all of that. Sometimes I feel lazy and try to find the shortest way to get something done. In my family, we had six kids.

We all had to do chores. I thought the solution was get it done fast. I only learned that meant I got more chores.

## Basic Numbers

**How many transactions did you close in 2005?**

We did 166 transactions and $178 million.

**Are you a Billion Dollar Agent or do you believe you will hit that level during your career? Are you over a billion for career sales or what do you estimate?**

Yes, probably at about $1.5 billion total.

**What is your current staff including: yourself, listing agents, buyer agents, managers, and assistants?**

Right now, we have two listing coordinators, a field coordinator, a marketing manager, a receptionist, a closing coordinator, office manager, and four buyer agents, and myself. I sell my listings. We have about 12 people total. I am building the infrastructure to get to the next level. Right now, I have a listing inventory of 59; my goal is now to get to 100.

I want to get to $6 million gross commission but I want to do it with five buyer agents.

It will be 90 buyers and 135 sellers; that is 225 total to make our number.

## Goals

**Do you believe goals are important to your success?**

No, I do not believe goals are important for my success. In fact, I did not work with goals for years. My quality service was the key to my success and I just did as much business as I could. Now, as I have a team, goals are an integrated part of our business.

## Marketing

### New Customer Marketing – Lead Generation – Prospecting

**What are your top five methods for new client lead generation and about what percent of new customers are generated from that approach?**

My goal is to sell houses, not to list houses. If I am selling houses then I am going to generate business. If I have a house for sale, someone calls me on that house, they buy my house and I list their house. Having a similar inventory allows me to be known as the person with "that kind of inventory". My market niche is move-up buyers.

The homes I have for sale are newer, perfect homes (move in quality). They are in good districts and communities and they are priced right.

All of my marketing is to get buyers to buy my property. I spend a lot of money on the web to advertise my properties on the web and in print.

I do top quality brochures and flyers. I like my advertisement to impress people when they receive it.

**What is the one most effective form of marketing that you have constantly done?**

Direct response target marketing with direct mail. Also, high exposure print marketing. I buy the back cover of the magazines and local newspapers. I advertise on the web with

AOL, MSN, Yahoo, Craigslist, Ebay, RE/MAX, Homes, Homesdatabase, Realtor.com, Luxuryhomes.com, and about 12 websites.

For advertising, we spend about $250,000/year from about $4 million GCI. It ends up being about 6%. Overall, it has been about $500k total, about 12%. This year will be about $800,000.

We spend about 1% of the sales price on all listing expenses.

**What marketing advice would you give to someone at $100,000 who wants to get to $200,000 and more?**

It is easy to get started in real estate. One hundred thousand dollars is a very small amount of money to make if you are willing to put in the hours that it takes in real estate. You have to gain experience. When someone calls me and tells me the name of the street, I know who built it, what property is worth there, and exactly where it is.

Very early on, I was told to get billions of dollars worth of inventory. Then all you have to do is to get a license, a cellular phone, a fax number, and a computer, and you are in business. You need lots of inventory and there are no expenses for floor plans for inventory. In any sales business you need to know your product down to the last screw.

You need to know community as well. You are selling the neighborhood and community as well as the house.

I tell potential buyers that if the real estate agent needs a map, then they need to find a new agent. When I started, I marked every home on the market with a color dot. Green was one price range, etc.

## Client Marketing – Repeats/Referrals

**Of those, about how many do you have in current database?**

We have about 3,000 past clients and we have about 4,000 total names.

**What percentage of your business is referral?**

About 35% was repeat. About 50% total with referrals. Most people who do business with me end up doing business with me repeatedly.

I do not rely on just my past clients. If you look at 3,000 people and look at the average person sales every seven years, you are only going to do so much business. I need to do business with new people as often as I do with past clients.

So last year, about 80 deals were related to past clients. I think the goal should be 80% of past clients. Some past clients move out of town. We are doing campaigns to our past clients telling them it's a good time to sell your house. In years past, I could not market to past clients. There is a lot of variety in real estate.

**What client marketing activities do you do with past clients?**

We do some client marketing. I do a Fall client party.

# Ronnie Matthews

## Introduction

Mr. Matthews has over 20+ years experience in the Houston real estate market. His goal is to provide his clients, with the utmost in professional Realtor services. His unique turnkey services include marketing properties with sound planning, expert marketing advice, loan processing assistance, creative decorating tips, persuasive skills and a strong company support system. He has received the #1 RE/MAX team award in Texas for eight years out of the past 14 years; # three RE/MAX Team in the world in 2005. Other awards include: Circle of Legends Award, RE/MAX Lifetime Achievement Award, and winner of the Chairman's Club Award.

## Background

**How many years have you been in the real estate business?**

I began working in real estate in January 1988.

**What is your personal background and how did you get into real estate?**

We got in by default. I owned a plumbing utility business, employing about 65 people. Then the Houston economy started to collapse. From 1985 to 1987 several big developers went out of business. We lost everything. One day we looked at each other and said, "What do we do next?" There were not a lot of job opportunities for high school drop outs or ex plumbers. We had always been interested in real estate, so here we are.

**What lessons did you learn from your family, friends, previous jobs, and life experiences that helped you most to succeed in your career?**

I think the basics are "he who works hardest is usually the most successful". You have to always be looking for ways to grow and improve your business:
- How to increase business,
- How to cut costs,
- Where is the next potential growth spurt?

Our business is not like the insurance business; there is no annual renewal. You have to always be marketing yourself.

**What do you enjoy most about the business?**

I am fortunate that we have a great staff and the real estate business almost runs itself.

I am a partner in a subdivision development business and I have invested in starting up a radio station. I enjoy the freedom, flexibility, and new challenges these other ventures bring. I can be the leader and idea person. I invest in other businesses as a passive investment. I am on the board at a local bank. I am also involved in a new real estate software business, a radio station, and a title company.

## Basic Numbers

### How many transactions did you close in 2005?

We closed 920 homes in 2005 for about $187 million. The average price is about $200,000. My net profits were around 25%. My goal is for the employees to own the business over the next few years. My payroll ran close to 40% last year. My entire team consists of employees. I have no independent contractors.

### Are you a Billion Dollar Agent or do you believe you will hit that level during your career?

I think our career totals are over $1 billion.

### What is your current staffing, including: yourself, listing agents, buyer agents, managers, and assistants?

I have about 30 people working for us. I have four buyer agents and two listing agents. We do listing appointments Monday to Saturday, but not on Sundays. We make our last appointment at 6pm. Inside the office, I have one main person who negotiates contracts and helps with management. I have three other people who do other duties and rotate weekends for contracts. Weekends are divided between four people. Everybody in our office has to work some weekends. That is the nature of the business. Our office staff has a rotation. I personally do very few listings at this point. Our listing agents bring it back to the listing department for processing. Then they pass it on to the three people who handle it by keeping in touch on weekly basis. We have a total of 12 licensed people.

We have an inventory of about 175 listings right now. With many listings you can have higher productivity because of having two people doing listing appointments. We have been weaker on buyer agents and we are trying to build a buyer agent department. Last year we probably had 150 buyers and 700-800 listings. Our listing agent and buyer agents get a salary and they get a bonus for each listing that they get. There is not a higher split because they are not generating the lead, etc.

Our listing agents go on 400-500 appointments for listings and they will get 75% of those.

## Goals

**Do you believe goals are important to your success? If yes, describe your approach to goal setting for your business and life?**

I have never been one to set goals on January 1st. You automatically expect to do more than previous years. On a personal note: if we are always doing the best we can, and working hard, then the growth will come automatically.

## Marketing

### New Customer Marketing – Lead Generation – Prospecting

**What are your top five methods for new client lead generation and about what percentage of new customers are generated from that approach?**

We have two big new pushes: expanding our buyers' agent department and getting involved in the foreclosure business. The foreclosure market, unfortunately, is going to be a dramatically growing business. The market has been financing homes for people that can't truly afford a home, especially in an environment with very little appreciation.

We have started to market to companies who handle foreclosures. We have one person building those relationships that generates referrals. I want that person to chase relocation business and foreclosure business. We are going to focus on the foreclosures after they have gone to the bank. The pre-foreclosure people here are not good prospects because they have no equity in their house.

Once a house is foreclosed on, it is going to be sold. The negatives of the foreclosure business are that there is potentially a lot of repair – management work involved, but you know that they are going to sell.

### Client Marketing – Repeats/Referrals

**About how many past clients have you worked with?**

We have about 10,000 past clients in our database.

**What percentage of your business is referral?**

Approximately 60-70% of business is referral. We get about 600 client deals per year from repeat/referral.

**What client marketing activities do you do with past clients?**

We send a 5 x 8 four color postcard, with our pictures and names on it. We send that every six weeks.

We make up three or four cards. I order 100,000 postcards at a time for about ten cents each. We mail the same cards to our farm market areas.

# Best Agent Business

We are in the process of starting email campaigns. Our contact program, currently, does not have email capability. But we are working to correct that.

I mail out around 8 - 10,000 postcards a month to farm areas. This is not as effective as it used to be because everyone is doing it. We also have billboards on the north side of Houston where we advertise.

# Blake Mayes

RE/MAX Capital City

Boise, ID

## Background

**For how many years have you been in the real estate business?**

I was licensed in 1995; so, for about 11 years.

**What is your personal background and how did you get into real estate?**

About 11-12 years ago, I met an agent who sold me a house. It was a difficult transaction and the agent thought I would be good in the real estate business. I was a barber and only 23 years old. The house I lived in had a fire and I ended up losing much of the house. I decided I wanted to move. The agent listed my house and sold me her own home.

**What lessons did you learn from your family, friends, previous jobs, and life experiences that helped you most to succeed in your career?**

While growing up, my family did not have much money. I was used to working hard for my parents. I was tired of being poor. I was willing to work as hard as necessary to make money. I was able to watch a successful agent as a mentor.

**What do you enjoy most about the business?**

I like the freedom and diversity. It is not mundane.

## Basic Numbers

**How many transactions did you close in 2005?**

I closed about 600 transactions.

**What was your total dollar volume in 2005?**

The total dollar volume was about $87 million.

**Based on that, about what was average price of a sale?**

The average price was about $150,000.

**Are you a Billion Dollar Agent or do you believe you will hit that level during your career?**

I am over $500 million so far and it is very early in my career.

**What is your current staffing including: yourself, listing agents, buyer agents, managers, and assistants?**

I have two buyer agents and one listing agent and one administrative assistant. That is about 125 deals per agent. I personally do 80-85% of the deals.

Listings are 75% of the business. My business is two categories. The first is we do a lot of foreclosures and REOs and handle many banks in the area. That is the driving force of my business. It is a machine. The other category is I work with one of largest developers in Idaho and we sell him a lot of bare ground that becomes development land. I was in my second year of real-estate and the lending company I worked with referred me to Washington Mutual to handle foreclosures. From there I tried to develop more bank relationships. I flew to different companies. I work with Fidelity, Washington Mutual, and Countrywide. Sometimes I will pay a referral fee, or as much as 1%. I can do more foreclosure listings. I think I net more. I do not have to do advertising or open houses, etc.

## Goals

**Do you believe goals are important to your success? If yes, describe your approach to goal setting for your business and life?**

I think goals are extremely important and I set goals a lot. I started in goal setting with my coach, Walter Sanford. I went out to Walter Sanford in 1996 and 1997 and he coached me a bit. I did some one-on-one coaching and flew every three months to Long Beach for him to coach me. It worked out really well. I read my goals daily. One of my goals is to be a coach or motivational speaker.

## Marketing

### New Customer Marketing – Lead Generation – Prospecting

**What are your top five methods for new client lead generation and about what percent of new customers are generated from that approach?**

I stay on top of the foreclosure market. I keep track of who has assignments in Idaho. There are about 50 different organizations that handle foreclosures. For buyers, I have someone who works on the development side who spends eight hours a day cold-calling landowners and farmers to see if they want to sell. They cold call everyday.

For land development, I have a developer who I have worked with for many years. He buys enormous amounts of land. We find him land. I meet with him for 2-3 hours each week. We go through all the land we found.

We have programs of each piece of dirt and pieces of land that becomes available. He buys properties and pays commissions directly. We average about one deal a month on land. We are very focused on who is out there and what they plan to do. We try to find out who the players are. An average size of a land deal is $2-3 million.

There is no other agent on that, so I am getting both sides, which means we get the whole 6%.

We keep in touch with the entire valley for over 1,000 pieces of property. We are marketing to about 50 contacts a day.

**What marketing advice would you give to someone at $100,000 who wants to get to $200,000 and more?**

I do not think there are any magic words. I think new agents are looking for magic words. For me, it is direct correlation in work effort and what comes from it. There is not an easy way to do this business.

You should create a machine in the business. It is better to have one client who can give you 20 listings than 20 clients with one listing each.

**What client marketing activities do you do with past clients?**

My buyer agents do a lot of repeat and referral business. We do thousands of pieces of mail a month to past clients. We have affiliations with different lenders as well.

## Growth of Business

**What single quality has made you more successful than others?**

When I started my foreclosure business, I made sure I was in the air once a month. Idaho is very remote. People did not pay attention to the market. I was more willing to go meet clients in-person, especially the banks. They would say I was the only one from Idaho who flew to Florida to take someone to lunch. I was able to develop face-to-face relationships. I used to do pop-bys bringing cookies. When they got a foreclosure in Idaho, of course they gave it to me. I did face-to-face sales.

## Building a Team

**How did you first start to delegate and out source and build a team?**

I got to a point that I had so many listings and signs up there that I started to not return all my calls. I had so many messages from people who wanted information on houses. I started to refer my leads to people in the office. Then someone asked to join me as a buyer agent. When we reached 75-100 listings, we needed to divide up by county.

It developed over time and we developed a team, as we needed one. I was able to handle the business and grew it until it took off. It really took on a life of its own and became a machine. I found myself learning as I went along. I put stuff in motion and it took off in ways I did not realize it would happen.

My buyer agent was, at first, based on volume and I received 20-40% of commission check depending on the volume.

# Best Agent Business

The first chunk I received was 40% and then it went down to 20%.

I would start them at 60/40 split. And then moved them to a 70/30 split.

I bought my own RE/MAX franchise after two years. We have 33 licenses and that is considered small.

The total sold in my office was $140 million, of which I was $87 million. The franchise is not profitable; it does not make money. The only reason I own it is that I want to run it myself. In Boise, many brokers will recruit from each other's offices. I wanted a national name. I was at an office for two years and it was in financial trouble. I bought it for $30,000 and I owned it for ten years. I used to have 70-80 agents. I had a big business, but I sold and shrunk it a bit, and that has been good. The agents in the office pay the bills. It pays the salaries of all of my assistants, etc.

# WILLIE MIRANDA

## Introduction

Willie Miranda began his real estate career in the Capital Region in 1999 with Coldwell Banker. He left there and worked for Re/Max Premier until 2002. In July of 2002, he decided to go out on his own and established Miranda Real Estate Group. This decision was made by Mr. Miranda's desire to form a Real Estate Team of Professionals to serve the Capital Region. His innovative and progressive approach to real estate has been the driving force behind the continued expansion and success of his unique "Sales Team System." Mr. Miranda is a Certified Trainer of the Brian Buffini "100 Days To Greatness" program and member of an elite group of the Top Realtor's in the Country. Miranda Real Estate Group won the Business Reviews' 2005 - Great Places To Work Award. Willie was also a recipient of the Business Reviews' 2006 - 40 under 40 award.

## Background

**How many years have you been in the real estate business?**

I have been in real estate since 1999. About 7 years.

**What is your personal background and how did you get into real estate?**

Growing up, I was a paperboy and I had a farm area of about 500 homes. In college, I wanted to be a state trooper. I took the exam and I had to wait for about 6 months to be approved. I had a Discover Card bill to pay and no job; so, I found a job selling insurance with Prudential. Mike Mali was my boss and first mentor. He taught me how to run a business, both good and bad. Six months later I was making much more in commissions than I would earn as a state trooper.

I would go knock on doors. An older guy, Sam Stern, was another agent and mentor who told me to get out of the office and knock on doors. My goal was 150 knocks in 3-4 hours, which is about 30-40 knocks per hour. I left a letter at each door if they were not at home.

I achieved the Gold Record Award for getting a commission of $13,000 in the first 15 weeks. I was rookie of the year in 1990. I switched to Allstate and became an Exclusive Agent there. I soon realized that I was sending a lot of referrals to Realtors and they earned more commissions on my referrals than I did on my clients in insurance.

At Coldwell Banker, they had a Mike Ferry training session and that was very helpful.

235

**What lessons did you learn from your family, friends, previous jobs, and life experiences that helped you most to succeed in your career?**

My mother and father have been instrumental in raising us to believe you really have to work for what you have. I paid my own way through college. My father worked as an electrician for CSX, the rail company, for 37 years. It amazed me that no matter how sick or tired he got up everyday and he was a great provider to our family. I am the oldest of three boys. It has been instilled to me that I am the role model for my brothers. My mother always told me to strive to do my best and go to school. I went to a local community school for my first two years, then, I went away to finish my Bachelors' degree in Business Economics and Finance.

**What do you enjoy most about the business?**

I love building things. I love growing the company. One of the things Mike Mali taught me was to surround myself with good people and never burn bridges. Do not surround yourself with negative or bad people and always protect your name. I enjoy building my team and watching them become successful. I enjoy teaching and showing other agents how to build their own center of influence.

I am trying to figure out the best model for myself using Michael Gerber methods. I am also trying to figure out the best training/learning program for my team and staff.

## Basic Numbers

**How many transactions did you close in 2005?**

In 2005, we closed about 363 for $54,445,000 million with an average sale price of $150,000. I started in 2000 with 13 sales, then 53, 76, 106, 204, and 363 in 2005. Our target is 500 in 2006.

**Are you a Billion Dollar Agent or do you believe you will hit that level during your career? Are you over a billion for career sales or what do you estimate?**

I am a future Billion Dollar Agent. I have sold about $200 million so far.

**What is your current staffing, including yourself, of listing agents, buyer agents, managers, and assistants?**

I operate as an independent brokerage with 43 agents. We have about 5 full-time assistants. I do about 10 deals myself. We have about 55% listings and 45% buyers. My top three salespeople do about 50 deals each. That group does 150 deals. About 20 of the agents are part-time and do about 4 deals a year. Another 12 agents do about 12-15 deals per year. For listings, we take 25% off the top and then do a 50/50 split for overall split of 37.5% to the agent, plus transaction fee of $595, which is not negotiable. For buyers agents we do a 50/50 split.

My GCI was about $1,400,000 last year and will be $2,500,000 in 2006. We spend about 10% or $130,000 on marketing. My net profit was about 20% or $280,000 in 2005.

We were voted as one of the "Great Places to Work" in Albany, NY for 2005 and 2006.

## Goals

**Do you believe goals are important to your success? If yes, describe your approach to goal setting for your business and life?**

My approach to goal setting is, that every year I do an annual goal and then break it down into monthly goals. I then break that down into weekly goals. I also do that with my agents. I need to give it to someone else. I have peer agents outside of my company. Most of them are in Craig Proctor's Platinum Group.

The other person that holds me accountable is my coach at Brian Buffini. His name is Nick. We talk twice a month and it is all about team culture and the culture of the office and P/L statements.

## Marketing

### New Customer Marketing – Lead Generation – Prospecting

**What are your top 5 methods for new client lead generation and about what percent of new customers are generated from that approach?**

I would call from 9-12 with a focus on my farm of about 500, FSBO and Expireds. I kept a box of information in my car that I left at the doors of any FSBO that I saw. I asked a friend who worked at the utility company to watch for new FSBOs. With FSBO's, for every ten I met face-to-face I ended up getting about 2-4 listings.

We do radio, television and classified ads.

We are starting a new venture called The Miranda Referral Network, which encourages inactive agents to provide us with referrals.

The majority of my marketing is from the Craig Proctor system, which is reverse prospecting lead generation.

## Client Marketing – Repeats/Referrals

**About how many past clients have you worked with?**

I have about 300 right now. We have had 800 transactions since I started. My agents, who are selling, will put the client into their client appreciation program. Our group does mailings to a total of around 700 clients right now.

My own personal clients number about 300.

**What percentage of your business is referral?**

About 40% of our business is repeat/referral. I started to use the Brian Buffini methods, besides Craig Proctor, a few years ago.

**What client marketing activities do you do with past clients?**

I do a monthly mailing with an item of value.
I do a market watch newsletter.
I send them out a birthday card.
I send them an anniversary card for the home purchase.
They are contacted about 26 times per year.
They all get a phone call from me, as well, throughout the year.
With that alone we are at 26 touches.
We do an annual golf tournament for the Local Children's Hospital.
We have special listings that we get and send something to our whole customer base a few times a year.
I also give them a magnet calendar.
I also have a referral contest. To be in the drawing they have to send me a referral, which is buying, selling, or relocating.
For every person they refer, their name gets thrown into the hat. In June of every year we give away a trip for two people to Las Vegas. We have a second drawing in November where we pick two winners. Each wins $500, for a Christmas shopping spree. All they have to do is refer someone to us. It has been very successful.

## Growth of Business

**What single quality has made you more successful than others?**

I think my leadership qualities. I want to share and help people grow.

# GREGG NEUMAN

NEUMAN & NEUMAN REAL ESTATE INC.
PRUDENTIAL CALIFORNIA REALTY
SAN DIEGO, CA

## Introduction

Whether they are showing a $100,000 condo or a multi-million dollar estate, Gregg Neuman and his partner, Debbie Neuman, always take a client-centered approach toward the real estate business with an 'it's our pleasure' attitude. They attribute this winning attitude to the sixteen years in San Diego that Gregg worked as a bartender, and eight years that Debbie worked as a waitress. "People in the bar business make excellent sales people because they interact with so many types of people," explains Gregg. In real estate since 1981, Gregg and Debbie both have developed strong skills, which complement each other. While Debbie oversees the office staff, listings, and advertising, Gregg handles the finances and sets goals.

Now Prudential California Realty, Gregg and Debbie are 20-time Pinnacle Award winners, two for each year they have been with the company. The award is given to Prudential's top ten agents in the United States, based on the number of units sold and commission dollars earned. The Neumans have been #1 in the USA four out of the last five years and #1 in San Diego County five out of the last six years.

One of the ways the Neumans have stayed innovative in the business was the creation of their "Fine Homes Division" in 1996. Discovering quickly that contacts and credibility were crucial factors for success, they hired retired businessman Paul Roberts, as their marketing director. "That was probably the smartest thing we did in creating the division. He happened to be a brand new agent who had connections in the high end of the market."

## Background

**What is your background and how did you get into real estate?**

I started when I was 35 years old. I was a bartender for about 15 years. Being a bartender helped me to learn to talk to all types of people at all stages of life - attorneys and truck drivers. I wanted to get into something that paid more money. The only thing that pays more than sales required lots of education, such as medical. I had a limited degree from 1.5 years of college. With sales, the bigger ticket price, the more you are paid. If I were a shoe salesperson, I would need to sell millions of shoes to make a lot of money. I wanted to increase my income.

**What about your background, lessons from your family, friends, and previous jobs helped you succeed in your career?**

I was raised with a Midwest work ethic. I am not afraid to put in hours and time.

**What do you enjoy most about the business?**

Doing the deal. The deal itself is the best part of business. I like to get a seller and buyer to compromise. In the middle of a deal, I say to myself that we do not have problems; we have challenges. Less than 1% of agents perceive problems as a challenge; they focus on the problem.

## Goals

**Do you set written goals for your business and life?**

Yes, I am a great believer in goal setting. Without goals you just have dreams. If you set it down, it is a map to your dream. They become manageable bites. I look at my goals once a week. I do not have life goals. I have financial goals. I started to write goals when I was ten years into the business. If not written down, the goals were more nebulous.

## Marketing

**What are your primary methods of lead generation for new customers?**

I use interactive voice response, IVR, of a product called Powerline. Powerline gives me the best impact for lead generation for new buyers. Agents give out too much information in advertisements, so people may not call. By providing less information that is specific, you get more calls. By using an 800 number, the call is captured and tracked by advertisement. Each property has a four digit code for which property and which ad. We also do postcard mailings of 2,500 with one message and 2,500 with another message. The call volume for print ad is declining. The Internet volume is growing to about 15-20% of business. We only advertise in color, no black and white. We track all leads and find we get 28% more response with color. We do some radio advertising but it is hard to measure.

**If you had to teach only three lessons about marketing, what would you tell someone who is at 100k and wants to get to 200k?**

My income took off when I realized I had to have people make a bigger effort to contact me. I changed the way I advertised and stopped giving out so much information. Each listing generates about two new buyers.

**What percentage of your business is referral?**

About 25% of our business is referral. Early on in my career I was not so methodical about referrals and this was a weakness. About 3-4 years ago I changed that.

**How do you encourage referrals? What is a target percentage?**

A target of 40% would be phenomenal. Past clients are about 10%. We stay in contact by sending a monthly postcard. We have a client party every other year.

We have season tickets to our baseball team, the Padres, which we offer when available. In the year after closing of a new client, we contact them once a quarter.

## Sales

**What is your closing ratio of qualified leads for listing proposals?**

We close about 80-90% of listing proposals. I would guess agents who are at the $100,000 level are closing about 50%. The key is to find out why you did not get the listing and learn from the feedback.

## Feedback on showings

For feedback on showings, we got 50% based on phone call, and now we get up to 70% based on e-mail. We use a service and it is very effective because it goes directly to the seller. The single biggest complaint of sellers is that they listed with an agent and never heard from him again. I believe that the reason other agents fail to provide feedback on showings is a mix of lack of professionalism among some agents, lack of respect, and lack of time.

## Listings

**What is your ratio of listings versus buyers and how has that changed over the years?**

Last year we had about 120 listings and 180 buyers. The ratio was about 40% listings. It fluctuates with the market.

**Do you have any comments on a suggested balance for someone at $100k or $200k?**

You should shoot for 70% listings. Listings work for you 24 hours a day. They are the most effective for an agent.

## Specialized Markets and Approach

**Beyond the basics, are you involved with any specialized niche markets that are part of your success or more than 10% of your business?**

We created a Fine Homes division to gradually increase our average price point. Our approach included better quality stationery and cards and was headed up by someone with long-standing ties to the community. It is about 10% of our business. We also have a downtown condo market focus.

## Growth of Business

**What single quality has made you more successful than others?**

Tenacity.

**How did your business and staffing grow?**

My first assistant came after five years in the business. She was an all around assistant who basically did everything. I believe that once an agent is doing two deals a month for a year they should add an assistant or at least share an assistant. Most agents spend too much time micro managing and not enough time on dollar productive activities. The year that I added my assistant, my production doubled in that year. It was a very sound and wise investment.

Next I added a second assistant and that was in my seventh year. Then I broke down their roles into a listing/advertisingassistant and a transaction coordinator for open escrows.

Interestingly enough in 1991, one of the toughest years in real estate in California, was when I added my first buyer's agent. I was doing a lot of trade-in and contingency management with builders and I got so many well-priced listings that I could not keep up with the calls that were coming in on the signs. I added a buyer's agent and began to advertise the listing. During 1991-1997 when the market was slow for many, we had six buyer agents.

In 1998 I noted that the market would be swinging toa seller's market, which is where it's been until recently. I built the team to as many as 12 buyer's agents since listings were going to be difficult to obtain and buyers were the way to make money. Now that the market has shifted, I have moved from buyer's agents (down to 8) and we are focusing again on listings.

As the number of calls increased, I added a receptionist, and as the demand for service increased, I added a courier. The team is now one listing coordinator, one escrow coordinator, one receptionist,one courier, and eight buyers' agents.

**What one thing would you tell a beginning agent to pursue to achieve success?**

Agents should expose themselves to people who are more successful. It was useful to meet people who did far more volume. I have been involved with groups such as Howard Brinton's StarPower and Mike Ferry. Also, focus on profitability. Our current structure is about 60% expenses and 40% net income.

**As you grew your business, what were the biggest mistakes that you made that you would warn others about?**

First, we did not track the source of business and the source of advertising. We did ego advertising that was a critical mistake that we made for a long time. I was thrilled to see my face but it was not financially effective!

Second, we did not work past clients. We have about 3,000-4,000 past clients and about 1,600 e-mail addresses. We do a monthly e-mail newsletter.

**f you could go back and do things differently,what would you have done at $100,000 that would have sped the growth of your business?**

I would have hired an assistant sooner. I waited too long to get an assistant. I was bogged down in doing paperwork and doing things that were not dollar productive. I spent too much time following transactions, giving sellers feedback, giving buyer's info, etc. The minute the transaction is placed in escrow it should be handed off unless there is a challenge to be resolved. The ideal deal is a listing that proceeds as follows. Someone on my team sends a package to prospective seller. They book an appointment in my calendar and I show up to present and take a signed listing. I turn the package over to my transaction coordinator and do nothing until an offer is generated. I bring the client into the office or on the telephone to present the offer and then turn it over to the escrow coordinator. The ideal deal is two hours of my time for the listing and one hour for the deal.

The reason that agents fail to hire assistants early enough is that they are afraid they cannot afford them and they think they do not have enough work to keep them busy. Also, by spending time to train them, it affects short-term productivity. Also, many agents have never hired and fired before. I think that at about 25 deals an agent should have an assistant.

**What do you use for client database?**

We use Act primary contact management and Online Agent for buyer agents.

**What are best books you have read in past ten years that helped with your business and life?**

Millionaire Real Estate Agent, Pursuit of Excellence, Who Moved my Cheese

# STEPHEN O'HARA

## Introduction

My business career started with a successful "Kool-Aid" stand at 5-years old. In Junior High, I began a business that led to my first automobile dealership in High School. Actually, my first car is still my favorite of all time – a Lincoln Continental. My automobile business grew to three dealerships and in 1976 I was the founder of what has become known as the "Certified" used car, which was marketed using a franchise business model.

On January 28, 1986, as the world and I watched the Challenger explode, I was on my first cell phone with my CPA. He was explaining why I was about to go through a multi-million dollar bankruptcy. With huge loss carry-forwards, I dusted off a real estate license I had since 1976. That began an incredible career in real estate, earning a slew of professional designations along the way CSCA, CRB, CRS, GRI, ABR and SRES.

In 2005 I was ranked #14 by RE/MAX from among 117,000 sales associates worldwide. It was at the awards recognition event that it dawned on me that the way I differentiated myself from other agents. I became the relocating family focal expert and it could also work nationally.

To support my real estate practice, I had created the Parent Relocation Council® Inc. (PRC) in 1999. In February of 2006 the PRC web site www.schoolfolks.com the nation's first website that catered to relocating parents went live. Today, the program is active in over a dozen states and growing daily. Today, hundreds of agents are visiting www.parentrelocationcouncil.org, to read my story and, to find out how they can be certified as a PRC Local Partner®. That way that they can set themselves apart from their competition.

In looking back, I know I needed to go through all I have experienced to bring me to this moment today. Without that Kool-Aid stand, without those incredible 20-years in the automobile and franchise business, and without that bankruptcy, "today" simply would not have happened. I would certainly not be who I am today, as a businessman or as a person.

## Background

**For how many years have you been in the real estate business?**

I have been in business since 1976.

**What is your personal background and how did you get into real estate?**

I had lost much money in another business. I had a $43 million bankruptcy. I had a real estate license and I never used it. I did 176 transactions my first year. My academic background was a mix of marketing, law, and accounting.

**What lessons did you learn from your family, friends, previous jobs, and life experiences that helped you most to succeed in your career?**

I was blessed to be able to believe that I could achieve anything. I always believed that I could do something that would make a difference.

**What do you enjoy most about the business?**

I like deal-making. Especially the creative aspect that no two deals are the same. I feel like I won the Super Bowl every time I see the meeting of the minds. The legal and "numbers" aspects of the real estate business keeps my mental juices flowing. And the money is not bad.

## Basic Numbers

**How many transactions did you close in 2005?**

I typically close about 50-75 transactions per year, so that's about 2,000 in 30 years.

My sales dollar volume is typically about $70 million – plus or minus.

**Are you a Billion Dollar Agent or do you believe you will hit that level during your career?**

You know, I've never totaled it up, but "quick math" would confirm that I've either hit that mark or am certainly close to the billion-dollar level. I have consistently generated over a million in commission for years – so I would have to be at that billion-dollar level.

**What is your current staffing including: yourself, listing agents, buyer agents, managers, and assistants?**

I have a personal assistant and an administrative assistant. I have two associate agents – I call them my partners. My business is a mix of 60% buyers and 40% sellers. I quarterback most of my transactions. Using my name and celebrity, I initially meet with a potential client along with one of my partner-agents at Starbucks. I never meet clients at my office. In truth, I have never met a client at my office in 30 years. It is too formal – and I'm the 'King of Casual'. It seems that no matter where my office is, the home the client wants is the opposite direction anyway. If it is relocation, we meet in the lobby of the hotel. Still, Starbucks is my favorite. It sets a professional – yet approachable business tone.

In this way, the client gets a "touch" from me but my partner spends the time with them. Once the client has settled on "the" home, I'll typically want to look at the property so I can be emotionally part of the process.

I creatively engineer the deal and my associate partner and my staff move it along through the escrow/closing process.

Think of it the way that most of the medical profession works. The nurse preps you and the doctor pokes his head in. They pull me into the picture for problems and other things. For buyers, we show an average of about 5-10 homes. We have it down to an art form.

## Goals

**Do you believe goals are important to your success? If yes, describe your approach to goal setting for your business and life?**

In the classical definition of goal-setting, I don't think it is important to my success. In an emotional sense I am a born perfectionist. I feel I am already born with a goal because I am focused on perfection and results. I drive myself. In fact, I am very driven. I don't really think about money. As long as I keep driving toward perfection and serving my customers, the dollars will follow.

## Marketing

### New Customer Marketing – Lead Generation – Prospecting

**What are your top five methods for new client lead generation and about what percentage of new customers are generated from that approach?**

First, we get on our knees and thank the Internet. Once I talk to a client I ask them key questions to figure out what they are looking for. Then, I send a sample of homes and ask the buyer to tell me what they do not like. Based on things the buyer does not like, I am able to focus and narrow to one more step.

I have a huge machine in place. I own the URL www.orangecountyrealestate.com and I have been offered a small fortune for it. I started it in the mid 1990's. I was laughed at back then. Now, I have standing offers for – well let's say, a lot of dollars for it. I remember an agent said to me, "$70 to register a name, that's stupid."

By having that website, I get traffic from all over the country. Generally 50% of our business comes from that. Once those people are here, they become part of my overall client base. The key to using the Internet was to find ways to filter leads from cold to warm. From a series of questions we profile and are able to identify the stronger leads – that typically lead to a closed sale.

500-1,000 cold leads per week may result in 150 warm leads per week. To filter, we ask questions like "are you going to be moving and in what timeframe?"

You would be surprised how many people get on our site for different reasons. While "basics" are always fundamentally important, working smart has taken center stage. The reality is that everyone who visits my site is NOT looking to buy or sell a home. So, there are a series of questions we will ask prospective customers.

We have many questions on the website form and if they complete it all, they are a serious lead. Our questions are designed to get rid of 75% that are NOT serious leads.

My guess is 5-10% of the warm leads end up being a transaction.

My Internet presence skyrocketed when I started www.parentrelocationcouncil.org, first in Orange County, then nationally.

I've never done much traditional farming. I have a problem associating recipe cards with million dollar homes. I did not think it was cost-effective when only 5% of a farm will sell in a given year you are wasting money on 95% of the people.

Most of my business is from my sphere of influence, repeat and referral.

## Client Marketing – Repeats/Referrals

### How many do you have in current database?

We have about 2,000 past clients. We also have a 10,000 person sphere of influence.

### What percentage of your business is referral?

I estimate the client repeat/referral is about 33%.

### What client marketing activities do you do with past clients?

That is a very good question. I view my clients in different tiers. My innermost circle – about 100 folks who give me multiple referrals, and with whom I have a special connection – is my most precious "tier." I invest "one-on-one" time with these folks. Since cooking is my hobby, and I'm good at it, I'll have their family join my family for what is usually an incredible evening of food and fellowship.

The next group is comprised of about 250-350 clients. From this group, I'll select people with similar/common interests and do special things with them. For example, one time I did a mystery trip. I took about 120, two busloads, to The Tonight Show starring Jay Leno. I take advantage of a lot of the free stuff in Southern California. Many of my vendors help by sponsoring transportation and meals.

My family also hosts a huge holiday party once a year at my home.

### What single quality has made you more successful than others?

First would be my communication skills and the ability to "think on my feet". Second would be my ability to "see" a deal.

I can see a series of facts and I immediately know what I need to bring the parties and the deal together to make it happen for everyone. There is an art to that. Problem-solving is easy for me. I like to "keep it real." My clients enjoy my folksy approach. My approachability is helpful. I want to be very approachable.

In my 30 years of doing this, 9 times out of 10, it is usually the ego of the other agent that is the problem.

**What does the average real estate agent fail to do which are among the reasons why they are average?**

They do not understand the business of business, let alone the real estate business.

They let their ego get in the way.

They are not capable of seeing the big picture.

They tend to get tied up in the minutiae of stuff.

There are many that do not understand that you have to work at it.

They do not understand commission sales because they come from salary background.

They fail to realize that they can put in a lot of effort and work and might not get paid for it.

They do not understand they need to spend money to make money.

**Did you make any big mistakes that you want to warn others about?**

The brokerage office is where you work. It is where you hang your license; it is not a marketing differentiator, it does not set you apart. About 15 years ago I walked into a listing appointment and walking out was the agent who sat next to me at the same brokerage.

I always knew that I didn't want to work for 30-years, and be only as good as my last closing. The challenge was to build a business that I could pass on to my daughter or sell. Agents who build the business around themselves are in trouble. They can't sell their business; they have to work 24/7. From day one, you want to run and build your business like a business.

## Building a Team

**How did you first start to delegate and outsource and build a team?**

The joke answer is, "when I got tired." The truth is I had to leverage in order to grow. The reality is there is only so much that one person can do. To grow you need to trust and get other people, with the right talent and skill-set, into place.

For me, I knew I needed to build a team when I reached the $75,000-$100,000 income level. Adding more people is relative to how much you are capable of quarterbacking.

I knew if I could build a system where my clients would not feel abandoned, and they knew they were dealing with me but ALLOWED me to use my team for all the 'busy work,' all I needed was good people who make me look good.

My team and I work well together. One of the girls has been with me for 19 years. She is probably so sick of my jokes she could slit her wrists.

I knew where I wanted to go and, as in any business, I knew I had to "bite the bullet" and invest in my own business. I think many agents are more reactive than proactive. The group of agents I "travel with" are very proactive. Like any forward thinking business- person, I reap rewards of investments later.

I cannot "will" business to just happen. I have to make it happen. If it's going to be, it is UP to me.

Most people wait until they have a heart attack to hire an assistant.

I am going to hire an assistant so I don't have a heart attack.

# Ray Otten

## Introduction

Having obtained his Real Estate License 1989, Ray Otten now has over 16 years of real estate selling experience. Some of his achievements during this time include the Associate Broker Designation, being President of Ottawa Real Estate Board (OREB) 2000, First Vice President Ottawa Real Estate Board (OREB) 1999, Chairman of Finance Committee (OREB) 1999, Chairman of Multiple Listing Service (OREB) 1998, Accredited Buyer Representative (ABR Designation), and Registered Relocation Specialist (RRS Designation).

## Background

**For how many years have you been in the real estate business?**

I have been helping clients with their real estate needs for over 16 years.

**What is your personal background and how did you get into real estate?**

I was working as an accountant when a good friend suggested I try real estate as I would be rewarded for working hard. My first year I sold 23 homes and from then on my business started to grow quickly.

**What lessons did you learn from your family, friends, previous jobs, and life experiences that helped you most to succeed in your career?**

My experience working on an oil rig as a young man, taught me great work ethics and how to work hard. My family was very supportive even though I knew they were thinking, as was I, what am I doing leaving a job with an good annual income and pension to try something with no guarantees. But I was determined to persevere in real estate. As my sales manager said, " The harder you work the luckier you get."

**What do you enjoy most about the business?**

I enjoy seeing the success of the Team as a whole. We have strong agents; excellent administrative staff and I have a great business partner. When one of our team members succeeds, we all share in the success. Knowing that I have helped a Team member to meet their goals makes all the hard work worth it.

## Basic Numbers

### How many transactions did you close in 2005?

Last year we had 168 sales and over $2 million in GCI. We do not track dollar volume. We only track gross commission income. We are located in Ottawa, Ontario, Canada and our average price is about $290,000.

### Are you a Billion Dollar Agent or do you believe you will hit that level during your career? Are you over a billion for career sales or what do you estimate?

At this point we are doing about $75 million per year. We combined in 2001 as a team. Between the two of us, we have probably done over $600 million in our careers and we will achieve $1 billion.

### What is your current staffing, including yourself, of listing agents, buyer agents, managers, and assistants?

My business partner and I have two other sales people that help us with listing properties. We have four full-time buyer agents, a closing coordinator, a listing coordinator, and a multimedia administrator who handles all aspects of marketing our properties and our team.

## Goals

### Do you believe goals are important to your success? If yes, describe your approach to goal setting for your business and life?

We look at our sales numbers very hard each year and set Team goals based on past statistics, current market situation, and projected markets. Goals are set in terms of number of listings, number of buyer sales, and number of listing sales. We review financial statements and cash flow on monthly basis.

Personally, my goal is to lead by example. That means working hard each day, prospecting, continually upgrading my skills, and staying focused.

## Marketing

### New Customer Marketing – Lead Generation – Prospecting

### What are your top five methods for new client lead generation and about what percent of new customers are generated from that approach?

The majority of our new leads are from the Internet. In a month we get approximately 100 Internet leads, which works out to 1,200 a year. Of those 1,200 leads we will get about 18 transactions. Our website, on average, has about 240 - 300 sessions per day, which averages to about 6,000 visitors a month.

We have found that responding to an Internet inquiry within 15 minutes makes a major impression on that consumer. We always ask someone why they chose our Team and they always mention our professionalism and the speed in which we respond throughout the entire process. If we respond quickly, the client gets a sense of our business style – that they, the client, are very important to us.

Our Team also has a policy to return calls within an hour. Our admin. staff is trained to ask the client where they can be reached within the hour and to get that information to the appropriate team member immediately. Also, our office is also opened 7 days a week and on weekdays we are open from 9 am to 8 pm, which allows clients to speak with a member of our staff personally.

When a consumer calls in to make an appointment to list their property, we get our prelist package out to them within four hours. When the prelist is delivered, a photo is taken of the property. We then add to the photo an image of our For Sale sign. The photo goes into the listing kit - when we meet the consumer and review our listing presentation, they get an immediate impression of what they home is going to look like when we sell it for them.

We use the print media to attract consumers to call us for information. We have prominent ads in our major newspaper plus bulk mailings to specific areas where we have a strong presence.

We also have four logo vehicles driving around the city – a moving truck (for our clients), VW Beetle (used by Buyer Agents), a Mercedes SmartCar (doing deliveries), and a Mini Van (delivering Open House signs). Consumers comment on how they see our vehicles around our community all the time.

Our Team keeps in touch regularly with prospective Buyers. We keep our name fresh in their minds by calling them every two weeks and sending them property matches as soon as the property comes onto the market.

## Client Marketing – Repeats/Referrals

**Of those, about how many do you have in current database?**

Our whole database if over 6500 contacts. The client/referral group is over 4500 people. Of those, about 3000 are past clients. Our buyer department receives about 75% of their buyers from client referrals. The listing side is higher at 78%.

**What client marketing activities do you do with past clients?**

We have implemented a Client For Life program. We offer a moving truck not only for moving but also for various charitable events in our community.

Our past clients are able to use our copiers and printers to do flyers for their charitable events.

They can use our fax machine and scanners. We send them a Home Inventory CD and coupons.

On our clients' moving anniversary, our Listing Agents personally give them a call to congratulate them. A week before we call, we send out a letter, and if they have been in their home two years or more, we send comparable sales in the neighborhood. Our clients appreciate our keeping up with them. We update our database after these calls with our client's current information and their family situation. My goal is to call 30 people a week between 9 a.m. to 5 p.m. Our database has their work, cells, and home numbers – if I do not reach them, I leave a voice mail but usually only happens about 30% of the time. After the call, we schedule another call in 6 months. We always ask for referrals.

To help us with our prospecting calls to past clients, we have designated each client into an A, B, or C category, with A clients being our raving fans – we focus more attention to the A's.

## Listings

**What percentage of your transactions are listings? What would be ideal and why?**

Our split is 45% buyers and 55% listings. We are trying to get it to 50/50 – we want to get one lead closed for every listing we sell.

## Growth of Business

**What does the average real estate agent fail to do which are among the reasons why they are average?**

Most agents work very long hours without achieving the success their hard work deserves. Here are some of my hard learned lessons:
They do not have systems; they recreate the wheel each time.
They do not have goals and they do not keep themselves accountable.
They go in work cycles. When they are out of money, they work, when they have deals, it is holiday time. They have a feast or famine cycle.
They do not practice their art. They do not do role-playing.
They shoot from the hip instead of having clear conversations with buyers and sellers.
They do not work on a budget. They do not have financial statements. They have no idea how they are doing until the taxman tells them how much they owe.
They do not focus enough on quality service. They get the listing and forget about the listing client.
They do not implement a "Client for Life" program.

**What <u>single</u> quality has made you more successful than others?**

Having a business partner that keeps me accountable and keeps me focused. We keep each other motivated and real.

# CRAIG PROCTOR

RE/MAX OMEGA REALTY

NEWMARKET, ONTARIO

## Introduction

At the age of 25, Craig Proctor was working as a janitor at a local hospital making $14,000 a year. Three years later, at the age of 29, he was named the #1 RE/MAX agent in the world — the youngest ever to achieve this. Craig has been selling real estate for 20 years.

For the last several years, Craig has sold over 500 homes a year to earn him almost $4 million in annual GCI. He has been the #1 RE/MAX agent Worldwide several times, and has been in the Top 10 for RE/MAX Worldwide for 15 years.

What makes Craig's real estate system unique is that 100% of his clients contact him first — he has not made a cold call in 15 years. He doesn't do *any* cold call prospecting, and he works *less* than 40 hours a week.

Importantly, Craig has achieved dual success, both as a real estate agent and as a trainer. By making his system easy and inexpensive to duplicate, Craig has been able to share his success with others. In fact, over 18,000 agents from across North America are Craig Proctor system students and users, including hundreds of top agents. This makes Craig the ONLY real estate trainer who is actually DOING what he teaches. In recognition of this, Craig was selected by Dave Liniger (chairman and co-founder of RE/MAX) to be a trainer with the RE/MAX Coaching Hall of Fame.

## Background

**For how many years have you been in the real estate business?**

I've been in the business for 20 years.

**What is your personal background and how did you get into real estate?**

After high school, I went to college, but I really struggled there. Not because I couldn't do the work, but because it bored me. I had to ask myself why I was investing my time and energy into something that really didn't interest me. So I dropped out. This was the right decision, but it was a tough one because I really had no clue what I was going to do with my life. I needed some time to think.

So, the year before I got into real estate, I took a part-time job working at the local hospital slinging garbage and making $14,000 a year. Three years later I was making $1 million a year.

# Best Agent Business

My Dad has been in real estate agent for about 35 years, so it's natural that real estate was one of the careers I thought about.

He tried to discourage me from getting into the business at first though; he was well aware of the high failure rate of new agents. He wanted me to find success at something and he knew how tough the real estate business could be — he was trying to protect me from further failure. But, like many young people, I did the opposite of what my parents told me to do. After all, my Dad made it look easy. He had always earned a decent living from real estate. How hard could it be?

What I learned once I got into it, though, is that my Dad's success came in a different way than mine could. Back then, there were probably only 50 agents in town (now there are over 500). My Dad had built a solid reputation, and he knew many people. He never had to do any marketing. People called him and said, "Larry, come list my house."

It didn't work that way for me, of course. When I started, I was perplexed that people did not just call me. I had to start from scratch in a business that was getting tougher, not easier. I was told that the way to build a business was to cold call prospects, work the expired listings program, and hold open houses. That's how I started, and every agent knows exactly how grueling and demoralizing that is. It's because of this rocky start that I ultimately built the business I have.

**What lessons did you learn from your family, friends, previous jobs, and life experiences that helped you most to succeed in your career?**

My 15-year-old son and I have been talking about this lately. I believe that *all* experience is valuable experience – good and bad. Experience shapes you. It's because I had some really bad jobs that I could better appreciate what a good job was. The two courses I was most interested in at college were psychology and marketing, but the way they were taught was very dry. Once I started to build my business in real estate, it's these two disciplines that I kept returning to. Effective marketing is really the basis of my success.

**What do you enjoy most about the business?**

I enjoy the strategic part of building my business. As mentioned, I love marketing and grabbed onto that right away. It made so much sense to me and I found it easy to understand and extend. I didn't have any degrees or experience to draw on, but my fascination with the subject drove me to learn as I went.

I took courses from some of the great mentors (Jay Abraham, Dan Kennedy, etc.), and read voraciously. Some of the best books I read on the subject, that have really influenced me, are My Life in Advertising by Claude Hopkins, Tested Advertising Methods by John Caples, etc. But, it goes beyond book learning. I observe everything. Even the junk mail – instead of throwing it out, I look at it and ask, "What can I learn from this?

What's good about it and what isn't working?"

I used to do me-too marketing because I didn't know any better. Like every other agent, I thought the way to get people to call me was to broadcast my name and face. The most important thing I've learned is that just because people know who you are doesn't mean they'll call you. Instead, you must get inside the heads of your buyers and sellers to compel them to contact you, and the way to do this is to offer them something they want. My marketing is very different from what most agents do. Instead of promoting myself with empty image advertising, my ads are all direct response – they offer prospects something they want – something they have to contact me to get. I have completely set myself apart from my competitors with strong USPs (Unique Selling Propositions) and information offers. My prospects cold call me, and all inquiries go to either my website or an 800 telephone hotline.

There were other traditional ways of doing things that I realized simply didn't work that well – like Open Houses, for example. I innovated a "Tour of Homes", where we have 12 houses open for 15 minutes each which really qualifies the buyers. This is a highly successful program that generates high quality buyers and causes my listings to sell faster and for more money. I was also responsible for making performance guarantees more recognized in the real estate industry. This includes my Guaranteed Sale Program where I offer to buy a seller's house for cash if it doesn't sell within a set time period.

## Basic Numbers

### How many transactions did you close in 2005?

We did 547 transactions for almost $4 million in GCI last year. That's over $200 million in volume. My average price is about $375k.

### Are you a Billion Dollar Agent or do you believe you will hit that level during your career? Are you over a billion for career sales or what do you estimate?

In the past 20 years, I have sold over 5,000 homes, so I have surpassed a billion dollars in sales volume. I'm probably close to $2 billion.

### What is your current staffing, including yourself, of listing agents, buyer agents, managers, and assistants?

I think I was one of the first agents in Canada to have a team. I have ten licensed agents and three administrative people on my team; we're pretty lean and mean. We have a group of very productive agents who work with both buyers and listings. I no longer work with buyers and sellers. Instead, I focus my efforts on the marketing engine.

Two of the ten agents on the team are inside sales agents. Their job is to qualify the leads, and I believe I was the first agent to create this division of duties.

Most agents just give the leads to their agents, but having extensive experience on both ends, I realized these were really two distinct jobs suited to two different kinds of agent. The problem is, agents who are good at working face-to-face with buyers and sellers don't tend to be the kind who will sit on the phone and follow-up all the leads. I have two great agents who do nothing but incubate the literally hundreds of prospects we have in our pipeline until they're ready to act.

## Goals

**Do you believe goals are important to your success? If yes, describe your approach to goal setting for your business and life?**

I take a day off the first week of each year. I unplug the phone and complete what I call my "One-Hour Business Plan". In one hour I write down my big objectives, break them down and then work backwards. I call it a living document. We are continually fine-tuning it. We set a yearly goal and look at it every month.

What's key about this planning – and I teach agents the importance of this – is that your personal goals must also be set at this time. There are twenty things I want to accomplish this year from a personal standpoint. I will accomplish them because I have built them into the plan.

My training business is important because I'm helping other agents set goals for themselves and engineer change in their lives. My real estate business is my laboratory. By running a successful real estate business myself, I'm able to continually test new and better ways of doing things, such as delivering quality leads at the least possible cost. That's a very important part of things, but these days I'm most passionate about the training part of it. It is immensely gratifying. I rarely get a seller calling me to say I helped change their life.

But, I could tell you hundreds of stories of agents who have dramatically bettered their lives because of what they learned from me. My big goals are in that area.

## Marketing

### New Customer Marketing – Lead Generation – Prospecting

**What are your top five methods for new client lead generation and about what percentage of new customers are generated from that approach?**

Small classified ads are my number one lead generator. Most of the leads I generate are from $20-$30 classified ads. The copy on these ads is deceptively simple but highly effective at getting the hottest prospects to contact us. One example is our Distress Sales ad (which offers a list of distress sale homes and bank foreclosures).

We convert about 10% of these prospects. Eight out of ten of these will sign a buyer contract with us and 60% will ultimately buy.

We send out 20,000 postcards or flyers every week. One side targets sellers (with an online home evaluation); the other side targets buyers by offering them priority online access to homes that match their criteria. These are very effective.

I have many other pillars to my lead generation such as: the Sunday Tour I mentioned earlier, my Unique Selling Proposition or Performance Guarantee ads, Web Display ads, and much more. But truthfully, I generate more than enough leads, just from the first two vehicles I mentioned. I invest about 12.5% of GCI back into marketing.

## Client Marketing – Repeats/Referrals

### About how many past clients have you worked with?

Farming past clients isn't an active strategy in my business because we simply don't have a problem generating hot leads. That being said, I've worked with over 5,000 clients in my career. When one of my past clients moves a second or third time, we usually get the business because my system generates such great results.

### What percentage of your business is referral?

Probably about 20% overall. Again, we find it so easy to generate leads that we don't have to rely on referrals the way some agents do.

## Growth of Business

### What single quality has made you more successful than others?

Persistence.

### What does the average real estate agent fail to do which are among the reasons why they are average?

I think there are three key reasons many agents don't achieve the success they could.

The biggest reason is that most agents don't have an effective lead generation system, and this is probably the biggest reason why 80% of agents do not make it through the first 5 years. I think many agents are good at working with buyers and sellers, but they fail because they don't have enough clients to work with.

You can be the best agent in the world, but if you don't have any clients to sell to, you'll starve.

Second, they fail to differentiate themselves. They don't give their prospects any "real" reasons to choose them over their many competitors.

Third, they don't treat Real Estate like a business. Most people who get into real estate, do so because they are good at the technical aspects. The problem with this is that — the only way they can build their volume is on their own backs. It winds up breaking them. I would estimate that only 5% of real estate agents are really running a business.

## Delegation and Leverage - Assistants

**We see a challenge of people right at point of needing to delegate and outsource and hire their first part-time assistant to leverage their time. What percentage of agents do you think are in that zone and why do they fail to take the next step? What would be benefit for them to take that step?**

I take an entire day at our SuperConference to discuss the important subject of leveraging yourself with people. I help agents calculate what they are worth per hour. The guy who makes $100,000 per year trades 2,000 hours of his life for $50/hour. Most of them never think of it in these terms. I get them to think about their typical day. I have them write down a list of what they do all day long. Then I have them make another list to the right where I have them specify how much it would cost to replace themselves for each of the tasks in the left column. What they discover is that about 70% of the things on the list could easily be done by an assistant making $20/hour.

I help them understand that what they really need to be in their businesses is the Rainmaker. I awaken them to this important concept. Rainmaker activities are those activities that make the change and growth happen in your business – they're the activities you couldn't hire a $20/hr assistant to do, because by doing these activities yourself, you can change the outcome in a way someone else couldn't. You have to draw the line in the sand and say: "If I cannot change the outcome, then I should not be involved in that activity". Banging in a For Sale sign, putting on a lock box, printing off a feature sheet – these are activities that are certainly NOT Rainmaker activities.

An agent will not change the outcome of a sale by wasting his or her time on activities like these that could easily be done just as well by someone else. You need to stop doing the $20/hour work because it takes your time from the things that truly will cause your business to grow and flourish.

# RUSSELL RHODES

## Introduction

Russell Rhodes is a licensed real estate consultant. He is a 1986 graduate from TCU where he received a BBA, with a concentration in Finance. He and his wife, Mandy, married in 1990 and have three sons. They live in a suburb of Dallas.

## Background

**For how many years have you been in the real estate business?**

I got my real estate license in 2000 and created a partnership with my family in 2001. My family has been in the real estate industry since 1981. We had lived in five states by the time my oldest son turned five years old. My wife got tired of the whole corporate moving environment and she strongly encouraged me to start a business back in Dallas to re-establish our roots.

**What lessons did you learn from your family, friends, previous jobs, and life experiences that helped you most to succeed in your career?**

The most important lesson that I have learned is to track sales, expenses and leads on a weekly, monthly, and annual basis. It was absolutely paramount in the apparel industry, and if you do not watch the market trends, and your competition closely, you could easily go bankrupt within six to nine months.

Another lesson learned was not to be a penny-wise and a pound foolish when compensating your employees. It is very important to pay them a little over market to ensure that you retain viable members of your team.

**What do you enjoy most about the business?**

The challenge of growing the business. I enjoy identifying the opportunity and developing the strategy to achieve our goals.

## Basic Numbers

**How many transactions did you close in 2005?**

Last year we sold 243 homes and approximately $65 million in real estate. In 2005 our average sales price was $275,000.

**Are you a Billion Dollar Agent or do you believe you will hit that level during your career? Are you over a billion for career sales or what do you estimate?**

We have sold approximately $650-$750 million. We should exceed the billion dollar in real estate sold plateau by 2009.

**What is your current staffing, including yourself, of listing agents, buyer agents, managers, and assistants?**

We have five administrative people, one inside sales agent and six buyer's agents. My primary focus is going on listing appointments and managing the overall business.

## Goals

**Do you believe goals are important to your success? If yes, describe your approach to goal setting for your business and life?**

Yes. I absolutely feel that setting high but achievable goals is paramount to growing your business. On a daily basis, I review the Keller Williams web site that reveals the top 100 agents within Keller Williams. I need to look beyond my own little part of the world to enable me to see the possibilities with the proper systems and personnel.

We have an internal goal of a minimum of 20% growth per year. We have exceeded 30% growth five of the last six years.

## New Customer Marketing – Lead Generation- Prospecting

**What are your five top methods for new client lead generation and about what percentage of new customers are generated from that approach?**

Geographical farming has become an instrumental component to our lead generation. We attribute approximately 70 transactions per year to geographical farming. We have now expanded our geographical farming from one subdivision of 2,500 homes to 10,000 homes. We dominate our geographical farm by selling approximately 20% of all homes in the area. What we are using to accomplish this is a custom newspaper; a monthly newsletter of market conditions in the specific geographic farm area, and by sending out Just Listed and Just Sold cards.

**What client marketing activities do you do with past clients?**

Approximately sixty-five percent of our business is derived from past and current clients and our sphere. We are extremely hands-on. I want to be the Nordstroms/Ritz Carlton of Real Estate. I set up a Client Appreciation Program where the whole concept is how to create the law of reciprocity.

**What are all the things that people only need once to three times a year and does not make sense to buy?**

We have separated our Client Appreciation Program into three categories: entertainment, household and moving. Examples of items in our entertainment section are: a margarita machine, bounce houses, etc. Household includes: air compressor, air guns, power washers, 24 foot extension ladders to reach high lights, post hole tools, etc. In moving we have: a pick-up truck, a 16' moving van, the dolly and blankets. I have spent approximately $45,000 so far over two years, and have allocated approximately $20,000 in new items to be added to our Client Appreciation Program every year.

We have coined the phrase: "All of my stuff is yours for life." The margarita machine is so popular that we are about to have to buy a second machine and even possibly a third due to the incredibly high use. My Client Appreciation Program has been an unbelievable success to help me strengthen my relationship with my clients.

## Growth of Business

**What single quality has made you more successful than others?**

The sales approach that I follow is one which is more of a consultant than as a "sales person." I personally do not enjoy working with sales personnel who are pushy. I prefer to work with someone who gives me the facts and allows me to make the decision when I'm ready to buy. This is the same philosophy that our team has implemented and has resulted in phenomenal retention and referral based business.

## Delegation and Leverage - Assistants

**We see a challenge of people right at point of needing to delegate and outsource and hire their first part-time assistant to leverage their time. What percentage of agents do you think are in that zone and why do they fail to take the next step? What would they benefit for them to take that step?**

I had a wife and two small children when I entered the real estate industry and came from a corporate background where I was making several hundred thousand dollars a year. I had no choice but to find a way to quickly duplicate my previous salary or I would have to go back to work for a large corporation. The only way that I could see to duplicate my previous salary quickly was to invest in leverage immediately, so that I could spend the majority of my time working with clients and prospecting. I hired an assistant in the first three weeks when I only had one customer at the time.

You would not believe it, but this approach gave me leverage and allowed me to accelerate my business. Anyone who is serious about catapulting their business should consider capturing leverage, through an administrative assistant, if in a financial position to do so.

# MICHELLE RIZZO

## Background

**For how many years have you been in the real estate business?**

I have been in the business for 22 years.

**What is your personal background and how did you get into real estate?**

I was corporate person in customer service. I had one semester of college. I was a mom; I had a new baby. I didn't want to be doing daycare only. I wanted flexibility of real estate.

**What lessons did you learn from your family, friends, previous jobs, and life experiences that helped you most to succeed in your career?**

I learned what drive is. I was told I had drive as a kid. I played sports. I practiced judo. I think that the habits and perserverence I developed with Judo taught me to excel. I had a great dad who believed in me, and a mother who probably thought I never did anything right. I wanted the flexibility.

**What do you enjoy most about the business?**

I still sell, but I am a partner in three offices. I love coaching my agents and helping people do better at what they are doing. The money is awesome. I do not think I could make this money anywhere else.

There are times when you make a difference in someone's life. Moving is a stressful time. You are dealing with divorce, death, and job changes. It is good to do a good job and make their lives easier.

## Basic Numbers

**How many transactions did you close in 2005?**

I think I did 34 transactions, about $12 million in sales.

**Are you a Billion Dollar Agent or do you believe you will hit that level during your career? Are you over a billion for career sales or what do you estimate?**

I am probably up to $100 million. The one year I coached with Floyd Wickman, I did $16 million, and I did 55 transactions. My best year was when Floyd was coaching me.

**What is your current staffing including: yourself, listing agents, buyer agents, managers, and assistants?**

My staffing is two assistants and one buyer's agent. I have a listing transaction coordinator and a selling transaction coordinator. I've structured the compensation for the buyer agent to be hourly with a bonus.

## Goals

**Do you believe goals are important to your success? If yes, describe your approach to goal setting for your business and life?**

Anytime I see my production floundering, I realize I do not really have a goal or my goal is not important to me. There are usually a few things that I want. I wanted to take my family to Hawaii one year, and to hit $300,000 in commissions. It has to be something that really turns me on. I am a Mom of three, and my kids are everything for me. It has to be something I like but often has to do with somebody else. My goal for next year is that I want to buy a house at the beach.

## Marketing

### New Customer Marketing – Lead Generation – Prospecting

**What are your top 5 methods for new client lead generation and about what percentage of new customers are generated from that approach?**

I have had a billboard on a main drag for the last three years. My kids go to private schools and I sponsor the school folders and work a lot with the school families.

I do Expireds. I mail out a "SOLD" flyer to Expireds and have my most recent sales with percentage of sales price and how quickly they sold. I mail to them the day that they expire. Within a day we mail to them. I mail a letter " Sometimes even the best properties don't sell" on the second day. If I can call them, I do. Out of 100 mailed to maybe 1 will call me. I then probably list 8 out of 10.

I do print advertising for my listings. I have a lot of referral business from Realtors all over the country. I keep in touch with lots of those people.

## Client Marketing – Repeats/Referrals

**Of your prior clients, about how many do you have in current database?**

I mail out to about 330 a month. Those are the ones I kept track of. They get a newsletter once a month. It is a personal letter from me and does not say much about real estate. It is a letter from me about the family and me. Everyone knows my kids. My daughter is a competitive gymnast. I put a picture of the kids almost every month. Someone in the office puts it together.

**What client marketing activities do you do with prior clients?**

I try to reach out to them sporadically. I get a lot of referral business from them. I would love to do client parties in the future. I estimate 60% of business is repeat/referral. If you do a great job, they know they can refer you and you will take care of that person.

## Growth of Business

**What single quality has made you more successful than others?**

Doing what I say I will do. I put my money where my mouth is. If I say I will call you, I will call you. Do what you say you will do. My word is more important than my signature any day.

**What does the average real estate agent fail to do which are among the reasons why they are average?**

We have 42 agents in our offices.
They fail to prospect.
They spend too much time doing paperwork.
They fail to plan.
They fail to have goals.
They fail to know their numbers.
They fail to work.
They fail to follow-up.
They fail to be skillful.

**Did you make any big mistakes that you want to warn others about?**

It is always a balance of my priorities. I have three children and I am a single mom twice. It is important to focus on my kids first. You can focus on being a millionaire and meanwhile your kids may become dysfunctional. It is a struggle all the time to balance my priorities.

I am a mom to my clients, my agents, and my kids. I am trying to set an example and do the right thing. You need to be a mom to your clients half the time. The business can suck you right in so you cannot be taking care of what you need to take care of at home. And then you are reacting to major issues.

**What would you have done differently if you could begin your career again to speed the process of getting to your current level of business?**

Get better quicker. Being at RE/MAX was big because it is more business-oriented real estate company. Joining the right company and acquiring the right skills helps to elevate you. Being around better agents helps too. I have taken Floyd's program eleven times. I get better each time I go through it.

## Building a Team

**How did you first start to delegate and outsource and build a team?**

Desperation. We are control freaks. You do not think anyone can do it as well as you can. Out of time constraints, I needed help. Sometimes I just have to delegate. I could pay someone to do something for $15-20/hour and go out and sell a house and make $8,000 commission. I need to be out talking with people, either listing and selling or negotiating. Anything other than that should be delegated. I have gotten good at the stack which is a bin I through stuff in all the time and my assistant handles everything in the stack.

I have two assistants and probably still spend 50% of my time doing assistant level work. It is a control thing with me.

**In what order did you add your first part-time and full-time staff?**

Assistants – Marketing,
Listing Management,
Transaction Closing Coordination
Buyer Agent,
Listing Agent.

**If you had to do it again, today, from a starting point of making $100,000 per year, what would you suggest for delegating, outsourcing and staffing?**

Business Management and Systems

**What are the top 3 recommendations you would make for a skilled agent who has been in the business 3-5 years and is making $100,000 and wants to double to $200,000?**

Delegation and Leverage - Assistants

**We see a challenge of people right at point of needing to delegate and outsource and hire their first part-time assistant to leverage their time. What percentage of agents do you think are in that zone and why do they fail to take the next step? What would be benefit for them to take that step?**

I would say out of 42 agents of them only 5-6 of them have assistants and almost 30-40 of them should have a part-time assistant. Even a few hours a week would help.I think one thing is control. You think you have to do all that. Sometimes it is a commitment to pay someone else's salary. You also have to step back and know what you can delegate.
You can't go to the next level until you do that and get an assistant.
In addition, it makes you look so efficient. My clients think I am so organized and it makes me look so good to my clients.

# Joe Rothchild

## Introduction

Joe Rothchild, who is the owner/broker and managing partner at RE/MAX Fry Road, recorded $470,000,000 in sales volume in 2005 with 2,680 closed transactions in that year.

Joe's numbers in 2005 were $148,996,546 in gross dollar volume in closed sales, and 916 closed transactions.

In 2005, Joe Rothchild was able to boast "Over one Billion Sold" in the Houston real estate market as he reached this new pinnacle. This is quite an achievement from his early years of helping people out of apartments and into their first home. Mr. Rothchild has achieved virtually every award that RE/MAX offers to agents and brokers, both nationally and internationally. He was #1 worldwide with RE/MAX, three years in a row, who boasts over 100,000 other RE/MAX agents. His other RE/MAX awards include the Platinum Club, Chairman's Club, Hall of Fame, Circle of Legends, and more. He is very proud of his accomplishment of being #1 nine years in a row through the Houston Business Journal who recognizes all Realtors in the Houston area and statewide.

## Background

**What is your background and how did you get into real estate?**

I began in real estate in my early twenties in 1980 with my first land sale. Then I started an apartment locator service in Houston, called A-1 Apartment Locators, which I still own today. This launched my career into the industry.

**What about your background, lessons from your family, friends, and previous jobs helped you succeed in your career?**

My father owned a home improvement company and I accompanied him to many of his "cold calling" appointments. That began as early as age 14. He spawned the hard working, long hours, entrepreneurial spirit, that I will carry with me for the rest of my life. My mom gave me my compassion and consideration for others.

**What do you enjoy most about the business?**

I enjoy helping people and knowing that I make a difference in their lives. I aid them in making good decisions that have an impact on their dream of home ownership and help them accomplish their real estate goals.

## Goals

## Do you set written goals for your business and life?

I find it difficult to set written goals in this business. With the nature of this business, it is ever changing from year to year. For me, I set mental goals and work diligently throughout the years to try to achieve them. With them being mental, my goals can and do vary daily depending on the opportunities presented to me. I feel you need to be somewhat flexible to change yet must stay focused on long and short goals.

## What are your primary methods of lead generation for new customers?

The Internet is beginning to far surpass all other advertising I had been doing in the past. Computers are definitely having an impact on the scope of the real estate business. I am spending more of my marketing dollars on Internet advertising and far less on print media and it's proving to be very effective thus far.

## If you had to teach only three lessons about marketing, what would you tell someone who is at 100k and wants to get to 200K?

First, you need to spend more money. The more advertising you do, the more recognized you become. Second, you should advertise just as much, if not more, in the slower months than in the stronger months. By spending more in the slower months, you may bring just one more buyer or seller in for you to help. Many Realtors miss the opportunity of planting seeds for future business this way. Third, always try a new marketing technique for at least a year. Consistency in marketing is critical to success.

## What percentage of your business is referral?

Our business is approximately 75-80% right now. I would like to see and increase to 90% in the upcoming years.

## What were your mot effective ways of generating consistent referrals from you existing clients and past clients?

Communication is the key. It can be done in so many ways and I try to cover them all. Staying visible is vital. Send a letter or an e-mail or pick up the phone and visit for even a few minutes.

## How do you track leads and what makes them a qualified lead?

Every call and e-mail is tracked. I leave the actual qualification process to the outstanding agents on my team. They have been extensively trained to immediately act on all leads, and schedule appointments for the potential client to begin their search for their next home or list an existing home.

## Do you think there is much of a difference in sales skills of a billion dollar agent versus someone who is making 100-200k?

I do not think there is a huge difference. I honestly explain, to the people I see, our approach to doing business with them.

Most people like and appreciate my frankness and directness. I explain to them, "Here is what I can do for you, and here is what I cannot do." If the fit is not right for both of us, I refer them elsewhere. I believe setting expectations properly up front is critical.

**What is your ratio of listings versus buyers and how has that changed over the years?**

I concentrate on the listing side which, for me, is a much more efficient use of my time. My ratio is 80% listings and 20% buyers. We maintain a listing inventory of 200-250 houses. We sell about 1,000 per year with a staff of 17 people.

**What is your closing ratio of qualified leads for listing proposals?**

Our closing ratio is approximately 80%. My best suggestion for agents is to tie into a national affiliation and leverage that marketing value. The general public recognizes brands like RE/MAX and if you can tie yourself to a national franchise you will gain instant creditability and recognition. People love "name brand" identification.

**Beyond the basics, are you involved with any specialized niche markets that are part of your success and more than 10% of your business?**

Not really! Our business encompasses first-time buyers and clients who are selling the first home and are now looking to move to a larger home because of the growth of their families. We also cover the empty nesters looking to downsize. We follow our clients from beginning to end.

**What are the top unique things that you do in your business that distinguishes you from other agents in you market?**

The marketing I do far surpasses any other agent in our area. We like to stand out where people start out.

## Growth of Business

**What one thing would you tell a beginning agent to pursue to achieve success?**

Don't just work hard, but work smart. Make everything you do count toward your goals.

**As you grew your business, what were your biggest difficulties?**

Because I am such a perfectionist, it's been difficult for me to let go of things to my employees. I have set the bar very high for myself and I expect them to reach for the same bar.

My next challenge was to stop worrying about what other people thought of me. You can please most of the people most of the time; but I am a business person. You cannot please all the people all the time.

**What were the biggest mistakes that you made that you would warn others about?**

Be meticulous with your paperwork. Make sure you dot your I's and cross your T's to minimize litigation issues. Do not do sloppy paperwork. This is critical to being successful.

**What would you have done differently if you could begin your career again?**

I would have advertised more and hired my assistant much sooner. It is difficult to grow your business when you are the only one doing the work. The best thing I was told was, "If you ever find yourself doing $5/hour work, you're doing something wrong."

**What are the top three recommendations you would make for a skilled agent who has been in the business for 3-5 years and is making $100,000 and wants to double to $200,000?**

First, increase our marketing dollars. Second, hire an assistant and delegate the work and concentrate on growth. Third, be consistent and follow through on all promises made.

# Brad Rozansky

Long & Foster

Bethesda, MD

## Introduction

With 30 years of experience, Brad Rozansky is the #1 agent in the #1 Long & Foster office, and has been since 1992. He has total sales volume in excess of $1,000,000,000. He is ranked in the top 1/4% real estate agents nationwide and has sold over 600 homes in the last three years.

## Background

**For how many years have you been in the real estate business?**

I have been in real estate since 1977.

**What is your personal background and how did you get into real estate?**

I was a house painter when I was young, but developed an allergy to the paint, so that didn't work so well. I had a friend who was in real estate, which sounded like fun so I thought I would try it. Lucky for me, I was good at it!

**What lessons did you learn from your family, friends, previous jobs, and life experiences that helped you most to succeed in your career?**

I think what motivated me was that I came from a family where both parents owned their own business. I was continually being educated in the business through seminars. I sat in on several Mike Ferry and Floyd Wickman seminars. In 1980, at the age of twenty-three, I started my own real estate company. Twelve years later, we had thirty agents. I ended up selling it to Long and Foster in 1992. Then, I joined the company then.

**What do you enjoy most about the business?**

Honestly, at this stage, much of the enjoyment comes from the satisfaction of winning. I pride myself on giving the best service I can. I probably go on about 75 listing appointments a year and I "win" about 70% them. Moreover, I enjoy working with nice people. I try to only surround myself with motivated and enthusiastic professionals, and avoid working with people who are difficult. I love working with my team everyday. We have a lot of fun.

## Basic Numbers

### How many transactions did you close in 2005?

We closed about 125 transactions in 2005, adding up to about $52 million. This year we will do over 200 transactions and about $85 million. 2006 will be our record year in volume. Our record year of transactions was 232 deals.

### Are you a Billion Dollar Agent or do you believe you will hit that level during your career? Are you over a billion for career sales or what do you estimate?

I have done many project sales and listings of whole communities, which have brought my total sales to over $1 billion.

### What is your current staffing, including yourself, of listing agents, buyer agents, managers, and assistants?

I have two buyer agents, two administrative staff, and my wife does the books. Everyone here is cross-trained. I believe that everyone should know everything that is going on, including me. If someone were out of the office everyone else would be able to cover. I have one person whose job is to manage me. I am doing a million things at one time, which make it impossible for me to keep track of everything I have to do. The other part of my administrative staff works with foreclosure listings, in which we have recently seen a huge increase. My two buyer agents are working hard on increasing their clientele. I have placed a huge emphasis on growing our business by the end of the year.

## Goals

### Do you believe goals are important to your success? If yes, describe your approach to goal setting for your business and life?

Goals are very important at our level; I am unsure how we would have gotten here without any goals. The goal can be as simple as numbers of listings, transactions, volume, etc. A good idea is to put your business plan on audio and listen to it every day.

Most importantly, you need to share your plan with everyone in your staff, and make them a part of it to succeed.

## Marketing

### New Customer Marketing – Lead Generation – Prospecting

What are your top 5 methods for new client lead generation and about what percentage of new customers are generated from that approach?
1) We get many referrals from local people who know us because I grew up here. I am a local boy.

2) We also do sales postcards to nearby zip codes.

\3) We just spent a good deal of money on a 12-page pamphlet printed by the company who produces the Long & Foster Extraordinary Properties Magazine. It recently hit the market and we have received a great deal of positive feedback. We place ads in Washingtonian magazine.

4) Overall, we spend very little on marketing, maybe 3%.

## Client Marketing – Repeats/Referrals

### What percentage of your business is referral?

Probably 30-40% of our business is repeat referral. I often feel that we don't spend enough time and effort on keeping touch with old clients; we are too busy going on to the next one. If you analyzed how much you lose each year because of lost clients, it is hundreds of thousands of dollars, so one of our goals this year is to do a better job here.

Our mindset is always on the new business and on the current transactions. You move so fast, when do you have time to think?

### What client marketing activities do you do with prior clients?

We try to keep in touch with our most valued clients by sending postcards and holiday cards. We also call or send e-mails periodically to keep in touch and make sure everything is well.

## Specialized Markets and Approach

### Are you involved with any special niche markets, which is more than 10% of your business and part of your success?

I am unique because I will work any market. I recently took a $250,000 listing but I will also have an apartment building or a home listed for over $3 million. I want my business to be recession proof.

## Growth of Business

### What single quality has made you more successful than others?

Me. I want to have a good time doing this. What they see is what they get. If they do not like what they see, they will not hire me. My ego is checked at the door. Just because I sell a house does not mean I do something great in my life.

### What does the average real estate agent fail to do which are among the reasons why they are average?

They fail to get sales training; there needs to be some sort of education in your background to be successful.

They fail to come to the office and treat this as a 9 to 5 business.

They do not have goals.

They do not have a business plan.

They have a lack of understanding of market.

They do not know how to talk to clients.

They are afraid to ask the important questions to a client, or ask for a price reduction.

**Did you make any big mistakes that you want to warn others about?**

I don't care how long you have been in the business; you will always be making mistakes. I had been working on a potential listing for 10 years and something happened. The trustee, whom I became friends with, saw it as a problem; and he decided not to give me the listing. The lesson I learned was not to negotiate a deal before you have the deal.

**What would you have done differently if you could begin your career again to speed the process of getting to your current level of business?**

It always comes down to the basics, which is getting listings. The person who controls the inventory makes the money. In this slower market, you need 20 to 25 listings and then you will make more money today than in a good market. The attitude of most agents is they don't want listings in this market because they are not selling. What motivates me to do well is that ... I can't go home and look my family in the eye and say we can't go to a movie.

## Building a Team

**How did you first start to delegate and outsource and build a team?**

I knew when I left my own company that I needed an assistant. So, I looked for one when I joined Long & Foster. I have had both good and bad assistants. A person should get an assistant when they are doing about $5 million or 20 deals. The assistant should be good for another $5 million in business.

# RON RUSH

## Introduction

Ron Rush has been with Long & Foster Realtors since 1979. In 2005, Ron sold over $296 Million in residential real estate. Ron closed 526 transactions. Ron has sold over $1.5 Billion in residential sales and closed over 6000 transactions.

Ron, the #1 agent in Virginia, provides clients with unparalleled Real Estate sales experience. Ron's knowledge of the Real Estate market and expertise in finance and contract negotiations enable him to close more transactions than any other agent. Ron's commitment to excellence and tireless effort on the client's behalf makes him a driving force in today's fast-paced Real Estate industry.

Called, **The Hot-Handed Realtor** by the Washington Post, Ron oversees each transaction from beginning to end with a unique style and flair that makes him #1.

• #5 Nationally (Realtor Magazine 2003)
• Licensed Realtor - 39 years
• Over $1.5 Billion in lifetime sales with over 6000 closed transactions
• Long & Foster's #1 VA Agent and Top Producer for 13 years
• $296 Million sold in 2005 with 526 closed transactions

## Background

**For how many years have you been in the real estate business?**

I have been in the business for 39 years.

**What is your personal background and how did you get into real estate?**

I graduated High School in 1956 and worked various part-time jobs. I attended the University of Pittsburgh for four years. After graduation, I worked for Union Railroad Company in Pittsburgh, PA while attending Duquesne University for my MBA. I entered the US Air Force in 1962. While stationed in Dayton, Ohio, a local broker asked me to get a Real Estate license. As a result, I sold Real Estate part-time; at that time the average sale price of a home was about $12,000. I came to the Washington DC area in 1971 and continued to sell Real Estate part-time in Virginia. In 1981, I retired from the Air Force and became full-time in Real Estate. I started my employment with Long & Foster in 1979.

**What lessons did you learn from your family, friends, previous jobs, and life experiences that helped you most to succeed in your career?**

The Air Force gave me my biggest strength — organization. I was a Branch Chief in the Air Force. With that, I learned delegation and organizational skills that allowed me to insure each staff member was capable of doing several jobs. In 1981, when I became a full-time real estate agent, I did not have the staff I currently have. My daughter Darlene helped me part-time; my youngest son, Michael, graduated in 1986 from high school and, after graduation, began working for me. My son-in-law, Wil Bell was active duty Air Force and decided to leave the Air Force to join me in Real Estate full-time. He is very technical and is my computer support expert. My other son, Jeffrey, was married and a physical education teacher for an elementary school in northern Virginia. In 1995 he decided to join the growing team full-time as an agent. He is also my office manager.

I never get tired. I wake up every morning knowing that I will meet a handful of new people and make lasting business and personal relationships that day. People know me; I am almost like an institution in this area. Being well known in this area is great for referrals and repeat business.

**What do you enjoy most about the business?**

My desire to win is what I enjoy most about this business. I went to the University of Pittsburgh on a full track scholarship and enjoyed winning. In Real Estate, I love to win for my sellers and buyers. I like facilitating a deal no one else has achieved. It's exciting to me to make things happen; also, to be part of such an important process and transaction in my clients' lives.

## Basic Numbers

**How many transactions did you close in 2005?**

In 2005, we did 526 transactions totaling $296 Million. In my career, we have done over $1.5 billion and about 6,000 transactions.

**What is your current staffing, including yourself, of listing agents, buyer agents, managers, and assistants?**

We have about 15 total staff members, ten of which are licensed agents. The remainder being office staff and administrative staff. All licensed agents can both list and sell. My son Jeff is my office manager.

## Goals

**Do you believe goals are important to your success? If yes, describe your approach to goal setting for your business and life?**

When I first started in the real estate business, I wanted to do the most I could and do it better than any one else. I did set goals and tried to exceed the goals of the previous year. I took a break from the sales side of real estate in 1990 and 1991 and hired a promoter.

I published some Real Estate books and tapes and went around the country speaking at seminars. My sales volume suffered quite a bit since, actually, I was not selling real estate. When I returned to sales, I started mailing 60,000 direct mail advertising pieces a month and became known as the direct mail king of the United States. I quickly reclaimed my #1 position with Long and Foster.

In the 1990's the real estate industry slowed down significantly and I stopped setting goals and focused more on the bottom-line.

# New Customer Marketing – Lead Generation – Prospecting

**What are your top five methods for new client lead generation and about what percentage of new customers are generated from that approach?**

We have a home sell hotline system; it is a call-capture system. We use a local vendor to document a caller's information and we receive that information within 24 hours of a call. This generates about 5-10% of ourbuyers. The conversion rate is approximately one out of 25. It is a wonderful listing tool. Also, our listing signage is very successful. We have a unique and recognizable way of placing the listing signage. I reverse the signage to expose the brochure box to passer-bys along the street with the home sell hotline number on the top of the signage for maximum exposure. Our Internet ads and our website have provided phenomenal leads. Approximately 10% of our business is generated from the Internet. Print advertising still proves to be a great lead generator. We have a large control of our farm area. We live and operate in a development called South Riding. We control a large share of that market. We sold 150 homes in that subdivision in 2005. That accounts for approximately 30-35% of that market share. There are approximately 5,500 homes in South Riding. The biggest part of our marketing and lead generation comes from having our Long & Foster office centrally located in that subdivision; it provides us with maximum exposure. The front door says "Home of the Ron Rush Team".

**What marketing advice would you give to someone at $100,000 who wants to get to $200,000 and more?**

Get an assistant immediately. Don't put this off because you don't have it in the budget. If necessary, borrow the money to afford an assistant who will support and emulate your values and work ethic. Your business will expand rapidly.

My best advice would be time management and accessibility to clients. Spend as much time with buyers and sellers. A perfect deal takes 2-3 hours of my time. Always go to your closings; do not have someone go in your place. This is the perfect opportunity to thank your clients for their business and present them with a small token of your appreciation.

I give my clients a leather portfolio with a calculator and my contact information. This is another way to promote your referral business by name recognition.

## Client Marketing – Repeats/Referrals

**About how many past clients have you worked with and of those about how many do you have in current database?**

We have about 2,000 clients in my current database. My database core is made up of approximately 250 clients. We maintain constant contact with them because they are responsible for about 50 % of the referrals.

**What percentage of your business is referral?**

Our business is about 10-20% repeat or referral.

**What client marketing activities do you do with past clients?**

We send out a Ron Rush calendar every year. We have a very detailed follow-up system; we use Long & Foster's business services department and send out contact/follow-up cards a few times a year to touch base with my clients. I carry a Rolodex in my car of all my past clients that I have worked with. If I am in an area and I remember I sold a house in that area, I may check my Rolodex and call the client associated with the area just to touch base.

## Growth of Business

**What single quality has made you more successful than others?**

I possess an innate desire to succeed. When I was a child, my Mother said I was always interested in making money. When I was 5-6 years old, I rode my bike to the store for my Mom. I would ask friends and neighbors if they wanted something from the store and would charge five cents to pick up groceries for them!

**Did you make any big mistakes that you want to warn others about?**

I did not focus on any one specific area when I started selling real estate. I tried to do too much, too fast. I ultimately spread myself too thin. It did not provide me with expertise in specific areas. I should have concentrated on one area and had more focus. When I was focused, I did better. When you drop pebbles in a pond it creates a circle and the circle grows wider. Earlier in my career, I should have picked a subdivision or farm and become an expert in that area. A lesson I learned later in my career. I now make notes every night. I write down everything I need to do to cultivate my business the next day in order to bring it to its fullest potential and make the most money I can. I make certain my employees know how much I value and appreciate them. I make sure to treat people fairly, as if they were apart of my family. To me, they are my family.

# JEFF SCISLOW

## Introduction

Jeff Scislow CRS, is a seven-time top RE/MAX Associate for Minnesota and a RE/MAX Hall of Fame, Lifetime Achievement, Circle of Legends award-recipient. He has sold over 2300 homes during his 20-year career. In 2005 Jeff closed over $35 million in sales and by August 2006 he had already closed over 200 transactions worth over $46 million in volume. In 1986 he was rookie of the year, selling 58 homes. In 1990 he was a pioneer when he hired an agent to specifically show homes for him; the buyer agent concept has grown in popularity ever since. In 1995 Jeff was the first individual Realtor® in Minnesota to have a personal website www.Scislow.com.

Through his www.Minnesota2Florida.com website, advertising and local seminars, Jeff continues to sell large volumes of investment real estate in Florida and other key markets in the USA. Today, using the franchising concept, Jeff is setting up other "investment-minded" real estate agents in their respective marketplaces around the country through his websites www.America2Florida.com and www.Europe2Florida.com. Jeff supplies these agents with all the tools they need to sell an extra 100 properties per year.

## Background

**How many years have you been in the real estate business?**

I have been in the business for 20 years.

**What is your personal background and how did you get into real estate?**

After high school I joined the Marine Corps for a four-year tour and was guaranteed training in the computer field. While I was in the Marine Corps, I developed an interest in real estate as an investor. I started to read books about how to wake up the financial genius inside of you. I got out of the service and stayed in the computer field for seven more years before becoming a real estate sales agent. I set a goal in my first year to become the rookie of the year with the large brokerage firm I had joined. I remember asking the president of the firm what it would take to become rookie of the year and to set a new sales record as a rookie. He said if I earned about $35,000 I'd likely be rookie of the year (based on what other rookies had accomplished over the years). I said, "Great, my goal is to earn $50,000!" He chuckled at my lofty determination and said, "Good luck." Those 58 home sales not only earned Jeff the rookie of the year, but also rewarded him with $75,000 in commission income.

**What lessons did you learn from your family, friends, previous jobs, and life experiences that helped you most to succeed in your career?**

In my life, I have developed the confidence that I can do anything I put my mind to. I believe that was instilled in me by my parents and at a young age. I was very inquisitive too, always wanting to understand the "cause and effect" relationship. I learned that hard work and a well thought out plan would bring results – every time. I recall a couple of times when my mother questioned my ability to accomplish certain "tasks". My tenacity and determination and the desire to "show them" I could do it fueled my accomplishing the very things I had put my mind to. Mom often tells the story even today, of how she will never doubt anything Jeff says he can do. If someone says I cannot do something that always inspires me even more to demonstrate that I can.

**What do you enjoy most about the business?**

Helping people accomplish their goals is really rewarding. It could be getting into their first home, getting their home sold or helping investors wisely purchase investment property. I like to impart my skill and guidance into their life and for them to be positively affected. I always feel good when my clients appreciate what I do for them. I love getting "results" for others.

## Basic Numbers

**How many transactions did you close in 2005?**

Through August 2006 I have closed over 200. My average price is just under $250,000 and my volume is a little over $46 million. I have averaged 113 transactions per year in my 20-year career, with 58 being the smallest number of annual sales (my 1st year).

**Are you a Billion Dollar Agent or do you believe you will hit that level during your career?**

I am already well on my way based on "one-sale-at-a-time-type-selling". With my new way of selling (volume sales) and helping investors nationally to purchase investment real estate, I believe I will hit the billion-dollar mark in just a few short years!

**What is your current staffing including: yourself, listing agents, buyer agents, managers, and assistants?**

My wife is the CFO, I am the CEO, and my nephew is my technology manager. I have a property manager and a courier. I do all the selling. I have had "sales teams" of "buyer agents" in the past, but at this point I choose to sell on my own. This year (as of August) I have already topped my previous best gross commission income (GCI) annual figure. My previous best was in 1998 with three buyer agents.

That year we all totaled 223 transactions with a volume of $34 million. Today I focus not only on selling homes locally in my Twin Cities marketplace, but also in the Florida marketplace. I conduct investment seminars and do considerable Internet-based marketing of investment property in Florida. I am an active investor myself and only market investment property to others that I like enough to purchase for myself. I write articles (like a Columnist) and send them out to our investor database and post them on my web site www.Minnesota2Florida.com. We have a large audience of investors and many repeat purchasers, along with their family and friends!

## Goals

**Do you believe goals are important to your success? If yes, describe your approach to goal setting for your business and life.**

Yes, I think goals are very important. No goals, no (significant) results. Set goals and you can move mountains! I also believe there are different ways and means of 'accomplishing' goals. I have been successful with different approaches. One approach is to set a goal and then determine what specifically must be done to achieve it. To cite an example: how many calls, how many appointments from those calls, how many listings from those appointments, how many listings sold from those listings. Another approach is to set a goal and then "focus on the end, rather than the means," as Stephen Covey so wisely wrote in his Seven Habits of Highly Effective People." Both of these approaches will work. The common denominator is that a goal is set, and put in writing! Today, however, I use "tracking" as my means to accelerate and accomplish. I need to know what works and what does not work. I measure the outcome of the dollars and activities I engage in. Each year I analyze a spreadsheet of expenditures and dollar returns for each expenditure. The spreadsheet clearly reveals what works and what does not. This gives me more insight into profitability than anything else I can do and keeps me focused on the activities that bring me the success in real estate sales. I don't end just here, however. I make it a point, possibly every five years or so, to intentionally come up with something new, something different in my business, and the way this business is done. I'm not talking about a new system or something relatively "minor", but something "totally major". It creates a big challenge for me, but it is fun.

When the idea comes along, I not only run with it, but I run with it with a new passion and enthusiasm that cannot come from the routine of doing business as usual. The sky is the limit and I intentionally engage my imagination!

## New Customer Marketing – Lead Generation – Prospecting

**What do you do, if anything that you feel is fairly unique and successful?**

I work out of my house and have for nearly 20 years. There are no agents hanging around a water cooler (ha ha). There are pros and cons of a home office. It is harder to have effective buyer agents, since I request they too work out of their homes. Most do better in controlled office environments, not their own homes. Expansion of a Team is tough too when you work out of your home. Home offices usually result in less "office expenses" and it is always easy to get to the office.

Most recently I have developed an outstanding way to help real estate investors purchase property out of our marketplace, predominantly in Florida. People always want to figure out how and where to invest for their retirement. There is a huge group of baby boomers that will be retiring over the next 20 years and they are very concerned about their finances.

Through a variety of advertising, we invite everyone to our Florida real estate seminars where we teach the basics of investing in real estate. We then show why Florida is the number one retirement destination in the country and convey lots of facts and figures about the various Florida marketplaces. We keep investors up with the changing marketplace. Just in the last year we have seen the red-hot buying frenzy replaced with a sell off in many markets. This is not necessarily happening in all price ranges however. And, the lower price ranges have performed very well. In the midst of this shift in the market and the psychology of buyers we are finding excellent buying opportunities and incentives offered by builders and developers. This is just one example of what we are bringing to our investors today!

I constantly use the Internet and work with people I know in Florida to find great buying opportunities. I evaluate roughly 1.5 projects each week. On average, I find an opportunity that I want to invest in about every six weeks. I look for great pricing, on site management, incentives, location, high occupancy rates, etc. Once I find a "winner", I work out a referral program with the developer or builder for other buyers I will be able to bring to them. I purchase for myself and then offer this same opportunity to my investor database. I pay the same price for a given property that one of my investors will have to pay. I only offer property that I am personally buying. I bring great deals to others and they know it. They buy again and again.

I am now in the process of adding Marketing Partners to this "system" of investing. I am showing other "investor-minded" real estate agents around the world these opportunities and helping them market the opportunities to their own respective databases of investors. They are able to earn excellent compensation through my network and from the relationships I have with developers! My program information is found at www.America2Florida.com .

We are several years now into this program and have learned so much. We can help other agents to get right in and begin selling investment real estate in large numbers.

I created a whole franchise package of instructions of how to do this. It will be a referral received and a referral paid. I receive enough in my referral fee to pay a referral paid to another agent. At this point we are not charging agents to become a Marketing Partner of this organization.

The idea has worked beautifully. Here is how it began: I was interviewed for an article in the Minneapolis Tribune about helping baby boomers buy 2nd homes and investment property out of state. I had done it once (a regular referral to Florida). So I managed to be quoted in the article saying, "I have even bought my own piece of property sight unseen." From that quote I got three phone calls from people wanting to know how to buy Florida real estate. Interestingly enough, there was no contact info for me in the article. So, the three callers needed to look me up. That gave me an idea. If three called, without contact info, how many might call with contact info? I had to find out!

I set a 30-day deadline for my nephew (and employee) to set up a web site. We would take out a half-page ad on the front page of the real estate section in our local paper on the day we launch the web site. I came up with the name www.Minnesota2Florida.com. We launched the site along with the half-page ad on August 14, 2004, the same day that hurricane Charlie slammed into the Gulf Coast of Florida. Not the best timing, but the phone began to ring and ring and ring over the next few weeks. The rest is history. I have held over 20 seminars to date and have sold well over 200 properties in Florida – all from my residency in Minnesota!

## Client Marketing – Repeats/Referrals

**About how many past clients have you worked with and what percentage of your business is referral?**

Florida repeat business is much higher than Minnesota. Part of that has to do with buyers buying multiple properties as investment and not for their homestead. Florida repeat buyers is running about 70-75% while Minnesota is in the 40-50% range.

# Bob Shallow

## Introduction

Bob Shallow was ranked the #1 RE/MAX agent in the World in 2005! He is a member of the Elite RE/MAX Circle of Legends, was in the RE/MAX Top 10 Teams Worldwide for 3 Years before being named #1 individual RE/MAX Agent. Bob was awarded the 2002 Top Office for a Small Market by RE/MAX International and also named 2002 Broker/Owner of the Year by RE/MAX International. Additionally, Bob was awarded the Distinguished Service Award.

## Background

**For how many years have you been in the real estate business?**

I have been selling real estate for 26 years.

**What is your personal background and how did you get into real estate?**

I served in the United States Marine Corps (Semper Fi), attended college, and became a dairy farmer prior to moving to Tampa, FL and starting a career in the real estate business.

It was my good fortune to be offered a position with a development company doing general marketing for several different projects in Gulf Shores, Alabama. I fell in love with the area and its natural resources. Shortly thereafter, I bought a Coldwell Banker franchise and began recruiting agents. But, unfortunately, I disagreed with the operating system and sold that franchise.

Joining RE/MAX in 1989, as a single agent, was my most positive career move! After several years with the company, I was asked to be the Broker/Manager and eventually became the owner of the local franchise, growing it to three offices and about 100 agents. In 2004 I sold the offices and retained a franchise for myself. Life is good!

**What lessons did you learn from your family, friends, previous jobs, and life experiences that helped you most to succeed in your career?**

Growing up on farm created good work ethics – it was important to get out of bed every morning and get to work! Every day is a learning experience and it's taught me to build relationships for life!

**What do you enjoy most about the business?**

I enjoy putting the deals together! You have to have a passion for the deal and getting buyers and sellers together to make it work. The Real Estate business has offered me the opportunity to make enough money to get back into farming after all these years!

## Basic Numbers

### How many transactions did you close in 2005?

Last year I personally sold $173 million dollars in real estate based on 151 transactions. This year I intend to sell over $200 million dollars in real estate.

### Are you a Billion Dollar Agent?

Yes, I am a Billion Dollar Agent. In the last 10 years, I have sold over a billion dollars by myself individually. (This does not include my *prior team* status and the licensed assistants working with me prior to selling the RE/MAX of Gulf Shores & Orange Beach franchises.)

### What is your current staffing including: yourself, listing agents, buyer agents, managers, and assistants?

My current staff includes my lovely wife as our bookkeeper, my executive assistant (who has worked with me for twelve years), one agent, our receptionist and myself.

## Goals

### Do you believe goals are important to your success? If yes, describe your approach to goal setting for your business and life?

Absolutely! Without a business plan you have no idea how you are going to accomplish your goals. My wife and I have put our business and personal goals in writing for the past 25 years! Goals and business planning go hand in hand.

Continually educating yourself is extremely important in this industry! In order to provide customers and clients with the best possible service and advice you have to be good, and you have to be there! One of the most important tools available in real estate is attending conventions! Attending RE/MAX conventions are a great way to stay abreast of the latest trends and happenings in our profession. You should seek out the top producers and learn from them; always taking home one or two things to improve your business.

## Marketing

### New Customer Marketing – Lead Generation – Prospecting

### What are your top 5 methods for new client lead generation and about what percentage of new customers are generated from that approach?

You must make an impact on customers and clients when they are in your area! I have a billboard, use local publication advertising, and keep my website www.bobshallow.com on the forefront of everything!

Associating with a respected brand such as RE/MAX is also a tremendous benefit.

**What marketing advice would you give to someone at $100,000 who wants to get to $200,000 and more?**

You need to be realistic within your market of what can be achieved. You should look at the top person in the area and see their quality of life. You need to formulate a business plan to determine how you are going to move to the top of the market! What assets do you have?

I always drive a great car for the image it projects and have never had a client mention it was too arrogant to ride around in a $140,000 car. It is crucial to project a professional image.

## Client Marketing – Repeats/Referrals

**How many do you have in current database?**

We have about 2,000 in our database of prior clients.

**What percentage of your business is referral?**

Our referral rate is over 90% from current and prior clients!

**What client marketing activities do you do with prior clients?**

With the close of each transaction a gift is sent! For Thanksgiving I send a card with a picture of my wife, animals, and myself and during the Holidays we send a case of wine to the top 10 and top 20 clients.

## Growth of Business

**What single quality has made you more successful than others?**

The Desire to Be the Best!

**What does the average real estate agent fail to do which are among the reasons why they are average?**

They do not have a solid business plan! They are not working when they should be - there are two things in Real Estate – You've Got to Be Good & You've Got to be There!

When RE/MAX agents attend their first convention, the following year those people increase their income about 40%. That holds true every year. How can someone hear that statistic and not go to all conventions?

**Did you make any big mistakes that you want to warn others about?**

My biggest mistakes were not recruiting the right agents and having the right staff. Your front desk staff should be someone that projects a positive attitude and has a smile on their face. This staff member should work from 8:00 am until 5:00 pm and move to another capacity after one year!

You also need to have an administrative assistant and have a good relationship with this person. I buy my assistant a new Mercedes every two years. Most administrative staff members would rather have a week off than an extra week of pay. Support staff is extremely important; they are the direct link between you and your clients.

# RUSSELL SHAW

THE RUSSELL SHAW GROUP
JOHN HALL & ASSOCIATES
PHOENIX, AZ

## Introduction

Russell Shaw (CRS and GRI designations) has listed and sold residential real estate since 1978, making him a 28-year veteran with John Hall & Associates. He has consistently ranked among the top 1% of all agents since 1991. In 2002 he and his team took 504 listings and ranked 28th among all agents in the United States for total number of transactions closed.

In 2005 Russell's team of twelve talented members closed 350 transactions for a total sales volume of $76 million. They are currently on target to take over 700 listings and easily pass $100 million in 2006.

Russell is a high profile, well-known agent in his area, thanks to the celebrity status afforded him by his weekly radio and TV ad campaigns. Together, he and his wife, Wendy, sell more homes than any other agent in Arizona. Russell has been a featured speaker during the past three years at CRS' Sell-a-Bration. He has also spoken at NAR conventions, as well as routinely speaking at various real estate offices and meetings across the nation.

Russell offers many thanks to his colleague and friend Gary Keller, who quoted Russell in his best-selling book, The Millionaire Real Estate Agent.

## Background

**For how many years have you been in the real estate business?**

I started in 1978 and it has been 28 years.

**What is your personal background and how did you get into real estate?**

I used to sell life insurance and hated it. I did tons of radio production and broadcasting from a comedy standpoint. I did not know what else to do. I needed to get some money and I knew that I did not want to sell cars, so I wound up in real estate.

My first year I lucked into a commercial deal and I wound up making $85,000 in the first year. I "brilliantly" used the money for down payments on things. The next year when the market crashed, my income was cut in half. In the first ten years I worked mainly buyers.

**What lessons did you learn from your family, friends, previous jobs, and life experiences that helped you most to succeed in your career?**

What was successful for me was when I took my background in broadcasting and radio and I would write comedy in exchange for ten free commercials a week. It took me a year until the phone began to ring. Then I tweaked the ad and it started to work. My radio ad is now copied by hundreds of agents. The first year I did 60 deals. When new owners took over the station, I had to go and buy the spots and I spent $20,000 that first year buying ads. Now, our media budget is over $650,000.

**What do you enjoy most about the business?**

I like strategic planning of how to move to the next level. I enjoyed, in the past, taking listings. I had wanted to be a top-listing agent for so long; I made cold calls and worked FSBOs. I developed an excellent listing presentation.

## Basic Numbers

**What was your total dollar volume in 2005?**

We did about $76.6 million in volume with 350 transactions. In 2004, it was $66 million with 420+ sides.

**Are you a Billion Dollar Agent or do you believe you will hit that level during your career?**

I am either over $1 billion or close to it.

**What is your current staffing including: yourself, listing agents, buyer agents, managers, and assistants?**

We have three buyer specialists, three listing specialists and a weekend person, research department, two transaction managers, listings manager, and a contracts manager, and my wife - who does everything! The total is about 16.

## Goals

**Do you believe goals are important to your success? If yes, describe your approach to goal setting for your business and life? What percentage of Realtors, would guess, have written goals?**

Goals are vital to my success. What I used to do was an involved and complicated effort. I used to spend a lot of time on affirmations and working out the correct affirmation. Unequivocally, the correct wording for affirmation is critical. I believe having the *exact* goal is critical. Now, I just decide to do something and do it. The key issue is 'have you decided' to move forward in that direction.

I think that ½ of 1% of Realtors have decent written goals.

# Marketing

New Customer Marketing – Lead Generation – Prospecting

**What are your top five methods for new client lead generation and about what percentage of new customers are generated from that approach?**

Radio and TV: We have now also started some geographic farms. We send to an entire zip code the following: a newspaper, zip code "news", and a monthly paper. My total monthly mailings are about 24,000 pieces. I have a personal mailing list. The total cost for the mailings is about $10,000 per month.

With radio and TV, it is now up to about $650,000 per year and our total marketing bill is about $64,000 per month. My business is listings driven because it is far more profitable.

In 2001, I had a serious encounter with cancer and I completely beat it. What was fantastic, during this difficult time, was that while I was away from the business for nine months, my business went up - not down! Our systems enabled us to move forward. Our business increased even though I was only there ½ day a week.

**What marketing advice would you give to someone at $100,000 who wants to get to $200,000 and more?**

I would tell them to read The 22 Immutable Rules of Marketing, by Ries & Trout. The principles will work. Whatever they are doing to get to $100,000, just double it. Do not go looking for something new. If you did a farm of 500, just double it to 1,000. Play to your strengths and just do more of it.

# Client Marketing – Repeats/Referrals

**How many past clients do you have in your current database?**

We have about 2,500 past clients in our database. If you work buyers, it is easier to get referrals. But, if you work sellers, a good example might be ... the client just left — he moved to Florida. We receive tons of repeat and referrals from investors.

**What percentage of your business is referral?**

We do 60-70 deals per year from repeat and referral.

# Listings

**What percentage of your transactions are listings?**

About 86% were listings.

## Growth of Business

### What single quality has made you more successful than others?

My willingness to see when someone else is smarter than me and to just step back and let them do it. My ability to delegate to others is a good quality too.

### Did you make any big mistakes that you want to warn others about?

About 80% of the people you meet are decent and have social graces. 20% are troublemakers and 2 to 3% are really crazy. If they are in the 20% category, you should just cut the line and go away. Do not do business with those people. Life is too short; find someone else. We focus on the 80% "nice and decent" people; they are happy and appreciative and will tell others about us. All top agents have developed some sort of system for detecting and sorting out the "nuts".

## Building a Team

### How did you first start to delegate and outsource and build a team?

My first real assistant was my wife. It was the team building that I give her the bulk of credit for. At each level she was overloaded; I unburdened her. I did not get myself help until I started doing poorly on listings. I then hired someone to do 20% of listings.

Someone should get a part-time assistant at about 30 transactions. I went to a number of classes at Keller-Williams University in Austin to learn about the DISC system. I learned a lot. There is a correct profile for an executive assistant or a transaction manager, etc.

# LESLIE SHERMAN

## Introduction

Leslie is committed to anticipating her clients' needs and responding to them thoughtfully and immediately. With an unwavering commit-ment to excellence, she will help each of her clients through the entire process of buying and selling real estate. Leslie has two beautiful children and four dogs. Leslie is surrounded by support from her parents, extended relatives, and many close friends.

In her personal time, she enjoys traveling, spending time with family & friends, dining out, cooking, reading, theatre, scuba diving, antiquing, garage sales, and investing in Real Estate. She is also known for rescuing stray or abandoned animals.

She often donates time, money and items of necessity to the Big Brothers and Big Sisters Foundations. Additionally, she devotes time to mentoring and offering support for adoptive parents in all stages of the adoption process. She spends a great deal of her personal time mentoring and supporting men & women to overcome personal obstacles and achieve their goals.

## Background

**How many years have you been in the real estate business?**

I have been in the business for ten years.

**What is your personal background and how did you get into real estate?**

I was very successful in marketing & advertising for five years before making the transition into Real Estate. Prior to that, I was a District Sales Manager for a chain of retail stores in Southern California. I have a very strong background in marketing, sales, management and communication.

When I came to Las Vegas I decided that I was tired of working retail. So I quit, not knowing what I was going to do. I opened the yellow pages and wrote down topics, one of which was radio. I started calling radio stations because I liked music. I asked if they had jobs available, and was told that there were positions for radio sales. They handed me the "dead list". I called people and decided I did not want to deal with those prospects. I bought a house from a builder and tried to sell the builder on radio. Within a month I got him to do a promotion of a new community. I ended up selling 12 houses for him that weekend.

He became my first client and I became the home builder specialist for radio advertising. At that time, I was having a child and wanted time-off. However, since the radio station would not give me a part-time position, I knew it was time to move on. The builder hired me and suggested that I get my real estate license.

My experience and zest for personal growth and development have been a huge contribution to the success that I have had in the Las Vegas real estate market.

And….I do not use radio advertising in my business.

**What lessons did you learn from your family, friends, previous jobs, and life experiences that helped you most to succeed in your career?**

Both of my parents were business people, so I was constantly exposed to every aspect of the business world. I was able to learn from their triumphs as well as their mistakes. I strive to find a lesson in each life experience and from every person who has been a part of my life. I see life as a journey of growth, so I try to stay open to learning and growing every day.

**What do you enjoy most about the business?**

I love what I do and have an undying passion for the real estate industry. Everyday I look forward to going to work. I face the challenges that the day will pose, and find solutions to the obstacles that the ever changing market brings. I do my best to satisfy my clients through a vast knowledge and my complete dedication to meeting their needs. I receive a great level of personal satisfaction when I am able to assist my clients in obtaining their goals and making their dreams a reality. I strive daily to build long-term relationships with clients by proving my worth and earning their trust.

Another aspect that is quite fulfilling is educating the people that make up my Team. From the receptionist to my "Senior Agents" to myself, we are all constantly learning! We learn together because we keep the environment open, friendly and honest. When someone makes a mistake, we share it with everyone. This way, we can all learn from the mistake and know how to prevent repeat issues. When a new challenge or issue arises, we work together as a Team; we have discussions and brainstorm for solutions and ideas. With all my experience in this industry I have a wealth of information to share. My door is always open and I encourage the Agents and support staff to spend as much time working with me as they can.

## Basic Numbers

**How many transactions did you close in 2005?**

I closed about 500-600.

**What was your total dollar volume in 2005?**

We did over $100 million.

**Are you a Billion Dollar Agent or do you believe you will hit that level during your career?**

I am probably at $300-400 million so far and I am only ten years into my career.

**What is your current staffing including: yourself, of listing agents, buyer agents, managers, and assistants?**

My staff is 16 people total. It consists of ten other agents, five assistants and myself. The agents do both listings and buyers. I am not a greedy team leader. I do not want to restrict my people from doing both listings and buyers.

About 90% of the business is listings and 10% is buyers.

## Goals

**Do you believe goals are important to your success? If yes, describe your approach to goal setting for your business and life?**

I am a firm believer in goal setting. It is a driving force in my life and I share this belief with my entire Team. In our office, every year I have everyone do a business plan for me based on a format I use. We also do an art project in which we each put down short term and long term goals in all aspects of life. We attach a plan of action to each item, then laminate it and keep it in our offices. For new agents, they have to laminate it and carry it on their key chain for 30 days. I want it to promote conversation and be present in their day-to-day activities. I learned it in Floyd Wickman. At appointments we have that thing dangling, it starts conversations. I read my own goals every morning and set a plan for the day of what I can do today to achieve my goals.

## Marketing

### New Customer Marketing – Lead Generation – Prospecting

**What are your top five methods for new client lead generation and about what percentage of new customers are generated from that approach?**

We do many just listed, just sold and just reduced mailing pieces. For each property we send 200 just listed in the direct area of that subdivision. Right now we have 120 signs in the market. For a short time we were using the services of a marketing company that made 2,000 phone calls a month to specific zip codes for me.

The cost was around $2,000-$3,000 per month, but they did not provide enough real leads to justify the cost. This year I subscribed to a membership with HouseValues.com and I receive buyer leads from their JustListed.com website.

For a better part of this year I would feature eight listings a week on a local Real Estate television show. The response was very low so I ended my participation.

I also use Realtor.com to feature each of my listings and have recently become a member of their sister website Move.com.

Out of about 300-400, I would say that probably 10-15 would be good leads.

Currently our monthly advertising expense is just about $2500. Until this year, I never spent additional dollars. I have always done "just listed" and "just sold" mailings. I recently added, "just reduced". If you buy into the five touches idea, it is one more method of exposure.

**What do you do, if anything, that you feel is fairly unique and successful?**

I attribute a lot of my success to my mouth – I have the gift of gab. I am constantly out talking to people who can bring me business. Additionally, I focus on building personalized relationships with my Clients. I pay attention to their individual needs, wants and lifestyles. I then incorporate those aspects into my communication with them both during the transaction and for years to come after the close of escrow.

## Client Marketing – Repeats/Referrals

**About how many past clients do you have in current database?**

The database has about 2,500 because I did not keep track in the first few years. I realized how much money I left on the table.

**What percentage of your business is referral?**

About 25% of my business is referral. I do a lot of contingency management for new home builders. The key is transforming those referrals into life long clients who will provide me with their own referrals.

**What client marketing activities do you do with past clients?**

Every month we send out a mailing piece. These vary from postcards that we create, to pieces that we order from Real Estate Marketing Companies, to seasonal greetings. I strive to keep each piece different, personal, and interesting. We follow these mailings up with phone calls to each Client. Every Client receives a card, signed by me, within three days of his or her Birthday. Currently we are working

# Patrick Stracuzzi

## Introduction

Patrick is ranked in the Top 30 REALTORS nationwide by sales volume and transaction sides by Realtor Magazine, a national publication of The National Association of Realtors. He is an international real estate instructor. Patrick is extremely proud of his team, which applies the highest quality level of service, open communication, expert marketing and negotiating techniques to all real estate transactions.

## Background

**For how many years have you been in the real estate business?**

I have been in business for 15 years.

**What is your personal background and how did you get into real estate?**

After high school, I received a college scholarship and attended for one semester. I had previously been working with my father in construction. He was getting older and asked if I would stay with him and not go back to college, which I did. I then worked construction, which is very hard work. At a young age of 21, I got married and we had a baby. When he was a week old, an uninsured Mack Truck that ran a red light hit me on the driver's side of a Pontiac Fiero. I had 9 broken ribs, 3 dislocated bones, needed hand surgery, and stitches.

Plus, I received a severe blow to my chest. I had no fault insurance, which was the epitome of poor and had to check out of the hospital after a week. It was at the point of having to use food stamps to feed our family.

I changed roles with my wife and I stayed home while my wife worked at a daycare center. My no-fault insurance offered me approximately $30,000 to settle. Twenty years ago, that was about one year's salary, so I accepted it and moved on. Two years later, I developed chronic back pain. The doctors found an aneurysm on my heart and I had to have open-heart surgery. They discovered it had paralyzed a vocal cord and I needed two ribs removed, a transfusion, and back surgery. I had a throat operation and heart operation. To top it off, I was in the middle of building a home. I decided to hire a Realtor because I needed help. It turned out to be a bad experience. I also knew I had to change my career and worked in sales for my father a little. When I was 25 years old, I did a seven-day course in real estate and crammed to pass the exam. I felt I could do a better job than the Realtor I had hired!

I started out at ERA and changed to RE/MAX. I was with RE/MAX for ten years. During which time I was number 1 in the state of Florida for a few years and I was #10 in the world. I went out on my own about four years ago. My wife and I now have 4 children ages 20, 18, 12, and a surprise baby who is 3 years old.

**What lessons did you learn from your family, friends, previous jobs, and life experiences that helped you most to succeed in your career?**

My mother and father were my biggest inspirations. They were both first generation immigrants and they instilled a lot of love. My Mom always taught me to be a gentleman and be polite. They taught us about manners and Dad instilled hard work. Mom would teach us games and was always helping out. Working with my father I was always pushing and looking to be recognized. I was always doing amazing things in time. I ran a crew and did a month long job in two weeks. We would tile ten bathrooms in a day. In the end I spent a lot of time with my Dad, my Mom having died at an earlier age. My father died two years ago and the great thing in my life was spending so much time with him in his last years. In the final chapter of his life I enjoyed being with him. I would spend the nights in the hospital with him. There was no doubt about how much he loved you and he was proud.

**What do you enjoy most about the business?**

I enjoy that every day is different from the day before. I enjoy the challenge of taking on a house and marketing.

I like seeing my team all grow in their lives and succeed. It has been an amazing career. I enjoy taking people who have nothing and creating and building them into amazing producers.

## Basic Numbers

**How many transactions did you close in 2005?**

Last year we did $221 million on about 500 transactions. In 2004, and the years preceding, we did about $200 million, $173 million, and $86 million, and $50 million respectively.

**Are you a Billion Dollar Agent or do you believe you will hit that level during your career? Are you over a billion for career sales or what do you estimate?**

Yes, I have sold over $1 billion in my career.

## Goals

**Do you believe goals are important to your success? If yes, describe your approach to goal setting for your business and life?**

I would say definitely yes. The coaching with Howard Brinton made me see life in a totally different way.

My life experiences also shaped me. During my heart surgery, I went code red and needed a transfusion. They had to bring me back. You begin to look at life differently after an experience like that. You don't sweat the small stuff.

I was working probably the first 11 years of my career. Looking back, I probably should have done something other than trying to be #1. It drove me but for the wrong reasons. At RE/MAX it mattered to be number 1 agent and where you ranked in the world. I wish I did the first 11 years differently. One of the major growth things, opening up my own companies, and from it I had many plaques and statues. I must admit the one thing that my driver said, when I asked him if I should hang them up. He said to throw them away. I took four boxes of trophies, and I felt the power to throw them away, all that I worked hard for, medals and stuff.

I went to an incredible funeral three weeks ago, the kids got up and said, "My Dad didn't have any trophies, but his kids were his trophies." You are not working for a statue. I have my team do a dream board once a week. They cut out all their dreams of what they do and every week we share those dreams out loud.

As a team, we get together and throw out ideas and brainstorm. The team can judge and critique the idea and then we put it into action.

Always stand out - be different. If there are 100 white sheep, you want to be the black one. You constantly want to use a unique selling proposition. Everything happens by the law of attraction; so always be conscious of laws of attraction. Nothing happens by chance. When you can, look at life outside in.

# Marketing

### New Customer Marketing – Lead Generation – Prospecting

**What are your top 5 methods for new client lead generation and about what percentage of new customers are generated from that approach?**

I have become a household name. It is not uncommon for people to say they are listing with me because of my reputation.

The three most important things about buying or selling real estate is location, location, location. When selecting a Realtor the three most important things are reputation, reputation, and reputation. The number one thing people look for in a Realtor is reputation. When I ask people why they call me, their answer is because they have seen the results we get. You should cold call, knock on doors, and sit in open houses. The problem today of why many Realtors are not successful is that they are busy trying to buy a new computer program. They need to get back to basics and do belly-to-belly relationships. The agents who do the basics will always succeed.

Always let everyone know that you are a real estate agent. It is like you have to run for President every year and every day. If you slack off for a year or two there will be someone else coming up right behind you. Always be different.

You should have a phenomenal website. Our website is an information source. People really enjoy that there are community things there. They like the downloadable brochures. Every property has a downloadable brochure for our listings.

# JIM STRIEGEL

REAL LIVING LONE STAR FLOWER MOUND

FLOWER MOUND, TX

## Introduction

Jim Striegel's sales and marketing career spans more than 32 years. After building an exceptional business in automotive sales, he joined the growing international real estate company Keller Williams and moved to the booming area of Flower Mound Texas in 2000.

Once there, Jim began formulating an all-encompassing plan to become the top real estate team in the entire state.Within a few short years, he developed a flourishing Keller Williams Realty office committed to comprehensive customer service based on honesty and integrity. Jim participated in more than 1200 home buying and selling transactions since his entrance to the industry. He was continually named #1 Keller Williams agent in the nation, as well as the #1 agent in Texas for 2002, 2003 and 2004.

In 2005, Jim was with Keller Williams and was the #1 Residential Agent.That year, Jim Striegel and his team closed 489 transactions for $189 million.In 2006 he started his own company, Real Living Lone Star Flower Mound, and plans to close 600 transactions for $250 million.

## Background

**For how many years have you been in the real estate business?**

This is my sixth year in the real estate business.

**What is your personal background and how did you get into real estate?**

Previously, I was involved in the ladies apparel industry; I ran all of sales for Izod LaCoste. From there, I started to acquire car dealerships. I built them up and sold them. When I sold car dealerships I decided to get into real estate. I thought real estate had a lot of people who did not know how to run a business. There was a major gap of people who did not know how to run a business.

From car dealerships, you want to own your inventory. When you own six car dealerships and $50 million of inventory and at 8% interest how much is that? A smart businessperson will take profit, and have cash to pay their sales agents. When you have a lot of inventory and are charged interest, you'd better turn the inventory into salesor go broke. You'd better know how to manage inventory. You need to turn inventory, and you need to understand the back end of building a business and service. The third is in owning your own warranty company; because there is 60% net profit margin.

Two of my friends, a major oil person and the head of Nintendo said to me, "You would do phenomenally in real estate."

My goal was to be the top agent in the United States. My first year I did $320,000 GCI; the second year I did $1,200,000; my third year I did $2,400,000; my fourth year I did $4,400,000; and I did $7,600,000 in my fifth year. My opinion is you should run 42-52% net profit for top level real estate agents. I believe you should spend 12% advertising but to grow fast you can spend 25% and then you can come back down to 12%.

Now, I coach agents around the United States. I tell them they should take 40% of what they make and put it away. Why? Because it forces you to run a business and market properly.

**What lessons did you learn from your family, friends, previous jobs, and life experiences that helped you most to succeed in your career?**

It all comes from your belief window, when you were born. My father built a belief window that I would always be number one. All I needed to do is work hard and run my own company. I was brought up that way, and I was selling Fuller Brush and Amway as a kid and knocking door-to-door. I was going to college and selling Fuller Brush products to wealthy people. All of these people were entrepreneurs and positive thinkers. Attitude and vision have a lot to do with this. I was raised in a small town in southern Illinois. My father was a veterinarian. I was raised middle class.

**What do you enjoy most about the business?**

I enjoy the people and challenge. I enjoy lead generation. I enjoy being bold and different.

## Basic Numbers

**How many transactions did you close in 2005? What was your total dollar volume in 2005? Based on that, about what is average price of a sale?**

We did 489 transactions for about $189 million. My goal is to be the #1 agent in the United States based on net profit. The average price is about $390,000. I own part of a company called Real Living. It is the 4th largest real estate company in the US.

I started with Keller Williams. They were entrepreneurs and thinking differently.

**Are you a Billion Dollar Agent or do you believe you will hit that level during your career? Are you over a billion for career sales or what do you estimate?**

My career total is $610 million.

**What is your current staffing, including yourself, of listing agents, buyer agents, managers, and assistants?**

I have total staff of 24 people. Out of that 12 are agents. I have some buyer agents, and some listing agents, and some do both. I still do listings, but I am picky and selective with what I do. Buyer agents are paid 50/50; and listing agents are paid 30%. I take $1,100 off the top. That is a fee for operating the company, marketing, advertising, everything. That is about a 45% split to buyer agent. We split about 50/50 on listings and buyers. Most businesses do 20-30 deals per agent, we do 40 or more.

We are better at booking appointments and training than other people. We train every week. It comes down to one thing; when you are selling - are you confident you can close the door? Are you confident and secure on the phone or in-person? I have hired/fired about 25 agents. I hired/fired over 100 people as a car deal salesperson. Maybe 20% were top sales people.

The top attributes of a top buyer agent is someone who comes into your office and treats it like a business, and is there everyday early in the morning. You go in and from 8:30-10:30 you do nothing but call back clients, and prospect, and ask for business, and send notes. From there, the buyer agent should be booked from 1pm onward. The ones doing 40-50 are high D and high I and can close at a higher rate and pick up the phone and hustle everyday. The other ones want the leads and the gimmies. The high D is also tough to control.

They do not want to be told anything. You need to hire them and understand the rules up front.

## Goals

**Do you believe goals are important to your success? If yes, describe your approach to goal setting for your business and life?**

Goals are very important and so is a full business plan. When I was 18 years of age, I took a business class and the guy told me I would never succeed in life if I did not have goals and know where I was going.

I guess only 5% of agents have solid real estate goals. I think that they, down deep, do not know how to run a business and do not know how to execute.

My BHAG is to have one of the greatest coaching businesses there is, as well as a successful real estate business that can run without me being there at any time. And, to continue at the level.

I started two years ago working with KW agents. I started doing my own one-on-one coaching. I have run other companies in other industries.

## New Customer Marketing – Lead Generation – Prospecting

**What are your top 5 methods for new client lead generation and about what percentage of new customers are generated from that approach?**

I do USPs, 'your home will be sold in 39 days, guaranteed, or you pay zero percent commission.' The consumer cares about one thing - what is in it for them. I guarantee to sell their home for over 110% of asking price. You have to do a call to action to get business. You have two seconds to get business. Jim Striegel sells a home every 14 hours. People are into instant gratification.

We get about 3,000-4,000 per month from Internet leads/inquiries. Once the lead comes in, I have a department called inside sales. My inside sales department returns the phone call within 5 minutes of getting the lead. If you respond within 5 minutes you get appointments quickly. With all Internet leads, if you cannot respond within an hour, you lose 60% of them. People want instant results. They are generation X, they want text messaging, and they want to do things totally differently. The goal is return phone call within 5 minutes, 25 minutes, or one hour. If someone wants me, they want instant results. We make 18,000 calls a month. We have three inside sales people. We look for high D and high I.

An Internet buyer will buy way faster than someone not using the Internet. There is an art to creating instant success. We categorize them into 'now' business, '3 months', etc. We throw away the junk. About 5-10% of leads are good leads and we close about 40% of those good leads. That is about 2-4% of total leads.

Our marketing costs were about 12% last year. I started my business doing 25%. As my business grew, I pulled it back. You also have to look at what effectively generates the same leads for less money. I do a lot of TV.

## Client Marketing – Repeats/Referrals

**About how many past clients have you worked with? Of those, about how many do you have in current database?**

We have a marketing e-mail database of 13,500 people. I update it every quarter. We have about 1,800 past clients.

**What percent of your business is referral?**

About 20% is repeat/referral. We do a lot of relocations. We do not have a lot of people that stay here.

# JEFF THOMPSON

## Background

**For how many years have you been in the real estate business?**

I have been a real estate agent for 4.5 years now. Previously, I was one of three founders of a software company that employed about 65 people. After I sold that, I went into corporate travel. When the travel industry was hit by 9/11, I left that business to go into real estate. My family has been in real estate for a long time. My father has been an appraiser for 30 years. When I got ready to enter real estate, I sat down with the top producer in my market, joined his team, and spent a year learning from him. Then I came across Craig Procter, who taught me about low-cost lead generation, and I did about 25 to 30 transactions.

**What lessons did you learn from your family, friends, previous jobs, and life experiences that helped you most to succeed in your career?**

A lesson learned was to be a self-starter and entrepreneur. When I was six or seven years old, my parents used to put Zig Ziglar motivational tapes in the hallway outside mine and my brother's room's as we slept. What I enjoy most is entrepreneurial creation and marketing.

**What do you enjoy most about the business?**

I enjoy the back-end of the business, the marketing side, and lead generation. I also enjoy the overall management of the business.
I do not enjoy the front-end of working with clients as much.

## Basic Numbers

**How many transactions did you close in 2005?**

We did about 50 transactions and about $25 million. I aspire to be a Billion Dollar Agent.

**What is your current staffing, including yourself, of listing agents, buyer agents, managers, and assistants?**

Our current staffing is one full-time administrator, six full-time agents, and two part-time agents. I do most of the listing presentations. Approximately half of our staff just started with us this year.

## Goals

**Do you believe goals are important to your success? If yes, describe your approach to goal setting for your business and life?**

I do not do goal setting.

## Marketing

### New Customer Marketing – Lead Generation – Prospecting

**What are your top five methods for new client lead generation and about what percentage of new customers are generated from that approach?**

For marketing, I do 54% of my business from Internet pay per click. I have about 14 different ads, that I use across seven different types of market segments; with about two ads per, I spent about $2,500 per month.

I started television at $5,000 per month using a different website, but the same phone number and a guaranteed sale approach. I pick up 2-5 leads a week from TV.

I also created a service called Optiagent to track property ads, instead of rotating the ads. Client repeat referrals and SOI are 38% of my business. For RMG we created a client for life program based upon a quarterly gift such as a key rock. We wrote letters and set people up with My Home Management, a website that finds affiliate partners and provides a discount for services.

### Client Marketing – Repeats/Referrals

**About how many past clients have you worked with?**

We have about 200 to 250 past clients.

**What percentage of your business is referral?**

Adding SOI and clients together, we run at about 30%.

**What client marketing activities do you do with past clients?**

I am transitioning right now from a Buffini monthly mailing to our client for life program.

## Listings

**What percentage of your transactions are listings? What would be ideal and why?**

Right now, our transactions are mostly from buyers. We do probably 25% listing and 75% buyers.

## Growth of Business

**What single quality has made you more successful than others?**

Two things. One is my entrepreneurial spirit. The other is a passion for technology. I quickly embrace and seek to use technology to its fullest extent.

**Did you make any big mistakes that you want to warn others about?**

I wish I had spent more time on branded advertising versus almost everything on unbranded advertising. When I came into the industry there was a huge push on unbranded effort. But those people failed to point out that they had already spent lots of money branding themselves. Craig Proctor shifted from branded to unbranded advertising. Everyone already knew who he was. You need to maintain a balance between branded and unbranded advertising.

# LARRY THOMPSON

VENTURE REALTY
FAMILY FIRST MORTGAGE
CHARLOTTE, NC

## Introduction

Larry is 33 years old and runs four different businesses. They include a mortgage company, a real estate office, an investment business, and one for marketing of the mortgages.

## Background

**What is your personal background and how did you get into real estate?**

I worked in the mortgage business for about four years and was number 13 in the country as a rookie. I did $37 million in production in my first year.

**What lessons did you learn from your family, friends, previous jobs, and life experiences that helped you most to succeed in your career?**

I previously worked as a stockbroker in a call center. I covered three cities, dealing only with million-dollar clients and up. I learned while dealing with those people, that if you give them the best service ever — they will love you. Communication, having rapport with people, and giving them whatever they want are the keys.

**What do you enjoy most about the business?**

Making the deal itself. I love figuring it out.

## Basic Numbers

**How many transactions did you close in 2005?**

In real estate, I closed about 85 transactions totaling 25 to 30 million dollars. My goal for 2006 is 120 transactions.

**What is your current staffing including: yourself, listing agents, buyer agents, managers, and assistants?**

We have eight people on staff: an in-house attorney, three full-time agents, a full-time office manager, a closing coordinator, and part-time inside salesperson.

## Goals

**Do you believe goals are important to your success? If yes, describe your approach to goal setting for your business and life?**

Absolutely. I started a few years ago after reading a book about setting goals and keeping them in front of you. I have a journal that I write in. It's more of a life journal. I write about how the business is doing and reflect on things. When my father died last year, I wrote about that. I also write about the status of the business. My journal helps show me where I have been. My goal for this year is 120 transactions and 200 transactions for 2007. My long-term goal is to do 300-400 transactions a year.

My goal for the real estate business is to break even. All the leads that are generated for the mortgage business are where I will make my profits. I put all the capital for marketing on the real estate side of the business. I have a very large equity line for my investment business that allows me to buy investment property. One advantage of that is if I find a one million dollar foreclosure, there are not a lot of people who have one million in cash that can buy that house. This ability opens the market for me. I can invest in foreclosures, and moreover in listings that I compete for to improve their home with my own money. Not many agents will spend their own money to fix up a customer's house. That makes me different. I am spending $120,000 on the TV and $20,000 on the Internet. I have a program that includes having a local flyer person do 10,000 flyers a week. Currently, I am spending 40%-50% on marketing. This is the entire profit of the business but remember that it is not my goal to make money for now off of the real estate side, only for mortgages. Next year, I will turn the real estate into a profit center.

## Marketing

### New Customer Marketing – Lead Generation – Prospecting

**What are your top five methods for new client lead generation and about what percentage of new customers are generated from that approach?**

For marketing, we use foreclosure flyers and home worth flyers. We recently started TV advertising and using Google. I'm also thinking about doing a radio commercial. For flyers, we hire someone who works 20-25 hours per week to put out my flyers and call the people getting them. That costs about $200 per week. We just started Google and running about 30-35% on marketing costs. We also do a weekly foreclosure newsletter which goes to everyone we have ever talked to. We may send that to 500 people and hope they will pass it on to their friends.

## Client Marketing – Repeats/Referrals

**What percentage of your business is referral?**

Right now over 50% of our business is referral.

## Listings

**What percentage of your transactions are listings? What would be ideal and why?**

We are about 50/50 right now. We have about 25-30 listings right now in inventory. We have closed about 50-55 transactions so we are on track for our goal of 120 for the year.

## Specialized Markets and Approach

**Are you involved with any special niche market that is more than 10% of your business and part of your success?**

I have been involved in bidding against a 1-800-PAY-CASH, which is a franchise to buy homes and flip them to other investors. This branch will fuel our foreclosure mix. We have way more buyers than sellers for foreclosures. We get 200 new ones each week from the courthouse. It is a lot of work to do it.

## Growth of Business

**What single quality has made you more successful than others?**

Personally, I have a way of talking with people and putting them at ease and making any deal doable.

**As you grew your business, what were your biggest challenges and what were the solutions that worked the best?**

One of my biggest challenges is delegating work to other people. I also need to track results, hire five more Realtors, four more mortgage brokers and a processor.

**Did you make any big mistakes that you want to warn others about?**

I feel my biggest mistake is that I did not give up control quickly enough; I need to delegate more — instead of continuing to put myself in the business to win a deal. I have been reluctant to give that up, although I know that I need to hire mortgage people to get this load off of my shoulders. My goal is to start hiring people and become more of a manager. My businesses have grown well. But, I have been too involved in each one of them. On the business side, I am constantly creating processes when I am up at five am by myself. I spend a few hours working on systems and processes.

# Gitta Urbainczyk

Keller Williams Heritage Realty
Lake Mary, FL

## Introduction
*The information presented here is from a combination interview with Gitta and her husband Ernest. Together they present a unique point of view.*

## Background

**How many years have you been in the real estate business?**

I have been in the real estate business for 18 years and my husband joined me 8 years ago.

**What is your personal background and how did you get into real estate?**

We have been married for 35 years. She was a housewife for most of the marriage. When I met Gitta she was a fashion model in Germany. We came to the United States and she could not work because she did not have papers. We had our children and she stayed at home. Her background is in banking. When we came to Florida, I did not have a job. My son was a top tennis player in the United States so we moved to Florida to be near the tennis association. I could not find a good paying job. I was managing hotels and I took up a job in Orlando for Orlando Sheraton. Gitta said she wanted to make at least $3,000/month. Little did we know that she would make $3,000 a day!

I had a full-time job and she was Mom and she traveled a tremendous amount of time with my son. She was gone all the time and she was doing real estate on the road over the phone, using those big old cell phones. She used to negotiate contracts over the cell phone while watching a tournament. That was a large part of her first 8-9 years. Then I decided after four years of commuting to Orlando, that we needed a change. I managed a resort and after two years I decided to go into renovating and reselling houses. After doing that for several years and not making any money I decided to join her.

Listening to tapes from Howard Brinton we got the concept to develop a team and do it on a systematic basis. So we formed a team.

**What do you enjoy most about the business?**

She loves the money. It gives an individual like us with relatively front-end investment to get in the business and make a lot of money. We can develop a team and have some freedom. I like to deal with people.

# Basic Numbers

### How many transactions did you close in 2005?

We did $84 million with 283 transactions. The average was about $295,000. Our GCI was $1,600,000 last year. Last year the buyers agents had 1.5% commission, 2% commission. It was a dogfight to get listings. The discounters moved in and took over the market. We had to compete against the Assist To Sells. We had to cut commissions. Now it is much better. Now we charge 6.5%.

### Are you a Billion Dollar Agent or do you believe you will hit that level during your career? Are you over a billion for career sales or what do you estimate?

We are currently at about $375 million. Our goal is to get to $1 billion in our career.

### What is your current staffing, including yourself, of listing agents, buyer agents, managers, and assistants?

We have 12 people on our staff. We have an office manager, a receptionist, a client service manager, a listing manager, a graphic design person, and a virtual company that assists us and our buyer agents. We have 6 buyers agents. We do 50/50. It is hard to find buyer agents at 50/50. They usually do 2 deals per month.

# Marketing

## New Customer Marketing – Lead Generation – Prospecting

### What are your top 5 methods for new client lead generation and about what percent of new customers are generated from that approach?

Last year we did thousands of mailings. We did both branded and unbranded. We did 20,000 or 40,000 per month. We also did unbranded lead generation. We had our own newspaper with 23,000 pieces. We have a tremendous web presence in Orlando area. We are on first page of all Google pages.

We do newspaper advertising of a full-page ad, which is seen by 240,000 homes. We also do magazines.

This year, when we realized the market was tanking and the postcards would not work we were really scratching our head because we were going from extreme sellers market to extreme buyers market. We got an email from Matt Wagner who does radio advertising. I looked at it and it was very costly, about $10,000 a month. We took the risk to do the radio advertising. It has been one of the best marketing things we have ever done. It is phenomenal. It opened some doors that would never have been opened up. Sean Hannity endorses us here.

We cut out postcards and spend more money on radio advertising. We also have a company called ProQuest with our IVR system. All advertising links back. We advertise payments like for cars. We just put a picture of house and payment of $1,250. People call us and it goes to the main office as a text message, which we then give to a buyer agent. The conversion rate is very low. Maybe .5% converts. We get massive numbers of leads.

All of our signs have our 1-800 number as well. The direct calls for yard signs have a conversion rate of about 30%.

We receive about 10 Internet leads per day or 300 per month. Many of the Internet leads are always further out. The conversion rate is pretty low, maybe 3%. About a year ago I spoke to HomeGain. You can buy leads from them. He said that out of all the leads you get like 6% are good and out of the 6% you will get 1-2%.

If a lead generation gives you 50 leads, 7% of which are viable, that is only 3 leads and you end up with only 1-2 transactions. The conversion rate is very minute.

The ones without a phone number are low priority. The ones with a phone number are top priority. We go after them immediately and contact them right away. Last year we had a lead manager in the office and the position became too overwhelming after 30 days. You have 10 then 20 then 150 people to deal with and call them to pre-qualify them. We were looking at having to hire 5 people to handle all these leads. It is inefficient to give the leads to the agent because they take the top priority. We have yet to come up with a good system. We have a company that is acting as our virtual agents and they get all Internet leads and feed it into our eprospecting system. They are being contacted and followed through. We use Top Producer. Some leads go into Top Producer automatically and some do not.

We spend about $30,000/month or $360,000 in marketing with is about 22%. We are trying to expand our business. You have to always plow into marketing. It has always helped us. Radio advertising while it is costly reduces our overall costs. The postcards were a lot more expensive. Radio has been better for us.

## Client Marketing – Repeats/Referrals

**Of those, about how many do you have in current database?**

We have about 3,000 past clients in our database.

**What percent of your business is referral?**

I would say about 40%. It probably could be better if we stayed in contact more. This is a sort of weakness. We use myhomeownersclub.com. We do not have the Brian Buffini system or the by referral system.

## What client marketing activities do you do with past clients?

We do a broadcast voice mail message. We record a message and broadcast out a message. It goes out to all the clients and as long as they do not pick up the phone, they get the voice mail. It only goes to their recording. We have been doing that for three years. People love it. We send birthday cards. We get their birthdates at the closing.

We send out Blockbuster gift certificates with birthday card for all the children. We send out movie tickets when they list with us.

Enjoy a movie on us. We send out cups with Gitta's name and candy. If we go on a listing presentation and do not get it we have a courier take a cup with candy saying thank you for inviting us to your home.

We send out the Brian Buffini item of value each month. We send it out to 300 of our top clients.

# Growth of Business

### What single quality has made you more successful than others?

With past clients I would say reputation has a lot to do with it. I have been in the business for 18 years. People know that I am very honest and straightforward. People like that.

### As you grew your business, what were your biggest challenges and what were the solutions that worked the best?

The biggest challenge in the beginning was not to spend more money than you have coming in. When I started out Ernst still had an income, which made it easier on me.

The challenge is to at least break-even. You come to a point that you have more money coming in then going out.

The next challenge is to grow your business. It took me 6 years until I hired my first assistant. That is when I really started to grow. I should have hired an assistant much earlier. You have to start much earlier. I was afraid to spend the money. If you do not spend the money then you do not grow.

Finding the right team administrative people to really help you in the process. It is a risk you have to take. You have to go out and spend $50-60k to get an office manager and all these different people.

Currently, our challenge is to find the right people to be part of our team. Finding the right buyers agents and finding the right people as a support system in the office. The biggest challenge is getting the price reductions to get out homes sold.

People are still in a denial stage right now. They cannot understand why their $500,000 home is not selling. On a weekly basis we have a very comprehensive report we are sending to our sellers which gives us a detailed market analysis. In Orlando, April/May 2005 was the peak. As of September 2006, the price has dropped by about 10%.

# TODD WALTERS

## Introduction

For 17 years, Metro Atlantan's have relied on Todd Walters' unsurpassed commitment to service, unique consumer programs, leading edge technology, and specialized knowledge to achieve success in their home sales and purchases.According to the National Association of Realtors, Todd Walters has been recognized as one of the top 20 Team Agents in North America, #1 Agent at RE/MAX Communities since 1995, Top 10 with RE/MAX Worldwide out of over 100,000 agents, and #1 at his local Board of Realtors. Todd has received numerous coveted awards through out his real estate career such as the RE/MAX Hall Of Fame Award, Life Time Member of the Million Dollar Club, Phoenix Award recipient, as well as the rare Craig Proctor Quantum Leap Award for outstanding achievements in marketing, for selling over 4,000 homes and earning over $20 million in commissions.

On June 1 of 2004, Todd Walters took another giant leap in the industry by launching the Real Estate Company of the Future; Todd Walters & Associates, The Realty Team – Metro Atlanta's #1 Home Selling Team. The company's mission statement is "To provide value added life experiences to our clients and each other, serving all, and making real estate dreams realities".

Todd attributes his success to an ongoing relationship with God through Jesus Christ, support from his wife Kristi and strong family values instilled by his parents who are dedicated to hard work and commitment. Todd plans to pass along these same ideals and beliefs to his daughters Morgan and Mackenzie. "Faith in God and Family are not just words but actions to live by" says Todd.

## Background

### How many years have you been in the real estate business?

I have been in the business for 17 years.

### What is your personal background and how did you get into real estate?

I got my real estate license when I was 21 years old. Prior to that, I was in college for one year, and hated it. I had a real entrepreneurial spirit. So I borrowed $50,000 from my grandmother and father and bought a pizza franchise. I worked really hard for three years, but going into the third year, I realized it wasn't going to provide me with what I wanted.

In reality, I had only bought myself a job. Seeing the end coming, I went to real estate school and needed to sell houses immediately. I was flat broke. I had lost the $50,000 initial investment plus I had another $50,000 of accumulated debt. That sort of hole is real motivation. When I was in high school, I developed a fascination with real estate. I looked around the world at guys who were very successful and most seemed to be involved in real estate, so that appeared to be a logical place to succeed. I liked it because real estate is something you can own, touch, feel and physically work with.

**What lessons did you learn from your family, friends, previous jobs, and life experiences that helped you most to succeed in your career?**

Both my mother and my father were hard working people. They had very strong work ethics. My father grew up on a farm - 'early to rise', 'stay focused on the job', and 'do not leave anything left undone' were values he passed on to me. My mother worked for the local county government, and I watched her work her way up through the court system. She was very people-oriented, seeing their needs as priorities.

**What do you enjoy most about the business?**

I enjoy the opportunities and the freedom of opportunities. There is a sea of opportunities out there to do well in this business. I also like the idea building something bigger than me and being a part of what is most likely the single largest investment most people make.

## Basic Numbers

**How many transactions did you close in 2005?**

We have been consistently closing around 400 transactions for the past several years. And although that's good by industry standards, I took my team from RE/MAX and went independent to get to 1,000 annually. It has proven to be much harder that I thought it would. It takes serious leverage of awesome people to do it.

I was RE/MAX for 15 years and became independent about 3 years ago. I worked myself into top spot at that office as well in the top 10 at RE/MAX International.

The biggest reason I took my team and left was I wanted to put some team members in different parts of town. RE/MAX said I could not do that because of area infringement on other franchise grid areas. I am still a big fan of RE/MAX though, especially that office I was a part of for so long. In my last year there, I paid $140,000 in fees to RE/MAX. Now, I estimate that I am saving about half of that or $50,000-$70,000 per year.

**What was your total dollar volume in 2005?**

The dollar volume was about $100 million. I am knocking on the door of $1 billion career sales.

**Based on that, about what is the average price of a sale?**

The average sale is $230,000.

**Are you a Billion Dollar Agent or do you believe you will hit that level during your career? Are you over a billion for career sales or what do you estimate?**

I once dreamed about making a million dollars a year in commissions selling real estate. Then, I blew right past that several years ago. I am around $800 million in career sales now and with God's blessings, I should scoot past $1 billion dollars over the next year or so. My sales really took off in 2000 thanks to awesome coaching from Craig Proctor. His system has been my biggest reason for the results.

**What is your current staffing, including yourself, of listing agents, buyer agents, managers, and assistants?**

We have 12 agents out selling and three inside sales agents following up the leads and setting appointments. I have a full-time courier, setting up the new listings, and taking them down when they sell. I have four administrative staff, a listing coordinator, a leads coordinator, a marketing coordinator, and a bookkeeper. The bookkeeper does the commissions as well as the transaction coordination. The leads coordinator pulls all the leads from the various websites and systems, adds them to our contact management database and makes sure the best inside sales agents get the best leads. We use Agent Office currently. It's a very good program but one problem is they do not have an online web version yet. So we created our own using a terminal server solution.

My inside sales agents are organized with an inside sales manager and three inside sales people. They come in everyday and work about 12pm-8pm and they call back all of the leads. They set appointments for the outside sales guys. This is a very good system. Outside sales agents, pretty much, would rather have appointments instead of just leads.

I recently partnered up with one of my longtime successful team members, Cindy Burson to create The Realty Team.

She handles the sales management and finances, allowing me to focus on what I do best, create.

## Goals

**Do you believe goals are important to your success? If yes, describe your approach to goal setting for your business and life?**

Goals are very important to me. My goals have always been set much higher than I could ever achieve and they keep changing or evolving. You can equate it to dreams, that you write down, and would like to see come true in your life time. It is an evolving paradigm for me.

My BHAG is to have a 10,000 transaction a year team system. I have had this goal since I left RE/MAX. I figure it will take me about 10 years to see it materialize.

## Marketing

### New Customer Marketing – Lead Generation – Prospecting

**What are your top five methods for new client lead generation and about what percentage of new customers are generated from that approach?**

We use all types of direct response marketing and we employ all mediums, including ads, signs, info lines and websites. I have worked with Craig Proctor and his systems for many years; he is the king of direct response real estate marketing and has taught me the value of our prospects "WIFM" – what's in it for me.

Our biggest lead generator is telling people that we will sell their home or we will buy it. Last year we did not buy any homes, since we sold them all. In Atlanta, price has not dropped, but sales volume has dropped by 5%. We consistently sell about 75% of our listings before the end of expiration date. The average in Atlanta is about 40%. So we are way above industry standard on that.

We generate about 1,000 leads per month, or 12,000 per year. My estimate is that about 3% of leads convert to transactions. The leads come into a funneling system – either a web site of an info line. They are sifted and sorted automatically. We do not reach them all of course, but have very aggressive follow up systems, including email, direct mail and personal phone calls. When we do connect up with them, some are already committed to another agent or already bought a house. We set appointments with the ones who can buy/will buy or can sell/will sell.

Our appointment conversions run at 70-80% to signed agreements.

I believe the biggest problem in our system is conversion. Craig and I have been working with marketing experts like Dan Kennedy to solve this dilemma. It would be great if a lead comes in and the lead is presold on us; and, then calls us up and says, 'come list my house'. The problem is, if we rely on people to do it, we will always need really good people - who are hard to find. If we can improve the lead conversion system without being expert dependent, it will make it easier to convert our leads and be more profitable.

But like I said, that is one I am still trying to figure out.

Our leads are split 50/50 between now and future business. Our inside sales agents follow-up the leads. They will send the buyer a snapshot of houses for sale in the area, find out buyers' moving plans and timeframes, and schedule calls for half that time. We also send them information that will help them in their move such as free reports and market news letters.

We really go after sellers. We spend $200 a day on postage for direct mail to area FSBOs, Expireds and other seller prospects. Offering to buy their home if we don't sell it keeps those sellers calling us daily.
We spend about 11% on marketing. Our GCI is usually around $3 million or so. That means that we spend over $20,000 per month on marketing. That does not include staffing, which is just hard core marketing cost. Our inside sales agents make about $50,000-$80,000 in the first 12 months and in the second year, around $100,000. They get paid a base salary plus 10% of gross commission. Everybody is on a 50/50 split after any corporate assessments. A Corporate assessment would be a 20% franchise fee that comes off the top for example, and then the agent gets 50% of the balance. For $1,000, the buyer agent gets $400, the inside sales gets $100 allowing us to keep our cost of sales at 50% My net profit is just under 25%. I am very comfortable with that number considering I do no selling personally and really do have a business that can run on autopilot without me.

## Client Marketing – Repeats/Referrals

**About how many past clients have you worked with?**

We have about 4,000 past clients. I estimate that those past clients had probably 200 or so transactions last year. We did not see much of that unfortunately.

**What percentage of your business is referral?**

A very small percentage of our business is client repeat/referral. Maybe about 10-15%.
We do very little to cultivate that business, it's just too easy for us to generate new business.
But, I understand that to make my goals -- I will have to do a better job of picking up a higher percentage of past clients business.

## Growth of Business

**What single quality has made you more successful than others?**

I have a moral obligation to do a better job today, than I did yesterday. I mean a better job in all that I do. Whether it is father, husband, Team Leader, citizen – all levels of activities. My fundamental philosophy is 'good enough is not good enough'. That means I must be constantly working on my life and my attitude about life, in essence, my heart.

**Did you make any big mistakes that you want to warn others about?**

The biggest challenge for me was myself and my attitude toward money. I never really cared much about the money side of the business. If I wanted to do something, I just did it.

I never operated on budgets and budget models until recently. In the past, if I had money around, I spent it on marketing and other things to grow the business. The sad part of my real estate career is that I have made over $20 million in commissions and most of it is gone. I did not have a financial model and I had no exit strategy. My new business partner, Cindy Burson, has done a great job of helping me in this area. Now, I can still focus on growing the business and keeping more of what I earn. Budgeting and profits was not something I learned about until several years into the business. I would hope that everyone who reads this will adopt sound fiscal policy and budgeting and stick to it. Lead with the numbers, the rest will follow.

# Pat Wattam

## Introduction

Pat Wattam, a native of Arkansas, received her BA in Music Education from Arkansas Tech University, and her Master of Music in Clarinet Performance from Michigan State University. Pat and her team sell over 130 homes a year. She has been the #2 RE/MAX agent in the state of Louisiana and #1 in Baton Rouge.

## Background

**For how many years have you been in the real estate business?**

I was licensed at the end of 1983.

**What is your personal background and how did you get into real estate?**

I was a professional musician in Nashville, performing in an orchestra at Opryland, USA and had a teaching studio with over 60 students. My husband was offered at job at LSU in Baton Rouge and moved here in 1979. Music wasn't as big in Baton Rouge, as Nashville, so I commuted to Nashville for four years. That took its toll – living up there all summer, driving during the school year, and I had to make a decision. Go to New York, where I could make try to break into play Broadway shows, or find a new career in Baton Rouge. I'll never forget, when my husband said I would be great in real estate; my response was a hauty "I'm a musician!" He loves being right!

When I was trying to decide what to do, I took stock of my assets. I am great with people and great as a teacher. I thought that if I went into real estate, I would have lots of money to buy cool clothes, have time to pursue my music and ride my horse!

**What lessons did you learn from your family, friends, previous jobs, and life experiences that helped you most to succeed in your career?**

Two main things. Being a teacher was very helpful. You have to listen, and as a music teacher you really have to listen to the student play and then help them interpret the music, not just play the notes. The same with real estate – you listen to your client then you interpret what they really mean! I used to spend 12 hours a day in a practice room. To perform you have to visualize yourself performing flawlessly in front of a crowd. It took me a few years to translate that to real estate. We perform everyday as Realtors and don't even know it. When you do realize it, it can take you to the next level.

Visualization and affirmations help move me forward. If I am in a slump I need to get past it quickly. I use these techniques to help me. I visualize the outcome, affirm it in the present tense, and write it down to make it happen!

**What do you enjoy most about the business?**

I really enjoy so many aspects of the business. I love marketing and I love winning! I really enjoy coming up with new ideas to increase my business and making sure anything I do is colorful and reflects me. It may not appeal to everyone but it is clear who I am! I am very competitive and love to win – whether it's playing tennis or at work! Winning means getting my client what they want, it means working with the other agent to put the deal together (the win/win scenario), and it means helping my team members succeed and reach their goals.

## Basic Numbers

**How many transactions did you close in 2005?**

We did 134 sales last year for about $23 million. We were already on that before Katrina. Katrina slowed us down. I am probably in the top 5 Realtors in Baton Rouge.

**Are you a Billion Dollar Agent or do you believe you will hit that level during your career?**

I estimate that I have sold $200 million plus over 23 years with an average selling price in 2005 of $171,600. Our sales prices have increased due to Hurricane Katrina.

However, to reach the billion-dollar agent status, I have to do something different; so, I am also now partners in an office in another state where the average sales price is over $500,000.

**What is your current staffing including: yourself, listing agents, buyer agents, managers, and assistants?**

I have two part-time assistants who job share answering the phones and basically running the office. I have one licensed virtual assistant who works from her home and is a licensed Realtor in our area. I had one full-time buyer specialist but recently added a second buyer specialist in April 2006 to handle Internet leads. We are currently looking for a 3rd buyer specialist to add to the team.
The virtual assistant does listing and closing coordination and marketing. She is paid per transaction.
I handle all of the listings and about 10% of the buyers and the buyer specialists take care of all the other buyers. Our goal is for me to handle only the listings and for my lead buyer specialist to eventually help me with that.

## Goals

**Do you believe goals are important to your success? If yes, describe your approach to goal setting for your business and life?**

It has to be written down. You need time to think about your goals. You need to visualize your goals. I set my goals with my team at the end of the year to decide what each team member can do. I ask them to set their personal goals, which has nothing to do with real estate. Achieving personal goals will help them achieve their real estate goals.

I have personal goals as well as business goals. They are broken down by annual cycle. You have to understand where your business is and track accordingly. I know that when school gets out in May, business tanks for a few weeks. When school starts in September the same thing happens. Those are great times for me to take a big vacation!

The first time I heard about goal setting was at a CRS class taught by Ed Hatch. I could not understand what he was talking about – you know, you set a goal and it just happens or what? How on earth can you see 5 years down the road! I was doing about 16 deals a year and could not see how I could possibly do any more. I told Ed that and I will never forget what he said to me, "Until you can see it, it will never happen."

That was the beginning of affirmations. Every morning in the mirror I would say to myself, "I am a three million dollar producer and I love the benefits that it brings me." My mind would reject that thought . It would tell me 'no, no, no – you can't do that.' My mind was rejecting my affirmation. So I had to say it again to myself out loud – looking into the mirror. Very bizarre because it worked!

He also mentioned an agent who wanted to visit 100 countries in the world and had made a list. He has already been to 60 of them. I thought to myself," all I want to do is go to England and see where the Beatles started!" So, there was a personal goal that could be a benefit of the professional goal. (And it was – more than once!)

Move forward one year and I was doing three million in sales. I then focused on units and set goal of 50 units. Amazing, that worked too! Next I was stuck at 45 - 50 units for three years and I could not break past that number. Then, I went to a Star Power Convention in Naples Florida, I'll never forget. I was sitting in a class, and in my mind everyone was doing 100 deals a year. I looked around the room and a light bulb went off, "That is easy, I can do one hundred."

You can't just say you will do one hundred units and it will happen. You need to break that goal down. I learned that my part-time assistant should to be full-time and needed to be licensed. I needed help with more than just paperwork. I came back from that conference, fired my part-time person and hired a full-time person with a real estate license.

Education is so important in helping you take these steps. When I first heard about goal setting, I did not understand how you take a goal and break it down to steps. CRS classes were a huge step forward.

Whenever you want to break a habit or change a mindset it takes 21 days. You have to affirm it everyday for 21 days. If I am in a slump, I will do an affirmation while waking up and while going to sleep. When I left a company where I was a Top Realtor for 20 years and moved to RE/MAX, I got all this negative feedback from people. I turned it around. I started doing my positive affirmations to get on the fast track back to success at my new company. Some of my affirmations were: "I list 10 houses a month, I go on four listing appointments a week".

Since I love to travel, I fill my office with photos taken during various trips to help keep me motivated!

## Marketing

### New Customer Marketing – Lead Generation – Prospecting

**What are your top 5 methods for new client lead generation and about what percentage of new customers are generated from that approach?**

Internet marketing: I set up a second website with Real Pros Systems that is stealth marketing. That has been really big. Last year we did 19 buyer sides from Internet. Many of the leads come in late at night – after 10 p.m. I could respond immediately and would have a pretty good conversion rate – but that's not the best use of my evening time! I hired someone younger to do that. That has driven much business to us. People will get to our website, www.PatWattam.com, through a variety of other sites such as www.AllBatonRougeListings.com, or www.HomeValueBaton Rouge.com and sign up for a free home search or an automated CMA. We have to enter them into the MLS and set them up to automated searches based on the criteria they have entered. This also starts up an automated e-mail drip campaign. Along with the automated drip, my buyer specialist will also interject some personal e-mails – trying to get them to start a dialogue with her. It might be a year before they are ready to actually buy or sell. Someone may have a daughter starting LSU in a year. With this system, it is easy for us to stay in touch for a long time without requiring much work on our end. We get about 5 leads a day, about 1,500 per year. You should be able to convert about 1% of those if you work them. Of course, many of them are junk or they already have an agent. Some people have unrealistic expectations such as 10 acres of land, on a lake, for $100,000! The contacts who give us their phone number are considered hot - because it is not required. If they send us a note, a personal question, or phone number, we reply immediately. If the buyer puts in 10 areas of Baton Rouge they want us to search, we know they have no clue of what they are looking for and they REALLY do need our assistance! My buyer specialists and I both get copied on the leads so that I keep some control.

A very low percentage of leads gives phone numbers. We think we might improve the quality of the leads by requiring the phone number before they can access any information. We may consider doing that just as a way to save some of our time. We are already ahead of last years Internet lead closings, and will continue to tweak what we do.

I brought in my first buyer specialist to handle the calls I was just throwing away. When he got busy selling so many houses that he was throwing away the leads he couldn't get to, we decided to add a 2nd buyer specialist. We also do a lot of print advertising. After attending a Star Power marketing class, I changed my print ads to read: "Pat sells a home every 3 days." That really catches the public's eye. I get calls for potential listings from people who think it means that I will sell their house in 3 days! And, sometimes we do!

## Client Marketing – Repeats/Referrals

### What percentage of your business is referral?

Our referrals make up about 70% of our business.

### What client marketing activities do you do with prior clients?

We send colorful postcards. I sent a postcard of myself standing in snow at Christmas in Arkansas with a cute caption on the back in small print it said "Photo taken at Pat's Mom's house in 2004." When we travel I do postcards from famous places around the world. We always put on the back, just like post cards you buy, where it was taken and when. Many clients keep them and put them on the refrigerator!

I do all kinds of great things for my clients. In fact, this is some of my favorite stuff!

They get a Christmas ornament each year. I have a big Christmas party at my house that is a lot of fun! People love seeing my house and looking at all my autographed rock and roll posters. I go all out decorating and it is really a fun party! People talk about the party and call to see "Is the party happening this year?" They get a free Christmas CD at the party so they can stay in the holiday spirit as they drive home!

I also take a photograph of them because it is a dress-up party- holiday attire is encouraged. Photography is another of my hobbies and they also get to see my work displayed in my house. People look forward to these photos each year. They are mailed to them after the party with their Christmas card.

We schedule the party on an evening when we know many of the corporations have their big parties so everyone gets a well-designed invitation but everyone can't attend – thank goodness!

We do many things for kids. I didn't know how important this stuff was because I don't have children. First, we do Santa letters for the kids.

We send a letter to my prior clients with a form for them to fill out for any child they want to receive a Santa letter. We sent our over 200 Santa letters to children the first year! The best part for me was all the personal notes my clients put on the Santa Request thanking me for doing this. My team takes care of doing the letters, getting it all put together but it would be a job easily outsourced.

We also do birthday cards for everybody including the parents. From age 4-18, the children get a $5 gift card to Barnes and Noble, and if they give me a book report they get another $5. The parents get wedding anniversary cards too. The cards the adults get are oversized, plastic, and don't require an envelope! Something very different that no one else is sending them!

We are always stealing ideas from other agents and sharing our ideas. One of my team members came up with an idea for a 'formal' invitation to the closing. We send these out to all parties, reminding them of what they need to bring to the closing, where it will take place, etc.

## Listings

**What percentage of your transactions are listings? What would be ideal and why?**

We're a little heavier of the listing side, maybe 60/40.

## Growth of Business

**What single quality has made you more successful than others?**

Sheer determination. I have always been that way! Anything that I want to do I just make happen! I think it is the 60s thing, if you tell me that I cannot do something it just makes me want to do it even more!

**Did you make any big mistakes that you want to warn others about?**

The biggest challenge was myself. We get in our own way. The biggest mistake I made was being afraid to take risks. I should have gotten a buyer specialist earlier. I should have gotten an assistant earlier. But, as they say, better late than never!

In hindsight, after one year someone should get a part-time assistant. When you hire someone and you are paying for them, you will figure out something for them to do and that frees up your time to prospect. By having two buyer specialists, I feel pressured to bring in more listings to generate enough calls for them to make a good living.

The biggest mistake I ever made was not buying rental houses sooner. I should have started making investments earlier. I resisted owning them for years because I did not want the headache. So now when my clients resist buying investment property, I can identify with their fears and share my experience with them.

# RAE WAYNE AND JUDY SHELLER

THE BIZZY BLONDES
KELLER WILLIAMS REALTY
LOS ANGELES, CA

## Introduction

Judy Sheller and Rae Wayne have over 30 years combined real estate experience. Averaging over 150 sales a year, almost all of their business comes from their network of past clientele. Judy Sheller has a financial background and Rae Wayne worked in the legal field. The biggest advantage of working with 'The Bizzy Blondes™' is their team concept. Besides Judy and Rae, there are four full-time 'Buyer Agents'—you have six top-level experts helping you to buy or sell! They also employ three full-time assistants. Every detail of your transaction, from paperwork, advertising and negotiations, to inspections, financing, appraising and closing, is handled with meticulous care.

## Background

**For how many years have you been in the real estate business?**

Rae has been in business for 21 years and Judy for about 30 years. Prior to Keller Williams, we were with RE/MAX and prior to that, Prudential California Realty.

**What is your personal background and how did you get into real estate?**

Judy: I was dating a guy in Real Estate and I knew I was smarter than him so I decided to get my license too. Before Real Estate, I was a buyer for a major retail store where I used my financial background.

Rae: In my childhood & teen years I pursued show business, and then I became a paralegal. Judy was my real estate agent and she suggested I go into real estate.

**What lessons did you learn from your family, friends, previous jobs, and life experiences that helped you most to succeed in your career?**

Judy: My financial background was very useful. Through college, I learned how to get along with all different kinds of people to get where I wanted to be. My father was killed in the war before I was born and my mother worked a lot. I had to take control of my life from the age of 12.

Rae: My father had a very strong work ethic. I came from a divorced family and wanted to make my own way and not depend on a man. The legal background was relevant for legalities and the paperwork side of the real estate business.

### What do you enjoy most about the business?

Judy: I like putting the pieces together to make the deal. I get a thrill out of getting a buyer into a house. I like the excitement of the transaction. I like saving money for retirement and the thrill of moving on to the next deal.
Rae: In the early years, I really enjoyed the challenge of it all. I enjoyed being appreciated by the clients and loved the unlimited income potential. In later years, I liked the rewards of running a business instead of just being a salesperson. I enjoy the leverage of other people (under my direction) doing some of the work.

## Basic Numbers

### How many transactions did you close in 2005?

We closed about $86 million in 2005, which was comprised of 130 transactions with an average sales price of $750,000. In 2004 our sales volume was approximately $110 million with approximately 150 units sold.

### Are you a Billion Dollar Agent or do you believe you will hit that level during your career? Are you over a billion for career sales or what do you estimate?

Judy Sheller trademarked "The Bizzy Blondes" name in the mid-80's. However, the two of us joined forces in 1990. This year-to-date within Keller Williams Realty, we rank #3 nationwide among team production. In our joint career (since 1990) we've sold and closed total volume of approximately $660 million. We estimate to hit the Billion Dollar milestone within the next few years.

### What is your current staffing including: yourself, of listing agents, buyer agents, managers, and assistants?

Our staff normally consists of between three and five buyer agents. We have a head-listing specialist who is starting his 5th year with us and has become a third partner. We have three full-time administrative people; two of them hold active real estate licenses. We have a full-time showing assistant who sets up personal appointments with other agents and their clients. We have a full-time marketing person. We also have a bookkeeper one day a week. The two of us focus primarily on sellers, and Jeff does many listings as well.

### When bringing agents onto your team, do you prefer to hire new licensees, or agents with experience?

If we had our choice, we would hire an agent who has been with another real estate company and found out how hard it is to make any money.
In the past, we hired new people and trained them from the beginning. Gary Keller (founder of Keller Williams) has trained us to always be looking for ambitious and talented people.

In our early days, we hired almost anyone wanting to come on board. We are much pickier now. We like someone who has some experience. For buyer agents, we used to set goals of two or three sales per month, but very few of them could meet those goals. Our average buyer agent over the past decade makes approximately 18 sales each year. Buyer agents are paid 35%-off pure gross. Their average commission is $6,500, so if they sell 18 houses per year, that is $118,000. However, in the last couple years, with record-breaking Californians getting their real estate licenses, it's harder and harder for us to hit those numbers. Recently we have changed our minimum standards and increased training and support. Our buyer team is doing great! The new goal for them is four sales per quarter, which equals 16 sales per year.

## Goals

**Do you believe goals are important to your success? If yes, describe your approach to goal setting for your business and life?**

Judy: Absolutely. I got into goal setting from the start of my career in retailing. We had a Beat Yesterday Board and a Beat Sales From Last Year attitude. Each month we write on our blackboard what we have done in that month over the past five years. We compare where we are because we need a certain number of sales to break even. Each of our buyer agents compares themselves to the other buyer agents. They do compete with each other.

Rae: Successful people always set goals; written goals in particular. There are all sorts of theories about writing things down. We need to teach that to all the people on our team.

## Marketing

### New Customer Marketing – Lead Generation – Prospecting

**What are your top five methods for new client lead generation and about what percentage of new customers are generated from that approach?**

Since we have been around so long, it is harder to track the source of the lead. Rarely do we get a straight answer. Right now we are implementing a new system where we will be able to lead track with branded and blind advertising from different methods.

We do door-to-door flyer deliveries. We put out 1,000 to 3,000 flyers and have them delivered door-to-door.

It is more economical and we can control the day of delivery. We do in-house marketing here and have a service deliver the flyers. A color flyer costs us about 22 cents to deliver to the door.

We have a sign delivery service that puts out 100-200 signs throughout the areas pointing to our Open Houses. That runs us about $250 for delivery and pickup of directional signs every Sunday. We put out about 15-20 signs per Open House. Before hiring someone to deliver all the Open House signs, our agents would put out four or five signs per listing (because an agent cannot fit that many signs in their car).

With our massive signage on weekend Open Houses, this is also a lead source for listings. We train our buyer agents to look for sellers at every Open House, and we motivate them by giving them a percentage on any listing lead that comes to fruition. They get a 10% bonus commission if they find a seller that sells with us.

Last year our GCI was $2.5 million. Last year our marketing, advertising and promotion cost was $140,000.

## Client Marketing – Repeats/Referrals

**About how many past clients have you worked with?**

We have a few hundred past clients.

**What percentage of your business is referral?**

Our guess is 20% is referral. If we had to do it over again, we would do it better. We try to call our past clients and check-in with them regularly.

## Listings

**What percentage of your transactions are listings?**

For many years it's been 50% listings, and 50% buyer sales.

## Growth of Business

**What single quality has made you more successful than others?**

Tenacity. Determination. Desire to succeed. We are more adventurous and we were more inventive than the average agent. We branded early and tried to leverage ourselves. We were one of the first people to take our personal names off the signs. You will not see our names.

**Did you make any big mistakes that you want to warn others about?**

I think the biggest challenge for anybody is that most agents have no clue how difficult it is. They come into the business thinking it is part-time and they do not have enough work ethic or savings.

We tell everyone we interview that it is a job. People rob banks and kill for $200-300. Imagine if there is $10,000-$20,000 in commission on the line. These commissions can be $50,000-$100,000.

We should have worked with databases earlier. We should have had a schedule to stick to. We should have been more disciplined. It took us a longtime to learn about running a business. We did not start out as managers or business owners. Now when interviewing and hiring staff, we use personality profiles and behavior assessments.

One of our biggest business philosophies is that you need to get along with everybody. We go out of our way to be fair and work with other agents. In the long run, the biggest client is the other agent. We give classes on how to get along with the other agent.

# STEVE WESTMARK

## Introduction

Steve Westmark is a consummate veteran of the real estate industry, not to mention Minnesota's #1 superstar agent in lifetime unit sales, selling nearly 3000 homes during his illustrious 33-year career, and generating over half a billion dollars in total sales volume to boot!

Westmark first got into the business after graduating from the University of Minnesota in Business Finance & Marketing. During his first few years, Steve would call on FSBOs and Expireds and attend packed local social events to find likely buyers and sellers. Today, he still works with expireds crediting them for nearly 20% of his business. In 2005, Steve closed 154 transactions for a total sales volume of $54 million.

Steve believes a key element of growing his business lies in his ability to remain the earliest adopter of the most innovative ideas in his market. Steve recently served as President of Counselor Realty, an agent-owned company, which is currently ranked #71 according to RealTrends. He is a past president of the Minnesota CRS Chapter, Governor of Minnesota's Regional MLS, and a Continuing Education Teacher for the State of Minnesota on the issues of technology, teams, and customer service.

Steve enjoys golf, snowmobiling, boating, reading, Harleys, and sports events. He co-sponsors the building of a new Habitat for Humanity home every year since 2000. He is a advisor to a director of Youth Investment that help underprivileged teens.

Steve started selling real estate in 1973. He sold nearly 3000 homes with over $550 million in sales. He was in the original Star of the Month Club for Star Power and has contributed to Marketing You Scrapbooks 1 and 2, Stars Revisited, and Time For Assistants. Steve is a CRB, CRS, ABR, SRES, and GRI.

## Background

### For how many years have you been in the real estate business?

I have been in business for 33 years and I have no interest in retiring. I don't just want to take up space while on this planet. I want to continue to give back, whether it be in people's real estate needs, to the community through education, or raising funds for young people or helping through housing with Habitat for Humanity. I have a friend that just retired from her leadership position and says she works 24/7 – meaning she works 24 hours a week for 7 months of the year. I can see myself doing that in the next 5-10 years with my real estate team.

### What is your personal background and how did you get into real estate?

I have a business degree in finance and management. I thought I would get into property management. When I was fired from my first job, I discovered my strengths were not in property management. I took a job as a buyer with a company. I found I liked the sales side better. I started interviewing with real estate companies and started selling real estate two years out of college.

### What lessons did you learn from your family, friends, previous jobs, and life experiences that helped you most to succeed in your career?

I like the quote of Robert Schuller who says, "Successful people are just ordinary people with an extraordinary amount of determination." I found using my strengths. Doing them with passion brings great joy. Jesus said, "If you wish to be great, be a servant; to be the greatest, be a slave." I have had a servant's attitude in my business from the very beginning. If you follow the Realtor Code of Ethics, you will find that people will seek you out. Then, you must find mentors that will move you to the next level. Some of my mentors are Mick Lee, Howard Brinton, Alan Domb, Bobb Biehl, John Maxwell, Leith Anderson, Ted Engstrom, David Knox and many more. After that find like-minded business people that you can be open and honest with, regarding your and their businesses. This will help you grow, through Think-Tanks, Shadowing, or Accountability. I have many real estate and business friends to thank for helping me be a success. I have personal faith that is the cornerstone of my life. I start my day with a quiet time of reading, reflection and prayer.

I have not arrived, I have a lot to learn, and I want to continue growing every day. "Inch by inch, everything is a cinch."

### What do you enjoy most about the business?

I enjoy working in the business, and helping people. I recently started reading a book called, "Now, Know Your Strengths". I found my greatest strengths are: being strategic, a learner, an achiever, a maximizer and self-assured. There are 34 strengths shared in this book but the authors encourage you to focus on your strengths and not focus on your weaknesses. If you are 6 foot tall and can make great 3 point shots, don't spend your day trying to out rebound Shaq.

## Basic Numbers

### How many transactions did you close in 2005?

In 2005 we closed 150 transactions for about $54 million. The average was about $350,000.

**Are you a Billion Dollar Agent or do you believe you will hit that level during your career? Are you over a billion for career sales or what do you estimate?**

I am at $550 million in my career. God willing, I will achieve over a $1 billion in sales by the end of my career.

**What is your current staffing, including yourself, of listing agents, buyer agents, managers, and assistants?**

My team consists of two administrative people and three buyer specialists. I do the vast majority of the listings. As a team, we are about 50/50 on buyers and sellers. I also have a designated closer who does both seller and buyer sides. I have a full-time listing manager to help with listings and facilitate stuff with my closer. My other administrative assistant manages prelist packages, CMA's, buyer packets, or other information, and letters on a daily basis.

I want my buyer agents to do 24 deals a year. I would like to see them become even more productive. As a new buyer specialist, if they can do 12 transactions in their first year, I believe they have the talents to grow in the business. Most buyer specialists stay on the team 3-5 years.

New buyer agents start out with a 40/60 split and then go 50/50 split at earnings of $30-60,0000; 55/45 from $60-90,000 and 60/40 for $90,000 and above.

## Goals

**Do you believe goals are important to your success? If yes, describe your approach to goal setting for your business and life?**

Goals were important to me from day one. I took a goal-setting class in early 1970s through World Vision/Ted Engstrom and I learned the importance of having goals and plans built. Stephen Covey, in his book "Begin with an End in Mind", says to know where you want to go — look to your future. You need to know where you are going. It is important to begin 15-year goals. Look 15 years from today, and make goals in the 7 equities. Business, Financial, Social, Education, Family, Spiritual, and Physical. Make at least one goal in each area to have some type of balance in your life. Then make 5-year goals built upon the goals of what you want to accomplish in 15 years. Then make 1-year goals built upon what you want to accomplish in 5 years. Then break them into monthly goals with plans and strategies. Come up with a perfect week and communicate it to your team and those close to you.

Do you want more business? You need to find leads to turn into prospects, and then into customers, and later into clients, and finally into raving fans that send you referrals. One simple plan to implement is to have a hour of power every day to make out going calls to anyone that will move those leads into raving fans. "If it's going to be ... it's up to me."

## Marketing

### New Customer Marketing – Lead Generation – Prospecting

**What are your top five methods for new client lead generation and about what percent of new customers are generated from that approach?**

I think many new clients are being obtained through websites today. We are using pay-per-click ads, which are sending people searching for home information through our Stealth Web Sites. On the backside they are receiving homes ads daily with our picture on it. We can follow-up on the back-end to move these people from a lead to being a prospect.

Get a lot of listings and then market through your websites that share that information with other aggregators (like Immobel, Trulia, Google, Realtor.com, and others) where people can click on your listings. We have the IVR sign on the listings to follow-up on people. We also advertise houses for sale with print ads.

All these are the kind of things where we are going to marketplace and trying to get the buyers to come to us. Listings are the King. If we do not have listings, why would buyers call us?

I get 25% of my listings through Expired listing plan. Everyday we download Expireds from 8 or 9 areas of the Twin Cities.

We have an eight-letter plan, with calls mixed-in, that we work over a two-month period. We send more letters early in first month, totaling about six in first month and then two letters in the second month. We have a greater chance to convert the listing if we get to them within first 30 days.

We have a proactive plan and have something that is different in each letter. I get stuff through StarPower, Cathy Russell, Truman Ball, and Russell Shaw. Find the people that have programs that work and implement pieces of them into your program. I find different things to use, some may have to do with the experience of our company, myself, testimonials, what we are doing in marketing, etc.

We try to match the personality of the person we are contacting. We have letters that cut across all DISC personality types. We contact over 1,000 Expireds during the year and we end up with 20 listings from it. That would be about 2%. Of those 2%, or 20 listings, at least half of them will turn into buyers.

We have found that the best time to call is between 5-8pm. In order to be successful with any program, is to consistently plan. We use REDX to cross-check what we do. Their website is www.theredx.com.

## Client Marketing – Repeats/Referrals

**Of those, about how many past clients do you have in current database?**

We have 2,500 past clients in our database.

**What percentage of your business is referral?**

Our repeat/referral rate is 50%.

**What client marketing activities do you do with past clients?**

We do 12 mailings. Four are quarterly newsletters; four are postcards. We offer a free pumpkin in the fall. In February, we offer a free rose for Valentines Day. I work out a deal with the florist and if they show up at that florist they give them a free rose.

Our rose giveaway is the most popular. There are about 100 roses redeemed each year. We get wonderful responses from our client base.

We also have shelf-life pieces that we send of "Websites at a Glance, Golf Courses at Glance, and Restaurants at a Glance." We send an annual calendar that we get from Melco Marketing. This is very popular with our client base. Also, we send an end of the year gratefulness for referrals letter with the calendar.

We do birthday cards, anniversary cards, and house anniversary cards. We go to different restaurants and get FREE certificates for a dessert.

It costs us the postage and a birthday card but they receive something they can use with their family for celebrating. When they use the free dessert on their birthday card, they take 4-5 people and have a dinner for a free $5 dessert. I go to different restaurants and get this deal.

We have a 'Thanks a Latte' program. When we get a referral we send a $10 gift card for Starbucks or Caribou Coffee as soon as we get a referral. Our team goal is to get one referral a day or 365 a year.

## Growth of Business

### What single quality has made you more successful than others?

I am an ordinary person with an extraordinary amount of determination. In high school I graduated in the middle of my class.

I am Joe Average. Looking at strengths, I know I am strategic and like to learn and I am an achiever. It is the achiever part that creates a lot of determination. I have a "things to do" list every day. I love to check off my accomplishments. I keep working. I keep making calls. I follow-up and stay on task. I stay focused on what is the most productive for me to do with my time.

I have problem-solving skills. I want to figure out how to make a transaction work and I have the desire to serve my client. I have always believed in giving the best possible service to my client and to look out for their best interest.

**If you could go back and do things differently, what would you have done at $100,000 that would have speeded the growth of your business?**

I would have started building my team sooner. Even now, I know I still need to learn how to delegate better. Someone learns how to do a task, then they hire someone else who only does it 80% as well. Because of the 20% difference, the original person decides they will keep doing the job because they can do it better at 100%. What they don't realize is that while they are doing less dollar productive work, which could be done at 80% level, what they are really doing is standing in their way of future growth. I have stood in the way of team members because I thought I could do it better. Could I be doing proactive phone calls, showing homes, presenting offers, getting price adjustments, and listing a homes? Or, should I be writing ads, putting up signs, taking photos, and the like. Use your strengths and as you get too busy to do it all, either delegate it or ditch it.

I am amazed at the strengths of our team. John Maxwell has a book <u>17 Laws of Teamwork</u>. I am not an island. I need to work with others. I am amazed at those that are around me, to help me be successful; and, I want to be that to others also.

By having two buyer specialists, I feel pressured to bring in more listings to generate enough calls for them to make a good living.

The biggest mistake I ever made was not buying rental houses sooner. I should have started making investments earlier. I resisted owning them for years because I did not want the headache. So now when my clients resist buying investment property, I can identify with their fears and share my experience with them.

# Jeff & Marsee Wilhems

The Marsee Wilhems Group
RE/MAX Majestic
Tucson, AZ

## Background

**For how many years have you been in the real estate business?**

I have been in mortgage lending for eight years. Marsee has had her license for 2 1/2 years.

**What is your personal background and how did you get into real estate?**

I convinced her to get a license and I was the lender. I do not know how to do anything half speed. We were both in the mortgage lending business. We were fairly successful; we had about 35 employees.

**What lessons did you learn from your family, friends, previous jobs, and life experiences that helped you most to succeed in your career?**

I have learned to never give up and to never quit. If you can visualize a goal that you want, you can obtain anything. Our platinum rule is "treat others the way they want to be treated".

**What do you enjoy most about the business?**

I enjoy the constant change to stay ahead of the competition and to make sure we are on the cutting edge of technology and techniques. Even our television commercials are always outside the box.

## Basic Numbers

**How many transactions did you close in 2005?**

We closed 197 transactions and about $43 million. Our goal for 2006 is 350-400 transactions and about $90 million. Marsee's first transaction was only in May of 2004.

**What is your current staffing including: yourself, listing agents, buyer agents, managers, and assistants?**

We currently have five buyer agents and three full-time listing agents. They go out and present marketing materials.

We have a transaction manager, a listing's manager, an office manager/ client liaison and a receptionist. We have a full-time after-the-sale person who is a referral specialist. It is her job to get testimonials and referrals from past clients. We realized we missed the opportunity by not requesting written and video testimonials of past clients.

We wanted to adopt the buyers for our listings. We are about 80% on listings so we adopt the buyers. Usually within a year they believe we were the agent that sold them the house.

The other key person is our inside sales department. He books all the appointments from the TV and radio commercials that we do. He schedules the listing agents and gets the prelisting package out with the DVD to presale. Once we book an appointment from the branded advertising they are predisposed. We carry over 100 active listings.

We wrote a business plan to determine how much we plan to make on the business. We started out with one assistant, Marsee, and myself. I had enough revenue from my mortgage business to build the real estate business. You have to build enough critical mass with the listings.

We pay our listing agents about 20% so we can pay a lot more to marketing and other parts of our business.

I have tried to model my business like Russell Shaw in Phoenix. We have taken the front-end model of Russell and added a back-end. I spent about 30 weeks with various people; I have traveled extensively and made numerous site visits with Top Agents all over North America. I am a huge Student of Modeling.

## Goals

**Do you believe goals are important to your success? If yes, describe your approach to goal setting for your business and life?**

Absolutely. Marsee and I sit down once a month and review our goals. It is probably more me that is goal-oriented and driven. The goals are reviewed monthly.

Our goals are based on units sold and profitability. Our goal for profit is to run 40% of gross of profit. Right now we are closer to 30%. We just keep track of the number of listing appointments and work the numbers backwards.

I have been doing written goals since I was 17 years old. Tony Robbins was instrumental to my goal setting.

## Marketing

### New Customer Marketing – Lead Generation – Prospecting

**What are your top five methods for new client lead generation and about what percentage of new customers are generated from that approach?**

We are using television and radio heavily. We run a wide variety of messages to step outside the box. For example, we do a commercial where we address the American Idol Fans.

We do really good television. The main reason for our success is Alan Alexander with Brightside Advertising. He was a big media buyer who is able to go and negotiate the media so it is a fraction of other people. We get a good cost. We probably have 10 to 12 agents on Tucson TV. We were the first. Our budget is significant on TV and radio.

We go after pre-foreclosures. We pick up lists from the county courthouse who just received a notice of default. The whole key is in the delivery. There are about 400 per month. Out of 400, there may be 50-60 that we go after. We send our people to visit them face-to-face. The concern is if the work can justify the return.

Our Internet presence is phenomenal. We do lots of Google pay-per-click for buyer business. We are about to change to a total custom website. We probably have 3% conversion of leads from the Internet. Many Internet leads are just kicking tires so to speak. Still, the key is a much faster response time than we've had. Rest assured that we will be improving that greatly over the next few months.

I think our sign calls are one of the best leads. People see the sign and call with questions regarding a property.

**What is the one most effective form of marketing that you have consistently done?**

The best advertising approach in the world is your yard sign.

**What marketing advice would you give to someone at $100,000 who wants to get to $200,000 and more?**

I would be spending money on branded television, radio, or print. I would not spend money on non-branded activity. Branded activity lasts longer. They may not remember you today or tomorrow but if you keep in their face, they will keep you.

fWe have a national radio show host that records scripts for AM powerhouse station. People remember the name of the radio show host.

## Client Marketing – Repeats/Referrals

**About how many past clients have you worked with?**

We have worked with about 300 clients.

**What percentage of your business is referral?**

Our referral is very low right now because we are brand new. In five years I hope it will be 20%.

**What client marketing activities do you do with past clients?**

We do not do a lot with past clients. We send a nice closing gift. We try to stay in touch with a quarterly newsletter.

We send a newsletter once a year with their HUD-1 settlement statement and, also send a candy bar for their chance to bite back at the IRS with a chocolate bar that looks like IRS Form1040. We have not adopted a big after-client program. We recently had someone in our office go into this position full time. We are spending a lot of money on marketing. We should take some percentage and spend it on current clients. We are chasing new business.

**Do you have other significant referral sources other than past clients?**

The mortgage business is our main referral source. I am the mortgage expert for the local CBS affiliate here in Tucson. I am on the morning news and talk on a different mortgage topic each time I'm on TV.

## Listings

**What percentage of your transactions are listings? What would be ideal and why?**

We are running about 80-85% listings. After running one model we realized that unless you are going to do a lot of business yourself, the only way was going to be to focus heavily on the listings side. When you pay 45/45, plus ten for marketing on the buyer side, it seems more profitable for the listing side of business. But in a slowing market be careful, "No Buyer Business" could be dangerous.

The real key to getting your listings to sell is simple, PRICE. Be sure to price the home to sell in under 30 days. If the seller is not willing to do so after you show them all the statistics. Then, politely tell them you would be happy to refer them to a good property manager to manage their new rental home. If that doesn't help and you feel you have the listing priced right, then wish them good luck. Do not take the listing…period!

## Specialized Markets and Approach

**Are you involved with any special niche markets that are more than 10% of your business and part of your success?**

We do not have any niche markets. Our business is 95% selling single-family homes.

## Growth of Business

**What single quality has made you more successful than others?**

We are very driven. When someone says we cannot do something, we work three times harder to prove them wrong. We believe in each other and our Team. We are trying to prove ourselves right.

**What does the average real estate agent fail to do which are among the reasons why they are average?**

They fail to brand themselves properly.

They fail to plan their business appropriately. If you fail to plan, you plan to fail.

They fail to surround themselves with people who are vastly superior.

They fail to network with top agents.

They fail to learn from others' mistakes.

They listen to people who are at their level or below.

They fail to ask people outside their office or market for ideas.

They fail to try new things.

They don't allow themselves to fail. If you haven't failed, then you haven't lived.

They fail to take risk.

They fail to step outside the box.

**Did you make any big mistakes that you want to warn others about?**

We would have started spending more money on branding sooner. We spent money on non-branded advertising such as free online home evaluations, classified ads. You can get business on the front-end or on the back-end through your marketing effort. Craig Proctor teaches getting business on the back-end. But, I would caution against that plan for too long. However, I think Craig Proctor is the best in the business of real estate trainers to take a new agent from 0-50 transactions bar none.

# SHERRY WILSON

SHERRY WILSON & CO.
RE/MAX LEADERS
PURCELLVILLE, VA

## Introduction

Sherry Wilson has been ranked Loudoun County's top real estate agent virtually every year since 1984, which marked the beginning of her real estate career. What's more, during her first two years, she was still teaching middle school full-time! Her secret to success has been staying in close contact with her clients throughout their transaction and paying attention to detail every step of the way.

Sherry is continuously learning about the most innovative systems, ideas, and marketing techniques at conferences held throughout the United States. Sherry also teaches team building and sales strategies to other agents by speaking at conferences for RE/MAX International Inc. and Howard Brinton programs. Her interviews are quoted in books to teach and coach new agents all over the world. Sherry has been proud to call Loudoun County home since 1977. She lives in a delightful community, just west of the Town of Purcellville, where she enjoys gardening and entertaining friends and clients.

## Background

**For how many years have you been in the real estate business?**

I have been in the real estate business for about 23 years.

**What is your personal background and how did you get into real estate?**

When I started selling real estate in 1984, I was a full-time middle school teacher. I was teaching Math, English, and History in Loudoun County, VA.

**What lessons did you learn from your family, friends, previous jobs, and life experiences that helped you most to succeed in your career?**

One of the biggest lessons I've learned is to stay consistent. I practice consistency in everything I do. I also stay in constant touch with people. Throughout my career I've learned that to be successful, you must surround yourself by people who are successful themselves. Always look ahead and never look back. You've got to constantly focus on the positive to succeed.

**What do you enjoy most about the business?**

I enjoy the art of the deal. I enjoy putting it all together and then seeing the outcome – making someone happy. It makes me feel good to be able to do something that not all other's can.

I make the American dream happen, and through that I make relationships with people that last a lifetime.

## Goals

**Do you believe goals are important to your success? If yes, describe your approach to goal setting for your business and life?**

I have always had goals, but in the past I never used to write them down. In 2001, I attended a Brian Buffini seminar that made it all clear to me. To achieve your goals, you must write them down and review them every day. You can't go anywhere unless you know where you are going and how to get there. If you write down your goals and affirmations, and review them each day, you would be amazed at what you can accomplish in just one year. I've since shared this strategy with the rest of my team members and it's working for them too.

## Numbers

**Are you a Billion Dollar Agent or do you believe you will hit that level during your career? Are you over a billion for career sales or what do you estimate?**

In 2005 I did $185,000,000 and sold 343 properties. I estimate at least $1,200,000,000 (one billion two hundred million) in sales so far in my career.

**What is your current staffing including: yourself, listing agents, buyer agents, managers, and assistants?**

I have 5 core agents who have been with me for more than four years. I have another 7 agents whom I've personally trained and mentored over the last few years. On staff I have about 12 people. My staff includes a Listing Manager, Contracts Manager, Advertising Manager, Staff Photographer, Agent Manager, Office Manager, Bookkeeper, Agent Assistant, 2 receptionists, and 2 couriers.

## Marketing

### New Customer Marketing – Lead Generation – Prospecting

**What are your top 5 methods for new client lead generation and about what percentage of new customers are generated from that approach?**

The #1 method for new client lead generation is advertising. I advertise in 18 local papers throughout the area just West of Metropolitan DC. Then I have my courtesy vans, which I lend to clients and 3 PT cruisers that my couriers drive. They are wrapped in my logo and contact information. I even have my logo wrapped around a huge Loudoun County Transit Bus.

So, you can't go anywhere in Loudoun County without seeing my name or picture. We recently started a "Just Sold" campaign, where we will be sending about 100 "Just Sold" cards to neighbors of properties we list and sell. Repeat business and client referrals are also a huge source of business for me. I have never telemarketed or sent direct mail because I haven't needed to.

**What do you do, if anything, that you feel is fairly unique and successful?**

As far as my marketing goes, I put a huge effort into client parties and branding my name and logo. The Internet accounts for about 30% of my leads right now. My team agents keep in close contact with past clients.

**What marketing advice would you give to someone at $100,000 who wants to get to $200,000 and more?**

My advice for newer agents is to brand yourself and invest in your business. You've got to spend money to make money. Take out a business loan if you have to. Then stay consistent and persistent in everything you do.

**How much do you spend on advertising?**

I spend about 11 or 12% of gross income on advertising, but a good target is around 10 percent.

## Client Marketing – Repeats/Referrals

**About how many past clients have you worked with?**

My repeat and referral business makes up about 60% of my overall business. This is why follow-up and staying in touch is vital to our business.

**About how many past clients do you have in your database?**

My A plus list is about 1,200-1,400 people.

**What percentage of your total dollar volume is spent on expenses?**

In the past years, about 65% of gross income was spent on expenses and I net about 35%. Those numbers changed in 2006 to where the expenses are much higher and the net is much less.

**What client marketing activities do you do with past clients?**

I do an item of value from Brian Buffini's program.
I do a quarterly mailing of a newsletter.
I do a client party at my house for new clients and older clients every two months.
I have a huge party with about 450 people. They are from my list of 1,200 people we stay in touch with. We even put an ad in the paper a few months prior to ensure we don't miss anyone – the ad encourages any past or current clients to call and join the party.

**What one thing would you tell a beginning agent to pursue to achieve success?**

I would tell them to find a mentor and learn all you can. Find someone who knows what they are doing and can show you the right things to do. When I started my business back in 1984, I had an agent who was helping me, and of course I split the commissions 50/50 with this person. This is a necessity to succeed. Find someone who is successful and follow in their footsteps.

## Growth of Business

**What <u>single</u> quality has made you more successful than others?**

The key to my success has been persistence. I do not accept the word "no." It doesn't exist in my vocabulary.

**What does the average real estate agent fail to do which are among the reasons why they are average?**

The average agent will throw a deal together but never follow through. They might be busy with another job, or they are inexperienced and don't know any better. Having the transaction signed is just half the battle. Getting to closing and ensuring that your client is happy is a big challenge. Some agents don't feel the urge to bring themselves to the next level. If they are happy or satisfied with their current production level, then they are just average. But the agents that push themselves and never look back are the ones who succeed and are considered above average.

**What one thing would you tell a beginning agent to pursue to achieve success?**

I would suggest the agent practice persistence and follow up, and possess a strong knowledge of the market and inventory.

**Did you make any big mistakes that you want to warn others about?**In the beginning the biggest challenge for me was delegating tasks. I did not want to do this in fear of losing control and I was worried things wouldn't be completed the right way. Then I realized that delegating to others would give me more leverage and more time to focus on the income producing activities. The next challenge was finding and hiring the right people to work for me. This is one of the mistakes I made. At first I tried to find people that were just like me, but then I realized that was not the best thing to do. So, overall I'd say that hiring assistants and delegating tasks is a must, but be careful not to give away ALL of your control. I gave too much control to a previous Office Manager and I should have had more oversight and involvement with her tasks.

**What would you have done differently if you could begin your career again to speed the process of getting to your current level of business?**

If I had a chance to do things differently, I would have hired more experienced staff, people with proper computer and database skills. Also I would have concentrated more on Internet growth earlier in the game.

## Building a Team

**In what order did you add your first part-time and full-time staff?**

Within 6 months, I had hired my first assistant. I was teaching school full time; so I hired someone part-time to put up signs, do paperwork, faxing, etc. If you are not growing, you are dying. It's important to recognize when it's time to build a team. You need to give away some to get some. Otherwise, you will end up working 24 hours a day, 7 days a week, and you won't have any time to enjoy your successes.

## Learning

**What are best books you have read in past 10 years that helped with your business and life?**

I read 17 Indisputable Laws of Teamwork, Freedom from Fear, Leadership 101, and The Four Agreements.

**What are the best seminars/conferences that you attend, if any?**

I attended Peak Performers and Mastermind with Brian Buffini and both conferences of Howard Brinton.

## Questions

**What are questions you would like to ask of other billion dollar agents?**

What are three best ideas that have grown their business or that has made an impact?
What wouldn't they do if they had to do it over again?

**What are the top 3 recommendations you would make for a skilled agent who has been in the business 3-5 years and is making $100,000 and wants to double to $200,000?**

1. Join a team so you can just concentrate on the income producing activities and leave the details to someone else.
2. Go back to the basics and keep in contact with people, follow up, and be persistent.
3. Know your market better than anybody else and be the expert in something.

## Delegation and Leverage - Assistants
**We see a challenge of people right at the point of needing to delegate, outsource and hire their first part-time assistant to leverage their time.**
**What percentage of agents do you think are in that zone and why do they fail to take the next step? What would be benefit for them to take that step?**

Agents can double their income if they learn to leverage themselves. The team agents can take care of the income producing activities of writing contracts, prospecting for business, and following up with people. Agents need to leave the small details to other people (assistants) to handle. I think most agents fail to take that step. In my opinion, most agents do not add staff — whether it is a manager, coordinator, or an assistant — because they are scared of spending money and they are scared of losing control. It seems quite obvious that eventually one single person will max themselves out, and not be able to grow anymore. In order to continue growth, you have to expand your team.

# Billion Dollar Agent

## Scott Wollmering

RE/MAX Results
Apple Valley, MN

## Background

Pearl S. Buck once said, "The young do not know enough to be prudent, and therefore they attempt the impossible, and achieve it, generation after generation." This statement could not be any more true than it is for a wonderful group of 'thirty-something' REALTORS® who make up the Wollmering & Elliott Real Estate Team.

We call our clients back within one hour. If we go over even one minute, we'll pay them $25 per occurrence... although we have never had to pay yet!" Honesty by all Wollmering & Elliott team members is another key virtue.

We have sold 99 percent of our listings within one percent of our estimated sales price.

We were all introduced to a Web idea that was like nothing we had ever seen offered in the industry before. Among other things, it provided free access to search all MLS listings without customers having to sign-in. We make a commitment to contact our sellers at least three times per week through their own personal password protected web page that is accessible from our web site, www.hasslefreelistingsearch.com.

Our clients can easily access information about the progress of their home's sale, day or night, to know everything we are doing to sell their home as well as receive feedback from recent showings. We sell our own listings at a rate ten percent higher than that of the average agent," explains Scott.

Day or night, our clients can easily check on the progress of the sale of their home. They'll see everything we are doing to sell their home; plus they'll view feedback from recent showings. We sell our own listings at a rate ten percent higher than that of the average agent," explains Scott.

**For how many years have you been in the real estate business?**

I have been in the real estate business for eight years.

**What is your personal background and how did you get into real estate?**

I owned three daycare centers and bought and sold property. People said I should get into the real estate business. At that time, my wife was in new construction sales.

**What lessons did you learn from your family, friends, previous jobs, and life experiences that helped you most to succeed in your career?**

From the daycare business, I bought businesses that were not doing well. I met with the parents to find out what they wanted.

I also talked to many of my friends and family and found out good customer service approaches. Most people I talked with were unsatisfied. In real estate, I was an individual agent the first year and then I put together a team. Now we are a team of 15 agents. I brought the same interview style into the business as I had used previously.

**What do you enjoy most about the business?**

I love when people go out with me and the clients enjoy how excited I am about my houses. I love houses and helping people. I get a real high when I find someone that perfect house.

## Basic Numbers

**How many transactions did you close in 2005?**

I closed about 325 transactions in 2005.

**What was your total dollar volume in 2005?**

My dollar volume was $100+ million in 2005. We have been at about 65-100 million for the last five years.

**Based on that, about what is average price of a sale?**

The average house price is $324,000.

## Goals

**Do you believe goals are important to your success? If yes, describe your approach to goal setting for your business and life?**

I am not a real numbers guy. I believe service takes care of the client. I am not big on numbers with my team. I like to focus on customer service. Our website approach is an important tool. It is a great way to communicate with the client and satisfy their needs. I do a radio program every Sunday for one hour as well.

## Marketing

### New Customer Marketing – Lead Generation – Prospecting

**What are your top five methods for generating new client leads and about what percentage of new customers are generated from that approach?**

We receive about 150 leads per month from Google. We have a pay per click in Google. If they link from USA Today or other sites it is helpful. We end up conversing with 12%. We also have a referral coordinator. We sort of control the Minneapolis sites. We spend $3,000 per month and we get about 100 leads and then sell 13 home sales a month from Google.

I am bombarded with the large vendor lead generation; a lot are out of state and relocation. We also have a radio show every Sunday for one hour. It has gained popularity and we generally gain listings from it each week.

**What do you do, if anything, that you feel is fairly unique and successful?**

Our radio show and Google link have worked. We have also done seminars before.

**What marketing advice would you give to someone at $100,000 who wants to get to $200,000 and more?**

Do not believe the issue is a marketing thing. There are two characteristics I believe stand out: Having a likable personality and having great presentation skills.

## Client Marketing – Repeats/Referrals

**About how many past clients have you worked with?**

We do 90% of our business with past client sales or referrals of my personal business.

**What client marketing activities do you do with past clients?**

We do a newsletter as well as some events. We do a large client golf tournament which is a free event for past clients and we give away about $10,000 in prizes and have a big dinner and dance. It puts us in front of clients for an entire day. We have about 140 golfers and 250-350 at dinner. I used to spend money on Christmas tree giveaways but it was not as beneficial. We also have quite a few dinner parties at my house or somewhere. It turns out, a lot of past clients become friends.

**About how many past clients do you have in your database?**

We have about 2,500-3,000 overall and 1,500-1,800 are past clients. About one in ten is a repeat or referral client.

**Do you have other significant referral sources other than past clients?**

I work with relocation companies. I do not have contracts with these companies but my clients, such as Conagra Foods, have talked to me on the phone and said they wanted to work with me. This one contact alone has led to 30 new employees.

## Sales

**What are your top tips for turning qualified leads into closed sales? What do you do better than the average real estate agent?**

There are two ways to convert Internet leads. The Internet buyer is savvy.

They are looking for a WIIFM (What Is In It For Me) statement. If they are calling to look at one property, it is key to find out why it caught their eye because there are other similar properties to show them. Another tip is to work with bankers and lenders. Asking if they have chosen a lender yet and referring them to one of ours, gets us in the door too. People trust bankers more than they trust real estate agents. If they make the call to one of our bankers, that loan officer will also promote us. The client will save money and the bank has made another client. It really is a win/win for everyone. Taking the time to go the extra mile pays off too. The majority of people out there are loyal. If you give them information and do your homework on a property, they are loyal. They do not like being sold something or made to feel they have to do something in return.

## Listings

### What percentage of your transactions are listings? What would be ideal and why?

My listings are 90% and the rest are relocation. For the team, listings are 70% and the rest is relocation. My team consists of 3-4 people mainly Listing Agents and Buyer Agents. If a listing sits for 60 days, you should get one buyer for that deal. And sometimes you get a buyer and another listing. I get 3-4 emails off each listing a week.

### When your team makes a listing presentation to a prospective seller, about what percentage of appointments convert to a closed listing?

We have about a 94% closing rate. Part of the reason is that 90% of listings are mine. We have a detailed market presentation. It does not take a long time. I hired a marketing department and IT person to do an excellent presentation.

## Growth of Business

### What single quality has made you more successful than others?

We have good retention for agents who come to work with us.

# Debbie Yost

The Yost Group, Inc.
RE/MAX of Casa Grande
Casa Grande, AZ

## Background

### What is your background and how did you get into real estate?

Joe and I moved from PA in the late 1970s to a small desert town with a population of less than 10,000 people. Before I joined the real estate business I had been working in sales. I wanted to be able to deliver what I said I was going to deliver to my clients. Over the years I've learned just how little control you have over all the various aspects and personalities involved in the typical real estate transaction.

### For how many years have you been in the Real Estate business?

I started in 1980, so I have been in the business for about 25 years. I am a voracious reader and learner. I love to find new ways to get the job done. My husband joined me in the business in 1983 and we started working as a team. We were one of the first teams to split up the business. He worked with buyers and I worked with sellers.

### What about your background, lessons from your family, friends, and previous jobs helped you succeed in your career?

The belief that I could do anything that I decided to do is something I learned from my grandmother. My grandparents and parents taught me many things, such as there is more than one way to skin a cat or if something does not work one way, you try another way. I learned how to be creative early. If you can learn to be successful in a tough market, you really thrive in an up market.

### What do you enjoy most about the business?

It is an always-changing market. I like using trends and statistics to understand the market characteristics and then interpret that for my team members and clients. I love to find new ways to serve our clients, epecially if it makes the process more enjoyable for everyone involved.

## Basic Numbers

### How many transactions did you have in 2005?

We did 330 transactions for about $56 million in 2005. Our market values are still very low compared to most areas of the country.
The area is changing from a self-contained community separated from the metro areas by desert to a bedroom community for Phoenix.

353

We are always trying to analyze who the client is and how we can reach them. We have sold thousands of homes over the years. To stay competitive you have to keep reinventing the process and improving your systems to keep delivering improving levels of service.

**Are you over a billion for career sales? What do you estimate?**

I have stats since 1995. The last 5-6 years we have been very consistently closing 250-300 sales per year. I'd guess that we've sold a few hundred million. Probably we've sold over 4,000 homes.

**What is your current staffing: assistants, buyer agents, listing agents, other.**

Joe and I have two listing partners, four buyer partners, one property manager, four administrative people and one receptionist (office coordinator, listing manager, transaction coordinator, marketing person and office manager). We have moved from the point where we are actively working in the business and now just tweak the business systems and marketing. My job as the team leader is to do the marketing and create the big picture, as well as coach our team members. Joe supervises and backs up our buyer specialists and makes sure all the technology in place is running properly. He is also great at assisting our transaction manager with any financing or negotiating issues. There are only three things any business does: get the business, do the business, and manage the business. My job is to focus on systems that get the business. Joe assists our salespeople in doing the business. Our office manager supports the administrative team in managing the business.

Having so many people on our team gives the client a great experience and makes sure that all our team members have a life besides real estate. Joe and I are very fortunate to travel a lot, spend time at our place in the mountains and don't work the same kinds of hours we did when we first began our career.

## Goals

**Do you set written goals for your business and life?**

Yes, we do have goals. I used to think it was only about the numbers. I used to impose the goals on my team. When you have been in the business for a long time you start to shift priorities. I used to work 70 hours a week minimum and now I work about 30 hours. I want my team members to have a life as well. The epiphany for me was in 1999. I had to have time off for surgery and at that point I was the only person taking listings for our team. I took 125 listings a year minimum. At first I could not face the thought of being out of the office for the six weeks I needed to recuperate after the surgery because at that point the business couldn't function without me.

I had to bring in a listing partner and learn to delegate and stop micro managing.

## How do you work with goal setting?

We do annual goals, which we break down into monthly and weekly goals. We build team goals by determining the individual agent's goals and them combining them into a team goal. Everybody buys into the goal when we build it this way.

At the end of the year we analyze different things: Where did clients come from? What is your conversion factor? How many appointments do you need a week? How much money does each salesperson want to make in the coming year? We figure out their hourly rate and find their conversion ratio on closed transactions. We divide these numbers into a weekly and daily goal. Then, every month, we checkpoint where we are as a team and individually.

## New Customer Marketing – Lead Generation – Prospecting

What are the top 3-5 methods you use for new client lead generation? Can you discuss each one a little bit?

Buyers are either local or from out of the area:

### In-town:

Signs and brochure boxes. Our brochures are double-sided full color. We do everything in-house. On the backside, there is a list of all the other properties we are marketing. 72% of our local buyers come from our signs. Of course we are doing print advertising in the local newspapers and the typical real estate magazines as well.

### Out of town:

The Internet has really given us lots of marketing options. We have a great website that produces a lot of leads. We utilize the backdoor lead management systems to broadcast new listings and listing changes to approximately 2900 buyers who have signed themselves up on our system to receive instant notification of new listings. We absolutely use as many high quality photos and virtual tours as possible and our listings are represented well on Realtor.com and RE/MAX.com as well as a host of other real estate portals. Fortunately, we are well connected with many great agents across the country who refer their clients to us.

Sellers typically select a Realtor based on their image. Most sellers are local and they are very aware of our signs and how quickly we place the "bought" signs on them. They are also aware of our brochure boxes and that they always have brochures in them. They also notice the print marketing and the full color postcards that we mail to targeted neighborhoods with info on neighborhood home sales.

**We also:**

1. Twice a week we run a half page ad in the newspaper. I'm very aware of the concept of branding and staying consistent with branding the image that we create for every piece of marketing.
2. We do a lot of direct mail pieces but not direct response. Once a month we do a blanket mailing with all the properties we have sold. It is usually half letter size (8 ½ x five ½); a jumbo postcard. We show houses that we closed this month including pictures, address and price. We send it to 4,500 houses a month, targeted by neighborhood.
3. We have a great website that is updated frequently so it stays fresh and current.
4. I write a Real Estate column for a monthly local magazine that mails 25,000 copies. The column talks about market cycles, appreciation rates, appraisals, inspections. I write them myself and usually select a topic that is very timely. Those are also located on the left side column of the website for client reference as well.
5. We used to do a lot of new construction and we worked with builders to market semi-custom homes. Our focus was the move-up buyer. We were trying to list their home and sell them a new customized home, which meant that we represented them in at least three out of the four transaction sides. We used a guaranteed sale program to eliminate the risk of owning two homes.

**What are your most effective marketing efforts?**

Clean, attractive, fresh signs with brochures in brochure boxes are the most visible marketing effort. Neighbors driving past signs get the message over and over in their subconscious. Sold postcards reinforce that message. You can't beat the Internet for exposure to out of town prospects.

**To give advice to someone at $100,000 and wants to get to $200,000 and more, what do you think they should do more of and do less of for marketing?**

I would sit down and figure out from where my business came. Use a rifle approach rather than a shotgun approach in focusing on giving them great service. I would focus on my sphere of influence and turn them into raving fans. Referral and repeat business are the best business there is. Create a professional brand (not just a logo) and be consistent with that in everything you do.

## Client Marketing – Repeats/Referrals

**What do you do for client marketing to past clients?**

We put together a preferred partner program. We had an independent company do a survey of 500 past clients and it looked like it was unrelated to us in any way.

We found out that 68% of our business was referral based. As a result of that survey we found that our past clients wanted more contact with us after the sale. They also wanted names and phone numbers of other service people they could trust. The survey was done eight years ago. Our team sat down and figured out a list of referrals people asked us for. We came up with a list of categories and developed a list of businesses who gave the type of service we wanted our clients to experience. We invited all of them to a presentation at our house. I did a PowerPoint presentation on referrals and cost of obtaining new customers versus referrals. We discussed referrals and what people perceived as good customer service. Speed of responsiveness was important; they decided as a group that they needed to call back people within two hours. We offered to mail special offers from our preferred partners to past customers every month. We split the cost of the mailing with the vendor. They receive a lot of new business as a result, which is much more cost effective than placing ads in the newspaper.

**About how many past clients do you have in your database?**

About 15,000 households in geographic farms and about 4,800 past and current clients. They receive something quarterly from us at a minimum. We use Home by Design magazines; these are high quality magazines with photo logo on the front with customized inside and back covers. We are moving slowly to doing more e-mail marketing. For past clients we mail an offer to send personalized postcards from Santa to children and grandchildren, along with lifestyle pieces, beautiful scenic calendars, plus holiday poems and/or recipes. A very effective direct mail piece is our neighborhood update, which we mail quarterly. We take subdivisions and do an analysis of sales by each quarter of the year. We provide the average and highest sales price, along with days on market for each subdivision in the city. We tell them how the market is changing in their neighborhood compared with other areas in the city.

**What percentage of your business is referral?**

We just did another analysis and we found that we are close to 70% from past clients, repeat business and referrals. I would like it to be higher but cannot expect that to remain so high as our city changes and more and more people move in. We reward clients for referrals with a gift certificate to a local restaurant.

## Sales

**What is your closing ratio of qualified leads for listing proposals?**

I would guess it is about 90%. We have such a good system that people know we are the local experts. We have a great prelisting package that is beautifully bound and provides stats, and information on market trends, etc. It also provides all the things our sellers need to know about preparing their home for sale. It also explains the selling process.

## Growth of Business
**What single quality has made you more successful than others?**
Perseverance, innovation, and integrity.

**As you grew your business, what were your biggest challenges and what were the solutions that worked the best? What were the biggest mistakes that you made that you would warn others about.**

Delegation. Thinking you have to do everything yourself. Thinking your career is a business; instead of a job. Stepping from the role of working in the business, to working on my business. Empowering your team members.

If an agent is doing 25 deals a year, it is time to hire a clerical assistant. It is important to hire someone that complements us, not someone similar to us.

The biggest thing I hear when I am teaching and speaking about real estate is "that will not work in my market." Best thing I do is learning what's done across the country and finding out what other successful people are doing, and then learn to implement and tweak that system so it works in our business.

There are a variety of different approaches; not one-way to be a billion dollar agent.

The biggest change for me was when I attended a Starpower Convention in 1994. The focus of the course was your bottom-line. I remember walking away from that thinking, "They're right. It's not what you make. It's what you keep." I listened to Ralph Roberts, who was doing 500 transactions a year. He rented a bus and would take out four couples who were looking for the same style house in the same price range on a Saturday and show them three houses. He told them there were three houses and four couples.Only three of them were going to be able to buy a home that day, and he said they would negotiate between themselves to figure out who was going to buy which home. Then, I thought we were hot stuff in our market, doing 100 transactions a year between the two of us. I certainly came away with a different paradigm.

# Coach Interviews

During our interviews, it became clear that almost all of the agents interviewed are lifelong learners. Many of them are voracious readers, attend many seminars, and constantly listen to various audiotapes. A majority of them mentioned one or more national coach/trainer who had a major influence on their career success. In fact, most agents went out of their way to credit and thank other people such as coaches and trainers.

We reviewed the interviews and selected a few leading coaches/trainers who were mentioned by multiple people. We invited them to participate in the book and be interviewed. The interview questions were a mixture of questions that we asked the agents as well as coach-specific questions. We are very thankful for their time for the interviews. To our knowledge, this is the only book published in the real estate industry which includes interviews from some of the top coaches in the industry in the same book.

The following interviews are with:

Howard Brinton

Mike Ferry

Ken Goodfellow

Walter Sanford

Floyd Wickman

We congratulate them on their own personal career and life success and the amazing impact they have had on thousands of people in the real estate industry.

# HOWARD BRINTON

STAR POWER® SYSTEMS
BOULDER, CO

## Background

**For how many years have you been in the real estate business?**

I started in the real estate business in 1968.

**What is your personal background and how did you get into real estate?**

**How did you get into coaching?**

I began selling life insurance immediately after graduating from college. After five years, the fellow we bought our first home from convinced me that real estate was more viable. He had started a land development company when we were in Salt Lake City. I began selling dirt that turned into cities and communities. That took me to Colorado to open a new project. In 1974, I was President of my Board of Realtors. One of my competitors asked if I wanted to come teach a GRI course in Colorado. I had fun and enjoyed teaching it. I had never been shy about being in front of people. After that course, I was asked to teach the course alone. That led to teaching courses around the State of Colorado. In 1978, I was asked to nationally audition for the Council of Residential Specialists (CRS). I was accepted. Slowly, I was meeting people through teaching nationally. It led to more and more people asking me to speak privately.

I was teaching about 50% of the time, and the other 50% I was doing real estate. My future wife gave me What Color is Your Parachute? After completing most of the exercises in the book, I opened up my speaking/ coaching business in 1984. Ever since, I have devoted my full efforts to helping others achieve success.

**What lessons did you learn from your family, friends, previous jobs, and life experiences that helped you most to succeed in your career?**

I think of the values that are important to me. Those are the driving forces of my life. The values of honesty, integrity, joy, happiness, accomplishment, and responsibility all came from my parents. They were very hard working, industrious people who raised six boys on a farm. On the farm you learn some of life's greatest lessons, like: You do not, NOT milk the cow. Milk is the lifeblood of your family. You can't let them down AND the cow will dry up. You have to milk the cow. I learned responsibility early. Another lesson, from What Color is Your Parachute, was to do what you have the most fun doing — what you are passionate about. That led me into the education business. And while I'd found my niche in front of people, a challenge for me was in creating products for attendees to purchase. Recording in a studio, with no audience and only a microphone, was very daunting.

I could, however, sit down with someone one-on-one and talk to them for hours, and I knew some very successful people in the business. After asking the first one if they'd be willing to do a recorded interviewed, and gaining an acceptance, the cornerstone of my business was established. I've been doing a monthly interview with successful agents ever since. The sharing of their "Best Practices" in our STAR POWER Club has been the cornerstone upon which I built my business.

**What do you enjoy most about the business?**

I get great joy out of people's success and knowing that we've made a difference in their lives. Our mission is *"to have a profound impact on improving the quality of peoples business and personal lives."* And, it's most satisfying when we accomplish that mission.

**What single quality has made you more successful than others?**

Integrity.

## Mentors

**Who was the most influential person or mentor in your early career?**

Sark Arslanian: My college football coach, and at 84, he still inspires me today. Because of him, my first career interest was to become a football coach.

Hugh Pinnock: He sold me on sales and using my personality to my financial benefit.

Ken Reyhons: He taught me that there's so much more to education than making people laugh. He showed me that joy and integrity could be partners in the learning process.

**What are the most influential books you have read?**

The Good Earth was the first book that kept me up all night until I finished it. I fell in love with novels and prefer them to success books. How To Win Friends and Influence People was the first success book I recall reading, and possibly the best. Its principles apply today. In many ways, each interview with a different STAR is like reading a success book. I suspect I'm more of a student of people than books.

## Basic Numbers

**About how many real estate agents do you work with on different levels in your organization? What is the structure and levels?**

We work with 15,000 active agents, in our database, who are plugged into things we are doing, our Conferences, Summits, and University programs. I'll speak to over 4,000 annually, and on a one-on-one I still coach a select few.

**How many people do you think, in the country, have sold over $1 billion in their career?**

I estimate there are maybe 100 people who have achieved this level. About 18 years ago, when I was looking for agents who had sold more than 100 transactions, I only found about 16.

## Marketing

**If you were advising our target agent at $100,000 who wants to get to $200,000 or $500,000, what would be your top marketing advice?**

Develop a marketing plan; and budget every year — and follow it. Agents in a growth mode will invest as much as 25% in marketing; while 10% percent is a normal budget level. Have a message with your "Brand" going out to your marketplace at least twice a month. More, if you want to grow and dominate an area. Your message can vary each month; however, consistency is critical. Next, put lead generation systems in place (FSBO and Expired programs, Orphan programs, Referral programs, Post Sale programs, WEB lead generation and incubation programs) that will require little time or management. Lastly, and the most productively, get on the phone with people you know on a regular basis, and stay in contact with them. Handle their real estate needs and the needs of those they know.

Tracking the source of business becomes a larger part of an agent's evolution at this stage, particularly if profit is a desired byproduct.

Lead generation is the key, with systems in place to handle the extra business.

**For a top agent who has been in the business for 10 years, what percentage of their business should be client repeat/referral? What is the range you see in reality?**

I was told years ago that after 4 years, 40% of your business could be referral. That never occurs if you don't work it with a plan and a system. I've interviewed agents with as high as 80% coming from referrals, and yes — they have a strong follow-up and referral program. I know some agents who are successful, at 10% or less coming from referrals, because they gear their lead generation to cold calling and spending less than 1% on marketing. It works well for them.

**For listings, what is the suggested balance for target agent?**

Most successful agents attempt to keep a balance of 50-50 to buyers and sellers. The number of listings one carries is dependent on price range and size of team.

## Growth of Business

**What does the average real estate agent fail to do which are among the reasons why they are average? Name as many things as you can.**

They fail to get out of their own way (allowing their own fears and biases to dictate their actions).

They fail to take action on items that work.

They fail to realize the importance of continual education.

They fail to work "on" their business daily instead of working "in" their business.

They fail to see themselves in abundance and earning more than they can visualize.

**If you were interviewing an agent at $100,000 and you were trying to determine whether they can and will achieve $500,000, what would you want to know about them or ask them?**

I often ask people to write down their income goal for the next year. I then have them draw a line through it and double it. When asking how many feel they can reach the doubled figure, most hands do not go up.

What would your life look like earning $500,000? What would need to change in order for you to go to $200,000, $300,000, and so on? How would you go about making some changes? What would be the top three things you could begin working on today?

What kind of support program do you have at your office, your team, and at home to reach this growth?

What has kept you at the levels you're at currently?

**As you see agents grow from $100,000 to $500,000, what are the biggest challenges you see?**

The challenges range from redefining their role (from sales to leadership), surrounding oneself with good people (team building, hiring, policy manuals, job descriptions), to building a business of systems (getting them implemented). Another difficult challenge is the ability to "let go" of the outcome, when building a team to take you to higher revenue levels.

Then, you can start looking at a more global picture of your business. The more systems people have in place, the better the chance the consumer will receive the same level of service. It makes the workload of the team automatic and makes sure things are getting done.

**When should an agent get their first part-time assistant?**

I think they should hire an assistant from the very first day they start their business. Until you hire an assistant, you are one. Are you worth $20/hour or $100/hour?

Many things happen when you hire someone. It is like getting married. You start to do things because you have another mouth to feed.

# MIKE FERRY

MIKE FERRY ORGANIZATION
IRVINE, CA

## Background

**For how many years have you been in the real estate business?**
I have been in the business since I was 18. I am now 61, so 43 years!
**What is your personal background and how did you get into real estate?**
**How did you get into coaching?**
I worked at a title insurance company for several years and was doing training for them. I started out in Southern California. I was a Realtor for 2 years in my mid twenties. I went back to the title insurance company and at age 30, started speaking full-time in the Real Estate Industry.
I was doing 15-20 transactions per month. I was willing to spend the major portion of my day generating leads. I spent time qualifying those leads. I was going on presentations to buyers and sellers everyday. I worked about 40-45 hours per week. I tell people today to do exactly what I did then. I was probably doing about 130-140 sales per year.
I had a part-time assistant my first week in the business. I did not know another agent who had an assistant. I was constantly getting comments about why I wanted to do things so differently than other agents. I sold my small business to another real estate agent. Real estate was a stepping stone for me. I went into it, with purpose of going back into speaking and training.
In those days you had three choices:
1. Be hired by a state association.
2. Be hired by a franchise to train their salespeople.
3. Or, be hired by an independent company.

**What lessons did you learn from your family, friends, previous jobs, and life experiences that helped you most to succeed in your career?**
I had the good fortune to spend a lot of time with Earl Nightingale and 2 men named Gunther Klaus and Mike Vance. They were all highly paid professional speakers. They taught me a good part of the speaking business and I just applied it to real estate. All three of them were my mentors.

**What do you enjoy most about the business?**
I enjoy watching the evolution of the agents that we have trained for years. We have had hundreds of agents retire financially independent and thousands, whom we have worked with us for years, are some of the most successful in the country. I had a very clear vision from the beginning and that has made our system simple for our clients to follow.

**What single quality has made you more successful than others?**

I am not afraid of the response of the audience. I am not at all afraid of telling them what I think is right nor do I about their response. I have been the maverick for 30+ years. At one time or another I have been banned from nearly every Real Estate Organization.

I have said for many years there are two ways to get business. You can either buy it or go find it. The choice is what you are going to do. If you go to work everyday, you need to decide how to work, what are you going to do? This industry promotes sitting at an open house, sitting floor time and putting an advertisement in the newspaper. This industry is 100% behind the open house and advertising and waiting for someone to find you. I believe you need to find business — it will lead you to the more successful and productive outcome.

## Mentors

**What are the most influential books you have read?**

I became a ferocious reader at age 20 and I have read about 200 books a year for 33 years. One is called, The Art of Happiness by Dalai Lama. The second is called, This is Earl Nightingale by Earl Nightingale. The next is, Power of Positive Thinking by Napoleon Hill. Another is, Think and Grow Rich by Napoleon Hill.

I have also read every single book about or by Jack Welch.

## Basic Numbers

**About how many real estate agents do you work with on different levels in your organization? What is the structure and levels?**

We have about 40,000 agents per year go through our seminars. We have about 180,000 active customers who read our material, listen or watch our material. We have about 4,400 people involved in our coaching program. We will do about $50 million this year. We have 80 coaches working for us.

**How many people do you think in the country have sold over $1 billion in their career?**

We measure agents only by number of transactions. I would guess several hundred have hit a billion dollars. The industry is not sophisticated to measure by real business standards. The industry does not teach anything about good business sense. This is not a business industry. This is an ego and recognition based industry. They are going to sell huge volumes to get the recognition they want.

## Goals

**Do you believe goals are important to your success? If yes, describe your approach to goal setting for your business and life?**

Yes, 100%. I am a great believer in 70% short-term goals and 30% long-term goals. You have to have some goals in each of the following categories: physical, mental, personal, religious and financial.

I am a much bigger believer in short-term goals rather than long-term goals.

## Marketing

**If you were advising an agent at $100,000 who wants to get to $200,000 or $500,000, what would be your top marketing advice?**

I would tell them to work a lot. Set up a much better system for working their past clients and sphere of influence first. Second, do a better system to market around the existing listings to leverage their yard signs. Third, have them to do some type of institutional type of ad or marketing campaign which would give them some name recognition if they are talking to lots of people.

**For a top agent who has been in the business for 10 years, what percentage of their business should be client repeat/referral? What is the range you see in reality?**

I think that 30-35% should be repeat/referral if they want to have continued growth. A 30% repeat business is more profitable than a 50% repeat/referral business. If you are doing 30-35% from past clients, your costs are very low since you are not spending a lot of money on that business. If the other 60-65% is coming through actually going out to find business, the cost is very low. If the other is coming from advertising, showing agents and buyer agents, then it is very expensive.

In reality, I think that it is 60-70%. A lot of that is sphere of influence referrals.

A very profitable business would be personal time spent on going out to get the business, with lower advertising costs, no other staff besides assistants, and a 30-35% client repeat/referral rate.

**For listings, what is the suggested balance for target agent?**

I think it should be 70% listings and 30% buyers.

## Growth of Business

**What does the average real estate agent fail to do which are among the reasons why they are average? Name as many things as you can.**

They fail to have any specific lead generation system.
They fail to do any follow-up on the leads they generate.
They fail to manage their time so they can do any one of these two.

They fail to use specific scripts and dialogues.
They fail to use common sense when it comes to lead generation.
They fail to have canned presentations which gives them confidence.
They fail to master the answers to the basic questions and objections that clients bring up.

**If you were interviewing an agent who was at $100,000, and you were trying to determine whether they can and will achieve $500,000, what would you want to know about them or ask them?**

I would want them to tell me about their personal lifestyle. How complacent are they? How happy are they with their life the way it is versus the way their life could be? I would want to know about any big goals and dreams they have. I would want to know their history of executing. How well do they get things done?

**As you see agents grow from $100,000 to $500,000, what are the biggest challenges you see?**

There are two things. They are lead generation and delegation. For delegation, the key is the right mortgage company and title company as well as the right outside services and staff with them.

**What percentage of budget would you recommend for marketing expenses at various production levels?**

I would recommend 5%.

**What is target net profit percentage for an agent with a GCI of $200,000?**

It should be at least 60% at $200,000. At $1,000,000, I do not think it should change; they should target 60% pretax profit.

**When should an agent get their first part-time assistant?**

If they have any ambition to be successful, they should do it immediately. At 35-40 transactions they should have their first full-time assistant. They should have a part-time person at 15-20 transactions.

## Other Questions

### Who are the top 3 Real Estate Agents in Country and why?

Karen Bernardi because of her ability to build a large business and have time for herself and her business.
Chris Heller because of his ability to do large volume and make a high profit.

Deb Cizek because of her ability to do be in the business for an extended period of time and operate at high levels.

### Who are the top Real Estate Coaches and Trainers, besides yourself?

The only one I would recommend is Floyd Wickman. He is not a coach though, he is a trainer.

**What is your Unique Talent?**

My unique talent is my ability to keep things very simple and explain to real estate people in a simple way, which makes my ideas useable.

**How many methods of lead generation that you recommend someone at 100k-200k uses?**

There are about 20-25 methods. I recommend that they do 4-5 maximum.

**What are some daily rituals and habits that you would suggest agents' apply to their life?**

The ideal time is in the morning. I would suggest 8:30am-12pm. There is a higher percentage available and there are fewer distractions. I think that by having personal contact first by phone, and then e-mail, is better for developing business relationships. You need to do a little bit of each, every day.

# KEN GOODFELLOW

STEP INTO MASTERY
KANATA, ONTARIO, CANADA

## Background

**For how many years have you been in the real estate business?**

I have been in the business for 27 years.

**What is your personal background and how did you get into real estate?**

**How did you get into coaching?**

I am an entrepreneur. I still own many companies. When I was in my 20's I built a company that was not related to real estate; and, I sold it. Some friends told me to get into real estate, so I did in 1980. I sold over 100 houses in my first year. I then established my own company and had 180 agents. I sold that company to another independent in the 1990's.

I had a team with Century 21 after that. I built and sold that. I have now been coaching for eight years. One of my competitors called me and asked me if I wanted to get into coaching. And that is how it evolved. I left there, and went on my own 5-6 years ago.

**What lessons did you learn from your family, friends, previous jobs, and life experiences that helped you most to succeed in your career?**

My father was Vice President of Firestone, I learned I did not want to work for a corporation.

I have been married for 32 years. We had kids early. I always had time off for family. I coached hockey at a pretty high level. What I realized is that it takes discipline to do business. It takes discipline to train every day. A lot of my hockey coaching has helped with my business coaching. Everything is getting back to the basics everyday. People think of me as working with the top agents. My strategy is to turn salespeople into CEOs because they are running big teams.

**What do you enjoy most about the business?**

I love what I do. I get to speak to and hang around with successful people. We have a lot of fun and we help them move ahead.

**What single quality has made you more successful than others?**

Discipline. I am very scheduled. I am unbelievably scheduled. I practice what I preach. I always go over my profit/loss statement every month. I practice scripts and dialogues with my sales departments so they become better. I hold my people accountable. I work 4 days a week and no more than 5 days a week.

Everyday, I get up and go for a walk. I am in the office by 7am. I am on the phone for 5-6 hours everyday doing coaching. Three nights of the week, I like to do something with my family.

## Mentors

**Who or what was the most influential person, mentor, or book in your early career?**

Early in my career my father and my uncle were my mentors. In the hockey world, it was a coaching person who no one knows, Jim Daly. He was a great mentor. Now, Michael Gerber is a great mentor.

**What are the most influential books you have read?**

Good to Great, The Toyota Way, E-Myth

## Basic Numbers

**About how many real estate agents do you work with on different levels in your organization? What is the structure and levels?**

We work with about 180 agents. We suggest a minimum of $750,000 in GCI. We do not have other programs. We just do a mastery program with the top people.

**How many people do you think in the country have sold over $1 billion in their career?**

I would guess 100.

**How many people who are your current clients do you think have hit $1 billion?**

I would guess 20 of them.

## Goals

**Do you believe goals are important to your success? If yes, describe your approach to goal setting for your business and life?**

I think they are critical. My approach is that a couple of things can happen. People set goals as they move along. But, as they get to higher levels, they are not driven as much anymore. Goals are what make people get up in the morning. We always talk about both business and personal goals. I have people make lists of goals they want and we continue to check the list on a monthly basis.

I have been goal setting for probably 35 years. I honestly do not know where I was exposed to it; probably some seminar 35 years ago.

I have daily, monthly, annual, and life goals. I have yearly goals that I break down to the month.

## Marketing

**If you were advising our target agent at $100,000 who wants to get to $200,000 or $500,000, what would be your top marketing advice?**

To market at that level you need to do multiple things. You need to talk to past clients by touching them once a month. I think you should call them two or three times a year by phone. You need to have a website that attracts buyers and sellers but they have to make sure it is positioned properly without paying a fortune.

I think you can test market any other areas. You need to test areas to see if something works. You pick small areas to start with. You want to build your business or take the areas you are working on and get more people.

**For a top agent who has been in the business for 10 years, what percentage of their business should be client repeat/referral? What is the range you see in reality?**

The broad range seems to be 40-60% among my clients. It depends on their database, and if it is built properly. We really work hard with people on database systems and referrals.

**For listings, what is the suggested balance for target agent?**

I would normally say 70% listings and 30% buyers. Most of them have teams and buyer agents so they work with buyer agents. It gets as high as 60/40. I believe listings are the way to go.

## Growth of Business

**What does the average real estate agent fail to do which are among the reasons why they are average? Name as many things as you can.**

They fail to schedule themselves.
They fail to put a plan in place.
They fail to call people.
They fail to have a budget.
|hey fail to become knowledgeable on the Internet.

**If you were interviewing an agent at $100,000 and you were trying to determine whether they can and will achieve $500,000, what would you want to know about them or ask them?**

Are they interested in making $500,000?
Are you prepared to do what it takes to make it?
Handling a changing market.
Not burning out from working too much.
Keeping mentally positive.
Making sure with hires, putting the right people in the right place.

**What percentage of budget would you recommend for marketing expenses at various production levels?**

My group is 8-10% of overall gross. If they are at $100,000 I would also suggest 10%.

With a $1 million GCI, what is the net profit margin – minimum 50%

**When should an agent get their first part-time assistant?**

I would say after 30 deals.

# Walter Sanford

Speaker, Trainer, Coach
Sanford Systems and Strategies
Kankakee, IL

## Background

**For how many years have you been in the real estate business?**

I have been in the business since 1975, so about 31 years.

**What is your personal background and how did you get into real estate?**

**How did you get into coaching?**

When I was 16 years old, I entered into a lottery for $20. I borrowed $10 from Dad, and earned $10 from mowing lawns. I won an oil and gas lease in Campbell County, Wyoming. We sold it for $36,000. We, then, bought our first duplex in the early 1970's and kept investing in real estate. We bought about 400 units in just a few years. In my last year of college in USC, I was managing properties all over the western states. I estimate that I was probably worth $15-17 million in my early 20s. Interest rates went to 22% and we lost everything ... plus some.

I discovered that I went way past zero and had $1.7 million in debt. My dad told me, "You better sell real estate and sell a lot of it!" So, I went to work as a real estate agent. The broker had a one-line interview, "Why do you want to become a real estate agent?" I explained, "I have to make $34,000 a month before I can buy groceries." She said, "You're hired!"

My Dad told me that I could be anyone I wanted to be, by copying someone who had already been there. I took the top agents out to lunch. I asked various questions, and they "spilled the beans." You get by giving — so top agents look for every opportunity to make that happen. They told me what to do, and I copied them.

I became a top agent in California and then a top agent in the United States. Mike Ferry was an early mentor. He would tell people if they bought his books and tapes that they would end up like me.

I rebuilt my whole empire in 12 years and lost two-thirds of it by not paying attention to family, faith, and friends. I got divorced and started over a second time by putting my estate back together again.

In 1989, I started getting invited to speak to top real estate agencies. Based upon what everyone telling me, I was the top guy in the world! I got invited to events, and they began to pay me to speak there.

Shortly after these speaking engagements began to roll in, I started a newsletter. Mike Ferry suggested to his large crowds that they buy my $300 newsletter, and I made $60,000 in minutes.

I began to look carefully at the training business. I started taking my own business manuals and business plans then I started converting them into products to sell. I started getting invited to more and more events. In 2000, my income from my training company exceeded my income that I was making in real estate.

Personally, as a one-person office, I did about 350 transactions a year. I peaked at $86 million in sales in one year. In today's dollars, that is about $154,000,000. I had 4 assistants. I originated the use of assistants in real estate almost twenty-five years ago.

The first thing you do is master delegation. You delegate to your clients. Next, you delegate to your affiliates including your mortgage, title, and warranty companies. Then you develop checklists and systems. You have to create profitable systems and delegate those systems. Finally, you delegate systems to technology.

If you still need help with your business after the above delegation, then you delegate to paid assistants. Most assistants should be lead generation assistants. The lifeblood of your business should be listings so you need to determine the sellers who are most likely to list. We had sixty-seven seller lead generation systems running at all times. The next item for your paid assistant, after lead generation, is transaction coordination. Then comes investing, so your money works for you rather than you constantly working for your money.

The last item for a business is buyer agents. I eliminated the use of buyer's agents, for the most part, by having my buyers jump through "hoops" designed to help them. The first hoop was a series of thirty-five questions. If they didn't answer this question list over the phone, they were referred. They had to be pre-approved. They had to come to my office and meet me before I showed them a home. They had to sign an exclusive buyer broker contract. My buyer hoop systems eliminated 70% of the low percentage close buyers.

Referral fees from low percentage close clients paid for assistants. Less than 20% of leads I referred out ended up closing.

My business plan was developing systems for proactive seller lead generation to the most probable demographics. You develop a proactive, seller-listing machine. Have a great presentation, and have the lowest cost, most efficient system, which is getting the signs up.

**What lessons did you learn from your family, friends, previous jobs, and life experiences that helped you most to succeed in your career?**

The last 15 minutes of the day or the first half hour after 5pm are the least traveled areas. I could find myself doing things that other people did not want to do. I did the extra calls. I made sure I spent time, on most profitable parts of the business.

In 1993, we had over 500 listings expire on January 1. I listed 111 listings in first 2 months of 1994.

No one works the first week of the year so I went once again to the least traveled gold mine to reap my rewards.

**What do you enjoy most about the business?**

I enjoy changing my client's lives. I have changed outcomes and provided legacies for families. What is exciting about real estate is that with some tweaks and nuances, you can increase your business exponentially because the competition is so light in many specialized areas.

**What single quality has made you more successful than others?**

The one quality that stood out was my ability to concentrate on the most profitable aspects of real estate. The true pros determine what aspect of this business works most efficiently.

I would send a letter to mature people in large homes and get an 18% return. Hit the great demographics!

## Mentors

**What was most influential person, mentor, or book in your early career?**

In the 1980s, I spent time with Mike Ferry. He is a business systems genius. As far as mentors, there is no one who understands business systems like him. Jay Abraham and Dan Kennedy have also been influential.

**What are the most influential books you have read?**

Think and Grow Rich — I have always been my own best client. I wrote a book called Insider Investing in Real Estate. I am most proud of learning about real estate investing.

## Basic Numbers

**About how many real estate agents do you work with on different levels in your organization? What is the structure and levels?**

You can start with a free service on our website called "Ask Wally." See me speak all over the country. Buy my books, CDs, DVDs, and software. Some agents will take the most proactive step, which is personal one-on-one coaching.

## Goals

**Do you believe goals are important to your success? If yes, describe your approach to goal setting for your business and life?**

Goals are something we do weekly. I have a 5-year, 3-year, 2-year, 1-year and a life plan. I try to make sure that everything is congruent. I balance work, life, and family.

## Marketing

**If you were advising our target agent at $100,000 who wants to get to $200,000 or $500,000, what would be your top marketing advice?**

I would develop numerous systems for generating seller leads. Most agents spend the majority of time designing and implementing systems for generating seller leads.

**For a top agent who has been in the business for 10 years, what percentage of their business should be client repeat/referral? What is the range you see in reality?**

It should be 50%, and I see it is more often 20-25%. Most do not have proactive systems to generate leads from their current database. They may have a 1,000 person database, and they need to call XX people per day. Do the numbers and time-block the calls every day.

It is always more exciting, to find new business, rather then maintaiing existing business. The minimum database exploitation is to call your client database twice a year. Mail to them four times a year a custom, hand-signed, personal note. Plus e-mail them a monthly e-mail newsletter. With that, you are going to grow your database.

When you are a listing agent, your client (the seller), sometimes moves out of town. Add to your database the people who bought your listings. This is a segment of database leads that are sometimes forgotten.

**For listings, what is the suggested balance for target agent?**

I would suggest 80-90% of your income is from listings and 10% from buyers. Double-end transactions are always a goal! The last thing you increase is the buyer end of your business.

## Growth of Business

**What does the average real estate agent fail to do which are among the reasons why they are average? Name as many things as you can.**

1. They fail to do any proactive seller lead generation.

2. They fail to do custom direct mail with value.

3. They fail to maintain contact with their database looking for listings, buyers, and investors.

4. They fail to direct their website to hot demographics.

5. They fail to determine motivation of clients and work with low percentage closes.

6. They fail to invest for themselves.

**If you were interviewing an agent at $100,000 and you were trying to determine whether they can and will achieve $500,000, what would you want to know about them or ask them?**

I would ask them if they have the discipline to work two or three different systems every single day. Ask if they could write their entire calendar for the year, and time-block certain activities to get them done everyday. I would want them to choose two seller lead generation systems of their own choice. Some of the problems with trainers is that they are still talking about door knocking. Get excited about seller lead generation!

I made $150,000 net my first year working expireds, and that was over thirty years ago! If they could time-block two seller lead generation systems a day and time-block the activities, they would be in the top 5% easily. When you have a seller lead, it forces you to do everything else correctly.

Have affiliates aligned so they are putting out fewer fires.

**What percentage of a budget would you recommend for marketing expenses at various production levels?**

No more than 30% of your gross for all expenses. Your lowest cost client is your repeat/referral. Your cost of generating new leads should constantly go down.

**When should an agent get their first part-time assistant?**

I cannot see someone doing much more than 3-4 transactions a month without some help. I saw so much opportunity out there, but I was busy and could not generate leads any longer. There is much to do. If you have great systems, this frees you up to close for the appointment and take the listing. That is all I ever wanted to do.

# FLOYD WICKMAN

FLOYD WICKMAN TEAM, LLC
S. EASTON, MA

Floyd's exemplary career spans more than three decades. Among his many achievements he is best known as a top-producing salesman, manager, and creator of one of the nation's largest and most successful training organizations. Floyd Wickman is the author of six top-selling books, including Mentoring (McGraw-Hill Companies, 1997), The Wickman Formula, Successful Strategies for Sales Managers, and Successful Strategies for Sales Agents. He is the recipient of the *"Platinum Award"* for over a million audio programs sold. Salesperson Magazine described him perfectly when they named him "The Extraordinary Ordinary Man".

Floyd has spoken to over 3,000 thousand audiences, both in the US and abroad. He has graduated over 250,000 students through his Training programs. He is a member of the coveted, prestigious Hall of Fame of the International Federation of Professional Speakers. Among others honored with this distinction are Zig Ziglar, Dr. Norman Vincent Peale, Tom Hopkins, and Og Mandino.

Floyd's articles have appeared in such publications as: Today's Realtor; National Relocation and Real Estate; Professional Speaker; and Selling Power. Recently, The National Association of Realtors & Today's Realtor magazine named him one of the 25 most influential people in the real estate industry.

As a result of Floyd's years of experience, as a highly successful professional speaker, trainer and business entrepreneur, he brings to his audiences cutting-edge wisdom and firsthand knowledge in the fields of sales, interpersonal relationships, management, coaching and mentoring, recruiting and business development. Floyd's latest endeavor, The Starmakerâ Program, is a testament to his lifelong philosophy of "We Get By Giving." It is becoming a major trend in the training industry for Building Business Through Referrals, Relationships, Client Care, and Skill Development.

## Background

**For how many years have you been in the real estate business?**

I have been in this business for 40 years.

**What is your personal background and how did you get into real estate?**

**How did you get into coaching?**

I am more of a trainer than a coach. I spent 10 years in the Navy. I was roughly the same rank when I got out as when I went in.

# Billion Dollar Agent

My family has many members who worked milk routes. It was either stay in the Navy, do milk routes, or real estate. Someone nudged me into real estate; and I have been in it ever since. That was about 1966.

I've always failed at everything before I succeeded. That is usually the sign that someone will be a teacher, trainer, or coach. I was a failing salesmen; and then, I succeeded. It was April 1974 when I saw a speaker named J. Douglas Edwards. He said, "one of you has greatness in you." And like a dummy, I thought he was speaking about me. So, the next day, I had this overwhelming desire to do what he was doing, train real estate sales people. He was one of the best real estate sales trainers of all times. I began training for our seven office company and was managing about 8 agents in my office. All of a sudden my office sales meetings became mini-seminars. During this time my small office averaged 23 closings a month for 4 straight years. I knew how to train. Throughout my management career, I never really saw myself as a trainer. I thought every good manager should be a good trainer. I have a 9th grade education and it was very difficult to burn my bridges, you know, move forward right away. I never missed a speaker or trainer within 50 miles of my office. If a real estate board has 5,000 members and there is an event coming up where they are bringing in a speaker, they would be lucky to get 1 out of 10 to go to a free seminar. People are too busy — too busy to learn. As a result they continue to stay busy doing nothing and producing nothing. Non-producers are too busy to go learn. You start meeting other top producers at these events. They, too, are there at the learning session.

I am flattered that the top producers come to see me at my seminars. But I'm disappointed that the others are not there, the ones who really need the education. It's sad. People get into real estate and no one tells them this is a selling business. You need to learn how to run the business and you need to know how to sell.

**What lessons did you learn from your family, friends, previous jobs, and life experiences that helped you most to succeed in your career?**

I think the concept that 'you get by giving' is dominant in my life, my business and everything I do. I grew up in an impoverished family. My father was a successful milkman and a less than successful gambler. I remember we always hid when people knocked on our front door. My Mom used to hide her purse behind this dresser inside a hole in the wall.

When I started in real estate I felt a little like my father did ... nothing was working for me. I didn't have two nickels to rub together. One day I visited my Mom when I was broke. I remember her handing me $3 and telling me, "Sometimes, when a man has a few dollars in his pocket, he just feels better." I'll never forget those words. They impacted my life. All of a sudden my radar was up. I started practicing what my mom taught me.

Anytime I got within an arm's length of someone who was hurting, I would take out a few bucks and put it in their hand, just to give them that sense of hope, even if it's momentary. I never expect to get paid back. I think, I'm successful because of that.People know that I'm a giver and knowing what kind of man I am, has done a great deal for my company and me. For example, I hire people based on their character first and talent second.I only hire people who are givers. It grows and mushrooms.This awareness is created and, all of a sudden you are looking around and you see the power of 'get by giving'. Then you take it into the real estate business and teach this as a fundamental.

I learned how to succeed after learning how to sell.I became attached to Zig Ziglar early on.Zig has been my personal mentor for 30 years. I always pinch myself, "Why does he always take my call?"Whenever I needed a nugget, Zig took my call."Why me, Zig?Why would you always be there for me?"He said, "Floyd, I love helping people.Some I hear from.Some I hear of.And that's good.Some people I do not hear from or of.From you, I always hear from you and I am always hearing of you.I know whatever I am telling youhas value to you. You put it to use, and that is what motivates a coach and a mentor."

**What do you enjoy most about the business?**

I enjoy speaking. I enjoy that part of it because I love to see people laugh and learn. You know I speak for free — I just charge a lot to get there. J

My real passion is watching people grow — it takes time to develop.All of my training programs are what is called spaced training.When I first started teaching, all real estate training was compacted. Monday-Friday 9-4, *"We teach you everything you need to know in one week."*You can convey a lot, but people cannot learn much information, without first putting it to use. My students meet once per week for class.With spaced training I teach you a little bit and then I hold you accountable to apply it.Spaced training allows you to learn more and be more successful. My thrill is to see people grow and see them take control of their lives.I am teaching people how to be in control of their life.

**What single quality has made you more successful than others?**

I have been there.People say, "He seems to really care about us and he seems to really have been there." If you ever hear a speaker who seems to be speaking from the heart, it's probably because they are teaching what they needed to learn the most. People don't care what you know, until they know that you care.

## Mentors

### What are the most influential books you have read?

Og Mandino's, Greatest Salesmen in the World, Napoleon Hill's, Think and Grow Rich. I don't really read; I look for answers.

## Basic Numbers

### About how many real estate agents do you work with on different levels in your organization?What is the structure and levels?

Over 250,000 agents have graduated from my training programs.I have 17 trainers in my company and we train people on a daily basis.I run into 5-10 people a year who want to be personally coached by me.I enjoy that.Our #1 program is 7 once-a-week sessions called The StarMaker SMART Program.There is a one-year follow-up program to it called The Core Values Club.

We, also, hold an annual three-day event called the Master Sales Event. My students lovingly nicknamed it FloydFest.This is where education happens at a higher level.It is always in Chicago, in January, to kick off the New Year right. We have about 600 people at our annual meeting.

The R Mentor Group is something we do not charge to do and we tell agents to form their own R or Responsibility Group to interact.I just started calling it the R group, two years ago.

I wrote a book, published by McGraw Hill, called Mentoring.I am a real bug on mentoring versus coaching.To me there is a major difference.Mentors are people helping people without being compensated.That is the concept of mentoring.My job is to make you independent of me — not dependenton me. We suggest 3-4 people meet every two weeks as a mentor group.For years, I have been putting together mentor groups that meet once a month.But, the bottom line is, the cheese has moved. There is a major difference today. It was once common for people to take the time to meet in person. But, today people cannot always get in their car and drive to a meeting. It is getting harder and harder to do that.The R Group technique is telephone based.There is a maximum of 3-4 people, because if too many people are in the group, it cannot work over the phone. It would run over an hour long.

### How many people nationally do you think have sold over $1 billion in their career?

There is, perhaps, one out of 100 full timers who are doing $250,000 of gross commission income.

### How many people who are your current clients do you think have hit $1 billion?

I think maybe 5 or so.

## Goals

**Do you believe goals are important to your success? If yes, describe your approach to goal setting for your business and life?**

Obviously, yes, it's the only way you will have the energy. First, you need to find pictures of what you want in your life and what you want to accomplish. From there, everything translates down to activity. For every agent, I ask what turns them on; what are they looking for in life? When they come up with a number or picture of their goal, they need to ask themselves why? There are always five "whys" to our purpose. When you know your goal, ask yourself why. Take your answer and ask why this is important to you. Do this repeatedly until you've asked yourself why, five times. Asking "why" five times is very valuable. Your answer to the fifth why will give you your true inspiration and motivation to stay focused and achieve your goal.

## Marketing

**If you were advising our target agent at $100,000 who wants to get to $200,000 or $500,000, what would be your top marketing advice?**

I would say find 200 platinum relationships. That is finding multiple referral relationships from your sphere of influence. You can work 200 people efficiently. Why multiple referral contacts? Digging up prospects takes a lot of time. You can personally find only so many clients yourself. So, make sure your 200 relationships are multiple-referral sources.

You need assistance to get to that level. That might mean hiring an assistant or starting a team. You either need to outsource or bring in a right hand to work with you. I do not think you need a big team to do it. You have to be careful when you bring people to work with you. If they are not the right person, you find yourself having to go to work everyday just so *they* can earn a living. I run into some people who are all beat up and they say, "Oh man, I got my team and they are draining me." Was that the idea when you started to build the team? You have to recruit the right people.

**For a top agent who has been in the business for 10 years, what percent of their business should be client repeat/referral? What is the range you see in reality?**

I think it should be 70% at that point. There is a major distinction. The difference is, that for repeat business, you need to subscribe them to a follow-up program. When it is time to sell their home, it is pretty good shot that they will call you. Especially, if they have been on the receiving end of a mail-call-see program.

But, the day after closing, I might be able to pull two or three referrals from them that day. Referrals can be gathered and generated today, but repeat business takes time. That's why people get out of real estate; they run out of time.

Anyone can build a wonderful repeat and referral business. The secret is to have close personal relationships with your referral base. A lot of money is wasted on advertising for new business in an era when people can just sit down and shop the Internet. Why pay for Internet leads when you can generate everything you need from your referral base?

**For listings, what is the suggested balance for agents to target?**

Most of the big producers I know shoot for listings; and, they are just good at handling the buyers that come along. I do not think they proactively dig for buyers, though. They probably do 70% listings and 30% buyers.

I averaged 86 listings a year for 7 years. My personal goal was to go on 4 listing appointments per week.

## Growth of Business

**What does the average real estate agent fail to do which are among the reasons why they are average? Name as many things as you can.**

They fail to generate leads on a daily basis. As a salesmen I would be on the phone nice and early, and making my calls. You need to block out and take enough time to generate leads. Staying booked is the secret whether you are a rock star or a Realtor. Most agents go a whole week without any sales activity.

They fail to attend a minimum of three face-to-face appointments each week. They fail to consistently work their book of business.

They do not know how to be in control of appointments; they always adlib. They do not know how to control their time. They need to learn how to say "no".

**If you were interviewing an agent at $100,000 and you were trying to determine whether they can and will achieve $500,000, what would you want to know about them or ask them?**

I would start by asking, "What are your goals?" Then, following up, asking them the five whys.

**What is the most common mistake you see agents making?**

I think agents over advertise and rely too much on assistants. They're trying to win a tug of war pulling both ends of the rope. I don't care if you are at $100,000 or $500,000; there are still only 24 hours a day and you are going to work X hours a day. One of the mistakes agents make is they do not develop skills to increase their hit/win ratio. Let's pretend I am a two-stop lister at $100,000 a year. I'd better switch to becoming a one-stop lister if I want to double my income. My skills have to increase so my hit ratio increases.

## Bottom line — Skills save time.

### When should an agent get their first part-time assistant?

I think today you can handle 30 deals by yourself. Beyond 30, I think you have to get a little help.

Top 10 Things

### What are the top ten things that a real estate agent should do to grow from $100,000 to $500,000? Please be very specific.

1. Put your goal into your Purpose and your Purpose into your goal.
2. Translate your goal into a measurable activity so you know what to do on a daily basis.
3. Track activity and results so that you always know how much further you have to go.
4. Delegate minimum wage and lower priority tasks and eliminate time wasters.
5. Learn how to handle more problems.
6. Make life balance a priority.
7. Generate more leads, by cultivating multiple referral sources.
8. Stay trained.
9. Get a coach or a mentor.
10. Let go and let God, (Let go of responsibility for the end result and let God do the worrying).

# Conclusion
## *Thank You*

If you just finished the book, thank you for reading it.

Best Agent Business would appreciate any and all feedback. This is a first edition and we hope to get feedback, find more agents who have sold over $1 billion, and issue a second edition in the future.

I would like to acknowledge and thank some important people that helped me get to this point. I am thankful for my wife, Aileen, and our three daughters, who have helped me in many ways and always get a good laugh out of whatever crazy idea I am pursuing. I want to thank the Entrepreneurs' Organization (see www.eonetwork.org ) which has been critical to my personal development since 2001.

I would like to thank all of my colleagues who work with me at Lifebushido, the holding company of Best Agent Business. This project started in February 2006 and went to the printer in December 2006. The project involved phone calls and meetings with over 100 agents and industry experts. About 20 different people assisted in various aspects of the project. I would like to express special thanks to Tricia Nudelman, Project Editor. Tricia resides in Chevy Chase, Maryland with her husband Eric where she is a stay at home mom of three kids: Ben, Kendall and Samantha. She has been working part-time for Lifebushido since its inception in January 2006. In her spare time, Tricia is active in the community, enjoys playing soccer and traveling with family and friends.

I would like to thank Michael Goldstein, President of ContentNow (www.contentnow.com). Michael and I have been meeting every two weeks for business brainstorming during 2006 and his ideas have impacted this book positively. Finally, Guido would like to inform Jimbo that the score is now 3-1 and outer space is coming soon.

*Keep in touch,*
**Steve**

Steve Kantor
Best Agent Business
Bethesda, MD
December 2006

# Letter to Billion Dollar Agent Interviewees

This is a private letter to the 50+ agents interviewed for this book. I am sharing it with everyone else in case they can see the magic message written in this letter…

## Dear Billion Dollar Agent,

Thank you again for the interview. As you hold this book and read the interviews, I hope you see the potential. You are among the 1 in 1,000 in your profession. You are running a small business of a few million dollars. Many of you are capable of much more.

You are not only at the top, you are at the beginning. If you could achieve X, imagine what 100 of you could accomplish together: 1,000X. Since we are all about the number seven – BDA777 – here are seven final thoughts:

1. Explore your unique talents and focus on increasing time on your unique talents.
2. Leverage your time further with a higher ratio of assistants to agents in business.
3. Create goals and visions which go far beyond what you have set in the past.
4. Increase your profit margin to match the best in this book.
5. Focus on client marketing to increase profitable client repeat/ referral revenue.
6. Do it all by adding more revenue pillars to your business.
7. Learn from each other – we are here to help.

In a special way, none of you is truly a **Billion Dollar Agent**…yet. What do you think I mean by that sentence? Email me your BHAG. Better yet, come see me in Washington, DC for a day of brainstorming. I want to help you achieve your BHAG in anyway that I can help. Congratulations again on your incredible career and personal success!

# Biography of Author

Steve Kantor is an entrepreneur involved with multiple ventures to help people focus on their unique talents. Steve founded, grew, and sold Gnossos Software from 1986-2004, took a sabbatical year to recharge in 2005, and started new ventures in 2006.

Born in San Diego, California, Steve graduated from Harvard University and then from John Hopkins SAIS with MA in International Relations and Global Theory. Steve is a world traveler and spent 1985-1986 backpacking around the world. He has been to over 75 countries and is a strong believer in the value of diversity of backgrounds.

Steve is married to Aileen Kantor and is the father of three daughters and lives in Bethesda, MD. Based on their daughters starting the charitable effort of Project Backpack in September 2005 for the kids of Katrina, the family effort led to over 100 cities collecting and delivering over 50,000 backpacks to kids of Katrina in less than 100 days.

In 2006, Steve started Lifebushido LLC which is a number of ventures. These include the following:

1  The **Lessons Learned** book series at www.lessonsbushido.com. This includes **Lessons Learned by a Young Entrepreneur** and **Billion Dollar Agent – Lessons Learned**.
2  A resource of over one hundred compiled book notes on business, psychology, and science at www.bookbushido.com.
3  A synthesis of various goal-setting and personal growth pursuits at www.goalbushido.com and www.topagentgoals.com.
2  Orange Passion, a consulting firm helping companies to find their passionate customers and get innovative ideas from those customers. See www.orangepassion.com.
3  Best Agent Business, a real estate outsourcing business providing part-time assistants to top real estate agents nationwide. See www.bestagentbusiness.com.
4  Why Are You Here – Right Now? This book, www.yruhrn.com, is the world's first crowdsourced book written by over one thousand people.
5  Lifebushido, a company building a global network of people working part-time from home with flexible hours using their unique talents, with special focus on stay-at-home-moms. See www.lifebushido.com.

# Billion Dollar Bonus

**FREE FREE FREE**
**REGISTER YOUR BOOK TODAY!**

## Billion Dollar Bonus

Register your book today for free bonus material and content!

As an owner of **Billion Dollar Agent – Lessons Learned** you are entitled to hundreds of dollars worth of additional content.

Billion Dollar Bonus materials includes free additional content, goal tools, sample budgets, profit models, book summaries of other business books, and samples of systems.

Our goal is to share knowledge with you to thank you for buying our book and to introduce you to **Best Agent Business** for your current or future part-time or full-time assistant needs.

We are looking for 1,000 people to grow from $100,000 in GCI to $1,000,000 over the next 1,000 days.

**Do you have what it takes?**

**Register your book today for free Billion Dollar Bonus:**

Email your contact information to:

register@billiondollaragent.com

Call us and leave voice mail at: 240-396-5282

Complete this form and fax to: 240-751-4247

Complete form and mail to:

Billion Dollar Agent

7706 Oldchester Road

Bethesda, MD 20817

Name: _____

Company: _____

Phone: _____ Email: _____

City/State: _____